CRIMINALS
AND VICTIMS

CRIMINALS
AND
VICTIMS

A Trial Judge Reflects on Crime and Punishment

Lois G. Forer

W· W· NORTON & COMPANY
NEW YORK LONDON

Library of Congress Cataloging in Publication Data
Forer, Lois G   1914–
    Criminals and victims.
    Includes index.
    1. Sentences (Criminal procedure)—United States.
2. Reparation—United States. 3. Criminal justice,
Administration of—United States. I. Title.
KF9685.F67   345.73'0772   79-27465
ISBN 0-393-01349-9

1 2 3 4 5 6 7 8 9 0

For the People of Philadelphia

CONTENTS

The rarer action is in virtue than in vengeance.
—Shakespeare

ACKNOWLEDGMENTS

M y experience as a lawyer, law teacher, and judge are the materials from which this book was fashioned. I am grateful to Governor Milton J. Shapp, who appointed me to the bench; the people of Philadelphia who elected me to serve as a Common Pleas Judge; and the many great judges and excellent lawyers with whom I was associated and who have practiced before me. From them I learned the craft of law, the nature of the legal process, and also glimpsed the creative possibilities of more just and humane uses of the law. I acknowledge with respect and affection especially the late United States Circuit Judge John Biggs, Jr., the late Pennsylvania Supreme Court Justices Thomas D. McBride and Herbert B. Cohen and my husband, Morris L. Forer, Esq.

Lawyers and judges rely upon precedent. I, too, have built upon the scholarship of many lawyers, judges, psychiatrists, and sociologists whose works are cited. Carolyn Muldoon Weiner and Greta S. Cherry have made this task easier by their faithful and meticulous assistance.

My greatest debt is to the people whose lives and problems reveal the injustices and lacunae of the law and point the way to reform.

CRIMINALS AND VICTIMS

CHAPTER I

FROM
WHERE I SIT

No, I don't sin.
It worries me not to have influence
. . . I only turn screws, weld together
Parts of destruction,
Never grasping the whole
Of the human lot.
                    —Pope John Paul II

This book evolved from my experiences as a trial judge presiding over an endless torrent of criminal and civil cases in a large metropolitan city. I see a steady stream of criminal defendants, mostly young, unemployed, and undereducated, and an appalling parade of victims of crime. The victims are people of all ages and conditions, suffering losses which may be as little as twenty-five cents or as great as permanent disability and mutilation. Businesses of every size and type, from mom-and-pop stores to the largest corporate enterprises, are also victims. Ultimately the public pays not only for the criminal justice system but also for the losses caused by crime. The public pays for the disabled victims who must go on welfare. It pays for the business losses in higher prices. The public pays for the erosion of faith in the rule of law in our increasingly lawless society.

For an experienced lawyer or judge, the trial of a criminal case presents few difficulties. The law is reasonably clear as to the elements of the crime, the rules of evidence, and the procedures to be followed. Every aspect of conduct by police and prosecution from the moment of police surveillance, through arrest, interrogation, and preliminary arraignment is regulated by law. Pretrial hearings, the trial itself, or the plea bargain, if there is one, and the post-trial petitions and hearings are subject to statutes, rules, and decisional law. All of these proceedings are meticulously recorded. If there is the possibility that any rule or regulation has been violated, it will be presented on appeal and the conviction may be set aside. The defendant may be freed or tried again. Some may argue that the accused has too many rights and that the guilty escape punishment by reason of legal technicalities. This has not been my experience. On the contrary, I find that the poor and ignorant rarely exercise their legal and constitutional rights and that the great landmark cases in which the Supreme Court has enunciated and carefully specified the rights of an accused are meaningless to most defendants who appear in court. These people do not understand their rights and frequently waive them through ignorance. Most accused persons—rich and powerful as well as poor and ignorant—plead guilty. For all of them and for many who stand trial, the elaborate panoply of the law and the rights of the accused which occupy the attention of the public, the appellate courts, and the media is largely irrelevant. To lawyers and appellate courts, a trial is of great importance. To the defendant the sentence is really all that matters.

The sentence imposed on convicted criminals and those who plead guilty means the difference between freedom and prison. In a limited number of cases, it means the difference between life and death. Obviously, the sentence is a most important part of the entire criminal justice system. But it receives the least consideration under the law. Until recently, there were few regulations or limitations on the sentence which might be imposed and few restrictions or rules regulating the procedures to be followed in imposing sentence. The law governing the sentence to be imposed is still vague, the options limited, and the purposes of criminal penalties diffuse and contradictory.

Most aspects of law are tested and refined through the crucible of the appellate courts. Panels of judges in written opinions discuss the problems, establish guidelines for future cases, and provide an intellectual rationale or philosophy not only to justify the actions taken by the courts but also to contribute to the understanding of the community. Under our legal system, appellate courts rarely pass upon the question of sentencing in the sense of deciding whether the penalty imposed was appropriate. Was it too harsh or too lenient? Although appellate courts in Canada and in several American states routinely consider this most significant issue, the federal courts and most state appellate courts do not. They have been primarily concerned with whether the right procedures were employed—did the convict know he had a right to appeal? Was he provided with a lawyer? Did the lawyer raise all the issues of error in the trial that he should have raised? The problem of the sentence is left in the hands of the trial judge.

The statutes of most states establish the maximum period of incarceration and the maximum fine. The judge may order imprisonment up to the maximum number of years and a fine up to the maximum number of dollars, or both. The judge may instead place the defendant on probation or suspend sentence or impose a lesser fine or a shorter period of imprisonment. Fines are rarely imposed.

The real choice facing the trial judge is "in" or "out" of jail. This is the bottom line. Until approximately 1975, the sentencing judge had almost unlimited discretion so long as the sentence did not exceed the statutory maximum length of years. Rarely was a sentence reversed or modified for abuse of discretion. A young man was sentenced to twenty-seven years for possession of marijuana cigarettes. Another man was given a suspended sentence for beating his four-year-old son to death. A welfare recipient was sentenced to three years' imprisonment for cheating on her allotment in the sum of seventy-three dollars. None of these sentences was altered or set aside on appeal. Many big businessmen and public officials have not served a day in prison for defrauding the public of millions. Naturally, there has been tremendous dissatisfaction with these disparities in sentencing.

Numerous proposals for change have been offered by bar association committees, law professors, and criminologists. These proposals have been concerned with two issues: (1) How long a prison sentence should be imposed? and (2) Who should make that determination? A recent study phrases the question as "Who decides and when?"[1] Little thought has been given to other options. There are several basic assumptions underlying these discussions: that the choice of "in" or "out" is the only one; that if the crime is violent or the defendant has a prior record, then a prison sentence is appropriate no matter what the nature of the crime, the circumstances surrounding it, or the condition of the offenders; that if the offense is not violent and the offender has no prior record, "out" is appropriate regardless of the amount of money involved, the harm done to the public, or the intent of the offender.

Although only a trial judge can impose a sentence, few trial judges have written books on sentencing, and they deal largely with the mechanics of sentencing.[2] Rarely does one find a judge who is obligated under the law to impose sentence on criminals writing about this task. The opinions of judges who have imposed sentences upon hundreds of criminals are not sought. Some authorities explain this situation: "The experience of law makers and law enforcement officials is subject to serious limitations as a source of knowledge."[3] Of course, one person has only the limited experience of his own lifetime. But trial judges can observe the practices of their colleagues; they can study the research reports written by the scholars; and they can think and reflect upon what they have read and what they are doing. Trial judges are uniquely situated to observe the injustices and errors of the criminal justice system. They have an immediacy of experience to which few criminologists, philosophers, and legal scholars are exposed.

A judge who tries major criminal cases and accepts guilty pleas sees the actual criminals, hundreds of them if not thousands. A trial judge also sees the victims of crime. Most judges are so burdened with simply getting through the day and "disposing" of the allotted quota of cases that they are usually too weary to undertake the painful examination of the justice, morality, or common sense of the sentences which they impose. Trial judges are not given sabbaticals or furloughs to ponder these problems. Judges rarely apply for or receive grants to make studies or write books.[4] Consequently, the trial judge who sees the criminal and the victim of the crime, who makes the decision of "in" or "out," who sees the offender again if he is rearrested, and who must answer to the public for the sentence he imposed rarely has any significant input in the debates on sentencing, the design of the research, and the legislation. A state trial judge who deals with a multitude of offenders has, I believe, a useful contribution to make to the understanding of scholars and the general public.

The great Constitutional issues which are studied in law school such as the privilege against self-incrimination, the right to jury trial, the right of privacy, the prohibition against cruel and unusual punishment, and the duty to obey unjust laws are seldom raised in the hundreds and thousands of cases which are tried every day. Every day judges are faced with a problem of justice and fairness which is far from simple, and for which legal training provides little guidance.[5] The learned members of committees who have written about sentencing devise intricate schemes for figuring out how long is long enough but spend little thought on other options.

Most judges who write books are on the appellate courts, where they do not have the task of imposing sentences. They are removed from the often distressing presence of litigants, criminal defendants, and victims of crime. Many of the seminal philosophical works by leading American jurists have ignored the problems of sentencing or viewed it in abstract philosophical terms.[6]

The vast majority of books dealing with crime and punishment have been written by philosophers and sociologists. Sociologists working with teams of researchers look at facts, particularly those items that can be quantified, such as type of crime, age, sex, and race of offenders and length of sentences. From such data they seek to discern abstract properties and to establish relationships in quantitative form. Philosophers who deal with problems of crime and justice adumbrate principles of rights and responsibilities. They develop theoretical justifications for punishment which are logical, self-contained, and universal. Psychiatrists also discuss punishment but primarily from the point of view of its effect on the criminal, not on the rest of society. They are engaged in treating the ill, not in enforcing the law.

Trial judges look at crime and punishment very differently from these other professionals. A judge deals with specific cases and individuals, one at a time. What may be true of 90 percent of the population does not concern the judge. His duty is to deal with the individual in court who may or may not be average or typical, who may indeed be the rare, aberrant, and statistically insignificant individual who deviates from the norm of criminals. In each case, a judge is faced with a unique individual and a specific crime. The judge must be concerned with the rights of the accused, protection of society, and promotion of the rule of law. None of these other professionals has ever been faced with the necessity of imposing a penalty upon a single individual.

It is not easy to look any human being in the eye and say, "I am placing you behind bars for two years or ten years, sending you to a place where you will not be able to see your spouse and family except under degrading circumstances, a place which may not be physically safe, where you may be beaten or sexually abused, where most of your time will be spent in idleness or performing boring routine tasks for pay of perhaps fifteen cents an hour, where you will have no privacy, little opportunity to study, no opportunity to do meaningful work or support your family or make amends for the wrong you have committed." How does one justify such an action taken in the name of law and government? What are the facts and the theories which impel courts to impose sentences of imprisonment on tens of thousands of men, women, and children every year? Is there a choice other than prison which will vindicate the law, protect society and the victim, and do justice to the offender? These are the questions which sentencing judges ask themselves.

Sociologists proceed from an entirely different premise—the examination of how society behaves. They deal with measurable facts derived from large numbers of instances which afford averages and means. They do not purport to describe any individual or make a judgment or prediction with respect to any particular person. Sociological data are useful to legislators. But they must be received by judges with caution. An average family may consist of 1.9 children. A judge never sees that statistically important fiction—nine-tenths of a child. Nor can a judge deal with averages. Out of 10,000 people 9999 have never killed. A judge is not dealing in percentages but with a particular human being. Did he or did he not commit this unlikely and improbable act?

The importance of treating people as individuals was recognized in the Bible. According to the Scriptures, Satan told David to count the people of Israel and David did so. God then said to David, "You have sinned."[7] Many commentators have offered exegeses of this passage. The one that appeals to me explains that God was angry because David treated people as interchangeable units rather than unique human beings. A journalist, in describing a noted criminologist, wrote, "For thirty years [he] has been working not with real live criminals but with data about criminals."[8] This is an important distinction.

Philosophers do not deal with individuals either. They design ideal constructs, created without the disturbing emotional overtones which inevitably arise when one tries to apply a beautiful symmetrical theory to the untidy, irrational lives of people who find their way into the courts. In considering philosophical analyses of the justifications for criminal penalties and sociological reports, a judge is often reminded of the colloquy in Koestler's *The Age of Longing*. The Colonel, who believes in statistics, asks, "Is that a fact?" The Frenchman replies, "It must be, for it can be logically deduced." Judges are painfully aware of the illogical nature of the acts committed by criminal offenders.

Philosophers devote a great deal of thought to the fringe or hard cases, exotic situations which rarely come before a court, such as the moral right of shipwrecked survivors to eat one of their number in order to save the lives of the remaining people. They also discuss logical problems that do not arise under law. For example, can there be a wrong without a person who has been wronged?[9] Judges have no difficulty with this question. The law proscribes the sale of heroin. Any sale of heroin is a crime and a legal wrong. A sale to an undercover agent of the police is a crime although obviously the agent has not been wronged. Similarly, drunk driving which does not result in an accident is a crime even though no one has been wronged. The refinements of a symmetrical theory of wrongs and persons wronged which occupies much time of philosophers is irrelevant to judges except as an intellectual exercise, like a game of chess. Similarly, the problem of criminal intent raises interesting philosophical questions, but not legal problems. A philosopher asks: Should an individual who intends no harm but sells a commodity which poisons people be held culpable? If a statute proscribes the sale of this commodity regardless of intent, a judge will find little difficulty in convicting the vendor of this violation of positive law. The penalty to be imposed, however, will undoubtedly cause the judge great difficulty. If a moderate fine is imposed, the public will probably believe that the penalty is not commensurate with the harm done. A prison sentence, which is rarely imposed, may seem to be unduly harsh for a person who had no evil intent. Neither choice seems appropriate.

Philosophers seek to propound one overarching theory, valid in all situations. A judge faced with an infinite variety of circumstances under which crimes are committed and the unique qualities of each criminal and each victim has more modest goals—a theory that will morally justify what the judge is impelled by law to do in a particular case. A painstaking review of philosophical literature from Plato to Hart, Rawls, and Foucault, has failed to provide me or any of the judges I know with an acceptable rationale for the sentences we are obliged to impose every day.[10]

It is difficult to discuss sentences without using words like fair and just. These are the very terms which philosophers struggle to define. Indeed in a feat of intellectual tautology, a theory of "justice as fairness" has been propounded. Such semantic efforts provide little guidance to a perplexed judge who sees many aspects of the law and the administration of justice which are manifestly unfair. In civil cases, for example, a plaintiff who is ever so slightly negligent is, in many jurisdictions, precluded from recovering damages from a defendant who was very negligent. Such divergence between the law and a fair result is not uncommon in both civil and criminal cases.

A judge who takes seriously the oath of office to uphold the law must many times render a decision which most people, including the judge, consider unfair. What should a judge do when the law impels an unjust result? Blindly to follow the law reduces a judge to an amoral bureaucrat, an Eichmann who obeys orders regardless of the fairness or morality of his acts and regardless of the consequences. To render a decision which is "fair" to the litigants but violates the law undermines the entire structure of government which is predicated on the rule of law. It has been an article of faith in common-law countries like the United States and Great Britain since 1215, the signing of the Magna Carta, that no person is above the law. Certainly a judge should not violate the law.[11] A conscientious judge may often find that he or she is presiding over injustice. This occurs with great frequency in the imposition of sentence on an offender.

What is fair to the criminal? What is fair to society? What is fair to the victim? How should one reconcile these often divergent claims? In the enormous literature on the subject, there is little discussion of these questions which arise in almost every case. Even in the clearest case in which the accused admits his guilt and where there are no mitigating circumstances and the victim of the crime is entirely innocent, the fixing of a fair or just penalty is not easy. Take, for example, an unprovoked assault by a strong young man on a frail elderly man in the course of a robbery. This is a common crime. Most street crimes are committed by young men. Most victims are people unlikely to offer much resistance, such as women and elderly men. Reginald, the attacker, is not mentally ill or incompetent. He was not under the influence of drugs or alcohol at the time of the crime. There is no doubt that he is guilty. He came into court and pled guilty. I asked him, as I ask every accused person who wants to enter a guilty plea, "Are you pleading guilty because you did in fact rob Mr. Jones without any excuse or justification?" Sometimes, the defendant will say "No" and I refuse to accept the plea.

Reginald said, "Yes, I did rob the old man and I knocked him down. I didn't mean to hurt him. I just wanted to steal his wallet."

The facts are clear. There is no legal problem as to the crime, the voluntariness of the plea, or the competence of the defendant. The difficult question is the penalty. Pre-sentence reports which are supposed to offer guidance to the judge vary in reliability, sensitivity, and objectivity—as do the decisions of judges. Such reports are made by social workers, psychologists, and psychiatrists. These people are faceless employees who provide information, opinions, and recommendations. But they have no responsibility to the public, the criminal, or the victim. The report on Reginald discloses that he is twenty-two years old, did not complete high school, shifted from school to school until he reached age sixteen, and dropped out in the tenth grade, dull normal I.Q., no steady employment, no close family ties. His parents separated when Reginald was a small child. Reginald is unmarried, the father of one or more children whom he does not support. He spent two years in an institution for juvenile delinquents. He received an honorable discharge from the military after six months' service. He states that he has no sexual problems and no hobbies. Religion plays no part in his life. The board-certified psychiatrist who examined Reginald found no mental illness, but reported "poor internal control" and "low self-image."

No friends or relatives appeared in court when Reginald pled guilty. No character witnesses were presented. A judge knows that an honorable military discharge after only six months' service is the army's easy way of avoiding problems. Someone, perhaps a staff sergeant, recognized that Reginald was a misfit, the kind of person who is unreliable, who cannot be counted on to act with common sense and restraint. One can infer that the army, like the school system, simply wanted to get rid of him.

Under the law, Reginald is responsible. He did not plead not guilty by reason of insanity. The psychiatrist found he was not psychotic or suffering from any mental illness. In imposing a penalty, should the judge simply ignore Reginald's background? Are there no degrees of responsibility? Does not childhood deprivation affect the adult? The judge can only wonder what hurts have scarred Reginald. He is physically unattractive. He should have had orthodentia. He spits a little when he speaks. Who knows what slights an ugly, unloved, not very bright child must have suffered? He is not in touch with the mother of his child. He does not see his own child or support him. Is the terrible cycle of anomie and solipsism already being repeated?

It is easy to blame Reginald's mother, his missing father, an uncaring school system, a society that provided him with only the niggardly support of welfare. This deprived life evokes sympathy. But does it explain Reginald's behavior? Can or should it exonerate him from responsibility? The law does not, except in a few jurisdictions which have a doctrine of "diminished respnsibility," recognize gradations of self-control, capacity to reason and choose between the paths of licit and illicit conduct. The law presumes that if the defendant is not "insane," he is competent and must answer for his acts.

The elderly man, Archie Jones, who was knocked to the ground when Reginald grabbed his wallet, suffered a broken hip. He came to court hobbling on two canes. There was only five dollars and some change in his wallet. Reginald had spent the money before he was apprehended. The wallet with the identification was recovered. Medicare paid for most of Mr. Jones' hospital expenses. Before this robbery he was self-sufficient. He lived in a rented room with a hot plate and cooked his own meals. Mr. Jones can no longer do his own shopping or go to visit his cronies. He has difficulty taking care of his meagre room. He is in constant pain.

Without benefit of a clearly articulated public policy, with only the cold comfort of statistics—that Reginald has two chances out of three of being arrested and convicted again for another crime—the judge must decide "in" or "out." If he chooses "in," how long is long enough? There are no reliable statistics that can tell a judge that six months in jail is more beneficial than a year or vice versa. There is some evidence that more than five years in prison is more harmful to the individual than less than five years. But even this information is tenuous and depends on the individual, the crime, and the prison.

The social worker recommends probation. He believes that Reginald will benefit from the guidance of the probation department. Prison may be injurious to him. Any parent who has more than one child knows that it is impossible to be completely fair to two competing persons at the same time. To give one his due is to deprive the other to some extent. This is a problem with which the courts are wrestling in cases involving affirmative action.[12] This issue has not yet been raised in the context of sentencing. Reginald is in court. So is Archie Jones. For Reginald to walk out a free man, subject only to reporting to a probation officer once a month, trivializes the harm done to Archie and the entire principle of the rule of law. Should it be "in" or "out" for Reginald? Neither decision is satisfactory. The "hardliner" prefers prison. The "bleeding heart" tries probation. Most judges would prefer other options.

There is an infinity of variables in any criminal case. No two defendants are alike, as no two fingerprints are alike. A judge sees an enormous variety of human beings with their weaknesses and their strengths, their kindnesses and their cruelties. As each defendant appears before him, the judge knows that others, equally if not more guilty, have not been incarcerated. Does the principle of equal justice under law require the judge to take into account the sentences imposed in these other cases? The judge also knows that neither a harsh nor a lenient penalty will provide redress for the victim. Nor will the penalty contribute to public faith or disbelief in the rule of law. Most cases will not be reported in the press. No one will know or care what sentence is imposed except the victim, the defendant, and their families.

For several years I imposed the legally prescribed penalties of fines, imprisonment, and probation with growing unease and an awareness that I was presiding over legally sanctioned injustice. It was not until the case of Alfie that I decided there was another option available to the court which reasonably satisfied my imperfectly articulated and tentative philosophy of justice. Alfie's girlfriend, Lulu, had left him, taking the children, and had gone to live with her new boyfriend, Gerald. After brooding about this for several days, Alfie bought a gun and ammunition and went to the home of Lulu and Gerald in the middle of the night. Alfie knocked on the door. Gerald opened it. Instantly Alfie shot Gerald pointblank in the face, permanently blinding him.

At the time of trial, Alfie slunk into the courtroom. His lawyer presented a series of defenses: the gun went off accidentally; Alfie was just going to visit his children; Gerald had attacked him. Lulu led Gerald into the courtroom. He is a tall, handsome man who walks fearfully, hesitatingly. Clutching Lulu with one hand, he cautiously felt for a chair. Out of habit, he turned his sightless eyes in the direction of the speaker. Gerald was thirty-four years old. He had been employed as a foreman for many years in a factory manufacturing heavy and complex machinery. Since the incident he stays home all day and night. He is afraid to leave the apartment. The trial was short; conviction was inevitable. Again the only real question was what penalty to impose.

The prosecutor argued with passion that this heinous crime demanded the maximum penalty—ten to twenty years' imprisonment. He did not mention the fine, a maximum of twenty-five thousand dollars. If Alfie was sentenced to prison, obviously he could not pay a fine. Alfie had no resources except his modest salary. "Think of the victim," the prosecutor implored.

Defense counsel took the line of reasonableness. Alfie had not intended this unfortunate result. He was a young man who had no prior record, an unusual accomplishment in his environment, and he had good family ties. His father had a modest business where Alfie was employed. "What good will it do society or the victim to incarcerate Alfie?" the lawyer asked.

I knew that it would cost the taxpayers approximately twenty thousand dollars a year to keep Alfie in prison. Society would get no benefits from this expenditure. If Alfie was out and working, he would at least be self-supporting, pay taxes, and possibly contribute to the support of his children. The pre-sentence report indicated that Alfie was a high-school graduate, not psychotic, and not in need of rehabilitation or therapy. He was clearly no danger to anyone other than Gerald.

Both arguments were valid. Probation, which returns the defendant to society without punishment, would corrode the credibility of the law. Imprisonment for a long term would destroy the defendant and be costly to the taxpayers. Neither probation nor imprisonment would help the victim. I resolved to find a more appropriate penalty. I placed Alfie on probation for the maximum term which, combining all the charges, totalled nineteen years and conditioned it upon his paying Gerald, the victim, twenty-five dollars a week. This was a sum within his earning capacity. Alfie appealed, specifically alleging that the sentence was illegal. The Supreme Court of the state sustained this order of reparation. Since then I have ordered monetary restitution or reparation whenever it was feasible.

Such a sentence can only be considered rough justice. $25 a week does not compensate Gerald for his tragic impairment. If he had been blinded as a result of an accident and the responsible party was adequately insured, he would recover at least $250,000.

Most defendants I see are unemployed, often unemployable. A sentence of restitution or reparation may not be enforceable. On occasion it has spurred a defendant who has been on welfare for years to go out and get a job. It rarely provides adequate compensation to the victim. But the underlying principle seems to me to be valid. If people are to be held legally responsible for their acts, it follows that they should be responsible for the harm they have caused.

There are many problems not only in attempting to fashion individual sentences, but also in justifying a principle of reparation rather than retribution or rehabilitation or any of the traditional grounds for imprisonment which have been postulated by philosophers, legal scholars, and criminologists.

In succeeding chapters we shall consider the views of respected contemporary authorities and attempt to apply them to the ordinary cases which come before the courts. We shall also look back in history to see how we arrived at the extraordinary situation prevailing in the United States today. There are at least four hundred thousand adults in prisons and jails in the United States and perhaps one hundred thousand children in some form of secure custody.[13] It costs the taxpayers from $10,000 to $40,000 or more to maintain each one of them for one year. At least two-thirds of them will be convicted of another offense after release.

I believe that for many offenders there are choices other than "in" or "out" and that such choices are more consonant with our "evolving standards of morality" and with the needs of people living in a complex and impersonal society.[14]

It may be presumptuous for one individual to propose a change in the sentencing practices which have prevailed in American courts for two centuries. I have no special or unique qualifications for this task. My experience does not differ substantially from that of any other trial judge presiding over major felony and homicide cases in the courts of every big city in the United States. I have presided over scores of homicide cases and hundreds of felony cases and have been obliged to impose sentences on these offenders. I have seen them and their families. They write to me and come to visit me. I have seen the victims of these crimes and their families. Judges who sit in rural and suburban communities and in federal courts with ten or twenty years on the bench may preside over at most two or three murder cases and half a dozen rape cases. Their perspectives will, perhaps, be different.

A judge is not simply a bureaucrat dealing with problems of administration of government. The decisions of many of these government employees affect the safety and welfare of the public and may cause more widespread harm or benefit than the decisions of any judge. But the responsibilities of these government employees are different from those of a judge. A judge is elected or appointed to office. A judge has taken an oath of office to support and defend the Constitution. Implicit in this oath is the promise to ensure that no person shall be denied the equal protection of the laws and that no person shall be deprived of life, liberty, or property without due process of law. I have reluctantly concluded that our sentencing practices frequently do not meet these standards and rarely serve the needs of the offender, the victim, and society.

I am not alone in my dissatisfaction. The United States Congress is considering a federal crimes code which includes an important section on sentencing. Many states have enacted sentencing codes or are debating them. Sociologists and legal scholars are drastically revising their theories. This is an opportune time to present for the consideration of legislatures and the public a review of the problems, theories, and proposals now under consideration and to suggest other goals, standards, and policies in sentencing offenders.

My conclusions are based on the belief that every human being is responsible for his acts. Mr. Justice Cardozo declared the premise of responsibility clearly. All western civilization, he wrote, is "guided by a robust common sense which assures the freedom of will as a working hypothesis in the solution of [legal] problems."[15] We accept that assumption because there is no workable alternative. We must also assume that every offender owes a debt for the wrong he has done. The maintenance of a civilized society depends upon this responsible interrelationship among people.

In sentencing an offender, a judge should strive for proportionality between the penalty and the offense. A judge should also recognize the inequalities and differences among individuals and their rights to equality of treatment. I do not suggest that any one form of penalty is appropriate for all offenses and all offenders. I do, however, believe that every penalty must provide for the needs of the victim, society, and the offender. A penalty which requires restitution or reparation is, I believe, congruent with a humanistic and democratic concept of society and with decent treatment of criminals. It would provide a feasible alternative to prison and probation for many offenders.

CHAPTER II

THE SYSTEM

Friend: What is the Answer?
Gertrude Stein: What is the Question?

In most crimes there are two parties involved: the criminal and the victim. All of society may constitute the victim class when the criminal is a government official who betrays the public trust. A more limited group is involved when corporate officials embezzle company funds, in which case the victims are the stockholders. In street crimes, the immediate victim is most often an individual, the person whose purse is snatched, whose home is burglarized, who is mugged or raped. In homicides the relatives of the victim may also be victimized when the deceased had been the breadwinner. Under the criminal justice system the victim of crime is not a party to the prosecution of the case and is not entitled to redress for the harm done him.

The purpose of any legal system which has a tribunal for adjudicating disputes is obviously to do justice. What justice is, both in the abstract and in particular cases, presents extraordinarily difficult questions. For millennia philosophers have been attempting to determine what justice is. The statement attributed to Socrates in the first book of *The Republic* that justice is giving to each man what is proper to him provides a serviceable definition for lawyers and judges. In civil cases, this is roughly what American courts attempt to do. The parties to the transaction involved are in court and the judge or jury decides what is due each. Under our law, what is due is translated in terms of money. Occasionally, the court orders a party to perform a specific act or to refrain from doing certain acts. A seller may be ordered to deliver title to a particular house instead of paying the value of the house. Strikers will be ordered not to picket or to limit their picketing. But in most cases judgment is ordered in terms of monetary compensation as nearly equivalent to the loss or injuries sustained as the court or jury can approximate. This is what the late Justice Andrews of New York termed "rough, average justice." Although litigants are often displeased with the result of a civil trial, compensation for injury is regarded as a just and proper system.

When we examine the operations of the criminal law, we find that it is governed by entirely different principles. A crime is an offense against the state. The bill of indictment or information reads, "John Doe did feloniously and unlawfully rob Richard Roe of $1,050 on or about March 2, 1975, in the City and County of——, all of which is against the peace and dignity of the state." The parties to the prosecution are the state and John Doe. If Doe is convicted, the penalty will be exacted by the state. If it is a fine, it will be paid to the state. The court in administering criminal justice makes no effort to determine what is due the victim of crime or to give him that which is his due. From time to time courts are admonished to think of the victim of crime. A former Chief Justice of Pennsylvania, addressing the bench and the bar, declared, "Too often we in the courts, in dealing with those accused of crime, think only of the rights of the accused and forget the rights of the victim of the crime and society at large."[1] Such a statement probably reflects the dissatisfaction which many Americans feel today when they contemplate the ever-increasing lawlessness of our society and the apparent inability of government to prevent or control crime. It is a natural reaction to be angry at the offender, to sympathize with the victim, and to ask the courts seriously to think about the victims.

In the trial of a criminal case and in the sentencing of the criminal, judges do think about the victim, but there is little they can do for him. The criminal law is not structured to take into account the victim's needs or to give him what is due him. This failure of the criminal justice system to provide for the victims of crime is, in my opinion, a major source of public dissatisfaction with the law even though legal scholars have not considered it a problem.

Dean Roscoe Pound of the Harvard Law School in a seminal address to the American Bar Association in 1906 entitled "Causes of Popular Dissatisfaction with the Law" did not mention criminal law. Warren Burger, Chief Justice of the United States Supreme Court, has repeatedly called for reform of the criminal justice system and urged improvements in sentencing. In his address to the American Bar Association at the mid-year meeting on February 11, 1979, the Chief Justice stated:

No one can examine from a national perspective, or even the overall perspective within one district or one metropolitan area, the sentences of individual judges without being deeply concerned about seeming disparities. Of course there can be no such thing as perfect or uniform sentencing of convicted persons. Much depends upon the individual offender, the prior record, and the circumstances of the particular offense—and on the sentencing judge. In this sensitive area we cannot measure sentences with a computer or a slide rule. Yet, any serious examination of the subject leaves one with a sense of unease over the unreviewable choices sometimes made by individual judges.

Mr. Justice Burger focused on the crime, the offender, and the judge. He did not mention the victims of crime or suggest that criminal sentences take into account the needs of the victim. The average citizen, however, finds the failure of the criminal justice system to provide for the victims of crime a major source of dissatisfaction. I have not conducted a public opinion poll on the subject, but any number of citizens have strongly expressed this view. Prospective jurors often indicate their disillusionment.

A jury is drawn at random from all the registered voters in the jurisdiction. It includes men and women from the age of eighteen to perhaps eighty of all races and economic conditions. Since many poor and semi-literate people do not register to vote and certain occupations such as doctors and lawyers are routinely excused, a jury panel may not be wholly representative. But it is certainly a reasonable sampling of the community.

When a panel of citizens are called for jury duty in a criminal case they are asked if they can be fair to the state and the defendant. Their responses are frequently dismaying. Prospective jurors are questioned about prior involvement in crime. One of the first questions I ask every panel is: "Have you or any of your very close friends or relatives been the victim of a crime?" More than half of the forty people on each jury panel usually raise their hands indicating an affirmative response. When I ask how many of these crimes involved personal contact with the criminal, not the theft of a car or burglary of an unoccupied building, the response is well over one-third. Victimless crimes like drunk driving, numbers writing, and drug traffic are not covered by these questions. The illegal activities of organized crime rarely affect individual citizens who are not a part of the crime syndicate. White-collar crimes such as fraud and kickbacks by government officials, tax evasions, check kiting, securities frauds, and violations of environmental and health laws are also not covered by these questions.

Both the prosecutor and the defense attorney ask searching questions of the jury panel in an effort to select as jurors individuals who can listen to the evidence with an open mind, follow the instructions of the court on the law, and render a verdict based upon the facts and the law. Although some people try to avoid jury duty, the vast majority do not. They want to be good citizens. Most people believe that jury duty is a privilege and an obligation. They answer thoughtfully the questions which are put to them by the attorneys and the judge.

Each prospective juror who indicates that either he or a close friend or relative has been the victim of a crime of violence is closely questioned by both the prosecution and the defense. Many people say they will try to be fair. A sizeable number will somewhat reluctantly admit, "I'll try to be fair but I'm not sure that I can be." I question such people further.

A middle-aged man in work clothes declared that he couldn't give anybody a fair trial.

"Why can't you give this man a fair trial?" I asked him. "You're an intelligent person. It's your duty as a citizen to serve on a jury. There are not many countries where ordinary citizens can participate in the administration of justice."

"I'll tell you why," he answered belligerently. "I was robbed. I was taking the receipts from my auto body shop to the bank—over three thousand dollars. It was a very good week. We done a big job on a Mercedes. These two young punks jumped me and grabbed my money. I was in the hospital for two months. By the time I got out, my business was gone."

Q. Were the robbers apprehended?

A. Yes.

Q. And brought to trial?

A. Yes. The judge sent 'em up. But I didn't get a cent back. I still owe the hospital and the doctors. And I lost my business.

Neither the prosecution nor the defense wanted him on the jury.

I cannot forget a young college girl who was on one panel. She said she was studying psychology. "I'd like to serve on a jury, but I don't think I could be fair to this defendant," she said looking searchingly at him. "I was mugged on a subway platform. He—he grabbed my bag. There

was only a few dollars in it. But I screamed and he cut me with a knife.
People came running. They grabbed him. I guess I was lucky I wasn't
killed."

Q. Was he brought to trial?

A. Yes.

Q. And convicted?

A. Yes. They gave me back my pocketbook. But I have this scar. I
can't afford plastic surgery. I still have nightmares thinking about him.

Q. But this is a different man.

A. I know. I know it's wrong. Every time I look in the mirror, I'm
reminded of it, the unfairness to me, to my whole life. I just don't think
I could be fair to any robber.

Her hand trembled as she fingered the livid disfiguring scar on her
cheek.

A soft-spoken woman with neatly waved gray hair explained, "Your
honor, my brother was shot during a holdup six years ago. He's a hopeless
cripple. He lives on welfare. The criminal went to jail for a few years.
But he's out now, riding around in a new car. My brother can't move
off his bed. How can I be fair when the whole system is unfair?"

A judge seeing hundreds of victims of crimes who are left scarred or
maimed or simply deprived of their property also has misgivings about
the fairness of the criminal justice system. It is not easy to dismiss these
thoughts with the comment of a rich and handsome young president
that "Life is unfair." The purpose of a system of law is to provide a
measure of fairness in the transactions of life.

All too often in criminal cases, even when the guilty are convicted,
the result is anything but fair. Most crimes are committed for money.
Better-educated people steal with a pen or a computer. Less educated
people use a gun, a knife, a blow of the fist, or simply rely on the fact
that most people cannot guard their possessions every minute of the day.
The vast majority of criminal prosecutions brought in the state courts
involve such crimes.

Four seemingly disparate cases show that the victims of run-of-the-
mill crimes have no legal redress for their losses. Jerry was observed by
a supermarket detective lifting a wallet from Mrs. S.'s pocket while she
was doing her shopping. There was a scuffle and a chase. With the help
of a passing police car, Jerry was apprehended some forty-five minutes
later. The wallet was returned to Mrs. S. Somewhere along the way Jerry
had managed to pass fifty-five dollars which was in the wallet to his pal.

This fifty-five dollars was the amount which the S. family had allocated for their supply of food for the week. Jerry's pal was never apprehended. Norman, another crime victim, lives in a housing project. He is a jazz buff and works in a music store. The pride of his life was his elaborate and expensive hi-fi set. Despite three locks on the door of his apartment and a security guard on the premises, Norman's apartment was broken into while he was at work. The hi-fi set, a TV, and a tape recorder were stolen as well as his collection of cassettes. Several weeks later, the guard seized Allen in the act of stealing a TV from another apartment. In the course of investigation Allen confessed to more than half a dozen burglaries, including the burglary of Norman's apartment. Allen is a drug addict. He is a high-school dropout. He has never had a job. He pled guilty and was sentenced to prison where he will receive drug therapy and attend school. Norman testified that his hi-fi equipment cost over one thousand dollars. When I questioned Allen about the hi-fi, he said he had sold it for fifty dollars. He does not know the purchaser.

When Sally came into the courtroom everyone looked up. The bored court officers who have seen everything and try to forget most of it before they go home, looked at her with interest. Sally is a stunning, stylish redhead who looks much younger than her forty-seven years. She has been victimized by several criminals. Sally is a widow who owns a small dress shop specializing in low-cost, jazzy fashions. She supports her two children and a sister who has a serious heart ailment. The shop is in a rundown part of the city where it is impossible to get burglary insurance.

Nelson went into Sally's store with a girlfriend. While Sally was showing clothes to the girl, he sauntered over to the cash register and took all the money. When Sally turned around, Nelson pulled a knife. "Freeze," he ordered. Sally froze. The girl helped herself to quantities of clothes which she tossed into a bag. Just as they were leaving Nelson went over to Sally, pulled her earrings off her pierced ears, yanked a gold chain from her neck, and demanded her rings. She gave him two rings.

Sally testified, "I was crying from the pain. My ears were bleeding. He said, 'Give me the other ring.' I said, 'That's my wedding ring. It's not worth anything to you. Let me keep it.'"

Nelson laughed and snatched it off her finger. Sally gave the police a careful description of Nelson and the girl. This was by no means their first robbery. The police arrested Nelson a few days later. Sally had no trouble identifying him in a line-up of eight other males, all approximately the same height, weight, and complexion. She had been robbed several times and had learned by bitter experience to be extremely observant. The first two times her store had been held up she was so frightened that she could not even be sure of the clothing the robber was wearing, his height, or his weight. She had looked carefully at Nelson. In particular, she described the hand that grabbed her wedding ring. That hand had an unusual ring on the fourth finger. Nelson was wearing the ring that Sally described when he was arrested.

At sentencing I asked Nelson what he had done with Sally's wedding ring. He had sold it for two dollars.

Sally, like Mrs. S. and Norman, had to bear the entire loss of the crime. None of them had insurance. The merchandise which was taken from Sally's store represented more than a week's profit. She had medical bills for the savage rips in her earlobes. The only memento of her late husband is gone.

Mrs. L. is another widow who had no insurance. She is a black lady seventy-three years old who owns a three-storey rooming house. She had two flats on each floor which she rented furnished. Adeline and Joseph lived on the top floor front. One day Joseph and Adeline had been drinking heavily and began to quarrel. Joseph slugged her a few times, knocking out a tooth. He felt better then and dropped on the bed and fell sound asleep. It was around noontime. Adeline was furiously angry and drunk. She poured a can of kerosene on the bedding, lit a match, and walked out locking the door behind her. The flames finally wakened Joseph. He couldn't get out the door, so he took a flying leap out of the window, bounced on a porch, and landed unharmed on the grass. The other tenants were out at work. By the time a neighbor called the fire department the whole top floor was burned.

The tenants in the other third-floor apartment lost all their possessions. Mrs. L. lost the furniture in the two apartments. She could not afford to repair the house. At the time of trial, she was living on the ground floor. Joseph and Adeline and the tenants in the other burned-out apartment had moved. Mrs. L.'s income was drastically reduced by the loss of the rentals from two apartments.

Adeline was charged with arson and recklessly endangering another person. She had a novel plea to the second charge, self defense. She claimed that to defend herself from Joseph's assaults she set him on fire. When she realized that I was not impressed with that testimony, she said coyly, "Your honor, Joseph wants to drop the charge. We've made up. We got ourselves a new apartment and we're buying furniture."

"You're buying furniture," I expostulated. "What about Mrs. L.'s furniture that you burned! Who's buying furniture for her? Why don't you pay her back for all her losses and the other tenants, too?"

"But, your honor," she exclaimed, "How can I pay them? I don't work."

A pre-sentence investigation disclosed that Adeline is forty-one years old, a high-school graduate. She is literate and of normal intelligence, not psychotic or mentally ill. She has never had a job. She has a drinking problem. A sentence of probation conditioned upon attendance at an alcohol treatment center was recommended.

At sentencing Joseph was in court with Adeline. Both were dressed in new clothes. Adeline confided that they were going to be married. I suggested that she would be spending her honeymoon in prison. To the astonishment of everyone, Joseph asked for permission to speak. He offered to pay for the repair of Mrs. L.'s house and the losses of the other tenants if I would release Adeline on probation. Joseph is a successful numbers writer. I placed Adeline on probation and imposed a stiff order of restitution which she is paying off weekly. She now has a job and is off welfare for the first time in her adult life.

If Joseph and Adeline had negligently caused the fire and burned Mrs. L's home, she and the other tenants could have sued them and recovered damages for their losses. Because Joseph had not set the fire, I had no authority to order him to pay restitution to Mrs. L. and the other tenants. Adeline could not possibly have earned enough money within a reasonable period of time to pay for the repairs of Mrs. L's house. If Joseph had not sufficiently desired Adeline's company, Mrs. L. and the other tenants would have had absolutely no legal redress for their losses. Neither Sally nor Norman had any legal redress for the loss of their property and Sally's medical bills. Nor did Mrs. S. have any redress for the money taken from her pocketbook.

In civil cases people injured through the carelessness of others are awarded monetary damages. The judge instructs the jury that the purpose of damages is compensation, to restore the person to the position he would have been in if the accident had not occurred. The items to be included in the damages are medical expenses and additional household expenses, past lost wages, future loss of wages, compensation for pain, suffering, disfigurement, and loss of life's pleasures. The spouse of the injured person is also entitled to recover for loss of companionship and additional duties and hardships resulting from the injury.

The case of Mrs. Charlotte P. was an ordinary run-of-the-mill personal injury case. It involved no unusual questions. The jury deliberated less than three hours and returned a unanimous verdict in her favor. The defendant did not appeal. The bus in which Mrs. P. was riding to work sideswiped a car, knocking Mrs. P. off her seat. Mrs. P. was thirty-six years old and in good health. She sustained a broken arm and a bad back injury; she underwent two operations. For more than six months she was unable to do any housework or take care of her children. She was out of work more than three months. Mr. P. had to do the housework in addition to his own job and his usual chores. A neighbor was hired to help out for six weeks. Before the accident Mrs. P. had been an active and happy woman. She was a member of a bowling team. She was a girl-scout leader. She and her husband liked to go dancing. On their vacations they went on camping trips with their children.

At the time of trial, three years after the accident, Mrs. P. was still unable to sit for more than fifteen minutes. Her face was lined with pain. She looked at least fifty years old. She had returned to work because the family needed her income. But she was unable to do any of the things she had formerly enjoyed. Her life consisted of going to work, coming home, and going to bed. Her husband did most of the household chores. The jury awarded her damages of $175,000 and her husband $45,000.

Mrs. Maureen F. was in her early thirties. She, too, was married. She had four children. She sang in her church choir, baked cookies for the school fair, and made most of her daughters' clothing and her own. She and her husband were avid bridge players. On her way home from work she was accosted by two men who grabbed her purse and pushed her into an automobile. They drove her to a secluded spot in the park. Both men raped her, forced her to commit sodomy, and beat her. Then they put her in the back seat of the car and drove off. When they stopped for a red light she opened the car door and screamed. As the rapists sped away, Mrs. F. fell to the street. She broke both ankles. The open car door swung and struck her in the face. The driver of another car which was also stopped for the light took the license number of the fleeing car and drove Mrs. F. to the hospital. The assailants were apprehended and brought to trial.

Six months later, Mrs. F. came to court on crutches. She had a bad facial tic. The car door had damaged a nerve when it struck her face. She was unable to return to work. She was having constant nightmares. She was unable to have sexual relations with her husband. They cannot afford psychiatric treatment for her. They may lose their home because they cannot make the mortgage payments and pay for the children's food and clothing on Mr. F.'s salary even though he now works nights and Saturdays in addition to his regular job.

Mr. and Mrs. F. were in the courtroom when the jury returned from its deliberations. Mr. F. had been tense and nervous throughout the entire trial. He sat erect in the first row of the hard wooden benches for spectators, his spine ramrod stiff. When a guilty verdict was announced Mr. F. slumped in the seat. There was only weariness, no satisfaction, on his face. Mrs. F. was impassive. She did not look at the defendants or the jury. She did not even turn to her husband. They did not hold hands or touch each other. Mr. F. picked up their coats and handed the crutches to Mrs. F. Slowly and haltingly they walked out of the courtroom. The prosecutor provided a car to drive them home. Mrs. F. was paid five dollars a day for coming to court for the two days she testified.

The criminal justice system was finished with Mrs. F. In criminal cases, juries do not award damages. They only decide the guilt or innocence of the accused. The judge imposes the sentence. There is nothing that I as the trial judge can do for Mrs. F. to help her rebuild her broken body and her shattered life. Mr. F. is tight-lipped and harried. Will their marriage survive? They have two teenage daughters. What effect will this crime have on their lives? In what subtle ways will it alter their attitudes toward men, courtship, and marriage? I will never know for I will not see Mr. and Mrs. F. again.

My responsibilities for the two defendants, however, have just begun. Both men were convicted of rape, deviate sexual intercourse, and aggravated assault. I ordered pre-sentence investigations and neuropsychiatric examinations of both defendants. Six weeks later I received the reports.

Albert H. is twenty-four years old. He has a long history of arrests, but no conviction for a serious crime. He was acquitted of two prior rape charges. When he was tried on those charges the law required the jury to take the testimony of a rape victim with caution because of her emotional involvement. Albert may have been guilty of those rapes. He left school in the eleventh grade. He served in the army for three years and received an honorable discharge. Since then he has been unemployed except for an occasional temporary job. He is not married. He has two children whom he does not support. His I.Q. test score is dull normal. The psychiatrist reported that he is the youngest of seven children, that he has a warm family relationship with his parents and siblings, but that he has a sense of inferiority. His older brothers are established in homes of their own. He was diagnosed as a "passive aggressive" personality and in need of therapy. The prognosis for Albert with therapy is "guarded."

Douglas M. is only nineteen years old and has no prior record. He left school in the tenth grade. He has never had a job. Douglas has not seen his father for many years. His mother has high blood pressure and cannot work. His I.Q. is low.

The psychiatrist who had gleaned his information about the crime from Douglas reports that Douglas was an unwilling participant who was dragged into the incident by Albert and taunted with being a sissy unless he participated. Douglas is small and slight. The psychiatrist reported that Douglas is emotionally immature and having problems of adolescence. He recommended psychiatric probation.

The pre-sentence investigator and the psychiatrists do not know the evidence that was produced at the trial. Mrs. F. testified that the big one (Albert) dragged her into the car, that both men pulled her out of the car, that the little one (Douglas) laughed while Albert was raping her and then demanded "his turn." She testified that when the big one finished, the little one came over, slapped her face and then took his turn. The investigators do not know that none of Albert's family, with whom he says he has close ties, appeared at the trial and that none of them would post bail for him. Douglas's mother tried to raise bail but was unable to do so. She is on welfare. They do not report that Douglas is functionally illiterate even though he completed tenth grade.

Both men were sentenced to prison. Albert was placed in the psychiatric ward where he is supposed to receive therapy regularly. He attended school in prison and obtained his high-school equivalency diploma in a year. He is learning a trade. He has chosen welding. There are any number of trade courses in prison. Douglas is slowly learning to read and write in prison. He, too, is supposed to be receiving psychiatric treatment. Both men are in a unit of the prison which employs several board-certified psychiatrists as well as psychologists and therapists. The routine prison medical examination of Douglas disclosed that he has an eye disorder and very bad teeth. He has had an operation on one eye and is getting a prolonged series of dental treatments. One man was represented by the public defender, the other by a court-appointed lawyer paid with public funds. Both defendants appealed their convictions and were represented by the same lawyers on appeal.

The prison reports to me regularly on their progress. The prison authorities recommended at the end of a year that Douglas be sent home on furlough to care for his sick mother. They suggested that he continue his schooling and therapy at home. If he is released he will receive welfare support.

I shall continue to receive reports on these men until their sentences expire. If they are released before the maximum sentence, which happens in most cases, they will be subject to the supervision of parole officers who will report to me. If either one is arrested for another crime while on parole, I will be notified and have to hold a hearing to decide whether to incarcerate him pending trial on the new charges.

The public is paying thousands of dollars each year to incarcerate, educate, train, treat, rehabilitate, and supervise each criminal. It spends nothing to treat and rehabilitate the victims of crime or to compensate them for their medical bills, lost wages, pain, and suffering.

Life is unfair. It is unfair to Mrs. Charlotte P., who certainly did not want to be injured in the bus accident. But at least insofar as money can provide reparation for harm done, the law protected her and awarded her and her husband redress because the harm down to them was unintentional.

The law did nothing for Mrs. F. and her family. The harm done to them was intentional. It was a crime, prosecuted by the state. The penalty for crime is imprisonment or a fine payable to the state, or both.

When Albert has served his minimum sentence, the parole board will decide whether or not to release him. The parole board will have reports from the prison. They will know what, if any, infraction of prison rules are on his record. The authorities will report his progress in his academic schooling and in trade school. Albert may well earn credits toward a college degree. When he is released in five or seven or ten years the parole authorities and voluntary charitable societies will help him get a job.

Douglas, who was not released at the end of a year, will probably learn to read at a fifth- or sixth-grade level after two or three years. In prison, he may be raped and brutalized by the other inmates. It is unlikely that he will ever find steady employment. But until his maximum sentence expires a parole officer will supervise him, help him to find lodgings, and see that he gets his welfare allotment and medical treatment for his various ailments.

The criminal justice system may have helped Albert and Douglas. It may have harmed them. Both men have been isolated from women for a long period. The psychotherapy both have received may or may not be beneficial. Douglas probably will not have learned to read fluently but he will undoubtedly have received a graduate course in crime.

Until Albert and Douglas have been at liberty for at least three years, one will not know whether imprisonment has rehabilitated them or deterred them from further crime. Most recidivists commit another crime within three years of release from prison. At least, the system has provided both Albert and Douglas with schooling and medical care.

By the time the defendants have served their sentences and "paid" for this crime, the taxpayers will have spent well over twenty thousand dollars a year each on Albert and Douglas for at least five years. Society will also have paid for the expenses of police investigation, trial, defense counsel, appeal, pre-sentence investigations, and at least two hundred thousand dollars to imprison Albert and Douglas. The criminal justice system has paid Maureen F. ten dollars as a witness fee.

CHAPTER III

THE ROLE
OF THE VICTIM
IN THE CRIMINAL
JUSTICE SYSTEM

I am an invisible man.
—Ralph Ellison

Courtrooms in the United States come in all shapes and sizes. The
magnificent marble temple which houses the United States Supreme Court and the dingy little fly-specked room inside a police station
are both courts in which the law of the United States is declared and
administered. All of them have the same basic design. The bench where
the judge sits is on a raised platform centered against one wall. In front
of the bench on one side of the room are a table and chairs for the
defendant and his attorney. On the other side, a table and chairs for the
plaintiff and his attorney. In the back of the room are seats for the
spectators.

Although fewer than 10 percent of all civil and criminal cases are
actually tried, the courtroom is the paradigm of the justice system.[1] It
is a public stage, open for all to see, on which the drama of litigation

is played. On the basis of what happens in the courtrooms of America, the citizenry assesses the validity and fairness of the rule of law. A more apt metaphor for the court is an arena, a battleground in which hostile parties contend before a neutral arbiter, the judge. As in medieval tournaments, eighteenth-century duels of honor, and wars between enemy rulers, the battle is not waged by the principals whose interests are at stake but by persons hired, dragooned, coerced, or cajoled into doing the actual fighting. In a court of law, the combatants are, of course, the attorneys who are hired by or for the litigants. This is the adversary system of justice in which the evidence is developed by the lawyers for the parties and in which the judge's role is limited to ruling upon the evidence. In many other countries, the court itself inquires into the facts and takes an active role in developing the evidence.

Dean Wigmore described our mode of litigation as the "sporting theory" of justice. The theory is that in this battleground of the courtroom using the skills of the legal system—testimony, cross examination, and strict adherence to the rules of evidence—truth will conquer. Mr. Justice Holmes poetically declared that in the marketplace of ideas truth will prevail. A judge, like the referee in a boxing match, may often find that the Kaiser's maxim, "might makes right," is more accurate than that of the learned Justice.

Theoretically both parties have equal opportunities to develop the facts and prove their respective contentions. In civil cases, the plaintiff may be poor and illiterate and the defendant may be a billion-dollar corporation or vice versa. Both parties are in the courtroom; both parties are represented by counsel.

In criminal cases, which are frequently tried in the same courtroom before the same judge, the rules are similar. The physical arrangements are the same. There is one significant difference: the plaintiff's seat is empty. The victim of the crime is not in the courtroom seated beside counsel. Usually the victim is not permitted to be in the courtroom during the trial. Under our law, the victim is not a party to the litigation. He is only a witness, no different from the bystander who happens to see a holdup or an automobile accident. In the conduct of the trial, the victim is a non-person.

Technically a crime is not committed against the victim who was robbed, assaulted, raped, or killed. As noted, the crime is against the state, not against Richard Roe. He is only a witness.

The state prepares the case and prosecutes the defendant. If he is found guilty, the law provides that he may be imprisoned for a certain maximum period of time and that he may be fined up to a certain maximum amount. The fine is paid to the state.

The purpose of the law is clear. The state, as the representative of the public, has the duty to maintain law and order. When the law is breached, it is the duty of the state to prosecute the offender. The victim is not expected to track down the criminal, arrest him, and prosecute him. Obviously, few private individuals have the resources or the ability to undertake such a task. In a civilized community, private vengeance should have no place in the administration of justice. The vendetta, the blood feud, and the hereditary hostilities of the Capulets and Montagues and the Hatfields and McCoys are banned under our legal system. Prosecution by the state is also supposed to weed out false or frivolous charges so that innocent people do not have to stand trial for accusations made maliciously and without probable cause. This is the theory.

In practice, let us see what happens to the sporting theory of justice and the search for truth when John Doe is brought to trial. He is seated beside counsel. Usually Doe has been advised to dress neatly in a suit, white shirt, and necktie. The clerk of the court reads the bills of indictment and Doe answers in a ringing voice "Not guilty" to each of the charges. Defense counsel immediately moves for sequestration of all the state witnesses and thereupon, preserving the appearance of equality, the prosecution moves for the sequestration of all defense witnesses. The victim, the arresting police officer, and all the other witnesses are then barred from the courtroom. Of course, John Doe, the defendant, is entitled to be present throughout the entire trial.

Sequestration of witnesses—that is, isolating them from the courtroom—is a sensible device to prevent lying witnesses from concocting the same story. If witness A cannot hear what witness B says, obviously he cannot tailor his testimony to agree with B's. While the witnesses have probably conferred before the trial and discussed their testimony, they cannot anticipate what they may be asked on cross examination. Thus, if witnesses are sequestered, they will have great difficulty in falsifying the evidence consistently with each other under cross examination.

The purpose of cross examination is to bring out inconsistencies, to explore in detail the story of each witness in an attempt to show error, lies, and implausibility. The effectiveness of cross examination depends in part on the skill of counsel—the way he phrases the question, his intonation indicating lack of credence, magnifying inconsistencies, and suggesting implausibility. Counsel can by a nod indicate his apparent satisfaction when a witness is maneuvered into making an admission. Even if it is unimportant, the jury noting the attorney's pleasure may conclude that this is significant. Successful cross examination, however, must be based on the attorney's knowledge of the facts. Even the most brilliant lawyer must know the facts in order to know when a witness is less than candid, telling only a partial story, or omitting a significant detail. No matter how carefully prosecuting and defense attorneys have prepared their cases, things will come up during the tesimony at trial which only the parties themselves can know.

In metropolitan communities 70 to 90 percent of all defendants are represented by the public defender. In some jurisdictions private counsel is appointed for indigent defendants accused of homicide. Prosecuting attorneys and defender associations, like all bureaucracies, have excellent, mediocre, and poor attorneys. Usually, they have a large proportion of young and inexperienced lawyers. In large cities, a lawyer in a defender office handles several hundred cases a year. Obviously, unless the case involves a peculiarly heinous crime or a notorious individual, preparation cannot be very thorough or complete. Most cases which do come to trial are completed in one to three days. These are not the cases about which journalists write books detailing massive investigations and lengthy interviews with the victim, witnesses, suspects, and police.

In these everyday cases counsel must, of necessity, rely to a great extent on what he learns during the course of the trial. The press and the public are unaware of the vast majority of cases being tried in their communities every day. Few of them are reported. Rarely are there disinterested members of the public in the courtroom. But to the victim and the defendant and their families, this is the most important case in the world. The defendant may lose his liberty and reputation. The victim may also lose his reputation and his faith in American justice.

The defendant is seated next to counsel. He can and does whisper to his attorney pointing out errors and inconsistencies in the testimony so that counsel can hone in on the witnesses' weaknesses in cross examination. The victim who is excluded from the courtroom cannot do so. The prosecutor must rely on paper reports and instinct—not very reliable guides.

The victim is usually the first witness called by the prosecution. All witnesses are frightened. A courtroom is an unfamiliar place. Most witnesses have never been in a court before. Their notions of criminal law are gleaned from Perry Mason. The witness sits in a box, alone. Questions are asked by both attorneys. The witness is usually an unwilling actor, playing an unfamiliar role on a strange stage. There is drama. But this is not fiction. It is grim reality. On the basis of the witness's testimony, someone may go to jail. It is an awesome responsibility. Even lawyers who are in court every day become rattled when called to testify as witnesses. They hem and haw. They try to tell what they want to say rather than answer the questions put to them.

No matter how sympathetic a judge may be he has to follow the rules of evidence and order the witness to answer the questions responsively and not to volunteer information which may or may not be relevant. A witness is not allowed to ask questions. Once the witness has responded "yes" or "no" to a question on cross examination, he may be cut off by the attorney. "Thank you, that's all," the lawyer will say. The witness sits in the box speechless. Unless opposing counsel knows what the witness wanted to say or should have said or can surmise and ask the appropriate questions to bring out the rest of the evidence, the witness is excused. The story is only half told. The court and jury have learned less than the whole truth which the witness was sworn to tell.

The trial of Willie J. was not unusual. He was charged with burglary and robbery—felonies carrying a sentence of ten to twenty years—and with possession of drugs, a misdemeanor.

It was the state's contention that Willie entered Dr. S.'s apartment without permission and forced the doctor's wife at knifepoint to give him a large quantity of drugs.

Mrs. S., on direct examination, had been asked in the usual fashion:

Q. Now, Mrs. S., go on and tell us in your own words what happened.

A. Well, it was early in the morning and my husband had just left for the hospital.

Q. What time was it?

A. We had breakfast about seven-thirty, I don't know if we were watching the news or not. Maybe it was eight or a quarter to eight.

Q. Go on.

Mrs. S. has lost her train of thought.

A. There he was with a knife at my throat.

Q. What kind of knife?

A. I don't know. I could see the blade shining and he said 'Give me the doctor's drugs. I know he keeps them in the back room.' I looked at the knife and did what he told me.

Q. Did you know the defendant?

A. No, I never saw him before.

On cross examination, defense counsel questions Mrs. S. on only one issue. Did she know the defendant? He was a patient of her husband. Mrs. S. admits that she has since been told by her husband that the defendant was, indeed, his patient.

Q. And you keep the doctor's books?

A. Yes, I do.

Q. That's all. Thank you, Mrs. S.

Bewildered, Mrs. S. left the stand.

When Willie took the stand he testified that he did not force his way into the apartment, that he was a former patient of Doctor S., and that he came to make an appointment. He further said that Mrs. S. did not give him any drugs. He never threatened her with a knife.

The police had already testified that there was no sign of a forced entry. Defense counsel subtly suggested that perhaps the doctor and his wife have manufactured the charge to account for missing drugs.

Because they were both witnesses, neither the doctor nor his wife was in the courtroom. She could not whisper to the prosecutor to ask the defendant what he said when he knocked on the door. In fact, he told her that he was a meter reader. He was wearing a kind of cap and khaki shirt that looked to her like a uniform. The prosecutor did not ask Mrs. S. what Willie said to her or what Willie was wearing simply because he did not know these crucial facts. Nor had Mrs. S. had an opportunity to explain that although she keeps the books, she rarely sees the patients. They are only names to her. If Dr. S. had been in the room sitting beside the prosecutor, he would have told him the arrangements of his office, that even though his wife is the bookkeeper, a nurse sees the patients. Mrs. S. does the books at home. All this could have been brought out on rebuttal only if Dr. S. and his wife heard Willie's testimony. But they were not present. Less than the truth emerged despite the fact that all the rules were meticulously observed.

Why didn't Mrs. S. tell about Willie's deception when he knocked on the door? She was probably not told the necessary elements of the crime. Many lay people assume that burglary means stealing from a house. She testified that Willie stole the drugs, forced her to give them to him. In the jurisdiction where Willie was being tried, as in many other states, the gravamen of the crime is not stealing but unlawful entry with intent to commit a crime. Had she been aware of the importance of her testimony as to the unlawful entry she probably would have told exactly what happened. If the prosecutor had discussed it with her, she would have told him. Then if Mrs. S. forgot, he could have asked her questions designed to bring out these critical facts.

Mrs. S. is not a stupid woman. But she had been through a terrifying experience. When she came into the courtroom and saw Willie the fear and revulsion, the emotions she had been trying to overcome during the months since the incident occurred, came back to her. She was not only nervous, she was also frightened.

The witness who sits alone in the box being pelted with questions, sworn to tell the truth, is agitated lest he say something untrue. All eyes in the courtroom are riveted on the witness who gropes for words, confused by the questions and the strange situation. He suffers embarrassment, bewilderment, and stage fright.

Many victims of crime who testify in court not only suffer stage fright, but real fright. The victim who is a witness often has reason to fear for his own safety. The defendant may be free on bail. He knows where the victim lives. After this incriminating testimony will he come at night and assault the victim again? Even if the defendant is in custody, he may have friends, relatives, members of his gang. Are they the spectators in the courtroom? Usually the victim does not recognize anyone in the courtroom except the accused, and the prosecuting attorney who may have had a hurried half-hour conversation with the victim.

Even when a defendant is convicted and sentenced to prison, the victim may be frightened and with good cause. Jerry M, a teenage slum boy of sixteen, had the misfortune to be by chance on the scene of a gang slaying. Robert, the leader of the gang, in the fashion of an old western movie, had gone alone and stalked a member of a rival gang and shot him in the back. Jerry, who saw the crime, was shot while attempting to run away. He fell in the street where he was left for dead by Robert who then fled.

Neighbors hearing the shots summoned the police who rushed Jerry to the hospital. Thanks to exceptionally prompt and good care, he recovered. In the hospital he gave a long and detailed statement to the police. He knew the defendant from the neighborhood. He knew the deceased. There was no question of identification. Jerry's testimony would convict Robert of first-degree murder. Robert was well known to the police, but this was the first time they had been able to get evidence against him. It was an airtight case, they thought.

Jerry was summoned as the first witness. Wearing blue jeans and a T-shirt, he limped into the courtroom and climbed up to the witness stand. He placed a small brown hand on the Bible.

"Give your name and address in a loud, clear voice," the court crier intoned.

"Do not give your address," I instructed Jerry.

"Do you swear to tell the truth, the whole truth, and nothing but the truth, so help you God?" the crier asked.

"I do," whispered Jerry.

He sat down and looked around the courtroom. Seated at the defense table next to counsel was the defendant, Robert S., immaculately dressed and looking like a lawyer. In the back row of the courtroom were more than a dozen large, glowering males—members of Robert's gang and his brothers. Jerry turned ashen. He testified that he did not see anyone being shot. He did not know who shot him. He heard two gun shots; he was hit and fell. He gave the time and place. To all other questions, he answered "I don't know,—I didn't see,—I can't remember."

The gun had been found and traced to Robert. Ballistics experts identified the bullets taken from the deceased's body and from Jerry's body as coming from Robert's gun. The jury convicted Robert who was sentenced to life imprisonment. Two weeks later Jerry's body was found in an alley.

Fortunately, not many victims of crime who report it are physically harmed. Most victims, however, regret having reported the crime. Whether the case comes to trial or not, the victim is put through a long series of ordeals which are time consuming, costly, and often emotionally harrowing.

Let us review an ordinary, uncelebrated case, the trial of The People v. John Doe. Let us examine it not only in the light of the goal of the adversary system, which is the search for truth, but also in the light of its treatment of the victim. Doe was charged with burglary, assault, robbery, and terroristic threats. At approximately 12:30 in the morning, Doe forced his way into Jane Roe's apartment, hit her, threatened to rape her, and stole more than one hundred dollars from her pocketbook. This is a run-of-the-mill case. Hundreds like it are tried every day all across the country. This case was not reported in the press. It was simply another statistic, except to Jane Roe.

The fact situation is typical. Eighty-five percent of all crimes in the United States are committed by males. Except for homicides which, unless they are family crimes, are usually committed by males against males, forcible crimes—such as assault, aggravated assault, larceny from the person, and robbery—are committed by men against both men and women. With the exception of rapes in prison, almost all rapes are committed by men against women. In most domestic crimes, whether the parties are legally married or not, it is the man who assaults the woman. On occasion she responds by shooting or stabbing him to death. But, in the overwhelming number of these cases, the man is the defendant, the woman the victim.

A trial judge, who hears major felonies in a metropolitan city, writes:

> If there is a typical factual situation presented by my cases, it would be something like this: Defendant "X," alone or with others, breaks into a citizen's private home for the purpose of burglarizing the home and/or robbing the occupants, usually with a weapon. The victims are often carefully selected; children are present but no adult males.
>
> Not satisfied with simply burglarizing the home and taking the money and personal property of the helpless non-resisting victim, the accused then proceeds to beat, terrorize and often threaten with death the female and her children, eventually raping her one or more times, then forcing her to perform other acts of deviate sexual intercourse.[2]

Not all assaults are followed by rape and sexual abuse. But there is, certainly, a pattern of males seeking out females as victims even in ordinary cases of burglary, robbery, and theft from the person.

Until very recently, the entire criminal justice system was essentially a male preserve. Policemen and detectives were almost exclusively men. Prosecuting attorneys and defense attorneys were usually men. Most judges who heard these major felonies were men. Often the victim was the only female in the courtroom. The situation has changed only very slightly.

Let us return to the case of John Doe, and see what happens in this average uncelebrated trial in which the defendant and the victim are ordinary citizens, with the government prosecuting a suspect accused of serious offenses in order to protect society and vindicate the rule of law. Doe is seated at counsel table with the attorney provided for him by the state. The prosecuting attorney is alone. A detective who is not going to testify sits beside him from time to time. This detective has probably

interviewed some of the witnesses and read the reports of other interviews. All the witnesses are ordered sequestered and required to leave
the courtroom.

Jane Roe, the victim, is called as the first witness. The judge and jury
watch as she enters the room. Jane is breathless and terrified. Before
coming to court she had given the children breakfast and gotten them
off to school, called her employer to say that she would not be at work,
and hurriedly dressed and rushed to the subway. She is wearing a sweater
and slacks. Her nail polish is chipped and her hair needs a touch-up. She
looks around the courtroom and sees the defendant and the lawyers
dressed in business suits and the court officers wearing official uniforms,
the judge in a black robe. She feels out of place, inadequate. The
defendant smiles when he sees Jane. She avoids looking at him. The
jurors watch with fascination. They are instructed "to observe the manner and demeanor of the witnesses, how they testify. . . ." They scruti-
nize Jane avidly, critically. She becomes even more nervous under this
unblinking scrutiny by twelve strangers, the jury.

Direct examination proceeds slowly. Jane finds it difficult to talk or
think. The prosecutor begins by asking simple unemotional questions.
He establishes the date and place of the incident.

Q. Describe your apartment.

A. A living room, dining area, kitchen, two bedrooms, and bath.

Q. Is the sofa to the right or left of the door?

Jane answers first that it is to the right. Then she corrects herself.

Q. You mean when you walk in the front door?
Yes.

A. It's to the left.

Q. How many feet is it from the door to the table where your
pocketbook was lying?

A. I never measured my living room. It's not large. Just a few feet.

Jane testifies that two friends had been visiting with her the evening
on which the crime occurred. The children were in bed asleep. A few
minutes after her friends left there was a knock on the door. Thinking
that her friends must have forgotten something and returned, she
opened the door. When she saw the defendant she attempted to slam
the door shut, He forced his way into the room and demanded money.

Q. What did he say?

A. I saw you cash your check at the bank. I know you've got some
dough. Give it to me.

Q. What did you do?

A. I was frightened. I didn't want him to wake the children. He looked wild. I thought he was crazy.

Defense Counsel: Objection.

The Judge: Don't tell us what you thought, just what happened, what he said and did, and what you said and did.

Jane is silent trying to collect her thoughts. If she hadn't thought he was crazy, she would not have given him the money. She is dismayed that she cannot tell what seems so important to her.

The Judge: Proceed.

A. All right. After he asked for money, I went over to the table where my pocketbook was and opened it and give him one hundred twenty dollars and some change, which was all I had. He was very angry because I didn't have any more.

Q. What did he say?

A. He used an obscenity, 'Give me—' he meant have sex with him.

Q. Tell us exactly what he said.

A. You mean use those words?

Q. Yes, the jury understands that they are not your words.

A. Well—[she paused, stammered, and then blurted out]—He said "All right, bitch, give me some cunt, so the evening isn't a loss."

Q. What did you do?

A. I didn't think. I just reacted. The pocketbook was in my hand. I hit him with it and ran to the door, opened it and screamed. He hit me in the face with his fist and ran out. After I stopped my nose bleeding I called the police.

It seemed to Jane that she had been on the stand all day, but it was only half an hour. She wanted to go to the bathroom. She wanted to be alone. Telling about that horrible evening, watching the defendant sneer at her, she wanted to go home and cry. After more questions, the prosecutor finally smiled at her and stopped. She got up to leave. Defense counsel said,

Q. Just a few questions, Miss Roe. Is it Miss or Mrs. Roe?

A. Mrs.

Q. Is your husband living with you?

A. No.

Q. Who does live with you?

A. My children.

Defendant whispers to counsel.

Q. No one else?

A. No one else.

Jane was getting angry and rattled. What business did that lawyer have asking with whom she lived? She hadn't committed a crime. The defendant had.

Defendant whispers to counsel again.

Q. On the night of the alleged incident, what were you wearing?

A. A housecoat.

Q. You mean a bathrobe?

A. No, I mean a housecoat.

Q. Is that what you were wearing when you entertained your other guests?

A. Yes.

Q. They were male guests.

A. Yes.

Q. Not relatives?

A. No.

Jane clenched her fists in anger. The jurors watched her closely. Jane looked at them in dismay. Somehow having two friends at her apartment in the evening was made to sound immoral.

Q. And that is what you were wearing when you admitted the defendant to your apartment, isn't it?

A. I didn't admit him. He forced his way in.

Cross examination continued for the rest of the day.

At four-thirty when court adjourned Jane said to the prosecuting attorney, "I'm never coming back. I won't go through this any more."

Defense counsel handed her a subpoena. Jane Roe was told that if she did not appear the next day she would be jailed for contempt of court. The defendant was free on bail.

For the next three days Jane Roe sat in the dirty drafty corridor of the courthouse outside the courtroom unable to hear the testimony of the other witnesses, their confusions, and inconsistencies. Often the contradictions of witnesses are immaterial. But these minor discrepancies shake the confidence of the jury in the credibility of the witnesses.

Jane did not hear the testimony of her two friends, Roland and Walt. Both Roland and Walt were asked on direct examination what time they left Jane's apartment. They both replied about eleven-thirty in the evening.

On cross examination defense counsel, seeking to develop an inconsistency, questioned Roland about the time.

Q. You said about eleven-thirty. Are you sure it couldn't have been 12:30?

A. I'm positive it was before twelve.

Neither Jane nor Walt heard this testimony. On cross examination, Walt was asked:

Q. What time did you leave Jane's apartment?

A. About eleven-thirty.

Q. Are you sure it couldn't have been twelve-thirty?

A. Well, it might have been. I didn't look at my watch.

Q. Could it have been twelve-forty?

A. I don't think so.

Q. But you're not sure.

A. No, I can't be sure.

Jane Roe is not in the courtroom. If she were sitting next to the prosecutor, she could tell him to ask Walt on redirect what was playing on TV when he and Roland left. Jane, Roland, and Walt had been watching the eleven o'clock news. At eleven-thirty when it was over, the two men left together.

All that the prosecutor knows is that the police were summoned at 12:40 A.M. If Roland and Walt did not leave until almost 12:40, then Jane's story will not hold up. But there was nothing further to ask Walt.

Jane did not hear the testimony of the defendant that he came to her house at ten o'clock, that she admitted him, that she was wearing "you know a negligee—she wasn't dressed," and that she gave him one hundred dollars out of her pocketbook.

Defense Counsel: Why did she give you one hundred dollars?

A. She thought it was worth it. [He smiled blandly at the jury.]

John Doe was acquitted. If the jury had known that both Roland and Walt left Jane's apartment at eleven-thirty, they probably would not have had a reasonable doubt as to Doe's guilt.

Doe is free and on the street. He knows where Jane lives. She does not know where he lives. She does not know how to protect herself from him. She is terrified and trying desperately to find a new apartment in another neighborhood.

A victim who is not asked embarrassing personal questions and whose testimony is not emotionally distressing also undergoes an ordeal. He is put to great inconvenience and often substantial financial loss. He frequently regrets having reported the crime long before the defendant is brought to trial.

Angelo G. owns a little neighborhood butcher shop. He has been in business on the same corner for more than fifty years. Late one afternoon a young man came into the shop, walked over to the butcher block, picked up the meat cleaver, and said, "Gimme twenty dollars—quick."

Angelo is barely five feet tall and is sixty-nine years old. By the time he came to court he had spent two evenings with the police. This was his fifth day in court. At the trial he repeated the same story he had told before.

Prosecuting Attorney: After he demanded the money, what did you do?

A. I bargained with him.

Q. What do you mean?

A. I says, "Times are bad. I ain't got twenty dollars, sonny. Take this ten dollars and go away." We bargained back and forth. Finally he took the ten dollars and left.

Angelo called the police immediately after the robber left. They came within minutes and Angelo described the incident and the robber. He was sure he could identify the young man. They had stood face to face in the brightly lighted butcher shop and talked for several minutes.

The police wanted Angelo to go with them at once and look for the robber. It was Saturday evening, Angelo's busiest time, but he closed his shop and drove around the neighborhood for an hour. Angelo did not see his robber who was across the street hiding in a doorway and watching the police and Angelo. The police then took Angelo to detective headquarters to examine pictures. He pored through stacks of pictures for more than an hour before he found his robber. Angelo had not the slightest doubt when he saw the picture. "That's him. I know him like my own hand," he told the detective.

On Monday, Angelo appeared before a magistrate and a warrant was sworn out. On this day, he managed to get back to open his butcher shop by noon. However, most of his customers do their marketing first thing in the morning. They shopped elsewhere that day. A few days later, Angelo was again told to appear in court at 9 A.M. for a preliminary hearing. Angelo was there promptly but the case was not reached until late afternoon. Angelo testified and the magistrate ordered the man whom Angelo identified as the robber held for the grand jury. Bail was set. A day or two later, the robber's relatives posted bail. Angelo was not told that the man was out on the street again. Several months later, the case was called for trial. This time, Angelo had to go several miles to City Hall where major trials are held. Angelo again came promptly. He waited all day but the defendant never appeared. By the time he was told that the case could not be tried that day, it was too late to open his shop.

Angelo heard nothing for several months. One night about ten o'-clock, just as he was going to bed, the police called and told him they had picked up a fellow on some other charges. They thought he was Angelo's robber and they wanted Angelo to go with them to the detention center and identify him. "I'll come tomorrow," Angelo pleaded. But they insisted that he come at once. The police came for Angelo about ten-thirty and drove him all the way across the city to the prison-like center where the robber was being held. By then, it was after eleven. The detention center is a busy place—cops rushing around, people walking in and out. Someone gave Angelo a cup of coffee. It was past his bedtime and he had worked hard all day. Angelo dozed, his head nodding as he slept in the hard wooden chair. Finally, they awakened him and took him into a dark room. Standing under bright lights were six young black men, who all looked alike to Angelo. They were all about the same height, all slight, and all had the same complexion. Angelo was confused. He hesitated and finally pointed to one man who was in fact a policeman. This was duly recorded. Defense counsel was present and realized that now he had a possibility of getting his client off. Angelo had made a wrong identification.

A line-up, or stand-up as it is sometimes called, is an important safeguard against false identification. All too often the victim of a mugging or a purse snatching sees the criminal for only a second or two, usually in a dark place. The assailant is described as a young black male, average height, wearing blue jeans and a sweater. The city is filled with people answering that description. If the victim is shown one person who fits that description he will probably in all honesty say that this is the man who robbed or mugged him. By placing the suspect in a line with four or five other people who also fit that description and showing them all to the victim, an innocent suspect is protected against an erroneous identification. Usually the other persons in the line-up are police officers who closely resemble the suspect. Often a guilty suspect is freed because the victim simply didn't have an adequate opportunity to see the criminal, or, as was the case with Angelo, after an interval of more than six months he can no longer be sure. The police had the accused's fingerprints. They knew that this was the man whom Angelo had identified from the photographs. This time, bail was set very high because the suspect had failed to appear at the previous date when the trial had been scheduled.

Several months later, Angelo was told that the case would come to trial on a Wednesday. He was given a subpoena and told that he must appear. For the fourth time he did not open his butcher shop but went to court. But the case could not be heard because the arresting officer whose testimony was essential was on vacation.

Angelo was given another subpoena and ordered to be in court two weeks later. This time, the case went to trial. Despite Angelo's error in identification at the line-up the jury convicted the accused. He was sentenced to five to ten years in prison because he had been convicted of four other robberies. The judge ordered the prison authorities to see that the defendant attends school and learns a trade in prison.

Angelo's experience with the criminal justice system cost him not only the $10 of which he was robbed but also a night's sleep, the earnings he would have made when he went looking for the robber, and the earnings he would have made the five days he appeared in court. He was paid $10 and carfare for each day he appeared in court. (In many jurisdictions witnesses are paid only $5 per day.) His total net loss was more than $550. On appeal, the conviction was reversed because of Angelo's mistaken identification at the line-up. The appellate court reasoned that the jury could not be convinced beyond a reasonable doubt that the defendant was the culprit if Angelo himself was uncertain.

Martin C. is another crime victim who suffered more from the criminal justice system than from the criminal. He is a dealer in rare coins whose shop was burglarized. A skilled, professional team of criminals committed a series of burglaries of coin shops. They took about $75,000 worth of coins from Mr. C.'s store, almost his entire stock. A few weeks later, the burglars were apprehended in another city with a good part of the coins belonging to Mr. C. Like all dealers, Mr. C. had photos of each coin—front and back—catalogues in which they were listed, and a careful inventory. He was overjoyed to learn that at least a part of his merchandise had been recovered.

His delight soon turned to dismay when he went to police headquarters and discovered that the coins had been removed from their cellophane packets and were lying jumbled in a box on the detective's desk.

The condition of a coin is a significant factor in its value. If it is worn or nicked its worth is drastically depreciated. Mr. C. wanted his coins. But he was told that the police needed the coins for evidence at the trial and that he could not get them back until after the trial which might not be held for six months. Mr. C. could not collect on his insurance on the coins which had been recovered. Without the coins, which were his stock in trade, or money to purchase more coins, Mr. C. was effectively out of business. After consulting friends and other dealers, he retained an experienced lawyer who, after much difficulty, managed to persuade the prosecutor to return the coins to Mr. C. before the trial and substitute photographs for use at trial. Mr. C. promised to be available for interviews and to testify whenever he was called.

The burglars who had been caught with the fruits not only of Mr. C.'s burglary but also seven other burglaries, entered into a plea bargain with the prosecutor. They pled guilty to all the burglaries and were sentenced to prison without going to trial. Part of the bargain was that the sentence for each burglary run concurrently with the sentences for the other burglaries. In other words, the men who had committed eight burglaries paid the penalty for only one.

Although the burglars obviously had sufficient ill-gotten gains to pay a well-known private attorney, they were not ordered to pay Mr. C. or any of the other dealers whose shops they had burglarized for the stolen coins which were not recovered or for the loss in value of those that were recovered. The plea bargain was entered into by the prosecuting attorney and counsel for the burglars. Mr. C. and the other victims were not parties to the deal. Mr. C.'s lawyer was not notified. After all, Mr. C. was only a witness. The prosecutor was not representing him. Mr. C. and the other victims learned about the plea bargain only when one of them called the police to find out the date of the trial. By that time, sentences had been imposed. The judge never had the opportunity to hear the testimony of the victims or the arguments of their counsel that restitution to the victims be made a part of the sentence.

In discussing this case, his only experience with the law, Mr. C. said, "I had to get a lawyer to protect me from the justice system as well as from the criminals. I would have been better off if they'd never caught the burglars."

The prosecuting attorney, the police, and the judge were satisfied. The prosecution had eight convictions without the trouble or risk of trial. The police statistics showed eight major crimes solved by arrest.

The judge had disposed of eight cases in less than one day, cases which might have taken eight weeks or more to try. The backlog of untried cases was substantially reduced. The taxpayers had been saved the costs of these trials. No one asked Mr. C. or the other victims what they thought of the result.

CHAPTER IV

CRIME PREVENTION AND THE COURTS

What we demand is nothing peculiar to ourselves.
It is that the world be made a safe and fit place
to live in.
—Woodrow Wilson

The criminal justice system is not a coherent whole. It consists of police, courts, prisons, and all their supporting personnel. The powers and duties of each of these components are established by statute and practice and are limited by the Constitution. No one, including the founding fathers, ever sat down and wrote a theory of criminal sentencing. No single theory of sentencing has received explicit legislative approval on a national basis. The purposes of imposing sentence are vague and variable depending upon the times, the individual judge, and the particular crime and criminal. Although the procedures in the conduct of a trial are regulated by statute, rules, judicial decisions, and the federal and state constitutions, the conduct of the judge and counsel at sentencing was for centuries left to the discretion of the individual judge.

From time to time philosophers, scholars, and legislative codifiers have attempted to impose a rational and logical order upon a system which, like Topsy, just growed. The public, judiciary, attorneys, and defendants would undoubtedly like to have a clearly articulated goal or at least a list of priorities in sentencing on which there could be agreement. As is true of many other issues of public importance, there is no consensus with respect to the purpose of criminal sentences.

One authority on criminal law asserts that "every criminal law system in the world except one [Greenland] has deterrence as its primary and essential postulate."[1] If deterrence was, in fact, the only or the principal postulate of the American criminal justice system, that system would be entirely different from what it is. We would not restrict the power of the police to arrest on mere suspicion and to detain suspects for more than a brief period. The police would have unfettered discretion to arrest and detain suspects. We would not be concerned with improving and humanizing our prisons, which would be even more unpleasant and miserable than they are in order to maximize the deterrent effect of incarceration. We would not today be involved in agonizing reappraisals of our sentencing practices. We would not exercise scrupulous care to give all persons accused of a crime a fair trial. Instead, swift certain punishment of a Draconian nature would prevail with little regard for the rights of the accused. Summary execution rather than due process trials would be the fate of persons suspected of crime. Indeed, swift, certain summary execution of possibly innocent people might be far more terrifying to potential criminals than the prospect of a trial with constitutional safeguards and limited penalties.

In Iran and many other countries, people are executed without trials. The penalties for many crimes are death or mutilation. According to Dr. Ibrahim Yazdi, Deputy Prime Minister for Revolutionary Affairs under Ayatollah Ruhollah Khomeini, the penalty for serious offenses is death, for less serious offenses a hand and the opposite foot are amputated, and for minor crimes the penalty is exile.[2] In the Soviet Union, as any reader of Solzhenitzyn knows, many people are imprisoned or sent to Siberia following trials which lack any element of due process. Others are held for long periods without trial. This is a common practice in many nations.

The United States criminal justice system is very different. It is predicated upon the rule of law. This belief in law and justice, one might say, is a secular American religion. Any theory of criminal penalties and any scheme for establishing the nature of sentences and the method of imposing criminal sanctions is limited by this concept and should be designed to promote a belief in and adherence to the rule of law.

Jurists and legal scholars have propounded a variety of theories to justify criminal sanctions. Justice Oliver Wendell Holmes gave these reasons for imposing criminal penalties: the wicked conduct of the offender, usefulness in deterring crime, and an expression of outrage.[3] John Stuart Mill justified punishment as a means of benefiting the offender and protecting society. Mill expressed a dual concern: for the offender and for society. The theory for imposing criminal sanctions that I find most acceptable was enunciated by Lord Denning. He declared that punishment for crime is justified as an "emphatic denunciation by the community of a crime."[4]

Crime prevention is, of course, a most desirable goal. If people could be prevented from committing crimes, the community would be safer and more pleasant. The taxpayers would be relieved of the burdens of maintaining prisons. Police forces and courts could be drastically reduced in size. Although people speak of crime prevention as a purpose of the criminal justice system, it should be obvious that courts cannot prevent crime. Before a suspect is arrested, a crime has already been committed. The purpose of the trial is to determine whether the suspect is in fact the person who committed the offense. The imposition of the most drastic penalties imaginable cannot prevent the commission of that crime.

What is usually meant by crime prevention is deterrence. The theory of deterrence is based on the belief that what is done or is not done to A will affect the conduct of B, C, D, and all others who might be tempted to emulate A and commit a similar crime. It assumes that potential criminals are aware of this lawful and orderly system, that they know the penalties, and that they will exercise reasonable judgment and not risk the possibility of a severe penalty. According to this theory, potential offenders will refrain from committing crimes if severe penalties are imposed on wrongdoers. Many people adhere to this belief despite the fact that throughout history punishment of law violators has been brutal and harsh. Yet crime has always been a part of the human condition, from Cain to the present. Some proponents of the deterrence theory do recognize that there is no proof that punishment deters crime.[5]

Despite these obvious facts, deterrence is an appealing notion. It gives the public a false assurance that those in government can act in a manner that will protect all of us from the misconduct of others. We like to believe that life is not subject to random vicissitudes but that we, through our elected and appointed officials, can control the actions of others. This belief is our security blanket. The policeman is on the corner; the judge is in the courthouse; the criminals are in jail; all's right with the world. Similarly, we as citizens of one nation in a world of hostile nations like to believe that because we have more and bigger bombs than any or all of our potential enemies we are safe. This has been called the "myth of deterrence."[6]

I suggest that deterrence of crime by imposing criminal sanctions is also a myth. By jailing an offender the court can prevent him or her from committing other crimes against the public (not crimes against other prisoners) for the period of incarceration. But will what the court does to that defendant deter the commission of any other crimes? No one really knows. It is my belief that except for sophisticated, cold-blooded, calculating individuals who act with understanding and premeditation, criminal penalties have little deterrent capacity.

A scholar states as a fact, "Judges sentence offenders with the object that potential criminals will hear of the sentence and that this message will result in general deterrence."[7] Any judge who has tried a number of criminal cases knows that this statement is patently untrue. It is predicated on several fallacious notions: first that potential criminals will know about the penalties imposed on others, and second, that this threat of imprisonment or death will deter them from acting.

Except for a notorious crime, usually homicide, which receives sensational coverage by the media, no one knows or cares what happens to the run-of-the-mill criminals who are tried in state courts every day. There is seldom anyone in my courtroom other than the victim, the accused, and possibly his family. Occasionally a few relatives, friends, or neighbors of the victim are present. Reporters rarely attend these trials. When they do it is often for an extraneous reason such as the fact that the reporter knows someone involved or the prosecuting or defense attorney wants some publicity. Jurors who live in the city where the crime was committed are always questioned as to their knowledge of the incident. It is an extraordinary situation when someone who is not a friend or acquaintance of the victim or the accused has heard of the crime even though it occurred in the city where all the members of the jury panel reside, and sometimes within a few blocks of a juror's home.

Most people do not know what the maximum penalties are for crimes.

In fact, most lawyers do not know. Since they do not know what the penalty is, there is little in terrorem effect. The maximum penalty, of course, gives little guidance as to what the actual penalty will be. Even criminals who have been convicted several times do not know the penalties for for their crimes.

Obviously those who have served time in prison, been released, and then committed other crimes have not been deterred by the experience. Since more than two-thirds of convicted offenders commit other crimes, it is evident that punishment has little deterrent effect on them. It is also extremely unlikely that similar people could be deterred even if they knew what penalties had been imposed on other offenders.

For a person to be deterred from committing a crime, he or she must act with reasonable prudence and foresight and calculate whether the crime is worth the risk. Most criminals who are tried for crimes like robbery, rape, burglary, and theft do not act in this fashion.

Every person knows that homicide is a very serious offense and that a long prison sentence is the almost inevitable consequence of an unlawful killing *if* the slayer is apprehended. One would think that a person who commits homicide would have to be moved by passion or outrage or vengeance to risk such a penalty and that such a killer would act stealthily and cautiously to attempt to avoid detection. Most people who commit homicides, however, act without any calculation as to whether the crime is worth the penalty. They do not take the most elementary precautions to attempt to conceal the crime. The following are but a few of the scores of homicide cases tried before me. They are typical in that the killers knew what they were doing and knew that they would be apprehended immediately and would certainly be convicted.

Elbert killed his brother. He did it in his parents' home on a warm summer afternoon when the windows were open. The neighbors were out on their front porches. They had seen the brothers enter the home. A few minutes later they heard a gunshot and called the police. Elbert answered the door. The officers asked, "Is there any trouble here? We have a report of a gun being fired."

Elbert replied, "Yes, I shot and killed my brother. Do you want to see him?"

Audrey is a pretty twenty-two-year-old girl. She had been living with Amos, a wealthy man by whom she had a baby. For several years the course of their love ran smooth. He gave her a new Cadillac and set her up in a nice apartment. Amos then became involved with a new girl,

Melissa. On a nice summer evening when all the neighbors were sitting on their doorsteps enjoying the pleasant weather, Amos decided to take Melissa for a drive in his Jaguar convertible. Audrey in her Cadillac had been circling around Amos's house for at least a half-hour waiting for them. When Amos and Melissa came out of the house, they started to cross to the opposite side of the street where the Jaguar was parked. Audrey gunned her car and knocked down Melissa. Amos jumped out of the path of Audrey's car. Audrey then backed up and drove over Melissa. She drove forward and back three or four times until Melissa's body was flattened and shredded. Audrey then drove home. Everyone on the street knew her, knew her address, and knew the license number of her car. Within minutes she was stopped by the police. The officer approached her with drawn gun. She got out of her car and said to him, "I killed her, didn't I? I drove over her enough times."

James and his wife, Janet, went to a busy shopping center at noon on Saturday to do the marketing. For some weeks they had been discussing a separation and had agreed that Janet would move out the following week and get her own apartment. They parked their car and walked toward the supermarket. In full view of at least fifty people James drew a gun and shot Janet in the heart. She died almost instantly. James did not attempt to flee. He waited for the police to apprehend him.

Bill, nineteen years old and known to the corner boys as "Homicide," was lounging outside a bar. Three total strangers strolled down the street. One was wearing a white T-shirt. In the dusk he was a perfect target. Suddenly Bill asked one of his friends for the gun which was the common property of the gang. He took aim and shot the boy in the T-shirt in the back. Bill returned the gun to his friend and then strolled into the bar on the corner and ordered a drink. He was sitting there when the police apprehended him.

Helen is forty-four years old and the mother of three children. Her fifteen-year-old daughter, Nola, had a boyfriend, Warren, who lived a few blocks away. One night Nola came home from her date with Warren gasping with pain, blood trickling down her legs. Warren and six of his friends had repeatedly gang-raped her. Helen took Nola to the hospital where the police were promptly notified of the rape. Nola was hospitalized for more than two weeks. A few days after she was discharged, Warren came over to take her out again. Helen chased him away and called the police. She was outraged that Warren had not been arrested. The police told Helen the next time Warren came to see Nola she should keep him in the house until they arrived. The first thing the following morning Helen went to City Hall, obtained a permit to own a gun, and then bought one. A few days later, Warren appeared. Helen shot and killed him.

All of these people who had killed testified before me. They were all of normal intelligence. They told what they had done clearly and without hesitation. James had attended college for two years. He was a war veteran who had an honorable discharge. "Homicide" was a high-school dropout but he was literate and had completed eleventh grade satisfactorily. All of them were examined by court neuropsychiatrists. None was found to be mentally ill. Every one of them knew that he or she would be arrested and convicted. The prospect of a life sentence did not deter them. Nor would the death penalty have made any difference to them. None attempted to escape. Except for Helen, none of them had what could be considered a reasonable ground for killing. With the exception of "Homicide," they had planned to kill and they did it. "Homicide" was not drunk or under the influence of drugs when he killed the stranger.

These were not crimes of passion, as that phrase is known in the law. Melissa was jealous and angry. But neither she nor the other killers committed their crimes at a moment of stress inflamed by the sudden sight of infidelity or some other action that would cause a person to lose self-control. I have never encountered a crime of passion except on the operatic stage. Apparently contemporary Americans are not roused to sudden fury by the betrayal of a loved one. Homicides have occurred over disputes as to a parking place, arguments over small sums of money, and other subjects which seem to the court to be of relatively slight importance. Carol stabbed her boyfriend to death because he was two hours late for a date. As she testified, she was not particularly fond of the man. Before all her appeals were exhausted, Carol had a new boyfriend who accompanied her to court.

None of these killers attempted to conceal their crimes or to flee from certain arrest and conviction. Obviously such offenders cannot be deterred by a threat of a severe penalty or even the certainty of a mandatory sentence.

Almost every study of capital punishment has shown that there is no material difference in the rate of homicides in states which have capital punishment and states which do not.[8] The homicide rate per 100,000 in Michigan, which did not have the death penalty in the fifties, was

3.49. In Indiana, which did have the death penalty, the homicide rate during the same period was 3.50. This confirms empirical observation of the manner in which most homicides are committed.

The vast majority of those who commit other crimes of violence also act without calculating the risk of the penalty. Would any sensible person rob a bar or store a half a block from his own home where there is a strong probability that he will be recognized by the victim or bystanders? A cautious calculating robber would go to a section of the city where he is not known. However, most of the robbers who have appeared before me committed their crimes close to home. That is why they were apprehended and convicted. The witnesses were able to identify them.

Similarly much intrafamilial abuse will certainly result in prosecution and conviction. A man who beats his wife, girlfriend, or child so severely that the victim is hospitalized should know that the crime will be reported by the hospital if not by the victim. He may believe that he can get the wife or girlfriend to withdraw the charges and go free. Indeed, this often happens. The beating of an ex-wife or former girlfriend, however, is sure to be prosecuted. These cases which occur every day among wealthy, middle-class, and poor people baffle judges and juries. Why would any man who has already separated from a woman go to her home and assault her? Obviously, he is not acting under a sudden provocation. There is no immediate precipitating factor.

Months after they were divorced, Ronald went to his former wife's new dwelling. He was equipped with chisel and crowbar. He broke down the door. He then beat his ex-wife in the presence of the children. He knew that she would promptly report the crime and that she would see that he was prosecuted vigorously and relentlessly. There was no possibility that he would not be arrested and convicted. Neither knowledge of the penalties for crime nor the threat of such penalties deters most people who commit homicides and other crimes of violence.

It is often said that "if punishment would be made certain almost all crime would be eliminated."9 Proponents of such ideas generally favor mandatory sentences. The notion is that if the penalty is fixed by the statute and the judge has no discretionary power to alter the penalty, that punishment would be certain. Again a moment's reflection reveals the absurdity of such reasoning when applied to the criminal justice system in the United States. A due process trial with all the Constitutional safeguards is designed to ensure that no innocent person will be convicted. It also makes possible the acquittal of some who are guilty. Necessary witnesses may not appear. If they do, their testimony may not be coherent and convincing. The jury or the judge may be misled into believing a false story concocted by the defendant. No one can know for a certainty that the guilty person will, in fact, be convicted.

Even more uncertain is the arrest of the perpetrator of the offense. The police claim to clear 37 or 40 percent of reported crimes by arrest. This figure includes homicides which are intensively investigated and car thefts which are relatively easy to find. Many police departments also include in these statistics of arrest the drunks, prostitutes, and derelicts who are picked up each night even though they have not committed crimes. Many crimes are not reported because of fear of retaliation by the criminal and his friends. Other crimes, such as rape, are not reported because the victim does not wish to undergo the ordeal of trial. Other victims who are themselves marginal people—illegal aliens, ex-convicts, people in trouble with the law for many reasons—and people who simply don't wish to go to the trouble of appearing at the police station, at line-ups, and at trial do not report crimes. For these and many other reasons crime statistics are not wholly reliable. If law violators were better informed, if they were avid newspaper readers, if they studied crime statistics, they would realize that the likelihood of being caught and convicted if one is careful is not so great as to deter a reasonably cautious, calculating potential criminal. Since there is no certainty in either apprehension or conviction, the certainty of the penalty is of relatively little significance. This, however, is the only element which is discussed in proposing that punishment be certain.

It is also suggested that criminal sanctions would have a greater deterrent capability if punishment was swift. Even if the crime was reported promptly and the offender was apprehended quickly, however, the process of investigation, arraignment, preliminary hearing, pretrial motions, trial, post-trial motions, and appeals would take time. Not only does due process prevent punishment from being certain, it also ensures that it cannot be swift. With even the most efficient scheduling of all of the steps in the criminal process at least two to three months would be required before the case could be tried. Thereafter, under the speediest and optimum conditions, another two to three months would be needed before the appeal could be heard and decided. In most jurisdictions, there is the possibility of a further appeal to the highest state court. If there is a federal Constitutional question, further appeals and rehearings are possible. Punishment cannot be either certain or swift regardless of the nature of the sentence. Moreover, there is no reliable evidence that swift, certain penalties would so terrorize the population that potential criminals would be deterred from committing crimes.

Obviously deterrence is not the primary or essential postulate of our criminal justice system. It is apparent that neither the individual offenders who have committed stupid, senseless, violent acts nor the members of the public who are likely to commit such acts will be deterred by the penalties imposed by the courts. This is not to say that nothing can be done to prevent crimes. In later chapters we shall examine a number of types of crime and suggest penalties and other forms of legal action which could reasonably have a deterrent or a preventive effect. There are many nonjudicial measures such as better lighting, more effective burglar alarm systems and locks, regular patrolling of subway stations, more efficient accounting systems in industry, and better security in stores, banks, and other places where property is likely to be stolen that can prevent some crimes. Citizen cooperation in reporting crime and in testifying as to those crimes they witness is of immeasurable help in locating offenders and in convicting them. There are many things which the government and individuals can do to protect persons and property.

Some crimes cannot be prevented or deterred no matter what penalties are imposed, but one should not therefore conclude that the criminal law and the courts are engaged in a futile exercise. A United States study entitled "Federal Crime Control Assistance" points out that there are "two general models which characterize the criminal justice system —the crime control model and the due process model."[10] One seeks to prevent crime; the other considers concepts of individual rights, fairness, and the rule of law as matters at least of co-equal significance with the control of crime.

There is no reason to believe that the due process model provides less deterrence to crime than any other system of criminal law. Repressive police states which ignore human rights are also troubled with street crime and corruption. Russia has its "hooligans" and its corrupt officials. China has admitted that in one district in Shanghai alone there were approximately one thousand thefts and burglaries committed in 1977.[11] In eighteenth-century England when the death penalty was imposed for more than two hundred offenses and public hangings were a common sight, the streets of London and the highways were more unsafe than the city streets and turnpikes of the United States today.[12]

On occasion, legislatures moved by a desire to deter crime or simply in response to public clamor have enacted laws requiring long prison sentences for a particular offense. Under such acts the courts are forbidden to mitigate the penalty in accordance with the gravity of the offense or the culpability of the offender. A striking example of the folly of this approach is the so-called Rockefeller law in New York which mandated prison sentences for drug offenders. The results of this law have been drastic overcrowding of the prisons, excessively long trials, and innumerable appeals. As a consequence a heavy additional burden has been imposed on the taxpayers. There is no evidence that this law reduced the use of narcotics or deterred any potential narcotics violators. But the manifest unfairness of this law eroded public faith in the rule of law and led to strenuous efforts by courts and prosecutors to bend the law in order to avoid such sentences.

Even if there were positive proof that more arrests, prosecutions, convictions, and long mandatory jail sentences for narcotics offenders and serious street criminals could have a deterrent effect, it is doubtful that the American public would want to pay the price. The cost of an all-out war on crime is twofold: a diminution of freedom for all citizens and a substantial increase in monetary costs for more police, courts, and prisons. A policy of dragnet arrests, stop and frisk, and detention for questioning undoubtedly would turn up a good many law violators who would otherwise never come to the attention of the police. But the restraint, fear, embarrassment, and inconvenience imposed on law-abiding citizens would be considerable. These are onerous aspects of a police state which Americans have always deplored. The Constitution places limitations on random stopping and searching or questioning of people not suspected of crime. In addition, the financial costs of such a program would be almost intolerable. Today, prisoners are being released from jail in order to save the expense of incarcerating them.[13]

Americans are already spending vast and increasing sums on the criminal justice system. In 1971, the total state, local, and federal funds expended through the Law Enforcement Assistance Administration amounted to $9.5 billion. In 1975, these expenditures had reached almost $16 billion with little, if any, reduction in crime. These sums are in addition to the much larger amounts spent by federal, state, and local government on the routine operations of police, courts, and prisons. Americans are prone to believe that money will solve any problem. The experience of LEAA indicates that all too often money is simply wasted. The people who design and carry out the projects may be the principal beneficiaries. The problems remain. LEAA, for example, spent $.25 billion on college education for police officers. A recent study shows that this money has been wasted.[14] Despite all these programs and the expenditure of vast sums of money the crime rate continues to escalate.[15] To continue to spend more money doing what we are already doing will not bring about a reduction in crime.

Revision of sentencing practices is desirable in order to provide redress for victims, to promote equal justice for offenders, and to vindicate the rule of law. These are the values to be considered in weighing proposals to distort the criminal justice system into a crime prevention institution. Some changes in sentencing practices which are in conformity with these goals may also have a deterrent effect. This, however, cannot be proved or disproved.

To achieve these goals is not a simple matter of devising a mechanism or passing a law mandating a fixed penalty for each crime. All too often even intelligent people assume that once an accused has been found guilty, the imposition of the penalty should be automatic. Rebecca West in referring to Daniel Ellsberg declared, "He has violated the law. Now he must pay the penalty." This simplistic notion is based on several misconceptions. Such a statement assumes that for every crime there is a fixed penalty. This is simply not true under American law. For the vast majority of crimes, the legislature has fixed only a maximum penalty: a maximum number of years in prison and/or a maximum fine. Except in the few instances in which a mandatory sentence is required by statute, a judge may impose a lesser period of imprisonment, a lesser fine or no fine, place the defendant on probation, or suspend sentence. Any one or any combination of these penalties is legal. Such a statement also assumes that a judge may not consider intent, the harm done, or the good accomplished by the offender, or aggravating and mitigating circumstances. For centuries all these facts—the matrix in which the crime occurred—have been given great weight by wise sentencing judges.

Moreover, the nomenclature of crimes frequently does not distinguish between greater and lesser offenses. The name of the crime is used to define the prohibited activity, not its gravity. Burglary, for example, is commonly defined as entering wilfully without permission the building of another or a portion thereof with intent to commit a felony. Willie entered the unlocked door of the W. family home when no one was there. He intended to steal. A silent alarm went off. Willie was apprehended before he had taken anything. Arnold broke open the door of an occupied house, terrified the inhabitants, and stole jewelry and a coin collection. The value of these items was several hundred thousand dollars. Both men were guilty of burglary. Obviously the crimes were very different in their seriousness and the amount of harm done.

Drug offenses also vary enormously in degree of culpability although they are all violations of the same law. Under the laws of most states heroin, marijuana, and many other drugs are listed as controlled substances. It is illegal for anyone without a permit to possess any amount of a controlled substance. Melvin, a college student, was found in possession of one marijuana cigarette. Frank, a known drug dealer, was found in possession of several hundred thousand dollars' worth of heroin. Neither Melvin nor Frank had a permit. Both were guilty of illegal possession of drugs. Obviously no rational or due process model of criminal justice should impose the same penalty on both burglars or on both drug violators.

When one examines individual cases, it is apparent that the function of the judge in imposing sentence on a convicted criminal is not primarily to deter others from committing crimes. Nor is it a simple, automatic procedure to set mathematically computed terms of imprisonment. What penalties should a judge impose on Willie, Arnold, Melvin, Frank, and the tens of thousands of offenders who are convicted of crimes in American courts? To answer this question requires careful consideration of policy questions, fundamental philosophical concepts, the role and purpose of the criminal law, and the function of the sentencing judge.

If one believes in the Constitutional due process model of criminal justice, the penalty imposed on a criminal must take into account many factors other than crime prevention. The decision to mount an all-out war on crime raises significant questions of social policy because expenditures for this purpose, like expenditures for military purposes, inevitably reduce the amount of money available for other desirable objectives such as education, welfare, environmental protection, and economic development. There are also moral issues implicit in the way the state treats the individual. It is a fundamental tenet of American political theory that government exists to protect and further the interests and rights of the individual, not that the individual exists to serve the state. If in order to maximize the deterrent capability of the criminal justice system, a person is punished disproportionately for his offense in order to deter others, then, in effect, he is treated not as an individual entitled to due process but as a means to further the ends of the state. No one today would seriously suggest punishing the child or spouse of a criminal in order to prevent crime even though such penalties might well have a strong deterrent effect. In other societies penalties have been commonly imposed on the kin of wrongdoers. History does not record that there was less crime in those communities.

There are two diametrically opposed views on the propriety of using the individual offender for deterrent purposes. The Reverend Sydney Smith declared: "When a man has been proven to have committed a crime, it is expedient that society should make use of that man for the diminution of crime: he belongs to them for that purpose."[16] Professor Andenaes, on the contrary, suggests that it is indeed immoral to take into consideration while sentencing one person the effect that sentence will have on another person.[17] This is perhaps simply a philosophical refinement on the differences between the crime control and the due process models of criminal law. I believe it is not only immoral but also unconstitutional and futile to treat one individual as a means to a social end, even though that end may be desirable. When a sentence denies any individual his right to fair treatment, the sentencing court itself is acting outside the law.

There are other social and policy considerations which should be considered in sentencing. What are the obligations of society to care for and treat offenders? What are the obligations of society to care for and aid victims of crime? What sentencing procedures and penalties will enhance respect for the rule of law? These questions are certainly equal in importance to crime prevention or deterrence.

I suggest that the following goals and aims should be paramount in the imposition of criminal sanctions in every case: proportionality—that the penalty should not exceed the seriousness of the offense; fairness—treating similarly situated offenders similarly; and individual responsibility of the offender to the victim of his wrongdoing and to society—providing redress to the victim. No simple formula will yield a mathematically exact sentence for every offender if criminal sanctions conform to these criteria.

In succeeding chapters, the various theories of criminal penalties promulgated by philosophers, sociologists, and legal scholars and the sentencing proposals now being considered by the Congress and state legislatures will be examined. They will be reviewed in the light of these goals and will be tested as to their applicability to and effect upon the ordinary offenders who are convicted and sentenced in American criminal courts.

CHAPTER V

THE CONTROVERSIES

Logical method and form flatter that longing for
certainty and for repose which is in every human mind.
But certainty is illusion and repose is not the destiny
of man.

—O. W. Holmes

"R adical chic" is a phrase used to describe the tendency of a coterie
of well-known people to embrace new causes and new ideologies
and to create trends. The tastemakers decide whether blue jeans or
crinolines will be worn, whether abstract or representational paintings
are in vogue, whether serial music or tonal music will win prizes, and
a host of other issues in the arts and fashions.[1] A relatively small group
of people who hold no public office and have no responsibility to the
public create these changes in taste. Their views have a drastic effect on
which music will be played, the value of paintings, the success or failure
of manufacturers who do or do not follow their lead, and many aesthetic,
social, and economic decisions in which they do not participate. But
their ideas and preferences are of critical importance.

A similar phenomenon occurs in scientific and intellectual fields. For
many years Linus Pauling, the Nobel prize-winning chemist, espoused
the notion, based upon his studies, that Vitamin C (ascorbic acid) could
shorten the time period of the common cold. This idea was met with
ridicule until another study showed that it had validity. Recently, some

medical researchers have discovered through testing that vitamin C does prolong the life of terminal cancer patients, as Dr. Pauling suggested years ago.[2] Scientific history is replete with examples of the establishment accepting false data as true and rejecting theories later proved to be true. The hoax of the Piltdown Man, a somewhat crude fake of the skull of a prehistoric creature thought to be an early precursor of man, is a notorious example. For years the scientific establishment firmly believed in the authenticity of Piltdown and based many theories of evolutionary development on this false evidence.

In the field of criminology, evidence has not been falsified; it has been interpreted. Like all interpretations, these reflect not only the facts but also the views of those who gather, collate, and analyze the statistics which form the raw data of criminology. For more than a generation the American criminal justice system has followed the views of the academic and scholarly authorities who believed in the rehabilitation of criminals through the penal system. In 1969, the Report of the American Bar Foundation's Survey of the Criminal Justice System on Sentencing stated without qualification: "One of the major goals of the correctional process is the rehabilitation of the convicted offender."[3] Within the past few years this view has been repudiated by the criminology establishment in favor of a "lock them up" approach. Few people doubt the accuracy of the statistics from which the conclusions were drawn. They are gathered from government reports and collated and analyzed with refined techniques, skill, and admirable objectivity. Allowance is made for error, incompleteness of reporting, and innumerable conditions and anomalies which skew the results.

Although data gathering is much more complete today than formerly and statistical analysis is more sophisticated and refined, figures are not wholly reliable. Some statistics are based on crimes reported, some on arrests, and some on convictions. Many people who the public believes are guilty, such as Senator Passman, have been acquitted. Some innocent people are convicted. It is impossible to know who is actually guilty. But we must accept the verdict of the court until it is overturned on appeal. It is clear, however, that there has been no drastic change in the number of crimes committed or the amount of recidivism in the past few years. The change in theories arises not from the data but from the conclusions of those who analyze it.

Some crimes, such as rape, have risen faster than others. But this change in statistics is probably due to increased reporting of this crime.

The same is probably also true of child abuse. The public has been sensitized to these problems. There are laws which mandate reporting. More reports are made. In fact, no one knows how much child abuse there was in former decades or generations. Dickens' novels reveal childhood as a time of suffering, beatings, and crime. As we look on it, the common practice in the nineteenth century both in England and the United States of putting children as young as three or four years of age to live with other families was certainly fraught with the possibility of abuse.

Similarly, the recent spate of prosecutions of public officials must be viewed with caution. Obviously Watergate, like Teapot Dome, was an extraordinary episode of corruption and faithlessness. But the prosecution of numerous congressmen, senators, and state and local officials for accepting bribes and kickbacks may or may not indicate a rise in this type of crime. It may only be the result of more energetic investigative press reporting, a more aware public, and more politically ambitious prosecutors eager to ride the wave of this new crusade against crooked politicians. In addition, the laws are more stringent now than ten years ago. It is impossible to know with statistical certainty how many congressmen in the sixties or the fifties took bribes or accepted campaign contributions in return for favors. When there was no law requiring the reporting of contributions, it was more difficult to learn of this type of corruption. All these facts may cause one to conclude that on the whole public officials are no more corrupt today than they were ten, twenty, or thirty years ago. On the other hand, one may conclude from this data that public officials are indeed more corrupt than formerly.

Judges and lawyers who have been trying criminal cases for twenty-five or thirty-five years have seen many changes in the law. A great many of them have made trials fairer and procedures more regular. Some have had little, if any, effect except to add extra procedures. There have been few changes in the kinds of defendants brought to court, who always have been and still are predominantly young, poor, and disadvantaged.

Some types of crime have changed. Drugs were not a widespread problem before the Vietnam War. Children do commit serious offenses at a younger age. But are defendants today less amenable to reform than they were twenty years ago? Lawyers and judges have not been polled on this question. However, I believe that few of them who are regularly involved with offenders have changed their ideas radically. There were always those who thought that there was no hope for the criminals:

"Lock 'em up and throw the key away" was their attitude. Others believed in imposing the least penalty consistent with the offense, hoping that offenders could be helped and believing that society should not, in effect, banish the offender by incarcerating him for long periods. Nothing has happened in the last ten years to cause prison wardens, lawyers, and judges who deal with these people on a daily basis to change their opinions, whatever they were.

One views with much caution a radical revision of theory. The new opinion, like its predecessor, is deduced from statistics. The criminological tastemakers who espouse the rehabilitation or treatment model and the "lock them up" or desert model are convinced that these are logical and empirically based opinions. They are not engaged in a hoax. Like the tastemakers in other fields, they set the fashions which are followed but they have no responsibility to the public for the consequences of their theories. These people are not public officials. They do not control the expenditure of funds. They are not legislators. They are not prison officials. They are not judges. But their views have a profound effect upon what all these officials do and how public funds are spent. Their theories can mean the difference between prison and liberty to hundreds of thousands of people in the course of a generation. Their views can be critical in determining whether we build more prisons or fewer, whether we lock people up for shorter or longer periods, and whether criminal laws and procedures are amended to be more or less stringent.

Theories of sentencing form the basis of legal decisions that mean the difference between liberty and imprisonment, hope and despair, faith in or distrust of law for hundreds of thousands of Americans. Some say that theories are unimportant and believe that the only question to be asked is: Do the theories work?[4]

Whether one concludes that the theories work or fail to work depends upon the standard of success and the reliability of the evaluation. While there are many theories of penalties, there are few if any standards for measuring their success. The usual criterion for evaluating post-conviction disposition of criminals is recidivism, by which is meant rearrest or rearrest and conviction. Under this test, imprisonment must be judged a failure because the majority of convicts after release from prison are rearrested and convicted again. Probationers fare better than those who have been imprisoned, although the rate of rearrest and conviction for them is also dismayingly high. Two obvious facts explain the difference between prisoners and probationers. A person with a record of prior prison convictions is unlikely to be placed on probation again. He is clearly a bad risk. Moreover, those who commit particularly brutal or heinous crimes will, in most cases, be imprisoned. First offenders and those who commit less serious crimes will be placed on probation. Thus, there is little comparability between probationers and prisoners. It is impossible to compare the remedial, rehabilitative, or deterrent effects of either imprisonment or probation based upon the recidivism rates of these two groups of offenders. Nor are there reliable statistics to show whether imprisonment failed because it was too long or too short. Neither fines nor restitution have been imposed regularly enough and on a sufficiently broad spectrum of offenses to permit a comparison of the recidivism rates of those who have received such penalties with those who have been sentenced to imprisonment or probation.

Recidivism is not the best measure of the effectiveness of criminal penalties although it is the easiest to verify and quantify. The aim of the criminal justice system is not merely to prevent the repetition of crime by those who have already been convicted but to assure the maintenance of a law-abiding and an orderly community. The phrase "law and order" has been debased by demagogues using the slogan as an excuse for repression. However, the large and costly panoply of police, courts, and corrections are supported by the public for the purpose of maintaining a free, orderly, and just society under law. Law in this broad sense is not a reign of terrorist oppression but a government based upon concepts of equal treatment of all individuals. It means a legal system that assures for every accused person a fair trial in which the individual's rights are enforced and adequate remedies for wrongs done are provided. It also means a system that does not impose arbitrary or capricious penalties on wrongdoers.

Popular attitudes toward criminal penalties fluctuate. Often they bear little relation to the facts. Capital punishment is a notorious and obvious example of beliefs that exist independent of facts. There have always been substantial numbers of people who abhor capital punishment, who believe that it is immoral, barbaric, and useless. There have always been other people who believe that one who wilfully takes life should forfeit his own life, that wilful killers must be killed by the state to protect society, and that imposition of the death penalty will deter others from committing murders. A decade ago the majority of the Supreme Court, criminologists, and commentators seemed to oppose capital punishment. Today the contrary point of view appears to be dominant. What has happened to cause this change in attitude? There are no objectively verifiable facts to account for this change. In the two decades prior to 1977, only two convicts were executed in the United States. Crime increased steadily but not at a substantially greater rate than in the fifties. Indeed, the rate of increase may have been levelling off at the very time when the death penalty was reinstated. There are, in 1979, 513 condemned killers on death row. Most of them are poor. The vast majority are blacks accused of killing whites.[5] This was the situation when the death penalty was declared unconstitutional in 1972. Nothing has changed except the attitude of the public and criminologists. This book will not discuss capital punishment, which is applicable to only a fraction of a percent of convicted offenders. Although the death penalty is a significant moral and social issue, it is relatively unimportant as a practical matter in the administration of criminal justice. This book is concerned with the penalties the criminal justice system imposes on the more than 99 percent of offenders who are not subject to capital punishment.

For more than a generation the American criminal justice system operated under the theory that a primary goal of sentencing was the rehabilitation of the offender. The new approach being advocated in the late 1970s is based on a theory assumed to arise from data. The vocabulary is appealing: "justice as fairness."[6] In essence, the aim is to sentence equally all offenders who commit the same offense. The argument goes like this: Rehabilitation has failed; treatment is coercive; the purpose of sentencing is to give the criminal his just desert. It is simple fairness to impose the same sentence on all people who have committed the same crime.

The old theory was to make the punishment fit the crime and the criminal. The court was to do justice to the offender. Justice was seen as more complex than the mechanical imposition of the same sentence for the same crime.

It is curious that the "justice as fairness" theory of sentencing should gain popularity at the same time that the judicial and ideological battle over compensatory treatment for disadvantaged minorities is raging. Is it fair or just, assuming these words have different meanings, to give a black man a preference in employment or access to higher education than a white man? Or a woman over a man? Should a just social order take into account centuries when the black man and the woman were debarred from such jobs and such educational opportunities in the approaching goal of the equality of treatment for all? These perplexing questions are not unrelated to the problem of criminal sentences. Should a court in imposing sentence take into account the economic and social deprivations that criminal A has suffered in his life in comparison with criminal B who committed approximately the same offense but did not have a deprived background? Should a court consider the intellectual and educational deficiencies of the offender? Should it consider his inadequate family life, poor health, unattractiveness, or simply the fact that the offender was unloved? These are questions that often trouble sentencing judges but play little part in the theories of sentencing.

Darryl is a poor black nineteen-year-old, a school dropout. He has lived in the slums all his life except for one year spent in a juvenile correctional institution. He reads at a sixth-grade level although his intelligence is average. He has not seen his father for years. His mother is asthmatic and cannot work. She is on welfare. Darryl has never had a steady job although he has worked in a car wash and in a fast-food restaurant. Darryl was convicted of auto theft.

Marvin is also nineteen. He is white, a high-school graduate. He lives in a good middle-class neighborhood. Both his parents are employed. He had a job in a factory for a year but quit. He was also convicted of auto theft.

A judge who is faced with these two young men finds that the imposition of the same penalty on both would be neither just nor fair. Darryl has been deprived of every kind of training, love, and care that one hopes will help a child develop into an honorable person. Marvin has had advantages but simply refused to lead a law-abiding life. Both young men committed the same crime. But equal penalties applied to unequal people do not yield equal justice. Neither justice nor fairness is simple.

Although the bases of these shifting theories of sentencing are "scientific data," it is important to understand the inherent limitations in any scientific studies dealing with human beings, particularly in the area of the law. Scientific studies are believed to be reliable if one researcher can take two identical groups of subjects, place them under identical conditions, and change one factor with respect to one group but not the other. Group A, guinea pigs or fruit flies or cells, is fed or injected with a certain chemical and Group B is not. Otherwise both groups are exposed to the same conditions. If Group A develops a certain disease and Group B does not, it can be deduced that the chemical caused the disease. This is particularly true if the experiment can be replicated.

It has been wisely observed that "In the administration of justice no experiments are feasible."[7] A judge cannot take defendants A and B— two nineteen-year-old boys from the same environment, with the same amount of schooling, and the same I.Q. scores—who jointly committed a crime and sentence one to a ten-year prison term and let the other go free in order to test the deterrent capabilities of prison. Due process demands that each individual be given the sentence appropriate to the crime and to him. Moreover, there are simply too many variables in human behavior to conduct such experiments. They cannot be replicated. The length of generations is too long and the changes in physical conditions, social climate, and ideas are so numerous and far reaching that it is impossible to have a comparable period. People do not live in a controlled laboratory environment. Even in the same prison, the experiences of inmates differ.

The most that can be done in attempting to learn about crime, criminal behavior, and the penal system is to gather data after the fact. We know that two-thirds of all persons convicted of crime are apprehended for other crimes thereafter. We do not know how many of them actually commit crimes. Some who do may not be arrested. Others may be innocent but are apprehended because they are known to the police and are likely suspects. Does this prove that rehabilitation is a failure?

Crime does not occur in a laboratory, a controlled environment where causative factors can be isolated and varied. Data are unreliable because the raw materials depend upon unscientific individuals. Will the victim report the crime? Many imponderables go into that basic decision. Is the victim afraid of the suspect? Does the victim want to avoid contact with the law? That is true of many poor non-white victims of crime. Does the victim want to avoid more anguish, as is true of many rape victims? Is the loss too small to make it worth while to go through all the appearances in court that will be required? For these and many other reasons, reported crime does not give an accurate picture of crimes committed.

The next problem is the arrest of a suspect. That, too, depends upon a multitude of circumstances that cannot be controlled. Did the victim give a sufficiently precise description? "Teenage Negro male, approximately 5'10", wearing dungarees and green shirt." This is a better description than most. But unless someone answering that description appears in the immediate vicinity within a short time, the criminal cannot be located. Almost every teenage male wears dungarees. There are thousands of green shirts. If someone fitting that description is apprehended, what assurance does one have that he is, in fact, the person who committed the crime? Identification evidence when the criminal and victim are strangers is most difficult and unreliable. When I was representing teenagers accused of delinquency and identification was in question, I would frequently have my client, the suspect, exchange clothes with a friend. Invariably the victim recognized the clothes, not the person. Try to describe your best friend so that a stranger would be able to recognize him on the street. Unless he wears an eye patch, or walks with a limp, or has a scar, or is over 6'5" tall or under 5', it is practically impossible to give a description so detailed that this individual walking down a crowded street could be recognized by a stranger.

Conditions in prisons vary from abominable to decent. What happens to the individual in prison will obviously affect his behavior on release. There are many other conditions about which no researcher can possibly know that will be critical in determining the future of the released convict.

John had been in prison three years. He was eager to make good on release. He had been counselled in prison. His wife had written to him regularly and visited him as often as possible during his imprisonment. They had a daughter who was three when John was sentenced. When he went to prison his wife was unemployed. She stayed home with the baby. She was a naïve young girl who deferred to John, who was older and more sophisticated. During the three years John was incarcerated his wife had worked and attended a community college. She had become an administrative assistant who earned good money and was respected by her employer and her fellow employees. She planned to continue her education and get a college degree. John is a high-school dropout. The daughter could not remember John.

When John was released from prison and moved into the apartment with his wife and child, he thought it was a dream come true. It soon turned to a nightmare. He could not possibly get a job comparable to his wife's. She was far better educated than he. They had no common interests, not even the child, who had become a stranger to John and resented his presence. It was intolerable to him to have to ask his wife for pocket money. Within a few weeks, he stole again. Life in prison was more bearable than life outside where he was a burden to his wife and an intruder in his own family. Was this a failure of the rehabilitative goal of prison or a situation beyond control?

Such human tragedies and the occasional triumphs are not items which can be fed into a computer to determine whether prison rehabilitation has failed or succeeded. They are significant facts which a judge can discover only at a violation of probation hearing if he or she takes the time and trouble and if the prisoner and judge have established an ongoing relationship.

Whenever I sentence a person to jail, I explain to him or her why I am doing it and I ask the prisoner to write and let me know his progress. Many of them do.

Rockland who was convicted of homicide and sentenced to eight to twenty years in prison writes to me regularly. Here are excerpts from two of his letters. His spelling and punctuation are reproduced.

Your Honor,
When I was sentenced, by you, on June 4, 1973 I expressed my desire to receive a college Education while serving my sentence, which is Eight (8) to Twenty (20) years for 2nd degree Murder and Agg. Robbery. At the Time of sentencing me you stated you would help me carry out my desire to do so.
. . .
My main interest lie in Sociology and Teaching. By tackling these and other feilds I shall used my skills to help less fortunate persons than myself, both old and young. I know that If I am allowed to continued my plans at——. I will no longer be a burden on Society but a valuable asset.
Respect.

Reviewing the files of several hundred people I have sentenced to jail, I find it impossible to draw any firm conclusions. Has prison rehabilitated them? Would they have been better out of prison? I know that Earl would have been. He is a homosexual, very pretty, and effeminate. He was raped his first night in prison. I had entered a special written order that he be placed in the homosexual wing, but somehow the order was never delivered to the warden. Luigi in the same prison earned his school diploma, stopped taking drugs, and is now out and holding a good job. Did prison therapy rehabilitate him? Or is he one like Richard who told me, "Prison didn't rehabilitate me. I did it myself." Was Richard helped or hindered? Who can say? Many, like John, are back in prison again.

One person has only a limited experience. Social scientists have the benefit of statistics dealing with tens of thousands of cases. They can extrapolate from those figures by sophisticated methods and give reliable predictive results over a broad range of numbers. Are they applicable to individuals? Is one dealing with the person who is in the 60 percent majority or the 40 percent minority? Are these figures meaningful? Do they provide answers to the questions which are significant to society and the offender? It is difficult to reply with assurance to any of these questions.

Regardless of the uncertainties of the facts and the conclusions to be drawn from them, one must proceed to deal with problems on the basis of a supposition, no matter how tentative or subject to error it may be. Theories of sentencing, I believe, are no more than suppositions. They are subject to error. They should be carefully evaluated and revised in the light of developing or changing facts.

The two theories of sentencing which are now seen as being in opposition are generally called the "rehabilitative or treatment model" and the "desert or justice model." Both are predicated on the concept that the choices available to the sentencing authority, whether it be a judge or a commission or a parole board, are prison or probation. For a generation judges have been urged to adopt the rehabilitative model in imposing sentence. Some did and some did not. Inevitably disparities in sentencing resulted. It is now urged that the desert model be adopted not merely as a goal but as a mandate in sentencing.

The current controversies over sentencing involve more issues than these two rival theories. There are disputes as to whether the sentence should be for a specific period rather than an indeterminate time between the minimum and the maximum. Some question whether the sentence should be imposed by the judge who tried the case or by some other body. As we have noted, the problem has been expressed with deceptive simplicity as "Who Decides and When?"[8]

It is generally assumed that the trial judge decides the length of the sentence. In most cases the judge does impose a minimum and a maximum penalty. This decision is subject to many qualifications. There are a few crimes in some jurisdictions where it is required by statute to impose a sentence. In murder, some statutes specify that sentence shall be life imprisonment unless the jury decides that it shall be death. In some states, a person who is convicted of a felony for the third or fourth time or for a second sex offense must be sentenced to prison. Except for such statutes, judges in most jurisdictions are free to decide whether to sentence a convicted criminal to a correctional institution or to place him on probation, the "in" or "out" decision. If the choice is "in," the judge in most jurisdictions and for most crimes sets a minimum and a maximum term. In some states the minimum cannot be more than one half or one third of the maximum.

Who decides what the actual sentence to be served will be? When is this decision made? Usually a parole board determines how much more than the minimum the prisoner must serve. This decision is made when the minimum expires, if he is released. If he is not released, the board reconsiders from time to time until he is released or the maximum term is served. At that time he must be discharged regardless of whether or not he has been rehabilitated and whether or not he is dangerous or psychotic. If he appears to be suffering from a mental illness, a petition for a civil commitment may be filed. A due process hearing will be held in civil court on this issue.

The purpose of an indeterminate sentence is to promote rehabilitation of the prisoner. The theory is that the prisoner can obtain an earlier release if he works conscientiously to improve or reform himself. He has a powerful incentive to change—the carrot of early release and the club of prolonged incarceration. Parole boards are composed of appointed officials. They are bureaucrats who are not answerable to the public. Their deliberations are not public. Whatever rules they operate by are, in the main, self-imposed. Except for rare and notorious cases, the public does not know who is released and who is denied release.

In many states, the parole board sends the trial judge a form indicating that John Doe is coming up for consideration for parole and asks for comments. In most cases the judge knows nothing of what has happened to John Doe since he was sentenced. Even if the judge is interested in the prisoner, communication is often difficult.

Willie Y. was convicted of robbery. He was totally illiterate but apparently of normal intelligence. He told me, "I'm ignorant, but I ain't stupid." I think he was right. I ordered the prison to see that he had basic remedial schooling. From time to time the prison, which was overcrowded, wanted to release him on work furlough. Approval of the judge is requested but not required before placing a prisoner on furlough. A cynic might say that this is one of the many instances of buck passing. If the convict commits a crime while on furlough, the prison can always blame the judge and vice versa. After persistent prodding, at least half a dozen letters, I learned that Willie was not in school. Willie, who was illiterate, could not write to me. Better educated prisoners write to me regularly. I notified the prison authorities that I would oppose Willie's release until he learned to read. Somehow word of my position reached Willie and he insisted on going to school. In such ways an indeterminate sentence can be of value to the prisoner.

The usual alternative to an indeterminate sentence, one with a minimum and a maximum, is called flat time. The judge imposes a fixed term. When it expires the prisoner is released even though he is still as illiterate, unemployable, hostile, and unregenerate as when he entered the prison. Each prisoner gets a fixed reduction for good behavior—for example, one day off for one month of good behavior. The stated advantages of flat time are that it is supposed to be fair. It eliminates arbitrary and capricious decisions by the parole board. Each prisoner knows how much time he has to serve from the beginning of his sentence and is not confused and resentful when he but not another is refused release. There have been many abuses by parole boards and obvious unfairnessess. Careful research in several states has disclosed disparities in the length of sentences served which most lawyers, judges, and citizens would consider to be outrageous. The figures with respect to incarceration of juveniles reveal the illogical results of this kind of indeterminate sentencing.[9]

> 1. In six of eight institutions shorter stay is associated with index offense categories [crimes] as opposed to status offenses [truancy, runaway, incorrigibility].
> 2. Institutions . . . invariably detained younger male residents longer than their older counterparts.
> 3. Although females were committed for less serious offenses, they average nearly one month longer in institutions than males.
> 4. Females stayed on parole longer.
> 5. Less serious [status] offenders remained on parole longer than felony index offenders.
> 6. Availability of bed space in institutions controlled length of stay.

Similar irrational disparities in length of stay beyond the minimum also prevail in many jurisdictions with respect to adult offenders. Exact figures are hard to obtain. Nor does the researcher know what these prisoners have done in prison which may affect the decisions of parole boards.

Parole boards were created by statute to perform a limited function.

They can be eliminated by statute. Some states, notably Illinois, Maine, California, and Indiana have abolished parole boards and substituted determinate or flat sentences for indeterminate sentences.[10]

Eliminating the parole board would do away with arbitrary and capricious decisions which that body makes. Judges could impose flat time sentences and obviate the need for parole. But we are still left with arbitrary and capricious decisions of judges. It is not easy to eliminate the judge. A judge may be arbitrary and capricious in the finding of guilt. This issue is appealable. A judge may also be arbitrary and capricious in sentencing. In most jurisdictions this decision is not appealable. The inequities and disparities in sentencing have been noted by many observers of the criminal justice system.

The director of the Federal Bureau of Prisons, James Bennett, noted some alarming examples of disparity in sentences. He wrote,

The average sentence for forgery in a recent year in the northern district of Mississippi was sixty-eight months, while in southern Mississippi it was seven months. Not long ago we received at Atlanta a middle-aged credit union treasurer with a sentence of 117 days for embezzling twenty-four thousand dollars. He found there another embezzler his own age, with an impeccable previous record and admirable family life, serving twenty years' imprisonment with five years of probation to follow. . . . In Texas in 1959, a stripteaser was sentenced to fifteen years' imprisonment by a state judge for possession of marijuana. In 1962, three pharmaceutical company scientists who pleaded no contest to holding back and falsifying test data on a drug that allegedly hurt many hundreds of people were given six-month sentences in a Washington, D. C., federal court.

Throughout my years in office, the appeals courts were crowded with cases that had little merit in terms of the difference between guilt and innocence. The appeals had been docketed not so much to upset the convictions as to overthrow unnecessarily harsh sentences. . . .

The President [Kennedy] was particularly disturbed that a teenaged epileptic had been sentenced to life imprisonment on a narcotics charge, a teenaged boy to fifteen years for embezzlement, an Army officer to eighteen years for passing two bad checks, and he reduced the sentences to what he considered to be reasonable penalties.[11]

An obvious and uncomplicated means of eliminating or reducing the arbitrariness of the sentencing judge is to permit appellate review of the sentence. Thirty years ago this was cogently urged by Judge Simon Soboloff. Recently Chief Justice Warren Burger has suggested that such appellate review be considered. Judge Irving Kaufman of the United

States Court of Appeals noted that "The United States is the only nation in the free world where one judge can determine conclusively, decisively and finally the minimum period of time a defendant must remain in prison without being subject to any review of his determination."[12]

Whenever I am called upon to decide an unclear issue I say to the lawyers, "This is my best judgment of what the law is," or, "This is my best judgment of the direction in which the law is moving. If I am wrong, the appellate court will reverse me." Under the civil law in many jurisdictions the trial judge may certify a question to be decided by an appellate court. This is a wise protection against the prejudices, foibles, and aberrations of any individual. But in sentencing the decision is, in most jurisdictions, unreviewable. I believe that most trial judges would welcome review of this most critical decision. Everyone has subconscious biases and prejudices no matter how dispassionate he may try to be. A panel of three or more other judges reviewing these decisions should eliminate most of the gross unfairness in sentences.

The "justice as fairness" theory, however, goes much further than eliminating parole boards. In answering the "who-decides-and-when" questions, proponents say that the legislature should decide the penalty and it should decide in advance of the crime. According to the proposal of former Federal Judge Marvin Frankel, the legislature should establish sentencing commissions which will determine within the narrow limits of discretion left by mandatory sentencing laws what the sentence should be. The arguments in favor of sentencing commissions are clear and logical. What the penalties for crime should be is a policy decision. Except for a few Constitutional limitations, there is nothing that requires a judge to fix the penalty. Since it is a policy decision, it should be made by the legislature. Common sense dictates that some two or three hundred state legislators who are overwhelmed with problems of taxation, subsidies, environment, education, health, and welfare cannot themselves take the time to decide whether the sentence for robbery of over five hundred dollars without a gun should be three years and with a gun, five years, and all the variations possible throughout a penal code consisting of more than one hundred offenses from arson to zoning violations. The Commission will make these determinations which will have the effect of law. The Commission will establish the factors to be considered in fixing sentence such as the crime, the injury to the victim, if any, the amount of property taken, and the presence or use of a weapon. Each factor is given a weighted number. By applying this scale to the case before him, the judge arrives at the "presumptive sentence." The judge will then impose a sentence that is certain. It is the same because all judges in the jurisdiction must apply the same criteria. According to Professor Dershowitz, "Only in truly extraordinary circumstances would a judge be permitted to deviate from the presumptive sentence."[13] The presumption is that if the sentence is equally imposed and certain, it is fair. Under the justice as fairness concept, it should then follow that the sentence is just.

In succeeding chapters we shall look at the rehabilitation and desert theories and the presumptive sentencing proposal from the viewpoint of a judge who must impose sentence.

CHAPTER VI

THE GOAL OF REHABILITATION

> With ready-made opinions one cannot judge a crime.
> Its philosophy is a little more complicated than
> people think. It is acknowledged that neither con-
> vict prisons, nor the hulks, nor any system of hard
> labor ever cured a criminal.
> —Fyodor Dostoyevsky

The quest for the cure of criminality, like the quest for the Holy Grail, the Fountain of Youth, Eldorado, and the Northwest Passage, has preoccupied many people for generations. For almost half a century the American criminal justice system has been attempting to cure criminals. The phraseology today is slightly different; we are now attempting to rehabilitate criminals. The goal has been to treat convicted felons in such a way that they would cease to be law violators and become good, productive members of society. Courts, prisons, and probation departments have been involved in this task. Today almost every American court system employs cadres of social workers, psychiatrists, psychologists, counsellors, and paraprofessionals to test, diagnose, and treat convicted offenders. In recent years special programs to treat drug addicts and alcoholics have been established. Group therapy with professional leaders and "rap sessions" with ex-offenders have been instituted. This medical model of providing therapy for law violators is an integral part of American courts and correctional systems. It underlies the present philosophy of sentencing.

These rehabilitative programs were not established by wild-eyed reformers or bleeding-heart judges. Most of the programs were initiated to comply with the mandates of state and federal legislation and to conform to the carefully articulated purposes and goals of the criminal law. The most widely accepted expression of the philosophy of rehabilitation is contained in the Model Penal Code of the American Law Institute. It is the culmination of decades of work by leading legal scholars and penologists. It was approved by the Institute in 1962. This code has indeed been a model for state laws and sentencing practices throughout the United States. Its authority is awesome and persuasive even in jurisdictions which have not expressly adopted the Code.

Section 1.02(2), entitled "Purposes Governing Sentencing and Treatment," lists, inter alia, the purposes of criminal sentences as follows:

a. to prevent the commission of offenses;
b. to promote the correction and rehabilitation of offenders;
e. to effect individualized treatment; and
g. to advance the use of generally accepted scientific methods and knowledge in the sentencing and treatment of offenders.

Similar statements are found in the sentencing codes of many states. The aims expressed are lofty and admirable. Who would not want to "prevent the commission of offenses" and "to promote the correction and rehabilitation of offenders"? The difficulty for the judge who must impose sentence on the convicted offender is that he or she does not know what, if any, penalty will prevent the commission of offenses or what, if any, treatment will rehabilitate an offender. The Model Penal Code requires the judge to employ "generally accepted scientific methods." Until at least 1978, the consensus of the criminology establishment was that offenders could be rehabilitated in prisons and also in the community under the tutelage of probation officers. This opinion prevailed even though irrefutable statistics revealed that at least two thirds of all offenders upon release from prison or discharge from probation commit other offenses.

The goals and standards embodied in the Model Penal Code are really little more than vague concepts which at one time were found palatable by the criminology and jurisprudence establishments. They do not provide precise modalities of treatment or clear instructions to the sentencing judge. It is interesting and significant that the word "punishment" is not used nor is the concept of making whole the victims of crime any part of the purposes of sentencing. Indeed, the victim of crime is not even mentioned except in a passing reference in Section 7 that a fine should not be imposed if it would prevent restitution. Neither restitution nor reparation is included in the purposes of sentencing.

Many trial judges and lawyers have been skeptical of the concept of rehabilitation for years. We have seen offenders who have records of six or eight or more crimes. We have seen convicts who have committed other crimes within a week of their release from prison. Nonetheless, the goal of rehabilitation seemed to be firmly established in the criminal law. Moreover, the attendant bureaucracies which administer the programs of rehabilitation have become an integral part of the criminal justice system and outnumber lawyers and judges.

In 1979, the pendulum swung from the goal of rehabilitation of the offender to the hard-line concept of punishment. Professor Marvin Wolfgang, the dean of criminologists, now believes that criminals should be punished, that they deserve punishment. Many legal scholars take a similar stance. Punishment is perceived as the traditional prison. Compare this position with the Model Penal Code which states, "The Court shall deal with a person who has been convicted of a crime without imposing sentence of imprisonment unless it is of the opinion that his imprisonment is necessary for the protection of the public." Prison under the code is the last choice, one to be used sparingly and then only to protect the public. But even this specific rule is difficult to apply. How can a judge know whether the commission of one violent act is simply an aberration or whether the offender is likely to commit other acts of violence which will endanger the community? Should shoplifters, white-collar criminals, and other nonviolent offenders never be sent to prison? Their incarceration is obviously unnecessary for the protection of the public.

The respectability of the notion of punishment in legal and penological circles is sudden and startling. In 1974, at a bench-bar conference where some five hundred lawyers and trial judges met, as they do annually, to discuss common problems of the courts and the bar, a debate was held on sentencing. An assistant district attorney who had been prosecuting homicide cases for many years advocated imprisonment for the sake of punishment. He is a sophisticated, bon-vivant, middle-aged man who rather fancies himself as a local William Buckley. He deliberately espoused a position he knew would provoke his audience. He is a lawyer who has cut corners many times in order to try to obtain a conviction. He is convinced, however, that these shortcuts were for a good cause and, therefore, moral. He is similarly casual about personal transgressions by members of the non-criminal class but harshly censorious concerning street criminals. He was opposed by a young professor of criminology who expressed shock at the notion of a vengeful society and abhorrence at the goal of punishment. The professor learnedly quoted statistics about the higher rate of non-recidivism for those sentenced to probation rather than prison.

Seated on my right, appropriately, was Judge M. with a reputation for being a tough judge. "Damn nonsense," he muttered. "I only place the good ones on probation. If I put 'em all on probation where would his statistics be?"

The professor went on to discuss rehabilitation, the psychiatric counseling now available in prisons, the use of furloughs to test the readiness of the prisoner for release, and the batteries of tests and treatment programs available. On my left was Judge S., a kindly man, much respected as being patient, thoughtful, and unmoved by the oratory of either prosecution or defense. Judge S. listened carefully and then admitted sadly, "When I send a man to prison it is not to rehabilitate him, because I know that won't happen. It is only because I have no alternative."

After a heated discussion, the moderator asked for a show of hands. How many agreed with the prosecutor that imprisonment should be imposed for the sake of punishment? Barely 10 percent of the audience agreed with the prosecutor, not even Judge M.

There are many reasons why punishment is a word which lawyers and judges do not use easily or comfortably. Lawyers by profession deal with behavior, both past and anticipated, which largely falls in an area of unclear legality. They are trained to be non-judgmental. In civil matters a client usually consults his lawyer for advice about a transaction in order to learn the means of accomplishing his ends, which may be of dubious morality, within the limits of the law. The lawyer knows all too well that those limits are variable, depending not only upon facts and circumstances but also upon the jurisdiction in which the matter will be litigated, the skill of the lawyer, and even the identity of the judge who hears the case. In giving advice the lawyer cannot permit his own notions of morality to intrude. If the law permits a corporate officer to reap enormous profits from inside knowledge or from the division of stock into different classes so long as there is "disclosure" then the lawyer is not justified in withholding this information from the client even though the result is patently unfair to members of the public.

A lawyer representing a client accused of crime is required by the Canons of Ethics to suspend his own moral judgment and defend the client to his utmost ability regardless of the client's guilt or innocence, moral turpitude and evil motives, or his claims to a "higher" morality. If the client is convicted, the attorney must exercise his skill to ensure that the penalty is within the limits of the law and to seek to overturn the conviction on appeal. A lawyer may know that his client has in fact taken money that was not his or even that his client has killed someone; the lawyer may abhor the act and loathe the client; but it is his duty to obtain dismissal of the charges if there has been a delay in bringing him to trial or if the client was improperly interrogated by the police. It is the lawyer's duty to obtain his client's acquittal if he can do so by casting doubt on evidence that he personally believes is reliable. With such training and experience, it is understandable that lawyers are uncomfortable with the concept of punishment and prefer to relegate it to the clergy or philosophers.

Many judges are even more reluctant than lawyers are to think in terms of punishment because they see the frequent disjunction of law and morality. Often in civil cases, the law requires the judge to impose liability where no fault exists. For example, a seller of a defective machine which injures someone may be liable even though he did not manufacture the machine and did not know how the purchaser was going to use it. A person whose employee carelessly injures another while on company business is liable even though the employer was not at fault. In civil cases, a judge often has to deny recovery to an innocent party who failed to read a contract, or did not anticipate the outcome of his improvident bargain. In criminal cases, as in civil cases, the jury may be unduly swayed by the oratory of counsel and the personality of the litigant or the lawyer. Juries are frequently convinced by irrelevant details and fail to comprehend the principle of reasonable doubt.

Like all judges, I have seen individuals who are evil and vicious. There are men who have deliberately beaten, maimed, tortured, and robbed again and again. But I have had to permit such an individual to walk out of the courtroom free, without penalty, because in the case before me there was insufficient evidence, or the identification was uncertain, or the statute of limitations had run, or the accused was charged with the wrong offense, or able defense counsel managed to cast doubt on a stupid witness and the jury acquitted the accused. The jury, of course, did not know that the defendant had a long prior record of similar crimes. Under the law no penalty may be imposed on such an individual regardless of his evil ways.

I have also seen good, decent people who acted impulsively or on misperceived facts or who were convicted on very shaky evidence. Rochelle is a barmaid. She lives at home with her parents whom she helps to support. One night she met Seymour, a fast-talking man with a shiny new car and elegant clothes. He courted her assiduously and in a very gentlemanly fashion. He drove her home. He did not pressure her to go off on weekends with him. He spoke of marriage. After several weeks of exemplary behavior he asked Rochelle to deliver a package for him. During the next month Rochelle delivered many packages for Seymour. He never told her what was in the parcels. Rochelle was arrested by undercover agents while she was delivering several pounds of heroin. Seymour was never seen again. A jury convicted Rochelle of violating drug laws. Should punishment be imposed for naïveté or stupidity when there is no evil intent or malice? Does Rochelle need rehabilitation? What treatment can make her more wary and self-protective? These are troubling questions which judges face day after day.

Both rehabilitation and punishment as goals of the criminal justice system have been postulated by professors of law, researchers at institutes on law and criminology, and philosophers—people who deal in abstract concepts and statistics. It is important to see how these theories operate when applied to flesh-and-blood human beings and when measured against the standards of a due process legal system.

Before examining the goal of rehabilitation, it must be recognized that probation or prison—"in" or "out"—are not the only options of a sentencing judge. Fines, restitution, reparation, and conditions of probation, such as attending school or performing public service, are available penalties. Two common misconceptions cloud the understanding of sentencing. First is the belief that a penalty inevitably follows conviction, and second, that judges have unfettered discretion in imposing sentence. Former Supreme Court Justice Abe Fortas, who was never a trial judge, expressed the view that following conviction there must be the imposition of a penalty. Fortas declared that once a person has been arrested, charged, and convicted, "he should be punished by fine or imprisonment or both in accordance with the provisions of the law, unless the law is not valid in general or as applied. . . . He may indeed be right in the eye of history or morality or philosophy. These are not controlling."[1]

This is an extraordinary statement. It assumes first, that there are only two penalties: fine and imprisonment; second, that the judge has no discretion in imposing a sentence; and third, that there is little congruence between law and morality. All of these assumptions are incorrect. As we have seen, there is a range of penalties including suspended sentence, probation, restitution, and reparation in addition to fines and imprisonment. The judge has discretion in choosing the penalty and, if it is imprisonment, in setting the length of the term within the maximum limits. Most judges, I believe, do try within the restrictions of statutes and precedents to achieve a just and moral result. Often this is not possible. But most members of the legal profession, including judges, seek to achieve a just result in the litigational process, including sentencing of offenders. Indeed, it is this effort to reach a just result that has been the impetus for new sentencing codes promulgated since the Model Penal Code and for innumerable studies, seminars, and books on prisons and sentencing.

In considering sentencing, it is necessary to bear in mind that crime and punishment are not symbiotic. In fact, no real penalty is imposed on most persons convicted of crime. They do not pay fines. They are not put to hard labor. They are not required to work and repay the victims of their crime. They are not imprisoned. Instead, most convicted criminals are placed on probation. A probationer lives at home. He goes to work or not as he chooses. If unemployed, he is entitled to welfare. The only restriction on his liberty is that he must report at certain intervals to a probation officer. Some sentences of probation prohibit the probationer from leaving the jurisdiction or from driving a car or from taking drugs. Essentially, however, a convict on probation is a free person so long as he is not rearrested. In the eyes of most people, including the offender, probation is a nominal penalty—a slap on the wrist. Many probationers are rearrested for other offenses, tried, convicted, and placed on probation again. The cycle continues. These offenders are known as revolving-door cases.

Although the sentencing judge has discretion, it is subject to limitations. The law sets a maximum limit on the length of the prison sentence and the amount of the fine which may be imposed for each crime. Even though a victim becomes a quadriplegic as a result of injuries received

in an assault, the criminal, in most jurisdictions, may not be sentenced
to prison for more than ten to twenty years. At the expiration of ten
years, if not sooner, he will probably be released on parole. Even though
the offender stole or embezzled more than a million dollars, the maximum fine for these offenses in most jurisdictions is only twenty-five
thousand dollars. A few statutes require mandatory prison sentences, but
more than 90 percent of all persons convicted of crimes are not subject
to mandatory penalties. In all these cases, the judge is required to fix a
penalty within the maximum limits of the statute, taking into consideration the goals and standards of the sentencing codes. The judge must
determine what sentence—between the extreme of no penalty, neither
fine nor imprisonment, and incarceration for the maximum number of
years along with the maximum fine—is appropriate. The judge may also
suspend sentence or place the criminal on probation.

The theory of rehabilitation assumes that by placing an offender in
prison or putting him under the supervision of a probation officer his
criminal tendencies will be, if not cured, at least curbed. Through these
ministrations robbers, rapists, and offenders of all sorts and conditions
will be transformed somehow into law-abiding citizens. There is absolutely no objective evidence to support this belief. There never has been
any evidence that imprisonment or probation transformed any substantial numbers of offenders into law-abiding people. The statistics have
always been dismaying. Nonetheless, for decades knowledgeable people
in the fields of criminology and law have clung to the belief in rehabilitation through imprisonment and probation.

Let us take an ordinary nonpolitical street crime and see the results
of a conscientious application of the principle of rehabilitation and the
guidelines which the law requires in most jurisdictions in the United
States. Rickey, convicted of assault, stands before the bar of the court.
He looks like any other man one might see on the street, in a subway,
or in a restaurant. Inevitably, a judge will ponder over the known facts
and the unknown, the tangibles and the intangibles—the impelling
factors that have brought Rickey to this point. I review the pre-sentence
investigation report. It discloses that Rickey completed eleven years of
schooling. His school record and literacy level are not reported. He had
no childhood diseases. His religion is noted. There is much information
about Rickey's family: four siblings and their occupations, father deceased, good relations with mother. I note that the mother, although a
resident of the same city, did not appear at the trial and is not present

at the sentencing. How good is this relationship? The pre-sentence report is based largely on hearsay and is strained through the philosophy of the reporter. The court psychiatrist reports that Rickey has a "passive aggressive" personality.

Is Rickey likely to stab someone else? This is the most perplexing and critical question. But there is no answer to this question in either the pre-sentence report or the neuropsychiatric report which I order, as recommended by an enlightened court administration. The pre-sentence report is compiled by a graduate social worker who has interviewed Rickey and four people who know him. The psychiatric report is made by a board-certified psychiatrist employed by the state; he has the assistance of a state-employed psychologist who has tested Rickey. None of these professionals knows anything about the crime except for the self-serving account Rickey himself has given them. None of these profesionals, employed at great expense to the taxpayers, ventures an opinion on the crucial issue: Is Rickey reasonably likely to assault someone else? However, the psychiatrist and social worker do recommend the sentence I should impose, even though they do not know the evidence upon which the defendant was convicted.

All that I really know is that Rickey stabbed Barrack during a quarrel. If Rickey had been a little slower and Barrack a little faster, Rickey might well have been the victim and Barrack would have been on trial. Barrack was injured and out of work for several months. The maximum penalty is five to ten years' imprisonment and/or a ten-thousand-dollar-fine. Rickey is unemployed. He has never had a steady job. He has never married. He has two children by one woman and is living with another woman.

What sentence should be imposed and why? Should Rickey be punished? Should he be rehabilitated? If so, how can he be rehabilitated? I review the stated goals of sentencing which are commonly agreed to be incapacitation, deterrence, and rehabilitation.[2]

Incapacitation. In twentieth-century America, the state cannot amputate the hand of a thief, blind a peeping Tom, or castrate a rapist. I cannot banish Rickey to a penal colony, order his right hand to be amputated, brand him, whip him, or execute him. Incapacitation is really only a euphemism for imprisonment. It is, however, not only inexact, it is misleading. By being imprisoned a person is not incapacitated from committing other crimes. Every judge knows that stabbings and other criminal acts of violence occur in prison. Moreover, Rickey will be incapacitated from committing further crimes on the general public (not the prison population) only so long as he is incarcerated. Incapacitation for five or six years will cost the taxpayers approximately one hundred thousand dollars, depending upon the prison. Incapacitation does not seem to be a compelling reason for imprisoning Rickey, particularly in view of the stricture of the Model Penal Code that imprisonment shall be used only to protect the public.

Deterrence. Here the statistics are more reliable than they are with respect to rehabilitation. The two-thirds recidivism rate is appalling. Day after day, every judge sees people who have been arrested for new offenses within weeks of release from prison. Imprisonment is unlikely to deter Rickey any more than it has his predecessors.

Deterrence as a reason for sentencing is often favored by the press. "Soft" judges are seen as a cause of crime. Swift, certain, severe penalties are frequently advocated as the answer to the ever-growing crime problem. If criminals are not punished, it is argued, everyone will feel free to violate the law. This is the theory. Most judges, however, are skeptical.

Both Austin and Plato observed that the law depends upon the consent of the governed. People must be in a habit of obedience to law. Some people are and some people aren't. Most people stop at a red light even if no policeman is present. They obey the law because it is the law. Fortunately, the vast majority of Americans voluntarily comply with the law. If they didn't, all the sanctions which the law can command would not be sufficient to achieve a viable democratic society. Only a police state can terrorize into obedience the majority of a community who do not wish to obey the law. The history of prohibition and anti-marijuana laws reveals the almost insuperable difficulties of enforcing an unpopular law.

If a jail sentence is not imposed on Rickey, will other people conclude that it is perfectly all right for them to commit crime? Conversely, if he is given a stiff penalty will others be intimidated and deterred from crime because Rickey is incarcerated? He is a faceless person in a sea of some three or four million people in this community. His crime was reported in a two-inch item in the press. The panel of forty jurors who were questioned had never heard of either him or the incident. No spectators have been in the courtroom, other than the family of the victim. Rickey is just a statistic. None of the public will know or care what penalty was imposed on him.

Some proponents of the deterrent theory argue that if no penalties are imposed, the law-abiding members of the public may well decide to become law violators. Deterrence is not effective, they say, on lawbreakers. But it is effective in keeping the vast majority of the population lawful. Obviously this belief can never be substantiated by evidence. I have seen engravings of scenes of seventeenth-century England which depict crowds watching the hanging of a pickpocket while other pickpockets are busily plying their trade. It is farfetched wishful thinking to conclude that the incarceration of Rickey will deter anyone from committing a crime.

Sadly I conclude that a jail sentence will not deter Rickey or anyone else from committing other similar crimes. Imprisonment will "incapacitate" him only for the period he is actually incarcerated. Since he is only twenty-four years old and has a life expectancy of almost fifty years and since the maximum sentence allowable is ten years, his incapacitation will not be significant.

Rehabilitation The third of the trinity of justifications for imposing penal sanctions, rehabilitation offers the most appealing arguments. If the judge, the attorneys, and the people employed in the prisons can be lulled into believing that what they are doing is for the good of the criminal, then it is very easy to deprive him of his liberty. Rehabilitation is sometimes called "treatment." Imprisonment as treatment? It would be laughable if it were not so tragic. Every week I receive letters from prisoners complaining that they are not getting any treatment. They spend their days in the cell and the prison yard. They watch television. They work at meaningless tasks for a few cents an hour. They fight with the other inmates. The prison to which Rickey would be sent is probably better than most. On arrival, he will be tested by a psychologist, given three weeks' indoctrination, and then assigned to a unit where he can work several hours a day making license plates. He can also attend school, if he wishes. Even an illiterate prisoner is not required to attend school unless the judge specifies that he must do so. I find that such orders are often ignored.

If the prisoner is sufficiently literate, he will write to me complaining that he has not been to school or that he is not getting drug treatment or that he is being molested. Occasionally an illiterate prisoner will get another inmate to write to me. Rickey claims he can read "some." If I send him to prison I shall have to write regularly to be sure that he is attending classes.

Is Rickey in need of treatment? He does not appear to have any physical illness or any diagnosable mental illness. What effective therapy is there for a "passive aggressive" personality? And how much therapy will Rickey get in prison? He will be seen and evaluated on his arrival in prison. If he is an alcoholic or on drugs, he will be put in a special unit and given some treatment. There is no indication that Rickey is addicted. He looks too healthy to be seriously into drugs. I did not see any tell-tale needle marks on his arms. He may be subjected to "guidance and counselling." This sounds therapeutic and enlightened. However, I cannot help wondering what a forty-five minute session of conversation now and then with a social worker on the prison staff can do to make Rickey a better-adjusted person or less likely to commit another assault.

Rehabilitation is such a comforting reason for jailing Rickey. A judge, like an angry parent, can say, "I'm doing this for your own good, not to punish you but to help you." But most judges have seen too many prisons and too many prisoners to believe the theory. My disillusionment with prison and "therapy" is bolstered by studies which appear to prove that such intervention in the lives of criminals and potential law violators produces worse results than leaving individuals untreated.[3]

It is very easy for people who study statistics, charts, and penological theories to draw up standards and guidelines and phrase them in socially acceptable language. It is not so easy for a judge faced with a flesh-and-blood human to deprive the person of his liberty and say to him, "I am doing this for your own good, to rehabilitate you." Very few judges believe that imprisonment is rehabilitative. They do not try to fool themselves into thinking that what they are doing is for the good of the individual.

So far as I know there is nothing clinically wrong with Rickey. He doesn't need medical treatment or psychotherapy. He has no overt sex problems or personality disorders. Even if he did, he probably would not receive any meaningful therapy in prison. The continual procession of recidivists, or repeat offenders, has persuaded most judges that the likelihood of any reformation of character occurring in prison is extremely remote. Rickey is no worse and perhaps a bit better than most of the young men in his neighborhood with whom he has grown up. This is his first adult offense. Psychotherapy and treatment cannot change the factual conditions of his environment. If I were to send him to prison, on his release he would probably return to the same neighborhood, to his friends and family. He would walk streets where fights are an everyday occurrence. He would probably continue to carry a knife, which is customary and perhaps advisable, although illegal. The mirage of rehabilitation is not a sufficient reason for incarcerating him.

But a man has been stabbed and injured. His family is in court. Should a judge simply follow the guidelines and place Rickey on probation? Should Rickey walk out of the courtroom free after committing such an act?

A recent opinion of the Pennsylvania Supreme Court indicates the difficulties of the sentencing judge. In that case, the defendant was convicted of aggravated assault and sentenced to six to twenty-three months in the county jail. She was eligible for parole in three months. On appeal, the Pennsylvania Supreme Court vacated the sentence because the sentencing judge failed to "articulate reasons for sentence imposed reflecting weight was accorded the statutory guidelines for sentencing."[4] The facts as related by the Supreme Court were these: The defendant, a young lady, was a passenger in a car driven by her boyfriend, who had made an illegal turn on the highway. The car was stopped and a struggle developed between the driver and two police officers. The defendant got out of the car and pleaded with the officers to stop hitting the driver. After her protestations failed, she struck one of the officers once on the head with a stick and kicked another officer as he attempted to handcuff her. The defendant had no prior record.

The trial judge expressed his bewilderment as follows: "I am not saying you might not have been disgusted by the fact your friend was being arrested, but to turn on a law enforcement officer is a mystery to me and since I know of not other solution but to punish you for it . . . well, I simply cannot tolerate what you did." One can sympathize with the trial judge. The defendant's conduct was illegal and intolerable. He thought it should be punished. He imposed a prison sentence. But punishment is not, under most sentencing codes in the United States, a legally acceptable ground for imposing a penalty. This kind of punishment may relieve the judge's frustration; it may satisfy the press; it may momentarily assuage the victim. But what does it accomplish?

We must assume that sentencing has a rational purpose. Let us look at the facts of Rickey's life and Barrack's life without being bemused by the incantatory words of incapacitation, deterrence, rehabilitation, and punishment and see what kind of sentence will accomplish a useful social end. Rickey is a normal young man. His behavior is not aberrant in his community. His intelligence is normal. His education is very deficient. Although he has worked from time to time, he has no job skills. He is last to be hired, first to be fired. He does not support himself, his children, or his paramours. What does he need? Education.

Barrack is twenty-five years old. He is married and has one child. He had a steady job before this incident and supported himself and his family. It is four months since the stabbing occurred. Barrack is still not back at work. His bills are mounting. His rent is unpaid. His job pays for his hospitalization but he has other medical expenses. He has borrowed from everyone he knows. What does Barrack need? Money.

I sentenced Rickey to five years' probation conditioned upon learning a trade, getting remedial education, and making reparation payments to Barrack. Rickey was not able to get a real job for more than three months, but he did attend vocational classes regularly. Eventually he began to make payments to Barrack. At the end of three years he had paid over $1,400, which covered Barrack's loss of earnings and unreimbursed medical expenses.

Was Rickey punished? Was he rehabilitated? It is impossible to say. If loss of pleasure constitutes punishment, then to the extent that Rickey had to forego $1,400 of his hard-earned wages he was punished. Rehabilitation is more difficult to define and discern. Rickey has not been rearrested during the period of his probation. However, he had not been arrested for three years prior to the offense. Possibly he would not have committed a crime even if he had not been on probation. He has been fairly steadily employed. Prior to the crime he had never held a job for more than a few weeks. Perhaps work, under the dominant Protestant ethic in America, is one of the indicia of rehabilitation. It is not a wholly reliable factor. Many hardworking businessmen commit serious crimes of fraud and embezzlement and mastermind corporate crime. Such people are often workaholics. It is simplistic to equate steady work habits with licit behavior and idleness and unemployment with criminality. Members of the jet set are idle, but they are not criminals. However, many poor people do shoplift and rob because they cannot buy the things they want. Many wealthy people also shoplift and steal. Education, a trade or work skill, and employment may indeed be a means to rehabilitation for many poor semiliterate offenders. I believe that the criminal justice system should offer these opportunities to such offenders.

Rehabilitation, however, is usually viewed as some form of psychotherapy. The coercive power of the state is used in an effort to restructure the personality of the offender. In the words of the Model Penal Code, the purposes of the law are "to forbid and prevent conduct that harms individual or public interests" and "to subject to public control persons whose conduct indicates that they are disposed to commit crimes." These are extraordinary powers for government to exercise over a free and democratic people. The Code has not been literally construed. No court attempts to exercise control over an adult simply on the belief that he or she is "disposed to commit crimes."[5] After a person has been convicted of a crime, courts do prescribe and compel various kinds of treatment. Whether this is called brainwashing or therapy depends upon one's point of view. Not many cases have questioned the power of courts to order therapy or drugs for the purpose of changing the orientation and proclivities of the offender. Drug addicts and alcoholics are routinely ordered to attend therapy sessions. Offenders who are diagnosed as having mental problems are required to attend therapy sessions. Drugs are prescribed for prisoners, often in massive doses. Mood-altering drugs are routinely administered without the informed consent of the offender.

Zeke, who was awaiting trial, was given the following drugs over a period of months: INH, 300 milligrams once a day; multivitamins, twice a day; elavil, 500 milligrams in the afternoon; and benadril, 50 milligrams at hours of sleep, plus trilafon, 10 milligrams twice a day, and prolixin. This medication includes mood-altering drugs, commonly known as "uppers" and "downers." When Zeke appeared for trial and I learned of this medication I asked him, as I routinely do, if he understood the crimes he was charged with committing and his right to trial by jury, trial without a jury, and his right to enter a plea. All of these rights had been meticulously recited to him for more than a half-hour by his attorney. At the end of each paragraph he was asked, "Do you understand?" Each time he replied somewhat hesitantly, "Yes." The written record which a court would read on appeal was letter perfect. But everyone in the courtroom had grave misgivings that Zeke did in fact understand anything that had been explained to him.

In answer to my questions as to whether he understood the charges Zeke replied, "I don't know, judge. I feel sort of fuzzy." Many prisoners who are regularly dosed with thorazine and other tranquilizers and sedatives feel "fuzzy" most of the time. They may be easier for the prison guards to control, but one wonders whether this can be considered therapy. From time to time an offender or an accused person in custody awaiting trial refuses to take the medication prescribed and seeks a court order protecting his right to refuse treatment. Psychosurgery and electric shock therapy are no longer approved modalities of treatment. When they were popular, both shock treatment and surgery were performed on prisoners. It is impossible to learn how many people were subjected to such treatments or whether these prisoners gave an informed consent to such treatment.

Therapy which consists only of conversation and psychological testing is not generally perceived to be either dangerous or significantly effective in creating personality changes. Few prisoners openly object to attending these individual or group sessions. Although they consist only of talk, they are not always pleasant conversations. Prisoners may be asked the most personal and humiliating questions. Sometimes they are stripped of their psychological defenses and are seen by the therapist and fellow inmates as pitiable, whining, snivelling cowards. Rarely does the judge who orders therapy know what it consists of or what effect it will have on the offender.

The new philosophy which emphasizes punishment rather than treatment would eliminate these sensitive and difficult questions. Ease of administration, however, should not be the controlling factor in deciding whether the function of sentencing is to punish or to rehabilitate. While there should be well-defined limits to the powers which government can exercise over the individual, both in prescribing conduct and in compelling treatment, I am unwilling to abandon the quest for helping offenders.

There are many useful services which can be offered to offenders on a noncoercive basis. At least they should be provided with an opportunity to refuse or to give an informed consent and accept. Programs similar to Alcoholics Anonymous for alcoholics and drug addicts are available in many prisons and in many community treatment centers for convicts who are not incarcerated. The effectiveness of these programs depends upon the willing participation and cooperation of the patient. Those who are present in body only, under court order, are rarely helped. They are probably not hurt either. But the use of so-called therapeutic drugs and psychotherapy under court order imposed on unwilling prisoners cannot be lightly dismissed as a permissible exercise of government power under the rubric of rehabilitation.

Persons who are not convicts or who have not been judicially declared incompetent have a right to refuse medical and psychiatric treatment. Before authorizing surgery, a patient must under civil law be informed of the benefits and risks of the procedures, the percentages of recoveries and failures, the possible side effects and dangers. Only after being furnished this information can a patient give what is called "informed consent." I believe that even though criminals have forfeited the right to liberty, they have not forfeited the right to exercise control over their bodies and minds. Convicts who are schizophrenic, or manic depressive or have other reliably diagnosed mental illnesses or overt sex problems but not gross retardation or incompetence should certainly be given the choice of accepting or refusing drugs and therapy, unless such treatment is necessary for the protection of the other inmates and the guards.

Education and job training do not present problems of invasion of bodily or psychic integrity. It is obvious that unwilling students are unlikely to learn anything. Most of these offenders have been physically present in public school for ten years or more without having learned to read or write. A court cannot order a prisoner to learn, but it can condition early release upon the achievement of certain basic skills. This is a form of coercion but not compulsion. The offender has the choice of learning and obtaining early release or of refusing to study and serving the full term of the sentence. Given this choice, most offenders prefer to learn. I do not consider such an option an invasion of privacy or unduly coercive. Certainly learning to read and learning a trade cannot adversely affect the offender even though it may not "rehabilitate" him in the sense of making him law abiding.

How does a judge know what kind of treatment to order for an offender? A conscientious and able defense attorney at the time of sentencing usually brings to the attention of the court those mitigating circumstances of the offender's life—not only his good qualities but also the areas of his needs and deficiencies—which help to explain his illegal conduct. Counsel often suggests a course of treatment or study for his client, a program which the client says he wants. Of course, many of these pleas are simply for the purpose of avoiding a longer prison sentence or more onerous terms. But at least the court under such conditions is not imposing treatment on an unwilling subject.

Good pre-sentence and neuropsychiatric reports often disclose the offender's emotional deficiencies and other problems and suggest areas of education. Appropriate sentences can provide some measures which will successfully rehabilitate many offenders. Functional illiterates and school dropouts, for example, obviously need remedial education. Mere presence, however, in a prison classroom, or in a class ordered as a condition of probation which has teaching methods similar to the offender's previous public school, will do him little good. Intensive education designed to teach older teenagers and young adults can be very effective. I have ordered as a part of many prison sentences and as a condition of many sentences of probation that the offender obtain remedial education. Many young men who spent ten years in public school and failed to learn to read and write have within two years become literate and obtained their high school equivalency diplomas in prison or under the supervision of a probation officer.

Economic dependency and unemployment are strong factors contributing to criminality. There is no doubt that it is difficult for young unskilled ex-offenders, especially minorities, to get jobs. I have frequently ordered such offenders to learn a trade in prison or as a condition of probation. Many of them have learned welding, carpet laying, electrical repairs, and other trades as part of their sentences. A fair number of these offenders have been able to get jobs with the aid of probation officers and organizations formed to help ex-offenders.

It is difficult, if not impossible, simply through individual or group conversation to inculcate a sense of responsibility in people. But this is the kind of therapy most commonly provided for offenders. Most rehabilitation treatment for offenders consists of "counselling." What this usually means is that the prisoner is seen for an hour a week by a social worker or "therapist" who talks with him. Some social workers are very helpful in making contact with the prisoner's family, arranging visits, contacting prospective employers, and performing similar services. But it is unrealistic to expect that such weekly or even daily conferences, no matter what therapeutic name they are given, can change an offender's point of view or give him deep insights into his problems, or enable him to cope with a society that has no place for him. Even the most optimistic, dedicated, and skilled psychiatrists working on a one-to-one basis with a patient who is motivated enough to pay for treatment require months if not years of almost daily, unremitting therapy sessions to effect such changes. A coerced prisoner is scarcely a likely candidate for successful psychotherapy.

Rap sessions with ex-offenders are now popular in many prisons and many community treatment centers. It is impossible at this time to know how useful such programs are. Group therapy is popular among the general population of non-offenders. Some claim remarkable gains as a result of these programs. Others consider them useless at best and at worst, a fraud.

Regardless of one's views as to the value of counselling and therapy, the issue of rehabilitation is a fundamental question. Should society consign some four hundred thousand people each year to custodial care without even attempting to help them? Most of these prisoners will be released sooner or later. In the interests of society, if not of the offender, correctional authorities should be charged with the duty of helping these people without infringing on their basic human rights. I believe that the criminal justice system has an obligation to society to attempt, within the limits suggested, to help these prisoners. There are also more than a million offenders who are placed on probation each year. At present, probation for most of these offenders is little more than a bookkeeping task of checking on the whereabouts of the offender and notifying the court when he is rearrested. Probationers, like prisoners, are potential risks to the public. These offenders should be provided with the same services, education, and treatment that the prisoners receive and with the same safeguards of individual rights and bodily and psychic integrity.

The way most prisons and probation departments now operate provides neither meaningful help to the offender nor the probability of protection to the public. Moreover, in the present state of knowledge about human behavior, motivations, chemistry, and genetics no one can offer any assurance that therapy or treatment of offenders will be successful. And yet failure to provide treatment leaves the future of the offender and the risk to society wholly to chance. The odds are not good. The criminal justice system and the public have for decades been oversold on the wonders of rehabilitation. Recently, however, the public and the same criminologists who once ardently espoused the theory of rehabilitation have suggested scrapping that approach and substituting the theory of punishment, or "desert." Give the criminal what he deserves. To date, few responsible people have suggested a regimen of bread and water, hard labor, or the return of the chain gang. But the implicit premise of the desert theory is that the offender has forfeited all his rights and does not deserve to be helped.

Understandable disenchantment with the kind of rehabilitation now being offered does not necessitate abandonment of the goal of rehabilitation. I do not believe that an offender can be transformed into a law-abiding citizen by even the best prison or the most gifted and dedicated probation officer. My aims in sentencing are more modest. If the criminal is functionally illiterate, I order that he be taught to read. If he has no marketable skills, I order that he be taught a trade. I do not know how anyone can be taught to have a sense of responsibility toward his fellow human beings. But I order as a part of the sentence, whenever possible, that the offender pay for the harm that he has caused. Few offenders can make adequate reparations, but each offender is ordered to pay to the victim a sum within his earning capacity.

Rickey, the fellow who stabbed Barrack, paid through the probation department for more than four years. Rickey has been sufficiently motivated to get a better job because at his salary level the ten dollars he pays Barrack is a difficult sacrifice. Admittedly Rickey is not a hardened criminal. His conduct, though dangerous, illegal, and harmful, was neither irrational nor deliberately vicious. Many offenders are like Rickey —young, undereducated, and unemployed. They need education, employment skills, and a sense of responsibility for their own conduct.

The proposed Federal Crimes Code has a section on sentencing.[6] It specifically authorizes, but does not mandate, restitution nor does it require, as factors in sentencing, the consideration of the harm done to the victim or of his needs. Among the reasons listed for imposing sentence under that Code are: "(C) to reflect the seriousness of the offense, to promote respect for law, and to provide punishment for the offense; and (D) to provide the defendant with needed educational or vocational training, medical care, or other correctional treatment in the most effective manner."

Although "correctional treatment" is as vague as rehabilitation, education or vocational training and medical care are concepts which both the judge and the offender can understand. A judge can order that such training and care be provided. The results are objectively verifiable. Did the offender learn to read? Did he learn a trade? Did he get treatment for ulcers, epilepsy, tuberculosis, or whatever his physical ailments are? Neither education nor medical treatment is likely to do the offender any harm. There is a strong probability that they may do him some good. In imposing a sentence, I often think of the admonition to medical doctors—do no harm. The harm that can befall a prisoner in jail is very real and often serious. Both men and women are sexually abused in prison by other inmates and guards. Prisoners are beaten. Prisoners commit suicide. The inevitable disruption of the prisoner's life, the weakening of family ties, and the loss of self respect are less observable, but clearly harmful. The Model Penal Code's limitations on the use of prison as a penalty to be imposed only for the protection of the public is, I believe, very wise.

The sentencing provisions of the proposed Federal Crimes Code are limited. Critics rightly point out that it "does not seriously approach the problem of reconsidering the goals of our criminal justice system or reforming the sentencing structure."[7] Certainly the code does not represent a careful re-evaluation of the philosophy of sentencing. It does, however, acknowledge restitution and reparation to the victim as elements to be included in the sentence and it specifies attainable services for the offender. Rehabilitation of offenders is a worthy aim for a humane, democratic government. Despite the difficulties it poses and the past failures, it should not be wholly abandoned in pursuit of another indefinable mirage—just desert.

CHAPTER VII

THE
DESERT MODEL

My object all sublime
I shall achieve in time
To let the punishment fit the crime . . .
—W. S. Gilbert, *The Mikado*

D esert is defined as the "reward or punishment that is deserved."
The concept of desert is logical and sound. It is based on the old
principle of proportionality in sentencing. Almost eight centuries ago
Magna Carta declared, "A free man shall not be fined for a small offense
except in proportion to the measure of the offense, and for a great
offense he shall be fined in proportion to the magnitude of the offense."
The notion of proportionality between the offense and the penalty is
self-evident and deeply rooted in Western thought. That this principle
is observed in the breach today is apparent from even a casual reading
of the daily press.

Within a month the United States Supreme Court upheld a sentence
of life imprisonment imposed on a man who wrote a bad check for
$88.30, and the appellate court of New York set aside a three-year
sentence and instead imposed a sentence of five years' probation on a
lawyer who stole $2.5 million in a series of thefts and forgeries.[1] The
lawyer repaid $500,000 and gave up a pension worth $1 million. Simple
arithmetic reveals that he profited by his crimes in the amount of $1

million. A nineteen-year-old college boy is serving a seven- to fifteen-year sentence of imprisonment for two marijuana sales.[2] While these are extreme cases they are not anomalous. All too often the penalty bears little relation to the magnitude of the offense. The goal of proportion or desert in sentencing is understandable and desirable. Many times it is not achieved.

Psychiatrists and sociologists who are dismayed by disproportionate and disparate sentences have analyzed individual judges in an effort to determine and predict the characteristics of the jurist that might be significant in the fixing of penalties.[3] There are many studies which tabulate the race, socio-economic background, childhood upbringing, education, and family of a sampling of judges. Such studies may reveal something about incumbent judges but they tell us little about law or rehabilitation or desert.

While grossly aberrant sentences may be the result of the biases and prejudices of the sentencing judges, most sentences are arrived at by conscientious men and women who seek to follow principles of law, the codes, and precedents that have been established to guide them in imposing sentence. I believe that in most sentencing decisions these factors are of greater significance than the characteristics or identity of the judge. Theories do make a difference.

The desert model of sentencing seeks to establish objective standard penalties that must be imposed upon offenders based solely or primarily upon the crime committed. The desert model abandons the goal of rehabilitating the offender. It recognizes that a sentence is punishment and it asserts that penalties should be imposed for the purpose of punishing law violators. Discretionary sentencing powers of the judge would be abolished to avoid disparities and inequities. The fixing of a penalty for the offender would be a mechanical process which takes into account only the crime committed, unlike the rehabilitation theory which requires the judge to consider both the crime and the criminal. There is but one constraining factor—that the penalty not exceed the "outer limits of justice." Words like justice and fairness elude precise definitions. They are as protean as rehabilitation. Although the desert model seeks to avoid vagueness and subjectivity, even its proponents recognize a limiting factor of justice. Most people would agree that justice means something more than a mechanical application of rules.

The concepts of desert and the outer limits of justice do not furnish a very clear guide to a perplexed judge. But the desert theory does considerably narrow the range of subjects which the judge may consider in imposing sentence. It eliminates the criminal from the sentencing criteria. No longer will the judge have to struggle with the competency of the criminal, his age, I.Q., education, social background, mental illness, drug addiction, alcoholism, or other aggravating and mitigating circumstances. The focus is exclusively on the act which the offender committed. It also eliminates consideration of the victim and the harm done to him. It does not require the offender as part of the sentence to make restitution or reparation to the victim of his crime.

There is a beguiling simplicity to the desert model that seems to please people who are frustrated by the complexities of human behavior and the constraints of moral philosophy. John Doe has broken the law. He has committed crime No. 123 for which the penalty is four years in prison. Sentence John Doe to four years in prison. If Richard Roe commits crime No. 123, he will also be sentenced to four years in prison. The sentences are equal. The old maxim, "equality is equity," at least subliminally comes into play. If the sentence is equal, it is fair. And justice is now considered as fairness. Should the law of sentencing be reduced to such a syllogistic concept? To do so involves a drastic change in philosophy and practice. Notions of degrees of responsibility, motive, and intent become irrelevant. The desert model ignores centuries of evolving moral philosophy, much of jurisprudence, and all the teachings of psychiatry.

Under the desert theory, a mandatory penalty is specified for each crime. The desert theory is presumed to be fair because all offenders who commit the same crime are given the same penalty. Under the notion that justice is fairness, the desert theory assumes that fairness is also justice. This may be good logic but it bears little relation to the facts of illogical crimes committed by illogical offenders who are prosecuted, convicted, and sentenced in the criminal courts of the United States.

The appeal of the desert theory cannot be ignored. The concept of desert is simple and straightforward. People should get what they deserve. This has a deceptive ring of old-fashioned morality. Desert, like rehabilitation, is a comforting word. But when one examines the idea more closely, the difficulties of applying the concept equal if not exceed those of rehabilitating or curing criminals. Today few people would literally apply the lex talionis—an eye for an eye, a tooth for a tooth. Although, as stated, no law in the United States authorizes mutilation, beating, starvation, or torture of criminals, many criminals have mutilated, beaten, starved, and tortured their victims. The proponents of the desert theory do not suggest that new penalties be devised to provide the criminal with the precise penalty that his crime deserves. They accept the premise that the only alternatives are prison or probation. They are concerned primarily with a scheme to make certain and equal the length of the prison sentence imposed on every offender who commits the same crime.

The desert model sets a fixed or determinate sentence for each offense. An articulate proponent of determinate sentencing characterizes it as "simple justice."[4] Certainly it is simple to plot the name of a crime on a chart and arrive at a fixed sentence untouched by human hearts or minds. It is much simpler than to go through the agonizing process of attempting to fit the punishment to the crime and the criminal. But does it provide justice?

The justice of a fixed penalty for each crime depends in part upon the appropriateness of the penalty. Is it really proportional to the offense? This is not a simple matter of matching sentences to crimes listed in statutes and codes. The name of the crime may not indicate the extent of the harm done or the evil intent of the offender. Under some statutes the intent of the offender and the extent of the harm may change the name of the crime or the degree of the crime. In many statutes neither element is included but only the name of the act that is committed.

All killings are homicides. Not all homicides are murder. Murder in the first degree is the unlawful killing with malice aforethought. Here the intent of the offender is of crucial significance. Homicide may also be murder in a lesser degree, voluntary manslaughter, or involuntary manslaughter. If the killing is in self-defense, it is not a crime. In order to determine guilt and the precise crime and degree, the factfinder must take into consideration not only how the crime occurred but the intent and mental capacity of the offender.

Assault is a crime that usually has several degrees depending both on the intent of the offender and the harm done to the victim.

There are degrees of theft which depend upon the value of the goods stolen. Other crimes such as rape and drug offenses depend primarily upon the physical act performed and do not include consideration of either intent or harm done. The name and degree of the crime are only rough and approximate indications of the evil intent of the offender, the harm suffered by the victim, and the dangerousness or seriousness of the offense. They do not indicate the dangerousness of the offender. Under present law, except in those states which have adopted presumptive sentencing laws, the trial judge who knows the facts and the background and history of the offender is expected to take into account all these variables in imposing sentence.

Let us see what would happen in a series of ordinary crimes under the desert theory. A and B are having an argument. A punches B in the face. B suffers a bloody nose. This is the crime of simple assault. However, if B has a heart condition and suffers a slight heart attack A may be guilty of aggravated assault even though he did not know of B's heart condition and did not intend to harm him. The penalty for aggravated assault is more severe than for simple assault. If B suffers a very serious heart attack which makes him a chronic invalid, A is still guilty only of aggravated assault. Should the penalty be the same whether B is hospitalized for a week or is an invalid for life? Few, if any, schema for flat or determinate sentencing make these fine discriminations. A judge under present sentencing laws and policies can consider both the harm done and the intent. If the only penalty which the judge can impose is a prison term, it will make little difference to B, unless he is vengeful, whether a longer or shorter prison sentence is imposed on A. B will have to cope with his medical expenses, his loss of earnings, and the changed conditions of his life. What penalty does A deserve in each of these situations? The desert model does not supply satisfactory answers to these questions. The penalty will be the same whether B suffers a mild heart attack or a disabling heart attack, whether he suffers a broken arm or a broken back. The penalty will be the same whether A intended to hurt him only a little or whether A punched him with extreme viciousness.

The interrelations of intent, harm, and the name of the crime arise in many cases. The name of the offense under present law determines the maximum penalty permissible, not the actual penalty imposed. The judge can make appropriate adjustments. Under the desert theory, criminal nomenclature assumes much greater significance.

Three typical cases show that the name of the crime does not always indicate the seriousness of the offense. Joe, Roggo, and Tyrone were convicted of assault. Their crimes, their intentions, and the harms actually done were very different.

Joe, a twenty-year-old, snatched a wallet from George Smith, a poor elderly man. In the course of a brief scuffle Smith fell and broke his leg. He was taken to a city hospital and placed in a ward where he developed pneumonia and died. Joe was charged with murder. The law is clear that a death caused as the result of a felony is murder. Purse snatching is robbery which is classified as a felony. A doctor from the medical examiner's office testified that the cause of death was pneumonia. The prosecutor argued that if Joe had not snatched the wallet, Mr. Smith would not have fallen, broken his leg, and been taken to the hospital where he developed pneumonia and died. The chain of causation was clear. Under the law, only a break in the link of the chain, a supervening cause, could save Joe from a conviction of murder.

The doctor was cross examined.

Q. Isn't it true, doctor, that old people are prone to develop pneumonia if they are hospitalized or even bedridden?

A. Yes.

Q. Is pneumonia often fatal in old people who are bedridden?

A. Yes.

Q. What are the preventive measures, if any, which should be taken to avoid pneumonia?

A. Very simple. Turn the patient, move him five or six times a day.

Q. Are you familiar with the conditions in the ward of hospital —— where Mr. Smith was a patient?

A. Yes.

Q. Is it possible that Mr. Smith was turned or moved six times a day or even four times a day?

A. No.

Q. Doctor, isn't it likely that any elderly person who was hospitalized in that ward for six weeks, regardless of his injury, would have developed pneumonia?

A. Yes, I'm afraid that's true.

Joe was acquitted of felony murder and convicted of robbery and aggravated assault. The jury, however, might easily have found Joe guilty of murder.

Roggo also robbed an elderly man. That man suffered only a broken arm. Roggo was also convicted of robbery and aggravated assault. Should Joe and Roggo receive the same sentence? I submit that Joe deserves a more severe penalty. But under the desert model, the justice as fairness theory, both Joe and Roggo are guilty of the same offenses and both will receive the same penalties.

Tyrone intended to kill. He had been in a fight with Lucas the week before the crime for which he was on trial. Tyrone was waiting for an opportunity for revenge. He stalked Lucas for several days and finally encountered him just as Lucas was entering a bar. Tyrone stabbed Lucas in the chest with a knife that had an eight-inch blade and left him lying on the doorstep of the bar with the knife in his body. By chance, a second or two later someone opened the door, saw Lucas bleeding to death, and called the police. They arrived almost immediately with a trained paramedic who administered aid on the way to the hospital. A team of skilled physicians worked frantically through the night. Lucas recovered completely. He walked into court the picture of health, laughing and joking with the prosecutor. Tyrone was convicted of assault and assault with intent to kill, for which the maximum penalty in every jurisdiction is much less severe than that for murder.

Had Joe been convicted of murder he would, under the desert theory, have been sentenced to prison much longer than Tyrone, who was convicted only of assault with intent to kill.

The desert model is predicated on the principle that a sentence is imposed as a punishment for the wrong done. Under this sentencing model the court is required to ignore the intent of the offender. The court would probably also have to ignore the extent of the harm done and look only at the name of the crime of which the offender was convicted. Tyrone did little harm but his intent was to kill. Joe's intent was to take a wallet. The harm done was death. What penalties do Joe, Roggo, and Tyrone deserve? Does justice or fairness require that they receive the same sentences because they were convicted of violating the same section of the penal code? I believe that neither justice nor fairness requires that result.

For many years jurisprudential scholars and philosophers discussed the retributive theory of justice. Retribution is defined as the requital for evil done. In essence the desert theory is simply the retributive theory renamed and updated. In 1968, Professor A. L. Hart of England optimistically and prematurely announced the demise of the retributive theory of justice.[5] He pointed out that retribution or desert is implicitly based on a free-will principle—that the person who broke the law had a free choice as to whether or not to commit a crime. A hundred years of psychiatry are erased by this theory. The influence of the subconscious, the background of the individual, his deprivation or poverty or ignorance, and his mental and emotional state are not to be considered at all.

Under a strict desert theory, the wrongdoer's prior criminal record is also irrelevant. Few proponents of the desert theory go this far, although the justice as fairness concept would theoretically require the same penalty for the same crime regardless of the offender's criminal record. It is obvious that a person who has a long record of other crimes should be treated differently from a first offender. Most proponents of the desert theory would permit the fixed penalty to be increased in the case of habitual offenders. In 1979, at this writing, no state has enacted legislation explicitly adopting the desert theory. But it has many distinguished, influential, and articulate adherents. Unless there is more discussion and understanding of the operation of the desert theory it may well supersede rehabilitation as the accepted standard and goal of sentencing.

The significance of a prior criminal record is clear to most lawyers and judges. It is now an important factor in the sentencing decision in almost every case. I believe it should be one of the most important factors. Elva is a typical shoplifter. She has made a career of stealing expensive luxuries. She appeared before me on only one charge—theft of a bottle of perfume worth eighty dollars. The prosecutor dropped a dozen other charges at trial because the witnesses and victims would not come to court to testify. Mary Jane is a high school senior. She wanted a new dress for the school prom. She went into a shop, tried on several dresses, and returned all but one to the rack. That one she folded and placed in the bottom of her school bag. She was apprehended before she left the store. The dress cost seventy-five dollars. These are about as equal crimes as one is likely to find. It was Mary Jane's first arrest. It was Elva's eleventh conviction. Under the desert theory both Elva and Mary Jane would receive the same sentence. The notion that equal punishment for equal crimes is fair and just founders on the hard rock of the habitual offender.

The desert theory encounters special problems when it is applied to atrocious crimes. Unfortunately vicious, sadistic acts are not uncommon. In New York City a young man pushed a girl off the subway platform into the path of an oncoming train. Her hand was severed. By extraordinary measures the hand was reconnected but it will never function properly. Under the laws of most states the most severe sentence allowable is a limited term of years in prison. What penalty does this man deserve? The desert model makes no provision for especially severe penalties for especially heinous crimes. It does not consider the dangerousness of the offender.

Kevin and Robert are young white men in their twenties. Both are school dropouts who held rather menial jobs in a factory. Kevin had a pretty red-haired girlfriend, Barbara, who also worked in the factory. Alvin, a black man, was employed in the same factory in a managerial position. Alvin was a high-school graduate who had taken some night college courses. He was a steady, responsible employe and had received several promotions. Alvin was married and was buying a house. Kevin and Robert who were inclined to "goof off," as the plant manager testified, had never received raises. They were on the verge of being fired. One day Kevin saw Barbara and Alvin having a lengthy conversation. A few afternoons later, Kevin and Robert drove to a dark spot near Alvin's house. When Alvin approached, they jumped him, threw him in the car, and took him to a garage where Robert had previously worked. There they tied Alvin's hands and legs. They burned his genitals; they tortured him; they mocked him. They kept up their obscene activities until well past midnight. Then they put Alvin, still trussed up with heavy rope, in the back of their car and drove to a small river and tossed him in the water. Incredibly, Alvin did not drown but managed to work his way out of the river and inch through the underbrush until he reached the highway. Somehow he managed to get himself to an upright position. A passing motorist saw Alvin, stopped, and took him to a hospital.

Kevin and Robert were examined by a psychiatrist and a psychologist. Both were of normal intelligence. Neither was found to be psychotic or mentally ill. Barbara was carefully questioned by the police. She voluntarily took a lie detector test which indicated that she was telling the truth. Alvin had never made any sexual advances to her. She had told this to both Kevin and Robert repeatedly. She also told the detective that Kevin, who was big, good-looking, and very macho in his manner and speech, was not much of a lover. The psychiatrist, of course, did not know what Barbara had told the police. He reported that Robert's sex life was normal and that he had had a long series of girlfriends. Under the desert theory Roger and Kevin would be sentenced for assault with intent to kill. There would be no additional penalty for the peculiarly atrocious nature of the assault. Neither the judge nor the prison authorities would be concerned with educating or treating Robert and Kevin.

Neither a life sentence nor the death penalty is permissible for assault with intent to kill in most jurisdictions. Robert and Kevin will undoubtedly be released from prison while they are still in their forties. Unless they receive effective education and therapy in prison, they will be just as hostile and dangerous when they return to the community. Should the mental or emotional condition of the offender or his drug or alcohol addiction be considered in imposing sentence? Most judges would say yes. But under the desert theory, the answer is no—all criminal acts shall be punished the same. It matters not whether the wrongdoer was a millionaire college graduate who looted his corporation of millions or a drug addict who embezzled a few hundred dollars to feed his habit. Nor does the desert theory make allowances for offenders with emotional problems.

Willis is one of many offenders whose conduct indicates that he is seriously disturbed. Mr. S. was driving along a limited-access highway at fifty miles an hour. The minimum speed allowable on the road is forty miles an hour. Suddenly he saw Willis standing on the highway in front of him. Mr. S. brought his car to a screeching halt—barely missing Willis, who immediately rushed over to Mr. S., yanked open the door of the car, and punched him in the face. The police testified that they had difficulty restraining Willis and that he did not answer their questions. He refused to give his name and address or tell them why he was on the expressway or how he got there.

Mr. S. stated that he thought Willis was drunk or crazy. The arresting officer testified, "He was a bed bug. That's what we call crazies." Willis was given a breathalizer test. He was not drunk. His urine was tested and was found negative for drugs. When Willis appeared in court, he was polite and responsive. He said he didn't know why he hit Mr. S. He said that he had not taken drugs or liquor. He was sorry he had hurt Mr. S.

In another case, the facts were similar, but the offender was a very different kind of person. Roger was driving his new Corvette home from work. He had a responsible job, a wife, and three children. He could not afford a new car but he had bought the car anyway. Roger stopped for a light in the right-hand lane. Mr. F., who was driving in the center lane, swerved to avoid hitting a dog and bumped Roger's left fender. Before Mr. F. could get out of his car, Roger rushed over, wrenched Mr. F. out of the car, and punched him. If passers-by had not restrained Roger, Mr. F. might have been severely injured.

Roger was sullen and hostile when he was brought to trial. After he was convicted and I had to impose sentence, I questioned him about his behavior.

Q. Why did you hit Mr. F.? You saw the dog, didn't you? You knew it was an accident?

A. I don't care about a damn mutt. Hasn't a man got a right to protect his property?

Q. You are paying for no-fault automobile insurance. Didn't you know you would recover the cost of repairs?

A. Yes. But the car is damaged. It's never the same after an accident.

Both Willis and Roger were convicted of aggravated assault. Both caused approximately the same harm. Should both be punished the same? Those who espouse the desert theory say yes. They contend that it is fair and just that people who have committed the same crimes be given the same penalties. Under the desert model of sentencing both Willis and Roger would have been sent to prison for approximately three to six months.

I ordered Willis placed on psychiatric probation and conditioned it upon paying Mr. S.'s medical expenses and loss of earnings for the days he was out of work. I sentenced Roger to pay Mr. F.'s medical expenses, the cost of his torn suit, and a stiff fine. I believe that reparation to innocent victims is simple justice. I also believe that in considering the sentence to be imposed a judge can benefit from the diagnoses, prognoses, and opinions of psychiatrists. Obviously, something is wrong with Willis. The psychiatrist confirmed my suspicions. He also suggested a course of therapy. I thought that probably Roger suffered from nothing more than a bad temper. The psychiatrist found that he was aggressive, under tension, and anxious but not mentally ill. Roger acted viciously and with a clear intent to do harm. I think he deserves a more serious penalty than Willis. Willis, under the law, is guilty of the same offense as Roger—aggravated assault. The nomenclature of the crime does not reveal the real nature of the offense or the offender. Under the desert model, neither is of any significance in sentencing.

A humane criminal justice system should, I believe, differentiate in its treatment of wrongdoers according to their intentions, capacities, and needs. The results will not come out neatly equal. In any computerized calculation of sentences, there will be disparities. A researcher will note that both men were convicted of aggravated assault. Many judges would sentence Roger to two to four years in prison and place Willis on psychiatric probation. No researcher will know the reasons for this disparity. Willis did not appeal. Therefore, the testimony taken at his trial was not transcribed. Even if a careful researcher wanted to compare the facts of the two crimes, he would not be able to do so.

The desert model makes no allowance for mental deficiencies. Samuel is probably the most stupid defendant I have encountered. His I.Q. was well below 60. He is big and strong. He seized a young girl standing on a street corner waiting for a bus, carried her to a vacant lot, and raped her. He made no effort to hide his identity or run away. Samuel has never been able to attend a regular public school. He is employed in a sheltered workshop for the retarded where he performs the most simple tasks by rote. He could not explain what he had done or why he had done it. Samuel was convicted of rape. Although Samuel is stupid, he is not mentally ill or insane.

Roy and James were also tried before me and convicted of rape. Roy was thirty-two years old at the time of the offense, married, with two children. He had a steady job. James was thirty and divorced. He was also steadily employed. It was a nice summer night. Roy left his wife and children at home and went out with James and a few men friends to go drinking at a series of bars. Later they all went to a section of the park where young people gather to play guitars and sing. Roy and James got into conversation with Jenny whom Roy knew slightly. The three strolled under the trees. Suddenly Roy grabbed her and forced her to the ground. While James held his hand over Jenny's mouth so she could not scream, Roy raped her. Then James raped her.

Roy, James, and Samuel are all guity of the same offense, but one of them is seriously retarded. The other two are not. Should the penalty be the same for all? Should the court consider intent and responsibility? Should the court consider dangerousness? Who can predict what any of these three men will do in the future? It was a first offense for all of them. Of course, they may have committed other rapes which were never reported or for which they were never arrested. Jenny knew Roy's name, so the police were able to apprehend him. If Jenny had not known him, he would probably not have been arrested.

These cases illustrate only a few of the injustices which would result from the adoption of the justice as fairness or desert model of sentencing. The philosophic implications of abandoning the goal of individualized justice cannot be ignored. Although there is a dreary sameness in many crimes, and many criminals appear to have the same characteristics of sex, age, race, schooling, and environment, no two cases are the same. Of course, no two individuals are the same. A society that values individual rights more than bureaucratic simplicity and efficiency should not lightly discard a long history of individualized sentencing in pursuit of the mirage of equality. It is obvious from an examination of even the most neatly paired sets of crimes and criminals that each case is unique.

Cohort groups which are used in sociological studies consist of people of the same age, sex, race, family background, I.Q., schooling, and environment. We can learn much about the behavior of different types of people from such studies. The predictions based on these statistics may be right 80 percent of the time. But under our Constitutional form of government each person is entitled to be considered as an individual. We do not convict accused persons without a trial simply because more than 90 percent of suspects accused of certain crimes are guilty. Each suspect is entitled to a due process trial with a presumption of innocence. Similarly each convicted offender should be entitled to be sentenced individually based upon the circumstances of the crime, the individual offender, and the harm done to the victim. Sentences should not be imposed on the basis of statistics, no matter how accurate they may be in the aggregate. The differences among offenders as well as their similarities are significant. Equal sentences imposed on unequal offenders do not result in equal justice.

American jurisprudence is now engaged in the difficult and sensitive task of trying to ensure equal rights, opportunities, and privileges for a population which has been handicapped by generations of unequal treatment and unequal opportunities. Society as well as the legal system is experimenting with compensatory programs, affirmative action, and many methods of trying to weight the scales of justice so that the treatment of unequal individuals will be equalized. Individualized sentencing permits a sensitive thoughtful judge to make those adjustments in imposing sentence. The desert theory precludes the sentencing judge from doing so.

One of the most dangerous but unintended effects of the desert model of sentencing would be to remove sentencing discretion from the judge and give it to the prosecutor. At present the majority of criminal prosecutions have non-trial dispositions. This is a polite euphemism for plea bargaining. The term is an unfortunate one and has sordid connotations. A bargain conjures up pictures of a backroom deal. In the argot of crime shows, the street-wise experienced crook "cops a plea" and walks out a free man. Many critics condemn plea bargaining as a perversion of justice and a means of letting criminals get off with lighter penalties than they deserve. This is, in part, a valid criticism. Some wealthy or powerful offenders with skilled and well-connected private counsel undoubtedly do get more lenient sentences than they would if they had stood trial and been convicted. But this is by no means the entire picture of plea bargaining.

Probably 90 percent of defendants prosecuted in state courts are represented by the public defender or court-appointed counsel because they are too poor to pay for a lawyer. Such people are unable to make the kind of deals for leniency that are rightly criticized.

Most guilty pleas are open pleas. That is, defense counsel and the prosecutor agree that if the defendant will plead guilty to certain offenses, the prosecutor will drop some of the charges. Careful prosecutors usually overcharge. They indict the suspect for every possible offense because at the time of trial the evidence may not support one charge but will be sufficient to sustain a conviction on another charge. In most jurisdictions, some of the offenses will merge and the court will be able to impose only one sentence for one criminal transaction regardless of the number of charges. Ironically, dropping a few counts may have no effect on the ultimate sentence. In an open plea there is no agreement as to the sentence to be imposed and the prosecutor makes no recommendation with respect to the sentence. A statement of facts agreed upon by the prosecutor and the defendant is read into the record. The judge obtains a pre-sentence investigation and a psychiatric examination, if it appears that one would be helpful. The judge may question the defendant and can inquire as to the condition and needs of the victim. After receiving all this information the judge then imposes a sentence which should reflect the seriousness of the offense, the danger to the public, the mitigating and aggravating circumstances, the needs of the offender, and the needs of the victim.

I have taken hundreds of guilty pleas. I know of no instance in which there was undue or improper influence in an attempt to achieve a more lenient sentence. If the facts indicate that the offense is more serious than the charges to which the offender is pleading guilty, most judges will not accept the plea and permit the more serious charges to be dropped or nol prossed. I do not believe an offender should be rewarded for entering a guilty plea or that an accused who demands a trial should be penalized because he did not plead guilty. Nor do I see any reason for requiring an accused who acknowledges his guilt to go to trial rather than plead guilty. To require a person who admits his guilt to plead not guilty and stand trial in effect forces the offender to lie. When an accused is arraigned, he is read the charge and then asked, "How say you—guilty or not guilty?" If he admits his guilt, he should plead guilty. He should not lie with the connivance of the court and say under oath, "Not guilty." I believe that the vast majority of guilty pleas are entered voluntarily and honestly and that the penalties imposed after a plea are generally no different from those imposed after trial and conviction.

Alaska is the only state that has abolished plea bargaining. All other states find it useful, if not necessary. But the desert model which prescribes the penalty for every offense would probably radically alter this system. Because the offender would know in advance what the penalty would be regardless of mitigating circumstances and voluntary offers of restitution and reparation, and because he could not hope to obtain needed education, job training, or therapy as part of a prison sentence, he would have no incentive to enter an open plea in the expectation that the judge would take into account all these circumstances and conditions. The judge would, under the desert model, be required to impose the fixed penalty on all persons who pled guilty or were convicted of a crime. The offender's only hope for individualized sentencing would be to bargain with the prosecutor for withdrawal of charges which carry too heavy a sentence. For example, an accused might plead guilty to simple theft rather than robbery because the penalty for theft under the desert model would be considerably less severe than for robbery of which the defendant is in fact guilty. Plea bargaining would not be eliminated. It would take place behind the closed doors of the prosecutor's office rather than in open court.

If the trial judge is precluded from considering mitigating circumstances, every defendant will quite sensibly insist on a jury trial in the hope that witnesses will fail to appear or that the jury may find him not guilty. In most jurisdictions the entire system would be so overloaded that it would grind to a halt. Administrative convenience does not, in my view, constitute a justification for unjust practices. But practical considerations should not be ignored in making choices when neither justice nor fairness is jeopardized. I believe that justice should be administered openly and publicly and be based upon the actual facts and the crime which was actually committed, not a lesser offense arrived at through bargaining with the prosecutor behind closed doors. In this sense I may seem to be more sympathetic to the "desert school" of sentencing than I am.

I believe that the sentencing decision should not be made in the prosecutor's office. Nor should the decision as to the release of the

prisoner be made behind closed doors by a parole board. Most proponents of the desert model would eliminate the parole board. The term
of imprisonment would be fixed at the time of sentencing. There would
be no need for any evaluation of the prisoner's rehabilitation to determine whether he should be released. Today most states have indeterminate sentencing. The parole board must decide when the prisoner is to
be released. Parole boards are supposed to be nonpolitical, fair-minded
agencies which carefully consider the release of prisoners who have
served their minimum sentences. The actions of parole boards are generally unreviewable. They operate behind closed doors with none of the
requirements of a public trial and due process imposed upon courts even
though their decisions may have infinitely more drastic effects upon the
lives of defendants. It is unnecessary to recite the usual litany of irrational and discriminatory actions of parole boards. A few will suffice.

One prisoner was sentenced to twenty years to life for the fatal
beating of a guard in the Attica uprising. Despite Governor Carey's
proclamation granting immediate executive clemency for all involved in
that incident, the parole board denied him clemency and refused to
reconsider his case until 1994.[6] The United States Supreme Court has
held that the sentencing judge cannot release a prisoner who is denied
parole at the expiration of his minimum sentence even though that was
the sentence the judge intended.[7]

Jeff was fifteen years old when he was sentenced as an adult to three
to eight years for a series of burglaries which netted him less than five
hundred dollars. No one was injured; no property was damaged. The
judge expected Jeff to be released at the end of three years. He was young
and found the confinement very difficult. He was sexually attacked but
was afraid to complain. Consequently, he spent most of his time in his
cell reading. Parole was repeatedly refused because Jeff was "not cooperative." The sentencing judge wrote to the prison and parole board asking
that Jeff be released, explaining that the offense did not warrant such
a long prison term. The parole board admonished the judge not to
overstep his authority. After five years in prison, Jeff attempted suicide.

But consider the unduly lenient treatment of Sam by the parole
board. Sam was forty-eight years old when he shot and killed his girlfriend. He claimed the gun had gone off accidentally. He was convicted
of manslaughter and sentenced to five to fifteen years. Before the end
of three years the parole board wrote to me suggesting an early parole
so that Sam could go home and support his wife and seven children. I

replied that at the time of the offense Sam's wife and children were on welfare while he was driving a new Lincoln and lavishing gifts on his girlfriend. He was a successful numbers writer and continued his business in prison. The parole board was either unaware of these facts or chose to ignore them. Sam was released the day his minimum, less time off for good behavior, had expired.

I agree with the Morgenthau Committee in New York City that "sentencing is a judicial function which should be performed in a public forum—the court room—and open to public scrutiny."[8] The termination of confinement in prison should also be a judicial function, performed in a public forum and open to public scrutiny. The parole board has outlived whatever usefulness it may have had. To date it has been abolished in Arizona, California, Illinois, Indiana, Maine, and New Mexico.

The values of indeterminate sentencing need not be eliminated in order to eliminate the parole board. The judge who sentenced the offender, who knows him, the crime, and the victim, and who imposed conditions to be met during imprisonment should be the official to decide when the offender should be released. If the offender was ordered to achieve basic education and job skills, the judge should determine on the basis of prison reports whether those goals had been met. A judge could also obtain the record of the offender's behavior in prison. On the basis of all this information the judge should decide when the offender should be released. It is unnecessary to abolish indeterminate sentencing or the goal of rehabilitation in order to avoid the evils which the desert theory is supposed to eliminate.

Fairness, defined as equal treatment for equally situated offenders, would not prevail under the desert system. However, the computer and the statistics would record equal penalties for equal offenses. At present there is no way that even the most diligent and careful researcher can learn whether sentences imposed are appropriate, fair, or equal. Very little research is based on reading transcripts of trials. Trial proceedings are not transcribed unless there is an appeal. The majority of cases are not appealed. Even if research were limited to cases in which the notes were transcribed, the research problems would be almost insurmountable. The transcript of a trial lasting only one day may be several hundred pages. It would take an army of scholars to read the transcripts of thousands of trials and the pre-sentence and psychiatric reports and evaluate the propriety of the sentences. It would be impossible adequately to compare these trials and sentences. There are too many variables to computerize. These are some of the problems faced by one who comes after the fact to evaluate the justice and fairness of the system. A judge who presides over trials and lives through them does not see statistics. The judge knows each defendant as a Raskolnikov, a Jean Valjean, a Lizzie Borden, and a whole host of three-dimensional people. A judge usually has good reasons for treating different people differently even though the nomenclature and degrees of their crimes are the same.

I think of Jay, whom I call Oedipus. He raped his mother. The crime was not reported by the mother. The neighbors heard her scream and called the police who broke down the door and observed the crime. Jay's mother and father came to court asking for help for their distraught son. What penalty does he deserve? Alan I remember as Cain. He killed his brother. The mother was in the courtroom pleading for treatment for Alan who is seriously disturbed. Should the law turn a deaf ear to these pleas? Every felon, no matter how trivial or atrocious his offense, is nonetheless a human being who cannot and should not be reduced to a punch card. I urge the legislatures of the states: "Do not spindle, mutilate, or destroy these people in pursuit of an absolutist scheme with the deceptive label of 'justice as fairness.' "

CHAPTER VIII

PRESUMPTIVE SENTENCING

A camel is a horse designed by a committee.

Between the present wide discretion of the trial judge in sentencing for purposes of rehabilitation and a mandatory minimum sentence for each offense fixed by the legislature under the desert theory, "presumptive sentencing" appears to take a median position of sweet reasonableness. Under this plan, the sentence would be fixed by a commission which lists certain factors to be considered by the sentencing judge and the weight to be accorded these factors.[1] It is presumed that this sentence will be equal to those imposed on others convicted of the same crime, and that it will be fair and just. Under this scheme, the judge has little discretion in deviating from the sentence fixed by the commission. Most presumptive sentencing plans avoid the choice between determinate and indeterminate sentences by narrowing the permissible range of length of sentence. Presumptive sentencing, fixed by the legislature or a commission, has the common-sense aim of avoiding gross disparities in sentencing. It also has the virtue of appearing to be scientific. It was first proposed by a trial judge.[2]

There are many variations on this theme. But the recurring melody is to have a presumptive sentence fixed for each offense based upon a point scale. After a verdict of guilty or a guilty plea, a clerk will add up the score and arrive at the number of months or years the criminal should serve in prison, and the judge will impose the sentence. The proponents argue that presumptive sentencing is fair because all offenders with the same score will get the same sentence. Such is the plan. It assumes that there are no variations or interpretations in applying the factors. As we shall see, no plan can be so precise that interpretation is not required. The appropriateness of the presumptive sentence, of course, depends upon the choice of factors to be considered and the weight accorded to each factor.

A commission can either take the sentences which the judges of the jurisdiction impose as the norm for the presumptive sentence, or decide for itself what the norms should be. The first plan has the virtue of using the experience and judgment of people who are actually imposing sentences. Between the extremes of the "hanging judge" and the "bleeding heart," a mean will be established that should be reasonable and provide a consensus. The disadvantage is that it freezes into law the foibles, prejudices, and ignorance, as well as the wisdom of the judges who happen to be on the bench when the commission adopts its standards.

Public attitudes toward many offenses change. War resistance, use of marijuana, deviate sex, abortion, and pornography are just a few of the crimes that within a few years have undergone the gamut from strict enforcement and severe sentences to failure to prosecute, minimal sentences, and decriminalization. In the past, such acts as poaching and employee strikes were severely punished under the criminal law. In time, poaching in England was simply not prosecuted. By the mid-1930s in the United States strikes were legalized by statute. Between the time public attitudes change and legislation reflecting the new views can be enacted, there is inevitably a time gap. Flexibility of sentencing can reflect these changes and ameliorate hardships.

Offenses like murder and robbery are always condemned. But opinion shifts as to many crimes. The public attitude to rape has undergone radical revision in the past few years. Until the seventies, in many states a rape conviction could not be had on the testimony of the victim alone. Corroborating evidence was required. Since rapes seldom occur in the presence of other people, except perhaps pals of the rapist, it was almost impossible to get a rape conviction unless the victim was white and the rapist black. In such cases, the penalty was severe, often death. If the rapist and the victim were the same race, the penalties were light. Today, rape is considered one of the most serious crimes. The penalties imposed in most instances are less racially biased and are much more severe than formerly for non-interracial rapes.

A commission, if composed of knowledgeable lawyers, judges, sociologists, psychiatrists, and concerned citizens, might fix penalties and establish factors that would be more appropriate and better reflect the views of the public than the widely disparate practices of sitting judges. But such a commission, like the now discredited parole board, would work in private and would not be directly answerable to the public for its decisions. People who have never imposed a sentence and who have spent little, if any, time with offenders may not have the experience and understanding to make these sensitive decisions which will affect the lives of countless people whom they will never see. The public's perception of the seriousness of offenses is not necessarily reliable. White-collar crime, for example, is consistently viewed as less serious than street crime although the detriment to the public at large is often much greater, as will be shown in chapter XIII.

The choice of factors which will determine sentencing, no matter by whom it is made, is a difficult task. Too many variables make the system unworkable; too few preclude the judge from considering significant circumstances surrounding the crime as well as many aspects of the offender's life and person. The weighting of these factors depends upon value judgments about which there is little agreement.

There are many reasons that impel state legislatures to adopt plans for a sentencing commission. They are under pressure from the public to do something about crime and putting criminals in jail. Mandatory sentencing, the other principal proposal, would require jail sentences for many people who are now released on probation. Such a proposal is fraught with danger and expense and is opposed by most judges, lawyers, and civil libertarians. Although the public wants more criminals in jail, no one wants to raise taxes to pay for new facilities or even to defray the additional cost of keeping more people in custody in the overcrowded existing jails and prisons.

The sentencing commission plan is attractive to legislators for many other reasons. It enables them to avoid the hard decisions of deciding how long a sentence is long enough for each crime. Is ten years too long for forcible rape or not long enough? Whatever the legislature decides, the decision will not be popular with many people. The public's views on such questions vary considerably. A study indicates that views as to a hard "law and order" attitude depend upon political affiliation, education, and income. Republicans take a tougher stance than Democrats.

The higher the level of education and the higher the income, the less tough the views of the citizen.[3] Most legislators would prefer to delegate these sensitive decisions to a commission. Moreover, state legislatures which are bogged down by problems of budgets and taxes can ill afford the time to analyze hundreds of crimes and circumstances under which crimes are committed to arrive at the appropriate or presumptive sentence for each crime and each of the variations included in the array of offenses. A survey of crime severity considered 204 different offenses— varied according to category of crime, harm done, and amount of property involved.[4] What legislature can decide on the appropriate sentences for 204 crimes? And this number by no means includes all the variations in circumstances under which crimes are committed. Nor does it include many factors involving the offender's life situation or mental and emotional condition.

All presumptive sentencing plans are predicated on the "in" or "out" choice. No provision is made for fines, restitution or reparation, or special conditions imposed as a condition of probation. Although most existing sentencing codes specifically permit all such penalties in lieu of or in addition to imprisonment and probation, presumptive sentencing plans ignore these other choices. If presumptive sentencing is mandatory, a judge will not have these options.

There is no doubt that presumptive sentencing would reduce some disparities in sentencing. That, indeed, is a desirable goal. But in the pursuit of this end, would there be more or fewer unjust sentences? This question is not asked. It is tacitly assumed that fairness will result if the same sentence is imposed for similar offenses.

Most sentencing commission plans take a median position between mandatory sentencing and judicial discretion. Under these plans there is a limited range of length of imprisonment if the decision is "in." No restrictions are placed upon the offender, other than reporting to a probation officer, if the decision is "out." Most commission plans also straddle the argument between the "justice as fairness" ideology which takes into account only the offense and the rehabilitation philosophy which focuses primarily on the offender. The plans scale offenses by seriousness of the offense, injury to the victim, weapon usage, amount of property involved, number of victims, and, in crimes not against a person, victim classification. In the plan which has been in operation in Philadelphia, Pennsylvania, for more than a year, there are only two categories in amount of property: under five hundred dollars and over five hundred dollars. The Philadelphia victim classification also has only two categories: large store or organization and private citizen or small store. There is no classification of victims in crime against a person.

To date presumptive sentencing has been adopted in four pioneer states: Maine, Indiana, California, and Illinois. Philadelphia has had a voluntary plan for almost a year. Pennsylvania has just established a sentencing commission. The first plan, that of Maine, went into effect in May, 1976. Obviously, there has been insufficient time to make a valid assessment of any of these plans or proposed variants. Before other states and the federal government rush to abandon a system of indeterminate sentencing with judicial discretion that has been in operation for centuries, the public should examine the concept and consider the proposed benefits and the problems that already are apparent. It is always more difficult to abolish a bureaucracy than to create one. Discretion in sentencing, which has been part of Anglo-American law for centuries, should not be abolished without careful consideration. As Mr. Justice White declared with respect to the abandonment of the search warrant by judicial fiat, "A heretofore acceptable enforcement tool should not be suppressed on the basis of surmise without solid evidence supporting the charge."[5]

The California and Indiana statutes establishing presumptive sentencing limit judicial discretion to a narrow range of prison terms. In California the judge must impose the presumptive sentence unless there are defined aggravating or mitigating circumstances. The range of these variations is also fixed and limited to one year more or one year less than the presumptive sentence. The parole board has been abolished and a community release board created which can give a maximum of one year parole. In California, the sentences are fixed by the legislature. All felons, except those convicted of murder in the first degree, are classified into four categories. The maximum presumptive sentence is six years.

The Indiana statute classifies all crimes into ten categories and requires the court to impose a fixed term. The presumptive sentence is fixed but the court has discretion to raise or lower the sentence based upon aggravating and mitigating circumstances. Indiana's presumptive sentences are substantially higher than those of California. For Class A felony (the most serious exclusive of murder) the presumptive sentence is 30 years with a permitted variance of 20 years more for aggravation or 10 years less for mitigation. Thus, the minimum sentence that can be imposed for a Class A felony in Indiana is 10 years as compared with

5 years in California. Illinois and Maine have abolished the parole board. Judges in both states impose a fixed or determinate sentence. In Maine, the judge has discretion within the statutory maximum. Illinois has not only a statutory maximum sentence but also a statutory minimum. For example, in the most serious category of offense, excluding murder and habitual criminals, the minimum is 6 years and the maximum is 30 years, with an additional 30 to 60 years for aggravation. It is obvious that there are gross disparities in sentencing between California and Illinois.

Within each state, disparities may well continue to exist. With fixed penalties for each category of crime, the judge's discretion is limited in jury cases. But these constitute, in most jurisdictions, only 5 percent of all cases. In a non-jury trial, the sentence can easily be reduced by a finding of guilt of a lesser included offense. For example, the defendant can be acquitted of robbery, for which the mandatory minimum sentence in Illinois is six years, and be convicted of theft, which in Illinois has a mandatory minimum of two years. In all cases under presumptive sentencing, the prosecutor still has discretion in fixing the charge. It may be that mandatory minimum sentences, like the desert model, simply transfer the discretion from the judge who operates in a public courtroom to the prosecutor who makes his decision in the privacy of his office. Under these four state presumptive sentencing statutes the character of the defendant is totally ignored. Nor is there any provision for redress to the victims of crime. All crimes, with their infinite variations, are lumped into a limited number of categories.

Let us examine some ordinary crimes to see how presumptive sentencing would operate.

Cool Hand saw Monkey, a member of a rival gang, walking towards him. Cool Hand drew his knife and slashed Monkey, who was hospitalized for two weeks. Cool Hand's testimony that he believed Monkey had a gun and would have shot him did not impress the jury. Cool Hand claimed to have acted in self defense. The jury undoubtedly reasoned that if Monkey was close enough to Cool Hand to be stabbed, he certainly had no intent to shoot. Cool Hand was convicted of assault with intent to kill and a weapons offense.

Walker approached Mr. S., an elderly man, and said, "Gimme your wallet or I'll blow your brains out." The terrified man fumbled as he reached for his wallet. In backing away from Walker Mr. S. fell and broke his right arm. He, too, was hospitalized for two weeks. Mr. S. is a bookkeeper. He was out of work for almost four months. Walker had a gun. He was convicted of armed robbery and a weapons offense. Under the Philadelphia presumptive sentencing plan and under most plans, Cool Hand would receive a much longer sentence than Walker. Assault with intent to kill is a more serious crime than armed robbery. Cool Hand used his weapon; Walker did not. That is a factor that increased the penalty. No property was involved in Cool Hand's assault. Mr. S. had only a few dollars. Property involved was treated the same. Both victims were injured, neither permanently, so both injuries were treated the same. However, the loss to Monkey was only his stay in the hospital. Mr. S. lost a considerable amount in wages. Most significantly, Cool Hand and Monkey were known to each other. Monkey had previously attacked Cool Hand. Mr. S. was a stranger, an innocent passer-by on the street. I believe that any person viewing these two crimes would conclude that Walker's offense was more serious than Cool Hand's, but the presumptive sentence for Walker would be less than that for Cool Hand. Neither justice nor fairness results. A sentence that does not provide reparation to Mr. S. is the most unfair aspect of the presumptive sentence.

Compare the cases of Paul and Vincent. Both were convicted of the same offense. The injuries to the victims were similar. But what reasonable judge would give Paul and Vincent the same sentence?

Paul, twenty-one, was in a fist fight with Arturo, twenty-three, who lives near him. They had exchanged blows before. The previous week Paul had suffered a broken nose at Arturo's hands. The crime that was tried before me was witnessed by the neighbors. In essence, they all told the same story. This is what happened. Paul was washing his car in the driveway when Arturo sauntered by and smiled.

"What're ya laughin at?" Paul demanded.

"Nuthin'," Arturo replied nonchalantly and began to whistle.

"Get offa my property," Paul yelled.

"The sidewalk's public," Arturo replied and didn't move.

Enraged, Paul seized the metal bucket of water and smashed it on Arturo's head. The soapy water spilled on Arturo and on the sidewalk. Arturo gasped, slipped, and fell, ripping his face on the ornamental iron fence surrounding Paul's lawn. Arturo suffered a skull fracture and a very bad cut. Paul was convicted of aggravated assault.

Vincent, twenty-two, was also charged with aggravated assault. He was in his car stopped for a red light when another car pulled to a stop beside him. Mr. J., the other driver, miscalculated the space and scraped the paint on Vincent's fender. Vincent was furious. He got out of his car. Mr. J., who was fifty-nine years old and a stranger to him, also got out of his car to look at the damage. Vincent punched him in the face, knocking him to the ground and breaking his jaw. Vincent was also convicted of aggravated assault.

Both crimes were the same. Both victims suffered injuries approximately equal. On a point scale under presumptive sentencing, both defendants get the same penalty: equal terms in prison. Obviously, both crimes are not the same. Paul and Arturo were engaged in a continuing feud. Vincent attacked a total stranger. Mr. J. was insured and was willing to pay for the damage to Paul's car. Arturo had deliberately taunted Paul and provoked the assault.

None of the presumptive sentencing commission plans takes into account the victims of crime. I ordered Vincent to pay Mr. J.'s medical expenses, his loss of earnings, and a fine. Vincent had to sell his car in order to make the payments. In my view, this penalty was his just desert. It also took into account the moral obligation I believe he owed to Mr. J. Although I have no way of knowing and no one will ever be able to plot statistically the deterrent effect of this sentence, I think that it will deter Vincent, but probably no one else, from other acts of violence. No one other than Vincent's family and friends and Mr. J.'s family and friends knows about the sentence. If Vincent had been sentenced to five or ten years in jail, probably no one would have learned of it except the appellate courts. Vincent would have made every effort possible to get the conviction reversed. He did not appeal this sentence. Angry as he was at having to sell his car, he recognized the essential justice of the decision. I like to think that every time Vincent rides on the subway instead of driving his car, this is a constant reminder that crime does not pay. Possibly one might find that this sentence had rehabilitative effects. Under some presumptive sentencing laws Vincent would have had to be sentenced to prison. There is no requirement under any of these laws for compensating the victim.

Lila is nineteen, a high-school graduate. She is nicely dressed and she has a steady job. She also had a steady boyfriend who was unemployed. At his urging, she went into a jewelry store. While ostensibly shopping for a gift, she filched a diamond ring worth more than one thousand dollars. She gave the ring to her boyfriend who promptly disappeared. The ring was not recovered.

Juanita is also nineteen. She, too, is a high-school graduate. She works intermittently. Juanita takes drugs. She steals to feed her habit. Although she admitted that she steals regularly, this was her first conviction. She stole fifty dollars out of a cash register. She asked the salesgirl to wrap with a ribbon a two-dollar item she had purchased. When the clerk went to get the ribbon, Juanita took the money. She was caught before she left the store and the fifty dollars was recovered. Under most presumptive sentencing plans Lila would go to prison and Juanita would not. Few judges who are permitted discretion in sentencing would sentence Lila to imprisonment. Most judges would require Juanita to enter a drug treatment program. If she resumed her drug habit, that would be a violation of probation and she would then be incarcerated. What is a fair or just penalty for Lila and for Juanita? Should each be sentenced without looking at her needs? Should each be sentenced on a scale which compares her offense to other crimes without considering the circumstances of her life and her needs and motivations?

Under some presumptive sentencing plans the judge is required to take into account certain characteristics of the offender. Under others, the judge may consider only the offense. Most commission plans require consideration of the crime and the offender, thus straddling the desert and rehabilitation models.

A description of the Philadelphia plan, which is similar to other plans, contains the following statement:

Information gathered falls into three (3) categories: (1) information concerning the circumstances of the instant offense such as victim injury, weapon usage; (2) information concerning the offender's prior record; and (3) information concerning the offender's background and social stability such as school and employment history. *An extensive analysis of these data using sophisticated statistical techniques was made to determine which factors were most important to the Philadelphia judges' sentencing decision.*[6] (Italics added.)

Sophisticated statistical techniques are always reassuring. If only we are modern enough and scientific enough, the results will be unassailably objective and fair. But in countless ordinary cases the results are not fair simply because human behavior cannot be reduced to six, a dozen, or even a score of items or factors. Moreover, the factors are imprecise. Darryl robbed a man by threatening him with an unloaded gun. Is this weapon usage? Tyrone had a loaded gun and fired in the course of his robbery. Should both be scored the same? Is an umbrella raised menacingly a weapon? Should it be scored the same as a knife or a gun? As we have seen, there are degrees of seriousness of injury which are not accounted for in these sentencing schemes.

The information about the offender is contained in five items. In some sentencing commission proposals, no consideration may be given to the offender, his prior record, or any mitigating or aggravating factors. The items in the Philadelphia plan are:

Item 1: *Prior Adult Incarcerations*	POINTS
0	0
1	+1
2	+2
3 or more	+3
Item 2: *System Relationship*	
No supervision	0
Supervision by criminal justice agency	+1
Item 3: *Prior Adult Convictions*	
None	0
1	+1
2	+2
3 or more	+3
Item 4: *Prior Felony Person Convictions*	
None	0
1 or more	+1
Item 5: *Social Stability*	
Unemployed *and* did not complete high school	0
Employed *or* completed high school	−1

As originally designed, Item 5 listed employment and education separately. The offender who had graduated from high school was given a preference over the offender who had not graduated, thus compounding the "unfairness" of a deprived youth. In my view, the more highly educated and favored offender should be held more culpable than the disadvantaged offender. This opinion, however, did not prevail.

A pre-sentence report, if it is good, provides the judge with much more information than these five items. The first three all deal with prior crimes. If the offender was fortunate enough to be placed on probation instead of being sentenced to prison, that conviction is not scored against him. Logic and fairness would seem to dictate that an offender who was placed on probation or given a suspended sentence was given a break by the system. Clearly he was not rehabilitated. The offender who was sentenced to prison has in a sense paid his penalty for that crime. He is now being additionally penalized because he did serve time. With respect to criminal record, the Philadelphia guidelines do not provide for consideration of more than three prior convictions. I have seen defendants with more than a dozen prior convictions. Such a record should weigh far more heavily than only three prior convictions. Moreover, there is no differentiation among types of offense. If a defendant convicted of armed robbery has a prior armed robbery conviction, I consider that far more serious than a prior drug offense. Similarly, with a rape conviction. A second rape is more serious than a prior robbery and a present rape. A man who has already been convicted of two rapes will probably commit more rapes when he is released.

The final component is social stability. Only employment and education are included. Although the pre-sentence reports and neuropsychiatric examinations reveal many things which most judges consider, no weight is given to them at all. For example, is the defendant's physical presence needed to care for a dependent? Does the defendant have an emotional, drug, or alcohol problem? Is the defendant a homosexual or transvestite? Is the defendant functionally illiterate or suffering from a physical illness? If none of these facts and many more are to be considered in arriving at the presumptive sentence, one must ask why the public pays for the elaborate pre-sentence investigations and examinations.

No list of factors can possibly include all the variations in human behavior and the almost infinite variety of circumstances under which crimes are committed. Obviously, the factors must be sufficiently limited so that a judge or law clerk can make the calculations without benefit of sophisticated computers. Many persons accused of crime act unreasonably and aberrantly and have a multitude of problems which cannot be coded into a feasible point system.

The criminal courts have experience with point systems. They have been used for many years by bail projects. Most bail projects are bureaucracies. They have staffs of employees graded in categories such as interviewers, supervisors, accountants, lawyers, administrators, assistant project managers, and a director, as well as clerical staffs, computer operators, and all the supporting personnel which a government or quasi-public agency requires. These organizations interview arrestees who are held for court and make recommendations to the judge or magistrate as to whether bail should be imposed or whether the individual should be released without bail pending trial. No one really knows how well or fairly these projects operate. There are reliable statistics as to the numbers who are released and abscond. But no one knows how many accused are held who should have been released. The judge has discretion to disregard the recommendation. In fact, in the rush of cases, most judges simply rubber-stamp the bail project recommendation.

The purpose of bail is to insure that the accused will appear for trial. The factors considered significant in most bail project point systems are:

1. prior record;
2. prior appearances in court on time;
3. employment;
4. verifiable residence;
5. community ties.

These are logical and sensible factors. A first offender who has a home, a job, and friends and family in the community is far more likely to appear for trial than an unemployed ex-convict who is a vagrant.

Examinations of only a few cases, however, reveal the limitations of any point system and the necessity for retaining judicial discretion. The New York bail project recommended that the multiple murderer known as Son of Sam be released without bail. On the point system he qualified for release.

1. It was a first arrest. He had no prior convictions.
2. He had never failed to appear in court when summoned.
3. He was employed.
4. He lived in an apartment on which he had a lease.
5. He had family in the community.

When the judge discovered this recommendation he was aghast and promptly ordered Son of Sam to be held in custody pending trial.

Geraldine is a fifty-three-year-old woman. She suffers from severe diabetes. She is losing her eyesight and her hearing. One leg was amputated. She is unemployed. She has no friends or family. She lives in a small tenement without a telephone. She was charged with arson. No one was injured. Only slight damage was done to the premises. When the lock on her apartment broke, she was trapped inside. Her neighbors would not come to her assistance. She set the fire in order to get the fire department to come and rescue her.

The bail project recommended that she not be released. True, she had no prior arrest. But she was unemployed. Because she had no telephone and the bail project employees did not take the time and trouble to visit her flat, her residence was not verified. She had no community ties. Geraldine spent almost four months in jail before she was brought to trial. How could this woman who had only one leg and no money flee the jurisdiction?

Any system that fails to take into account human differences will, in my opinion, cause injustices. It may be argued that Son of Sam and Geraldine are anomalous cases, that 90 percent of the time the point system works. Perhaps that is true. Ninety percent of the population are law-abiding people. We do not, therefore, abolish the criminal justice system because only 10 percent of the population commit crimes. Perhaps 80 percent of the people accused of crime plead guilty or are found guilty. We do not abolish the criminal justice system and jail all suspects simply because the number of innocent people is relatively small.

In the complicated relationships among the criminal and the victim and society no scheme, regardless of how sophisticated the design or how rigorously and undeviatingly it is applied, can provide fairness or justice. There must be a human mind and spirit that can weigh and assess needs, frailties, and differences among individuals and situations, as well as similarities. The judge who hears the evidence, sees the defendant, the victim, and all the witnesses and has the benefit of pre-sentence and psychiatric reports has the best information about the crime and all the parties involved. It is for that obvious reason that sentencing has been a judicial function under the common law for more than a thousand years.

A judge operates in a public arena, subject to direct criticism from the parties and the press. This may often be uncomfortable for the judge. It is not pleasant to be assailed as a fool, a dupe, a well-meaning bleeding heart, a hanging judge, a chauvinist, or any of the other epithets that are hurled at judges whose sentences displease some members of the press or the community. But it is far better to have the responsibility —credit or blame—placed on a public official who makes the sentencing decision than to have these decisions made by a nameless, faceless bureaucracy which has never seen the criminal or the victim and who is not responsible to the public. Nor should offenders be denied individualized consideration.

Presumptive sentencing is now being evaluated by a team of researchers in a project costing a quarter of a million dollars. Among the questions asked the judges is the following: "With which sentencing guidelines do you feel more comfortable?" I submit that sentencing should not be designed for the comfort of the judge. One is always uneasy and uncertain. Human beings are unpredictable. If one places a defendant on probation, one reads the morning paper with apprehension. Has this man committed another crime? Injured another person? If one sentences a defendant to prison, one is fearful of what may happen to him there. Will he be attacked? Will he give up hope? Will he commit suicide? The presumptive sentence may give a cowardly judge an excuse for an unpopular decision. It will not make a conscientious judge comfortable.

Appellate review of sentencing is an obvious and simple means of correcting excessive sentences. Almost every other aspect of civil and criminal trials is subject to appeal. There is no reason to exclude sentencing from the jurisdiction of appellate courts. At present, every convicted person has a right of appeal to correct errors of law and of fact. If that fails, he has a right to a post-conviction hearing at which he can attempt to prove, and often does, that he did not have effective assistance of counsel. The appellate courts will pore over the transcript to see if counsel objected to every possible question or bit of evidence that might have been objectionable and might have adversely affected the trial.

A convicted criminal can appeal everything except the most crucial question of all, the appropriateness of the sentence. On that issue, courts in many states have insisted that they lack jurisdiction unless the sentence offends the Constitution. Even this power is often narrowly construed. Under most presumptive sentencing plans, appellate review is limited to those cases in which the sentence imposed exceeds the presumptive sentence. S1437, the proposed Federal Crimes Code, provides for a sentencing commission and limits review of sentences to this question. It has been noted that, "Unless Congress can anticipate what the guidelines will be, it cannot evaluate the adequacy of appellate review of sentencing under S1437."[7] Limited appellate review is better than no review of sentencing at all. However, I maintain that it is unnecessary to establish this elaborate rigid scheme of presumptive sentences and create another bureaucracy—the sentencing commission—to eliminate disparities in sentencing. It can be done very simply by appellate review of the propriety of the sentence.

The present restricted appellate review of sentences often results in upholding outrageous decisions.

A man convicted of possessing and distributing nine ounces of marijuana was sentenced to forty years' imprisonment and a fine of twenty thousand dollars in Virginia. The federal court of appeals refused to set aside this sentence because it found that the sentence was not "grossly disproportionate to the severity of the crime" and did not "shock human sensibilities."[8] The court did not consider the propriety, justice, or fairness of the sentence. It limited its review to the constitutional issues. To any rational mind, this sentence is unjust regardless of one's philosophy. The public considers use of marijuana on a point score of severity of offenses only 1.34. Intentional murder of one person is scored 35.71. The length of the prison term in this case indicates that rehabilitation was not the purpose of the penalty. Under the desert model, the punishment should fit the crime. Obviously, it does not when one compares such a sentence with other offenders. The average sentence in the federal courts for bank robbery is ten years.[9] Appellate review which cannot correct such manifest injustice is a delusory remedy.

In order to see how presumptive sentencing actually works, I examined twenty consecutive major felony cases in which I imposed sentences. These cases were randomly assigned to me. No homicides were included. All twenty defendants were charged with major felonies although some were convicted only of less serious charges.

For each of the twenty cases the most serious crime of which the defendant was convicted, the presumptive sentence, the actual sentence imposed, and my reasons for the sentence where the sentence differed from the presumptive sentence are listed in the chart at the end of this chapter.

Of the 20 defendants, only 4 were first offenders. Under presumptive sentencing, 14 of the 20 offenders would have been released without serving any time or making any atonement to society for the offenses committed. This is the kind of revolving-door justice which the public rightly deplores. From an examination of these twenty cases, I am convinced that the sentences that were actually imposed are more consonant with justice and fairness than the presumptive sentences would have been and that they have a greater possibility of deterring and rehabilitating the offender.

Although there has been a rush to sentencing guidelines as the new trendy panacea for disparities in sentencing, a few dissenting voices can be heard.

"This bill [sentencing commission] doesn't cure sentencing disparities," Al Bronstein, head of the A.C.L.U.'s prison project, said recently.

"It just spreads around. The sentencing commission gets some of it, the judges retain some of it and there's still some parole and some rehabilitation in this sentencing scheme."[10]

Professor Franklin E. Zimring of the University of Chicago Law School also sounds a warning: "It's not clear to me that in the current rush to achieve legislation, these issues have been sorted out sufficiently. The only guideline that might be useful, and on a purely voluntary basis, would be the publication of statistics as to the average range of sentence for each crime. Judges could increase or decrease the severity of the sentence in light of all the facts and circumstances including reparation for the victim."

Complicated guidelines and point systems are unnecessary if there is adequate review of sentencing. A succinct and convincing explanation of the proper goals of sentencing—an individualized penalty which takes into account the needs of the defendant and society—is set forth in a New York case:

The proper imposition of sentence is probably the most difficult problem with which a Trial Judge is faced. The difficulty is not alleviated by the insistence of those who believe, simplistically, that long and severe sentences will provide the panacea for the burgeoning crime. A sentence must be fashioned strictly ad hominem, based almost entirely on how society will probably be affected by the strictures placed on the activities of a particular defendant. The process must take into account several factors. the rehabilitative, which is self-explanatory; the incapacitative, not here applicable; the deterrent effect upon him, as well as upon others who may be inclined toward criminal activity; and the vindictive, i.e., the measure of punishment to be inflicted upon the defendant by way of retribution for the transgression involved. It would, of course, be far easier to couple a particular punishment automatically with a particular crime, but such a sentence, completely ignoring the stated factors, would not, in most instances, be beneficial to society. Utter economic and emotional destruction of a defendant and of his family would rarely, if ever, confer a benefit upon the community.

Accordingly, the judgment of the Supreme Court, New York County, (Leff, J.) rendered June 29, 1977, convicting the defendant upon his plea of guilty to the crime of forgery in the second degree, and sentencing him to an indeterminate term of imprisonment with a maximum of three years, should be modified as a matter of discretion in the interest of justice to the extent of reducing the sentence to a term of five years' probation, remanding the matter to another judge to fix the conditions of probation, and the judgment otherwise be affirmed.[11]

An appellate court review which considers these factors *and* the needs of the victim would correct abuses, provide adequate guidance to trial judges, and obviate the need for the unduly complicated, restrictive, and inflexible sentences which would be mandated under a commission plan.

OFFENSES	GUIDELINE SENTENCE	ACTUAL SENTENCE	REASONS FOR DEVIATION FROM GUIDELINES
1. Robbery, Resisting Arrest	OUT	5 years probation conditioned upon getting an education, and $100 restitution	Functional illiterate. Prior conviction for aggravated robbery for which he had been placed on probation. Unless he becomes employable, he will probably commit other crimes.
2. Theft by unlawful taking, Receiving stolen property, Unauthorized use of car	2–4 months 1 ½–2 ½ years	18 months probation with intensive drug supervision	Defendant supports his wife and children. He is a drug addict.
3. Retail Theft	OUT	6–23 ½ months	Nine convictions between 1971 and 1978 for larceny, receiving stolen property, and various thefts. Probation obviously has failed.
4. 2 counts—Agravated Assault, 1 count Possession Instrument of Crime	6–12 months 1 ½–2 ½ years	2 consecutive 2–5 year sentences, one year consecutive probation	Defendant's wife and three-year-old daughter were severely injured during the aggravated assaults.
5. Criminal Trespass	OUT	1 year probation	3 prior convictions. Psychiatric report indicates need for supervision. Found

OFFENSES	GUIDELINE SENTENCE	ACTUAL SENTENCE	REASONS FOR DEVIATION FROM GUIDELINES
			hidden within a church, holding a crowbar.
6. Attempted Burglary	OUT	6–12 months, or until he gets G.E.D.	Defendant is in good health, has no prior employment, lacks an education, and is totally supported by parents.
7. Theft unlawful taking, Receiving Stolen Property	3–6 months 1 ½–2 ½ years	11 ½–23 months	3 prior convictions.
8. Theft Receiving Stolen Property	OUT	30 days–6 months	3 Prior convictions for theft RSP and retail theft. Prior probation had been ineffectual.
9. Attempted Theft	OUT	10 days	3 Prior convictions. In essence, he received time already served awaiting trial.
10. Simple Assault	3–6 months 21–25 months	$500 fine	Defendant is employed and is a transvestite, whom jail would harm physically and emotionally.

OFFENSES	GUIDELINE SENTENCE	ACTUAL SENTENCE	REASONS FOR DEVIATION FROM GUIDELINES
11. Attempted Escape	OUT	3 months psychiatric probation	Defendant attempted escape from a psychiatric institution. Psychiatric report indicates need for supervision.
12. Selling Controlled Substance	OUT	2 years probation, conditioned upon attending drug program and learning to read	First offense. Defendant is an illiterate drug addict who cares for helpless parent.
13. Criminal Trespass	OUT	1 year probation and $50 restitution	Elderly victim needs restitution.
14. Criminal Trespass	OUT	1 year probation and $50 restitution	1 prior conviction. Elderly victim needs restitution.
15. Criminal Trespass	OUT	1 year probation and $50 restitution	2 prior convictions. Elderly victim needs restitution. Sentence is motivation for this 41-year-old woman on welfare to get job.
16. Robbery	OUT	5 years probation conditioned upon inpatient treatment at	Psychiatric report indicates that defendant is delusional and needs inpatient care.

OFFENSES	GUIDELINE SENTENCE	ACTUAL SENTENCE	REASONS FOR DEVIATION FROM GUIDELINES
		hospital	
17. Carrying Firearms without License, in Public	OUT	$300 fine	1 prior conviction. Defendant earns $3.50 an hour and can afford to pay a fine.
18. Simple Assault	3-6 months 21-25 months	11 ½-23 months	
19. Burglary	OUT	3 years probation	Defendant is 21 years old, with a prior history of mental illness. He needs supervision.
20. Burglary	9-12 months 1 ½-2 ½ years	11 ½-23 months, $100 restitution	Restitution is imposed to force defendant to get a steady job after he leaves jail.

CHAPTER IX

THE ROAD FROM
VENGEANCE

Turn your eyes to the immoderate past.
—Allen Tate, *To the Confederate Dead*

The prison sentence is, as we have seen, the principal penalty in use in the United States. Almost every statute provides that the penalties for every crime shall be imprisonment or probation and/or fines. If the crime is serious, the sentence is usually imprisonment. There were in 1979 more than 400,000 people in custody in the United States. This is at least 100,000 people over capacity.[1] Some of the people in prison are serving sentences for homicides, rape, armed robbery, and other violent and serious offenses. Many are in prison for relatively minor infractions of the law. In New York State alone, from the time the Rockefeller law requiring prison sentences for all sellers of drugs went into effect on September 1, 1973, until September 30, 1978, 3,803 people had been sentenced to prison terms with a life-time maximum, some for selling as little as an ounce of cocaine.[2]

As crime increases, the public becomes more fearful and angry. The demand for more and longer jail sentences becomes ever more insistent. Judges are under pressure from the press and the public to lock up more people. If the only alternative to prison is the proverbial "slap on the wrist," a sentence of probation, inevitably more people will be imprisoned.

Imprisonment is an appropriate penalty for people who have committed violent crimes and who, if released, will probably commit more violent crimes. The majority of people in prison are not such offenders. They are there because probation is an unsatisfactory alternative to prison.

Today lawyers, judges, and criminologists are beginning to discuss alternative sentences to avoid the harshness of prison and still impose a significant penalty on the offender. Most of these alternative sentences have required some form of community service. Such penalties depend on the creativity of the judge and defense counsel. There is little comparability among these alternative penalties and no standards to guide the judge. Many of these creative alternatives are even less onerous than probation.

A penalty must, as Bentham pointed out, cause pain to the offender, but not necessarily physical pain. Deprivation of liberty causes pain. So does deprivation of money. It is questionable whether giving lectures on the evils of crime or working as a compulsory volunteer in a hospital or old age home, which are popular alternatives to prison sentences, provide the kind of pain or deprivation that is proportionate to any serious offense. A criminal sentence should not only cause pain to the offender but also reflect society's condemnation of violation of law. Such alternative sentences do not express adequate condemnation for offenders with a record of several convictions or offenders who have embezzled millions of dollars—nor does probation, which is the usual alternative to prison.

Prison is a very harsh penalty for minor crimes. Even for serious crimes prison is a manifestly inappropriate penalty for many offenders. It may be dangerous for young men who are not strong and assertive. It is dangerous for older men. If the prisoner is the provider for the family, his or her imprisonment may cause undue hardship to the innocent dependents.

When the offender is a mother, her imprisonment can be devastating to her children. Louella, who was convicted of five prior thefts, has four children. She was convicted before me of another theft. If she is sent to prison, the children will have to be cared for by the state, either in institutions or in foster homes, if such can be found. It is highly unlikely that any foster family will take all of these children. Should they be separated or institutionalized? Should the children be punished for the sins of the mother? The United States Bureau of Census reports that over two thirds of the women in prison or jail are under thirty-five years old. 42.1 percent are black. The American Civil Liberties Union conducted a survey of seventy-seven institutions with female offenders and discovered that the mean number of children per inmate was 2.4. Almost two thirds of the children were under ten, and one fourth were under four years of age. Is it any wonder that the other judges before whom Louella had been tried had placed her on probation?

Franklin is a twenty-six-year-old high-school graduate. He was tried before me on six counts of forging checks. Franklin is married and lives with his wife and three children. He has a good job. His wife is pregnant. If he is sent to prison his wife and children will undoubtedly have to go on welfare. In addition, it will cost the public from $10,000 to as much as $40,000 to keep him in prison for one year. It has often been remarked that it is cheaper to send a young man to Harvard than to prison.

Should Louella and Franklin be placed on probation because it is too costly to society to incarcerate them? A New York judge sitting in criminal court is quoted as saying, "There are so many cases—But there's no place to send them; there's no repository for them—There's nothing you can do."[3]

It is easy to be discouraged when one sees an unending stream of people for whom crime is a way of life. I empathize with that judge. But I do not believe that a "repository for them" is a solution. It is inhumane, ineffective, and unjust. We have been warehousing people for years. This practice has caused great hardship to the families of the prisoners and great expense to the taxpayers. It has provided little protection to the public except for the period of the criminal's incarceration. It has not provided redress for the victims of crime. The negative effects of imprisonment have been fully documented by the government and by scholars.[4] Yet, we persist in the belief that prison is the only meaningful penalty available to the courts.

What did governments do with criminals in the past? The treatment of common criminals was incredibly severe and brutal. The customary penalties imposed by the courts of England and France as well as most European countries in the eighteenth century were execution, torture, maiming, flogging, and banishment.[5] The death penalty was imposed in England for more than two hundred offenses, including poaching and smuggling. It was not until 1830 that branding of felons was abolished in England. Executions were performed in public. They were a popular spectacle. The public applauded a skillful execution of a criminal much as afficionados today cheer the matador who skillfully slays a bull.[6] The guillotine, as described in *A Tale of Two Cities*, was not the invention of bloodthirsty revolutionaries. In fact, beheading and hanging were among the less horrible forms of execution.

Let us not take our history solely from fiction. Blackstone, the great authority on English law whose Commentaries were a principal source of American law, described the penalties of the English law in mid-eighteenth century as follows:

. . . the court must pronounce that judgment which the law has annexed to the crime, and which has been constantly mentioned, together with the crime itself, in some or other of the former chapters. Of these some are capital, which extend to the life of the offender, and consist generally in being hanged by the neck till dead; though in very atrocious crimes other circumstances of terror, pain or disgrace are superadded: as, in treasons of all kinds, being drawn or dragged to the place of execution; in high treason affecting the king's person or government, embowelling alive, beheading and quartering; and in murder, a public dissection. And, in case of any treason committed by a female, the judgment is to be burned alive. [Burning was apparently considered less severe than the penalties inflicted on men.] But the humanity of the English nation has authorized, by a tacit consent, an almost general mitigation of such part of these judgments as savor of torture or cruelty: A sledge or hurdle being usually allowed to such traitors as are condemned to be drawn; and there being very few instances (and those accidental or by negligence) of any person's being embowelled or burned, till previously deprived of sensation by strangling. Some punishments consist in exile or banishment, by abjurgation of the realm, or transportation to the American colonies: others in loss of liberty, by perpetual or temporary imprisonment. Some extend to confiscation, by forfeiture of lands, or moveables, or both, or of the profits of lands for life: others include a disability, of holding offices or employments, being heirs, executors, and the like. Some, though rarely, occasion a mutilation or dismembering, by cutting off the hands or ears: others fix a lasting stigma on the offender, by slitting the nostrils, or branding in the hand or face. Some are merely pecuniary, by stated or discretionary fines: and lastly there are others, that consist primarily in their ignominity, though most of them are mixed with some degree of corporal pain; and these are inflicted chiefly for crimes which arise from indigence, or which render even opulence disgraceful: such as whipping, hard labor in the house of correction, the pillory, the stocks, and the ducking stool.[7]

Disgusting as this catalogue may seem it will afford pleasure to an English reader, and do honor to the English law, to compare it with that shocking apparatus of death and torment, to be met within the criminal codes of almost every other nation in Europe.[8]

Compared with Blackstone's account of penalties under English law, the American prison system is vastly to be preferred. It can, however, afford few Americans much pleasure to contemplate the fact that four hundred thousand of our fellows are behind bars, deprived not only of liberty but ordinary contacts with their families, and that many of them are subjected to indignities and attacks. It can afford little pleasure to Americans who are complaining about the ever-increasing cost of government and the ever-increasing burdens on the taxpayers.

Blackstone continued his description of enlightened British law in the Age of Enlightenment as follows:

And it is moreover one of the glories of our English law, that the nature, though not always the quantity or degree, of punishment is ascertained for every offence; and that it is not left in the breast of any judge, nor even of a jury, to alter that judgment, which the law has beforehand ordained, for every subject alike, without respect of persons. For, if judgments were to be the private opinions of the judge, men would then be slaves to their magistrates; and would live in society, without knowing exactly the conditions and obligations which it lays them under. And besides, as this prevents oppression on the one hand, so on the other it stifles all hopes of impunity or mitigation, with which an offender might flatter himself, if his punishment depended on the humor or discretion of the court. Whereas, where an established penalty is annexed to crimes, the criminal may read their certain consequences in that law, which ought to be the unvaried rule, as it is the inflexible judge of his actions.

Because the penalties imposed by the courts under law were so brutal, there was a popular revulsion. English juries refused to convict. Both in England and France mobs of citizens often helped prisoners escape. Today juries also refuse to convict when they are in sympathy with the law violators. Protestors at Rocky Flats, Colorado—site of a nuclear installation—admitted that they had trespassed and were convicted of that offense. The jury acquitted them of obstructing traffic, an offense of which they were also clearly guilty.

The situation in the eighteenth century evidently demanded a new approach. The intellectual rationale for the abolition of torture was supplied by the philosophers of the enlightenment. Cesare Beccaria, a young Italian, who had no legal background and was not a scholarly philosopher, provided the impetus for reform with a short book published in 1764, *On Crimes and Punishment.* [9] Beccaria was a contemporary of Blackstone. Beccaria opposed torture and the death penalty as barbarous. He also opposed banishment. His main thesis was the notion of proportionality, that the punishment be proportioned to the offense. Beccaria advocated the least possible punishment under the given circumstances proportionate to the crime. Beccaria's ideas hardly sound novel today. Indeed, some of his notions, such as corporal punishment, we find appallingly barbaric. But for his time, Beccaria was a flaming reformer. His little book, like Paine's *Common Sense*, had an extraordinary influence.

The idea of proportionality, that the penalty should be commensurate with the crime, seems to us to be obvious common sense. But in an age when people were killed for stealing a hare or a sheep, this was indeed a radical notion. Since Beccaria and up to today, the aim of fixing penalties has been to make them appropriate or proportional to the offense. The United States Supreme Court, as recently as 1972, held that the death penalty could not be imposed for rape.[10] Today, death can be ordered only for murder, and then only if certain procedures and restrictions are followed.

Proportionality was not original with Beccaria. The old Mosaic law, lex talionis—an eye for an eye—was in its day not a bloodthirsty cry for vengeance, but a limitation as to strict proportionality. For the putting out of an eye, the offender could not be hanged, he could only be punished to an extent equal to the harm that he had caused. Not only did this embody the concept of proportionality but of distribution, namely, that a penalty could only be inflicted on the wrongdoer. This strikes the contemporary mind as a statement of the obvious. The Mosaic law in this respect was a drastic moderation of the laws of Hammurabi which provided that if A raped the daughter of B, A's daughter would be put to death. Under Roman law, the children of the offender were punished. Proportionality and distribution as limiting principles require that only the wrongdoer be penalized, that the penalty be proportionate to his offense, and that the penalty not be more severe than the crime warrants in order to deter others from committing crimes.

Among the other Common Law penalties listed by Blackstone, banishment is not a penalty permitted by American statute law. The practical reason may be that the United States has no colonies such as England had in the seventeenth and eighteenth centuries to which to banish felons. Many English criminals were, as Blackstone noted, sent to America and Australia. France had its Devil's Island. Alcatraz is closer to mainland America, in fact, within sight of San Francisco. Until recently it was a federal prison. South Africa today has penal islands and colonies within its borders.

Mutilation, I hope, is inconceivable as a legal penalty today in the United States. It is not uncommon elsewhere. In Iran, under the Islamic law of Ayatollah Khomeini, according to Dr. Ibrahim Yazdi, deputy prime minister for Revolutionary Affairs, the penalties for "corruption on earth" are execution if it is a serious offense.[11] For a less serious offense, a hand and the opposite foot are amputated. For a minor offense, the penalty is exile. Significantly, under this law, there are both the limitations of proportionality and distribution.

What prevents the United States from instituting such penalties? None of the philosophical concepts of rehabilitation, deterrence, desert, incapacitation, crime control, or expression of outrage (which are posited as justification for the imposition of criminal penalties) would prohibit such penalties as execution, mutilation, and exile. In fact, capital punishment has recently been extolled as a legitimate expression of public anger and an affirmation of human dignity.[12]

We must look to other concepts for controls on the use of barbarous penalties. The most obvious is the Constitutional prohibition against "cruel and unusual punishment." This provision has rarely been relied on to strike down executions, corporal punishment, or shockingly harsh disproportionate sentences.[13]

Corporal punishment was widely employed as a legally imposed penalty in Colonial America and in the United States for many years. Every visitor to Williamsburg is shown the stocks where prisoners were exhibited for humiliation and shame in the elegant capital of Colonial Virginia, the home state of Thomas Jefferson. Whippings were common in the United States throughout the seventeenth and eighteenth centuries. After independence, courts sustained the constitutionality of whipping despite the Constitutional prohibition against cruel and unusual punishment. Under Virginia law, for example, a free Negro or mulatto convicted of grand larceny could be sold as a slave, transported, banished and given thirty-nine "stripes" or lashes on his bare back.[14] In 1973, the whipping post was finally abandoned in Delaware, the last state to retain this penalty. It was not declared unconstitutional or legislatively abolished. It could be revived. But in 1977, the United States Supreme Court held that the whipping of school children was constitutionally permissible.[15] Earlier, however, a Federal Court of Appeals had prohibited corporal punishment of adult prisoners because it was "degrading to the punisher and punished alike."[16] In 1952, the United States Supreme Court struck down the practice of pumping the stomachs of suspects to obtain evidence of their crimes. The court declared that the means were "too close to the rack and screw."[17] The more antiseptic and scientific extraction of body fluids with a syringe, however, was subsequently upheld.[18] The Supreme Court in *Funman* v. *Georgia* spoke of "the evolving standards of decency that mark the progress of a maturing society." However, no reference was made to these evolving standards of decency in the case involving corporal punishment of school children. By contrast, Sweden in 1979 prohibited the infliction of corporal punishment on children by anyone, including the parents. Even in the Mongolian People's Republic school teachers are forbidden to strike children.

If we turn to the year 1910, we find that the United States Supreme Court decided a case involving conditions of penal servitude, including shackling prisoners. A prisoner in the Philippine Islands, which were then under the jurisdiction of the United States, had been convicted of falsifying coast guard records. In addition to lifetime surveillance, forfeiture of property, and other penalties, this man was condemned to prison for twelve years. According to the opinion of the Supreme Court, this man and the other prisoners had to ". . . labor for the benefit of the state. They shall always carry a chain at the ankle, hanging from the wrists; they shall be employed at hard and painful labor, and shall receive no assistance whatsoever from without the institution. . . ." The Court set aside this conviction because they found that the penalties violated the Constitutional provision against cruel and unusual punishment.[19] Mr. Justice Holmes and Mr. Justice White dissented, declaring that the "mere fact that a chain is to be carried by the prisoner" does not cause repugnance to the Constitution. This rare case did nothing to halt the practice of chain gangs of prisoners who were used to work on the roads and farms, predominantly in Southern states. As to "evolving standards of decency," it is difficult to know where to look for a consensus on morality.

In the 1950s, I was involved in the case of a fugitive from a chain gang. Some twenty years before, Amos B., a black man, had managed to escape from a Georgia chain gang and make his way to Pennsylvania. He had married, raised a family, and lived a law-abiding life for twenty years. He had a small restaurant. Thinking that he might be able to increase his business if he could sell liquor, Amos applied for a license.

In checking his fingerprints for prior criminal record, the offense in Georgia was discovered. Georgia immediately demanded his extradition. His offense in Georgia was petty larceny. He had been tried and convicted without a lawyer, a jury, or any of the amenities and procedural rights known as due process. While imprisoned, Amos worked on the road gang ten hours a day, his legs shackled with heavy irons. Twenty years later he still bore scars on his ankles from the spikes on the leg irons. For any infraction of the rules he had been placed naked in a metal box, too short for him to stand, too narrow for him to sit. In the hot sun, it was a stifling oven; at night it was a freezing container that scarred his skin. There were no sanitary facilities. The chain gang did not operate in secret. It was not a surreptitious abuse of power by a sadistic jail warden. It was a lawful penalty, legally imposed, and publicly exercised in this generation in the United States. It is hoped that such conditions no longer obtain in the United States.

Public whipping is happily a thing of the past in the United States. But it may not remain as a quaint relic of history. There are some who would seek to reimpose the stocks and the whipping post and their number is growing. Judge Peter Krehel of Northumberland County, Pennsylvania Court of Common Pleas, is a vocal exponent of this point of view. Judge Krehel is not an illiterate redneck. He is a graduate of the University of Chicago. He was elected by the people of the county with whom he is very popular. Judge Krehel believes that the way to deter crime is publicly to humiliate the criminal. He has proposed restoring the stocks. "Had the stocks been present," he declared, "I would have had her (a shoplifter whom he had convicted) present for three hours in Market Street with a little sign saying 'I stole $1.79 from Grand Way.' "[20] The judge quotes admiringly the penalty imposed in his county court in 1772, citing the case of *King* v. *Williams*. The prosecution was brought in the name of King George III. The defendant was convicted of three thefts. He was ordered to make restitution of the goods stolen, pay a fine, and receive on his bare back twenty-one lashes. The whipping post—which stood in the public square in front of the old jail—was a stout piece of timber firmly planted in the ground, with a horizontal crosspiece above the head, to which the hands of the culprit were tied while the sheriff administered the flagellation on his bare back. Undoubtedly all the townspeople were there to watch. A whipping, like a hanging, was a public spectacle, a matter of entertainment for the populace.

One can deplore Judge Krehel's proposal and at the same time understand his frustration. Obviously no judge will send a person to jail for stealing $1.79, or a pair of pants, or a blouse, or a coat, unless it is sable or ermine. But the judge rightly believes that something should be done to show that the community and the legal system condemn stealing and other small and large violations of law.

Today there are many who urge the return of the whipping post and stocks. The death penalty is once again the law of this land. Executions had been stayed from 1972, when the United States Supreme Court held unconstitutional the death penalty in Georgia and by implication the death penalty in all other states, until the execution of Gary Gilmore in January, 1977. To date, the United States Supreme Court has refused to declare that capital punishment violates the Constitution or "the evolving standards of decency" in this nation.

Capital punishment is of enormous moral, social, and symbolic significance. As a practical matter, it is of minimal importance in the criminal justice system. Prior to 1972, the death penalty was imposed fewer than fifty times a year. Its abolition or reinstitution will not affect the plight of most of the four hundred thousand people in custody. Nor will it alter the principles of criminal sentencing except for an unfortunate few who commit particularly atrocious homicides in states which have reinstated the death penalty.

In the light of this relatively recent history of criminal penalties in England and the United States, prison can certainly be viewed as progress from brutality and barbarism towards civilization. The prison, as we know it, is an American invention. The first modern prison was established by the Quakers in Philadelphia in 1790. It was conceived as a humane alternative to the penalties then legally inflicted on felons. Solitary confinement, meditation, and prayer were the routine established for these wrongdoers. They were to meditate on their sins and learn the error of their ways.

The noble hopes of the proponents of prison have not been realized. Prisons have developed their own physical brutality. We now recognize the psychological brutality of solitary confinement. Most modern prisons have strict limitations on the use of this particular penalty.

For violent and dangerous criminals, those who have inflicted death or serious injury on others, prison is greatly to be preferred to the death penalty as a means of protecting the public. But for the vast majority of offenders who are not violent and do not pose a physical danger to the public, is there no alternative to prison other than the rack, the screw, the stocks, and the pillory? Must the judge's choice of penalty be "in" or "out"?

I believe that there is another penalty which is humane and appropriate: compensation to the victim of the crime by the criminal. It meets the tests of "desert," proportionality, and equal treatment for similar offenses. It offers as much hope of rehabilitation as any other penalty. There is no Constitutional barrier to the use of compensation today as an alternative to prison. Moreover, there is substantial historical precedent for this type of penalty.

England before the Norman Conquest and the Germanic tribes in Northern Europe had a well-developed system of criminal law and penalties, scaled precisely to the offenses. Although there were no trials as we know them, there was tribal justice in which the community or "Moot" sat in judgment. The tribe acted collectively. Such trials were perhaps somewhat like the "People's Courts" in China today, where the neighbors sit in judgment on alleged wrongdoers.[21] There were no lawyers and none of the rights and procedures rights which we call collectively "due process." These trials were not for the purpose of fact finding. Like many Biblical and classical trials, the issue of guilt or innocence was decided by battle, contest, or ordeal.

Outlawing or banishment was the penalty for the most serious offenses.[22] Often this was a sentence of death by starvation. The individual excluded from his tribe and thrust into a hostile world could not long survive. Outlawing, even though attended by the actual chasing away of the offender, is qualitatively different from hanging, disembowelling, and burning alive—the common penalties in seventeenth- and eighteenth-century England.

The penalties for most other offenses under early Germanic law were payment of money. The laws of Ethelbert of England in the sixth century provide, for example, that "Theft of God's property and the Church's, shall be compensated twelve-fold." The wergild, or price of a man, was a common way of buying off a blood feud or vendetta arising out of homicide. The victim's kin had a right to wage a blood feud against the killer. However, the killer and his family could buy off the feud by paying the wergild to the family of the victim. This was a common practice which sensibly avoided much bloodshed and death.

In England, the laws of Alfred in the ninth century specify in detail the payment to be made by the wrongdoer to the victim.

For a wound in the head if both bones are pierced, 30 shillings shall be given to the injured man.

If the outer bone [only] is pierced, 15 shillings shall be given . . .

If a wound an inch long is made under the hair, one shilling shall be paid . . .

If an ear is cut off, 30 shillings shall be paid . . .

If one knocks out another's eye, he shall pay 66 shillings, 6 1/3 pence . . .

If the eye is still in the head but the injured man can see nothing with it, one-third of the payment shall be withheld . . .

Here, indeed, is proportionality of penalty to offense precisely scaled. The penalty is certain and known. These are the attributes which are so greatly admired. Obviously, there is no barbarity or cruelty to the wrongdoer involved in the exaction of a monetary fine.

To the contemporary mind there is something incongruous about the notion of payment to the victim as a penalty for crime. A crime under our law is an offense against the state, not a wrong to an individual. But, in medieval law, as Maitland the great historian of English law pointed out, there was no clear distinction between civil tort, which is an injury done negligently, and criminal law, in which harm is willfully inflicted.[23] In both instances monetary damages were paid to the victim and his family by the wrongdoer and his family. The payment was to avoid the blood feud and keep the peace. In medieval times imprisonment as a penalty for common crimes was rarely used. Sir James Stephens, in *The History of the English Law*, comments ". . . the practice of fining was so prevalent that if punishment is taken as the test of a criminal offense, the fines are regarded as a form of punishment, it is impossible to say where the criminal law in early times began or ended."[24]

Fines or amercement were common for many acts now regarded as civil rather than criminal. One of the important provisions of the Magna Carta which was perceived to be of signal relief to the people was the limitation on amercements which allowed the circumstances of each case to be taken into account. Thus, instead of a fixed scale of penalties and fines which worked great hardship, the court could take into account the circumstances of the individual defendant and mitigate the penalty. Contrast this with the certainty which Blackstone extolled. It is extraordinary that today in the quest for "fairness" it is suggested that the courts be deprived of this mitigating power which was so dearly won.

Alfred's scale of fines may be thought of as diminishing the dignity of the law and the victim. Is the willful cutting off of an ear to be penalized by a mere sum of money? But if we look at the modern workmen's compensation laws we find a precise analogue. The loss of each part of the body or its use is given a fixed value carefully scaled for seriousness.

The Compensation Law of New York provides in part the following rates for the loss of parts of the body:[25]

INJURY	NUMBER OF WEEKS' COMPENSATION
Arm	312
Leg	288
Hand	244
Foot	205
Eye	160
Thumb	75
First Finger	46
Great Toe	38
Second Finger	30
Third Finger	25
Toe other than Great Toe	16
Fourth Finger	15

The employer must pay these sums to the injured employee. The conceptual difference is that the employer is sued civilly. It is assumed that he had no willful intent to injure his employee. The employee does not have to prove negligence. Statutory law provides for limited recovery without proof of fault. But can one say that a manufacturing corporation which fails to have effective safety devices and equipment is blameless? This modest compensation which is simply added to the employer's cost of doing business is not granted as a gift to the worker, but as a legal right enforceable in court.

This right of the employee to recover from his employer was created by the state legislature when the courts refused to impose liability on employers for injuries suffered by their employees. The courts required the employee to prove that he was injured by the negligence of the employer and not of another employee. Obviously a corporation can act only through its employees. The "fellow servant" doctrine, a piece of "judge-made" law, effectively prevented employees from recovering from their employer in the usual common-law civil action for tort.

Today, nearly a half-century after workmen's compensation laws were adopted over strenuous opposition, the situation can be examined with some objectivity. It would not be difficult today to impute criminal liability to many employers. Any reasonable person would know that if adequate safety measures are not taken, injury is likely to result to persons working around machinery, persons dealing with asbestos, and persons in contact with carcinogenic or radioactive material. The criminal law holds guilty a person who acts in reckless disregard of the safety of others. He is held responsible for the consequences of his act. For those who have a mind indifferent to the consequences of their acts, the criminal law supplies the intent to do wrong—the mens rea or guilty mind, on which criminal responsibility is predicated.

Such implied intent forms the legal basis of hundreds of convictions for ordinary crimes. Joe was drunk and hurled dynamite in the street, not intending to injure or kill anyone. A passer-by was severely injured. A jury had no difficulty in finding Joe guilty of aggravated assault. He was sentenced to jail. An employee injured by the employer's reckless disregard for the safety of his employees receives his compensation. This grants a measure of fairness to the employee. It will not help him if the employer is jailed. The injured passer-by would undoubtedly have preferred compensation by Joe rather than his imprisonment.

If one puts aside five or six hundred years of legal concepts and examines the conduct of the employer and its consequences, it is apparent that contemporary workmen's compensation laws are very similar to the medieval wergild and the laws of Alfred. We have simply applied different nomenclature. Under Alfred's laws the wrongdoer paid a fixed penalty based on a scale of seriousness of injury. The wergild provided that the payment for the injury go not to the state (that concept was still in the future) but to the injured party. Similarly, the Frankish Penitentials in the ninth and tenth centuries provided not only for prayers, vigils, and pilgrimages by the wrongdoer, but also for compensation and assistance to victims. Among the accepted penitentials, the offender might be required to pay for the medical treatment of the victim, to do his work, and to pay him compensation. Property that was stolen or property fraudulently obtained was subject to restitution.[26] Translated into our money economy, the wrongdoer would pay for the victim's loss of earnings.

In civil cases today, other than workmen's compensation, medical expenses and lost earnings are items of damages which the negligent wrongdoer must pay to the victim of his carelessness. In addition, the negligent tort feasor pays for pain and suffering and loss of life pleasures. I believe that willful wrongdoers should make similar amends to the victims of their crimes. As we have seen, there are centuries of precedent for this type of penalty. Compensation or reparation to the victim of crime has a much longer history than imprisonment.

The notion of restitution and reparation did not vanish from English law with the Norman Conquest. Significantly, in the case of *King v. John Williams,* in Northumberland County, Pennsylvania, Williams was not only sentenced to be lashed on his bare back but also to "do restitution of the goods stolen." Returning to Blackstone, we can see that monetary penalties, forfeiture of lands and movable property, were also common penalties. But these payments were made to the crown, not to the victims of crime.

The use of prisons developed slowly in England. In the Middle Ages prison was used primarily for detention and coercive purposes. Accused persons were held in various types of local gaols, often castles and dungeons, awaiting trial. People were also held in custody to force them to pay fines or debts or to compel juries to change their verdicts.[27] Today prisoners who cannot post bail are also held in custody awaiting trial. Spouses who refuse to pay alimony or child support are jailed until they do pay. Reporters and others who refuse to testify or produce evidence are jailed until they do so. Bracton, writing in the mid-thirteenth century, declared that prison is for confinement, not for punishment.[28]

In the late thirteenth and fourteenth centuries, the use of prisons increased, although imprisonment was still coupled with fines. Significantly, prison terms were short, by our standards. A year and a day was the most common term. The penalty for most felonies was capital punishment, although pardons could be purchased. With the rise of church jurisdiction, we find the use of long prison terms and the confusion of sin and crime. Clerks, who were a loose form of cleric, were given life imprisonment for their offenses in order to do penance.

It is interesting to note that in the Middle Ages, as is true today, the business of operating a jail was profitable to the jailer. At that time the jailer was paid on a fee basis. Today, jailers are civil servants who have salaries and fringe benefits. Throughout this early period, imprisonment as a penalty was a last resort, a coercive measure to be used only if fines and restitution were not paid. Forfeiture of the felon's estate was a common penalty. All of these old practices, with appropriate modifications, could be employed today as alternatives to prison for many crimes.

In later chapters we shall explore the use of monetary compensation as a penalty of choice and imprisonment as a penalty of last resort. This idea has been tentatively broached by a very few legal scholars and rejected or ignored by most. Professor Giorgio Del Vecchio suggests reparation as a penalty and deterrent to crime. He points out that the notion still prevails "that it is permissible to inflict pain on those who have committed crimes, not to obtain reparation (which, in fact, is not obtained thereby) but because the suffering of another causes a certain satisfaction." This suffering is inflicted by imprisonment. He proposes that instead the criminal should compensate the victim and that "the duty of compensation should be extended to cover the whole of the damage done, and this duty should be fulfilled by doing honest work, under proper control, but this should not be imposed for the sake of causing suffering."[29]

Although imprisonment today is viewed as the principal penalty for crimes, it is a very recent innovation in the common-law criminal system. Monetary compensation to the victim has a much longer history in Western law. In seeking creative penalties as options to prison, we find substantial precedent for restitution and reparation as the preferred penalties for many crimes and imprisonment only as the ultimate coercion used to enforce monetary compensation.

CHAPTER X

TYPES OF CRIME

Fungible Goods: "Those things one specimen of which is as good as another, as is the case with half-crowns or pounds of rice of the same quality. Horses, slaves and so forth, are non-fungible things, because they differ individually in value, and cannot be exchanged indifferently one for another."

—Black's Law Dictionary

Present laws cover all crimes. Judges are required to apply the same criteria to every offender and to impose the same penalties: imprisonment or probation and/or fines for crimes.[1] Under all the sentencing proposals now being considered the same penalties would apply to every crime although some offenses would result in longer prison terms than others. The judge would be required to use the same criteria or standards for every offender regardless of the nature of the offense. There is no differentiation among crimes or penalties. But it should be obvious to everyone that all crimes and all criminals are not the same. They do not pose the same risks to society. Their motivations and their needs are not the same. Rape and embezzlement, for example, are committed by very different kinds of people. Although all judges, criminologists, and writers on the subject of sentencing acknowledge the goals of crime prevention and deterrence, their proposals do not take into account the obvious fact that the penalty likely to deter an embezzler may be highly unlikely to deter a rapist. Nor do those who argue in favor of rehabilitation propose different types of penalties to rehabilitate rapists and embezzlers. Those who believe in justice as fairness assume that if rape is categorized as a class II felony and embezzlement is also categorized as a class II felony, then the same sentence imposed on the rapist and embezzler will be fair and just. Little thought has been given to devising differentiated penal ties for different types of crimes and criminals.

The tacit assumption of the legislators who enacted the existing sentencing codes and the proponents of the new theories and sentencing commissions is that the sentencing judge's options are limited to "in" or "out" of prison. If it is "in," the next question is: How long is long enough? One might paraphrase Gertrude Stein and say that sentencing codes are based on the assumption that a crime is a crime is a crime and a criminal is a criminal is a criminal. The offense may be child abuse, armed robbery, or breach of public trust. The offender may be psychotic and illiterate or a highly educated and sophisticated professional. Under present laws and the proposed codes every offender will receive either probation or a prison sentence. Every prisoner will spend his term of sentence performing a routine menial task for a few hours a day. Ultimately every prisoner (except those executed) will be released and returned to society after either a short or long sojourn in the same state prison regardless of his dangerousness, his ability to earn a living, or his mental condition.

A giraffe, a toad, and a polar bear are all animals. Their size, their habits, their diets, and their dangerousness are entirely different. No rational person would propose putting them in the same cage in a zoo, or suggest that fairness and equal treatment of all animals required providing the same type and quantity of food, the same type of shelter, and the same type of enclosure. The differences among criminals, their needs, their motivations, and their dangerousness to the public are as varied as the species of the animal kingdom. The penalties that are likely to deter crime, the penalties needed to protect the public, and the penalties which will provide for the needs of the offenders and promote rehabilitation are just as different for the types of criminals as are the needs for food, shelter, and restraint for the different species of animals.

If society is truly concerned about crime prevention, deterrence, rehabilitation, and protection of the community, then legislatures and judges should examine the types of offenders and offenses and fashion special penalties for each category which are specifically designed to promote the legitimate ends of the criminal justice system. Within the various classifications of crimes and criminals, every effort should be made to eliminate unreasonable disparities in sentences. Offenders who have committed the same kind of crime, caused the same amount of harm, and have the same characteristics and needs should receive similar penalties. Instead of making such rational distinctions among criminals, present law and the proposed sentencing codes and commissions classify all crimes into felonies and misdemeanors. Within those two categories several classes are established. Murder, for example, is a class I felony. Robbery, wife beating, and violation of environmental laws may all be class III felonies. Under most proposed codes, a judge would be required to impose the same sentence on every class III felon regardless of whether he is a wife beater, a robber, or a corporate official. All of these convicted felons would be sentenced to the same prison for the same number of years in the belief that this is fair and just or that the offenders will be rehabilitated.

It is obvious that these offenders are very different kinds of people who represent very different risks. What may rehabilitate one is not likely to rehabilitate the others. Neither fines nor imprisonment will provide redress for the victims of any of these crimes. Imprisonment of the wife beater will protect his wife only for the period he is incarcerated.

Most offenders and offenses can be grouped into five broad categories. They may be roughly denominated: (1) irrational crimes, (2) family crimes, (3) street crimes, (4) white-collar crimes, and (5) organized crime. The penalties for these categories which will protect the public, prevent or deter crimes, provide redress for the victim, and insofar as possible rehabilitate the offender are entirely different. I believe that most people who are involved in the criminal justice system recognize these basic differences in types of offenses. But nowhere in crime codes or literature on sentencing are such classifications to be found.

The Uniform Crime Reports of the United States Government use two major classifications: violent crime and property crime. Motor vehicle theft and burglary are property crimes. Murder, forcible rape, and aggravated assault are violent crimes. The codes do not differentiate between murders, assaults, and rapes within the family and those committed on strangers although most research studies draw this distinction. Nor do they distinguish among corporate or white-collar crime, street crime, and organized crime. I have not seen any code which suggests a classification of irrational crime, although the press regularly reports bizarre, senseless, brutal offenses which can only be considered irrational. Nothing in the criminal law or sentencing codes takes into account these major differences in offenders even though it is perfectly evident to lawyers and trial judges that the offenders who commit these different types of crimes are very different types of people. They have different motivations, different needs, different kinds of inner controls. One might almost say they are different species.

Lester is a wife beater. He struck his wife any number of times until finally she took the children and moved to her mother's home. Two days later Lester went to his mother-in-law's house, broke open the door, and beat his wife and daughter with a crowbar so severely that they were both hospitalized for several weeks. Lester wrote to me from prison asking for a reconsideration of sentence. He explained that he had a good job, which was true, and that he had no prior convictions. This was also true. Lester's employer, members of his church, and several fellow workers testified on his behalf. He is intelligent and a good, reliable worker. Lester concluded his letter with this telling sentence: "It wasn't a crime. It was only my wife and child."

Richard is a robber. When he was tried before me he had five prior convictions. He had served two short terms in prison. Richard is semi-literate and unskilled. He has no means of earning a living. He wants more luxuries than welfare provides. Each time he sees a likely victim, he holds him up. No one knows how many times Richard has robbed and not been caught. The robbery in the case before me netted Richard less than twenty dollars. Richard never plans his crimes. As he explained, "It just happened."

Herbert is an accountant who was employed by a medium-sized corporation. He planned very carefully and worked out a clever scheme for embezzling from his employer. He had been stealing approximately three hundred dollars a week for almost five years. He might have continued his careful thefts indefinitely. However, his employer sold the business. The new owners hired a management firm to review the records of the company and they uncovered the shortages. Herbert pled guilty before me. He had no defense and no excuse.

Wilbur has a record of three forcible rapes. He was on trial before me for raping an elderly grandmother and her twelve-year-old granddaughter. He had already served two prison sentences for rape. He was on parole when he committed these rapes. Wilbur is not a drug addict or an alcoholic. His IQ is about ninety-five. He is literate and employed. While in prison, he was given intensive psychotherapy. He was a model prisoner. He was released by the parole board the day his minimum sentence expired. The two victims who testified before me clearly identified Wilbur. The jury promptly returned a verdict of guilty. The problem was the sentence. Wilbur is only twenty-six years old.

Everyone knows that organized crime is a national problem. One reads in the daily press and in books and magazines of these elaborate criminal organizations. There must be innumerable people involved in the criminal underworld. Knowledgeable people declare that vast amounts of money are illegally obtained by organized crime and used to gain more untaxed money and wield more power. Movies like *The Godfather* graphically portray the brutality, power, and wealth of organized crime. There is no doubt that organized crime exists and operates in almost every city, large and small. But in eight years on the bench I have never had a case which overtly involved organized crime. Lawyers who represent such clients rarely appear in court. The police are, of course, aware of organized crime. But as the following case will show there is almost a conspiracy of silence.

Ralph was tried before me for a series of burglaries. He had stolen a large, carefully selected quantity of valuable goods. He was clearly not the usual run of burglar who simply takes easily salable things like TV sets and wristwatches. Many of the victims of Ralph's burglaries were in court. None of the stolen property had been recovered.

Ralph's attorney and the prosecutor came to me to discuss a guilty plea. The prosecutor said he would agree to drop many charges and make no recommendation as to the sentence to be imposed if Ralph pled guilty to a few charges. I told both attorneys that I would, as is my custom, insist on restitution but keep an open mind as to the question of a prison term.

"But restitution is impossible," both attorneys said. "He doesn't have the goods. He has very little money."

"He must know where the stolen property is, or to whom he sold or gave these things," I remonstrated. "Hasn't he told you who the fence is?"

"No," the prosecutor explained. "It wouldn't be safe for him to tell us."

"He knows that he is going to prison, doesn't he?" I asked.

Ralph's attorney assured me that Ralph did indeed know that in all likelihood he would receive a very stiff sentence. I suggested that if he cooperated, the sentence might be a little less severe. Both attorneys told me that if Ralph said anything his life would be in danger, whether he was on the street or in prison.

Ralph had no property, the family home was owned with his wife. He lived modestly with her and their three children. He attended church regularly. According to the neighbors, Ralph was a good family man, a good neighbor, a quiet man. He had lived in the same house for more than ten years. Ralph's participation in the burglaries was uncovered not by the police but by the company that had insured the property of one of the victims.

Under most sentencing codes and plans, Ralph would have been placed on probation. He had no prior record. His crimes were not violent. No one was injured. In fact, none of the victims ever saw Ralph. But I believed that it would be unconscionable to let a professional criminal, albeit a lowly subordinate, walk out of the courtroom a free man without returning the stolen property or making any atonement, and, moreover, without any assurance that he would not continue his life of crime. Even though some of the victims were insured, their insurance did not by any means cover all their losses. Some of the stolen property had great sentimental value which no amount of money could replace. I was of the opinion that regardless of the pre-sentence report, which recommended probation, I had to impose a stiff prison sentence. Perhaps after he has served time, Ralph will be able to get free of organized crime. But it is not likely to happen. It is also extremely unlikely that Ralph's bosses will ever be brought to trial.

Should these five men be given the same or similar sentences? No sentencing code and none of the more widely recognized sentencing reform proposals distinguishes among them. In order to answer this question one must examine the goals and purposes of the criminal justice system and the justification for penalties. Vindication of the rule of law, which I find the single most satisfying reason for the imposition of penalties, is predicated upon due process and the concomitant belief that the penalty should be proportionate to the offense. For many white-collar crimes, the penalty leaves the criminal in possession of the fruits of his crime.

Herbert, the accountant, managed to steal $75,000. A $10,000 fine, the maximum fine under the statute, is a signal example that crime does pay and that the rule of law may be flouted with relative impunity. Deterrence, if not the primary justification of the criminal justice system, is certainly an important and legitimate goal. Will the same type of penalty deter the wife beater, the rapist, the robber, the embezzler, and the member of organized crime? Prison sentences have had no deterrent effect on Richard, the robber, or Wilbur, the rapist.

Rehabilitation, although rejected by many, is still a valid and not to be discarded by-product, even if it is not an end, of the criminal justice system. Will the same prison routine rehabilitate all five men? Most pre-sentence examiners would report that Herbert, the accountant, who is nonviolent, intelligent, and well-educated, does not need rehabilitation. Prior prison sentences have not rehabilitated Richard or Wilbur. As for Lester, the wife beater, one finds little help or guidance from psychiatrists. I know that his wife lives in fear of the day of his release from prison. She is planning to change her name and move to another city. What, if anything, will change Lester's understanding of the role of husband and father?

What can prison do to rescue Ralph, the employee of organized crime? Unless Ralph's overlords in the underworld are brought to trial and convicted, he will probably have to continue to work for them and commit more crimes.

A judge who sees scores, if not hundreds, of people like Lester, Wilbur, Richard, and Herbert, and occasionally a Ralph, knows that they differ qualitatively from each other. It is my belief that they should be treated differently by the criminal justice system.

As I fill out my reports indicating the numbers of cases "disposed of," I have a mental picture of the kitchen sink into which the grapefruit rinds, the egg shells, and the leftovers are all poured; they go down the same drain, are ground up together, and disposed of in the same sewer. Sentencing all offenders to the same kind of prison to serve the same type of penalty is, in my mind, simply disposing of people. It is not doing justice to them, to society, or to the victims of their crimes.

Differentiation of treatment of offenders by types of crime is not perceived to be an important question by criminal justice specialists. The conference on Research Priorities in Sentencing by the National Study on State Courts, which was held with support from the Federal Law Enforcement Assistance Administration, did not consider this question at all. Only one participant, Professor Jack M. Kress, mentioned it. He questioned: "Is it possible to determine what type of sentence or sentence alternative seems to work best for a particular type of offender?"[2] The conference, however, voted pre-sentence reports as its number-one priority for research. Different penalties to be imposed on different types of offenders or for different types of crime was not even included in the list of research priorities by the conference.

In the next chapters I shall examine these different kinds of offenders and suggest ways which I believe the criminal justice system should treat irrational criminals, family criminals, street criminals, white-collar criminals, and children. I shall suggest different modalities for each type of offender which I believe would be more effective in protecting the public, deterring crime, providing for the victim, and treating the offender. I can make no suggestions with respect to organized crime because I have no experience with the bosses of such organizations. They are rarely prosecuted in state courts. There is little literature on the treatment of organized crime by the federal courts.

The views I express are based upon a limited but not unrepresentative personal experience. There is a paucity of published research on the question of differentiating sentencing according to types of crimes. Social scientists are measuring and quantifying all types of behavior by judges and jurors.[3] There are studies of offenders by cohorts and peer groups. We have data tending to show that treatment cannot rehabilitate or reform offenders[4] and that neither prisons nor capital punishment affect the crime rate but no data with respect to different types of criminals.[5] Lack of statistical information, however, need not paralyze the criminal justice system or freeze into perpetuity practices which are less than two hundred years old. Thoughtful observers who see the futility of existing policies must at least suggest other procedures which may reasonably be expected to be more effective and more just.

CHAPTER XI

IRRATIONAL CRIMES

To a reasonable creature, that
alone is insupportable which is
unreasonable.
—Epictetus

A lawyer making the closing address for the defense in a robbery
case eloquently argued: "My client was not hungry or shivering
in the cold. He has a job and a home, a wife and children. Is it reasonable
that a man like this would rob a store?" Of course, it wasn't reasonable.
But four eyewitnesses identified his client as the man who had held up
a grocery store. The license number of the car in which his client fled
was taken. He was apprehended with the stolen money in the grocery
store bag. He, like most people who commit street crimes, acted unreasonably.

Considered from the point of view of a reasonable person, most
crimes don't make sense. Would any sensible person knife or shoot
another for three dollars? Would a reasonable person kill a lover for
being an hour late to an assignation? Would any reasonable person
assault another and seriously injure him over any kind of dispute? Would
a reasonable or sensible person commit a murder in full view of scores
of witnesses?

The answer to these questions is a resounding "no." However, cases as bizarre and preposterous as these are tried in court every day. Indeed, those who are in criminal court on a regular basis soon wonder what is normal and what is aberrant behavior.

It is all too easy to excuse illegal conduct by saying that the offender is "sick." Mental illness is an umbrella phrase that covers everything from arson to zoning violations. Is a parent who beats his infant mentally ill? Is a twenty-year-old man who rapes an eighty-year-old woman mentally ill? Is a man who risks jail for stealing ten dollars mentally ill? Most people would probably consider the child abuser and the rapist mentally ill. Few people would consider the thief mentally ill. It is evident, however, that if most of these people thought in advance about the consequences of what they were about to do, if they reasonably calculated the risks and benefits, none of them would have violated the law. Cost/benefit theory plays little part in their decisions.

I have used the word "reasonable" as the litmus test of the actions of all these criminals because it is the standard by which the law judges most conduct. In all common-law countries, including the United States, judges and juries are asked to determine a multitude of questions by testing the behavior of the parties against the standard of what a reasonable person would have done under similar circumstances. The law presumes that people are reasonable. Such a presumption is necessary in any society. The law must declare norms of behavior to which the public is expected to adhere. Liability is imposed upon those who violate these standards of conduct. A simple example of the "reasonable-man" test which is regularly applied in courts occurs in automobile accidents. When an accident occurs at an uncontrolled intersection, the judge or jury must decide whether one or the other or both drivers were negligent. To answer that question, the judge or jury must determine what a reasonable person would have done under the circumstances.

In civil cases, the reasonable-man test does not present any of the grave philosophical questions of responsibility which haunt the criminal law. It is presumed that people who engage in the ordinary transactions of life, like driving cars, buying and selling goods and real estate, forming corporations, borrowing and lending money, manufacturing and shipping goods and the like are reasonable and should be held responsible for their actions. If they do not meet this standard they are liable in damages for the harms their unreasonable behavior caused. No one suggests that a driver who unreasonably speeds down the street and strikes a pedestrian should be relieved of liability because he is mentally ill or emotionally disturbed.

Although the reasonable-man test has been the touchstone of the Common Law for centuries, a little reflection reveals that it is a legal fiction, a myth. Many people are unreasonable. The actions which bring them to court are often patently unreasonable. But the mythical reasonable man is the standard against which real, unreasonable people are judged.

Lord A. P. Herbert, the distinguished and witty British lawyer and author, wrote a charming story entitled "The Reasonable Man" in which he describes, referring to actual cases decided in the English courts, how the rule of the reasonable man operates.

The Common Law of England has been laboriously built about a mythical figure —the figure of 'The Reasonable Man.' He is an ideal, a standard, the embodiment of all those qualities which we demand of the good citizen. . . . It is impossible to travel anywhere or to travel for long in that confusing forest of learned judgments which constitutes the Common Law of England without encountering the Reasonable Man. . . .

The Reasonable Man is always thinking of others; prudence is his guide; and 'Safety First,' is his rule of life. He is one who invariably looks where he is going, and is careful to examine the immediate foreground before he executes a leap or bound; who neither star-gazes nor is lost in meditation when approaching trap-doors or the margin of a dock; who records in every case upon the counterfoils of cheques such ample details as are desirable, who never mounts a moving omnibus, and does not alight from any car while the train is in motion; who investigates exhaustively the bona fides of every mendicant before distributing alms, and will inform himself of the history and habits of a dog before administering a caress; who believes no gossip, nor repeats it, without firm basis for believing it to be true; who never drives his ball till those in front of him definitely vacated the putting-green which is his own objective; who never from one year's end to another makes an excessive demand upon his wife, his neighbors, his servants, his ox, or his ass; who in the way of business looks only for that narrow margin of profit which twelve men such as himself would reckon to be 'fair,' and contemplates his fellow-merchants, their agents, and their goods, with that degree of suspicion and distrust which the law deems admirable; who never swears, gambles, or loses his temper; who uses nothing except in moderation, and even while he flogs his child is meditating only on the golden mean. [He] stands like a monument in our Courts of Justice, vainly appealing to his fellow-citizens to order their lives after his own example. . . .

Lord Herbert calls the reasonable man a myth, declaring he has never encountered one. Nor do I encounter many reasonable people who have committed crimes, particularly crimes of violence. Despite the unreasonable behavior of many persons, both the civil and the criminal law are predicated on the assumption that people are reasonable. It is a necessary assumption. No one could engage in any of the everyday activities of life if he did not assume that other people would behave reasonably. No one could walk on the sidewalk unless there was a reasonable expectation that motorists would drive in the street and not on the sidewalk. No one could go to a restaurant if he did not assume that the waiter would serve him food, not poison. No one could go to a hospital for treatment if he did not assume that the doctors were, in fact, licensed physicians, not imposters.

The law in establishing rules for civil liability and criminal responsibility must be premised on the presumption that people are reasonable. We cannot have one law for the rational and another law for the irrational. But when a legal presumption, which is a fiction, is treated as a fact, difficulties ensue. The legal presumption that people are reasonable causes no problems so long as we do not actually believe that all people are reasonable. If, however, we forget that the reasonable man is only a presumption, then when a person commits an unreasonable act, we are inclined to conclude that he must be mentally ill or emotionally depraved. Otherwise he would not behave irrationally.

Moral depravity or sin should not be confused with illegality. Many acts are made crimes which are not either immoral or inherently wrong. There is no ethical virtue in driving on the right-hand side of the street instead of the left. In England the law requires motorists to drive on the left side of the street. The purpose of laws mandating driving on either the left or the right is to ensure that a motorist can have a reasonable expectation that all motorists will be observing the same regulations. Without such assumptions there would be chaos. The law recognizes the distinction between crimes evil in themselves, malum in se, and those which are simply violations of rules, malum prohibitum. There is no moral dereliction in driving on the left or in selling liquor without a license. These offenses are prohibited by law. If an individual violates such a law, he is guilty regardless of his intent. He is subject to penalties even though he was morally virtuous, or unaware of the law, or mentally ill. Courts do not inquire into the mental state of these offenders or their sanity or evil intent. In imposing sentence, the court does not consider whether the offender needs rehabilitation or whether others will or will not be deterred by the imposition of a penalty. With respect to these offenses, the law is morally neutral.

The law retreats from this neutral stance, however, in many crimes, particularly when the offense is also morally wrong. The theological notion that punishment should be visited only on sinners comes into play. For centuries, under the common law the rule has been that fools, idiots, and infants were not responsible for their acts and could not be found guilty of crime. In a theological sense, of course, that accords with our notions of divine retribution. It makes sense in dealing with small children. Who would suggest that a six-year-old who sets fire to a house, even though it burns to the ground and a dozen occupants are killed, should be prosecuted for arson and murder? The law presumes that the child is incapable of criminal intent regardless of his intelligence or emotional maturity.

When adults commit senseless, brutal, and dangerous crimes, I suggest that the inquiry as to intent, mental capacity, and mental illness should be irrelevant. The perpetrator of an illegal act which injures another may not be morally responsible because of his mental condition, but he is no less dangerous to society than a man who acts illegally and with premeditation and intent. In these cases we should put aside the fiction of reasonableness and avoid the confusing welter of psychiatric and legal definitions of insanity. It should be obvious to anyone that John W. Gacy, Jr., who was charged in Chicago in 1979 with murdering more than thirty boys and young men, Son of Sam, and others who have committed brutal, senseless crimes should be incarcerated permanently for the protection of society. Moral responsibility is irrelevant compared to the need to protect the public from further senseless and brutal acts which may be committed by these individuals.

Even when the fact that the accused committed the illegal act is evident beyond a reasonable doubt, courts engage in the most lengthy and meticulous trials to prove to the satisfaction of a jury or judge the sanity of the offender. Sanity is considered a fact, not a legal conclusion or a scientific opinion. This is also a legal fiction. Sanity is proved like any other fact. In most cases involving a shooting, the prosecution must prove that the bullet which struck the victim was fired from the accused's gun. This is a physical fact. Was it fired from that gun or wasn't it? The bullet which was removed from the victim's body is present in court. The judge and jury see the bullet. But simply from a visual inspection they cannot decide this question. Expert testimony is necessary. A qualified ballistics expert who has examined the bullet and the gun is called to testify. He describes his examinations of the bullet and the gun, the instruments used to make the examinations, the criteria and tests which are employed by ballistics experts, and he explains his findings and conclusions. On the basis of such evidence the judge or jury decides an issue of fact: Was the bullet fired from the defendant's gun?

Similarly, in a personal injury case, doctors testify as to the fact of injury. Did the plaintiff suffer a whiplash injury or didn't he? There may be a difference of opinion on this question. A doctor for the plaintiff will show the jury the X-rays, describe the examinations and tests he made, and give his conclusion as to the fact of injury. A doctor who is called as a witness for the defense will also testify with respect to the X-rays, the tests, and examinations he made of the plaintiff and testify as to his opinion with respect to the alleged injury. One doctor will state "with reasonable medical certainty" that the plaintiff did suffer a whiplash. The other will testify, also "with reasonable medical certainty," that the plaintiff did not suffer an injury. On the basis of this conflicting evidence the judge or jury must decide the issue of fact: Was the plaintiff injured? Assuming that the defendant has been proved to be negligent, if the plaintiff is found to have, in fact, been injured, he will recover damages.

When this method of proving facts is applied to the question of the accused's sanity, courts become mired in a confusing welter of opinions as to an issue which is not really a fact. Sanity is only a matter of opinion. The doctor may conduct tests and examinations, he may state his opinion "with reasonable medical certainty," and the jury may find as a fact that the accused was insane at the time he shot the victim. It is difficult to conceptualize a state of mind as being a fact, and even more difficult to make a finding with certainty as to a state of mind. And even after the jury has made the findings, the "fact" of sanity or insanity is essentially irrelevant to the bottom line question: What shall society do with this person? It is interesting to note that in most notorious cases, the trial becomes a battle of psychiatrists. Several authorities stated with certainty that Patty Hearst was brainwashed and was not responsible. Others stated with equal certainty that she was not brainwashed and was responsible. Two psychiatrists testified with certainty that Son of Sam was incompetent. One psychiatrist testified that he was competent.

I believe that in the trial of persons accused of patently irrational acts which have resulted in death or serious harm there should be only one issue of fact decided by the judge or jury: Did the accused commit the act? If it is proved beyond a reasonable doubt that he did, then he should be incarcerated until he is so old that he is not physically a threat to society. His mental state and his sanity may mitigate the "sin." But they do not make the offender less dangerous. On the contrary, his irrationality makes him more dangerous. Since his conduct is not reasonable, it is unpredictable. Because he is irrational he cannot be deterred by threats of penalties. Nor is it logical to assume that counselling and therapy can transform an irrational person into a reasonable one. Indeed, the few studies that have been made of sex offenders indicate the contrary. Of course, not all offenders are irrational. It has been pointed out that some criminals are neurotic and can't help what they are doing. Others are "normal."[1] One can substitute the words insane, psychotic, or schizoid for the word neurotic. Whatever terminology is used, the judge or jury can determine the question of irrationality from the facts and circumstances of the crime itself. In most cases, no expert testimony would be needed.[2]

What should be done with the irrational offender who commits dangerous crimes? If we look at a few of these patently irrational crimes, it is readily apparent that the legal and psychiatric issues which befuddle the courts and dismay the public are really irrelevant. Gary has forcibly raped two teenage girls that the police are aware of. Gary has the mentality of a five-year-old. But he has the body of a twenty-five-year-old —his chronological age. He is 5' 10" tall and weighs 220 pounds. He did not know the meaning of the word rape until he was arrested. He was brought to trial before me for the second rape. He was never tried for the first rape because the victim refused to testify. She was so distraught that her parents would not permit her to undergo the further trauma of trial. What should be done with Gary? The maximum penalty for rape is twenty years. At age forty-five, when his prison term expires, Gary will still have a mental age of five. He will still be physically strong and capable of committing more rapes. He cannot be sent to a mental hospital because he is not mentally ill. He is not amenable to therapy.

In California, Lawrence Singleton, a merchant seaman aged fifty-two, was sentenced to fourteen years in prison for kidnapping and raping a fifteen-year-old girl and hacking off her arms. Superior Court Judge Earl H. Maas, Jr., who imposed sentence, said, "If I had it in my power, I would send him to state prison for the rest of his natural life."[3] Most people would agree with the judge. However, California's new determinate sentencing law designed to ensure equal penalties for all offenders specifies the number of years for each offense. But is there another offender in California who has committed a crime equal to Singleton's? Under the law, a fourteen-year sentence is the maximum allowable for rape. It will automatically be reduced to nine and one-half years less the 194 days Singleton spent in custody since his arrest. Singleton must be released at age sixty-one. It is likely that he will still be physically able to commit another such crime. It is highly unlikely that even if he is given intensive therapy he will be "rehabilitated."

Wade was twenty-two years old when he was brought to trial. He was accused of killing three elderly white women and attempted murder of a fourth elderly white woman, Mrs. R. She miraculously survived and was able to explain the circumstances of the crime against her. Wade is a soft-spoken, attractive, gentle-looking black man. He knocked on Mrs. R.'s door and told her he was selling magazines to work his way through college. Mrs. R. had never seen Wade before. She didn't want to purchase any magazines and politely told him that she had all the magazines she wanted. Wade then asked her for a glass of water. She turned to go to the kitchen to get it for him. He knocked her down, then pulled a heavy china closet down, smashing it over her. Wade left, closing the door which automatically locked behind him. Fortunately, the mailman came a few minutes later. He rang the bell because he had a package. Mrs. R. did not answer. The mailman knew that she rarely left her home. He looked in the window and saw her legs protruding from under the china closet which was lying on the floor. He immediately called the police. The three other victims had been killed by being suffocated or smashed by a heavy piece of furniture. There had been no signs of a forcible entry in any of the crimes. The police had had absolutely no clues to these deaths until they found Mrs. R.

The psychiatrists who examined Wade and investigated his background explained that Wade had been abandoned at a very early age. He was brought up in a home for foundlings. One of the matrons of this institution was an elderly white woman who treated Wade with great harshness. Wade was a bright boy and did satisfactory school work. He graduated from high school. He was employed and lived alone. His fellow workers and neighbors reported that he was a quiet, well-behaved young man. When told of the crime, they were shocked and incredulous. Wade was diagnosed as severely mentally ill. The only evidence against Wade as to the three deaths was his confession and the circumstances of a "common scheme or design." The confession was obtained without the presence of counsel and without adequate warnings to Wade as to his rights. The confession was excluded. It is difficult to convict for murder upon such evidence without the confession. The maximum penalty for attempted murder is only ten to twenty years. In ten years Wade will be only thirty-two. He will probably be released when his minimum term expires. He will have thirty to forty years in which to murder other elderly white women.

The psychiatrists agreed that Wade is psychopathic. Most lay people would agree with that diagnosis. It may explain his behavior. But should it condone it or exonerate Wade? Should Wade be in a prison or a mental institution? How long should he be confined? None of the codes or theories offers a satisfactory answer to these questions.

Alvin lured young men, usually college boys, to his interesting tobacco shop. He collected rare pipes and imported tobaccos. He was educated and had traveled extensively. He was a good raconteur. His shop was attractively decorated. It was Alvin's practice to invite a young man to come to see some new find just before closing time. After the young man arrived, Alvin would close the shop and take his guest into the back room where he tortured and killed him. Alvin dismembered each body, placed it in a trunk heavily weighted with stones, and dumped it in the river. Alvin pursued his arcane murders for months without detection or suspicion until he strained his back. He could not lift the trunk alone so he paid a neighbor boy to help him carry one of the trunks to the river. The boy who had not seen what was in the trunk became suspicious and told his older sister who promptly called the police. The river was dragged and the trunk was recovered. The police discovered the dismembered body. An ironic but not unusual twist to this bizarre case was the fact that the boy, who was only fifteen, was promptly jailed as a juvenile delinquent. Alvin was arrested. As an adult he was entitled to be released on bail. Bail was set at $100,000. Ten percent cash bail was permitted in this jurisdiction, as in most states. Alvin was able to post $10,000. He was released while the boy remained in custody. Alvin was found to be mentally ill, psychopathic.

What should be done with irrational offenders such as Alvin, Gary, Wade, and Lawrence and people like them? I strongly believe that all such irrational persons who have committed crimes resulting in death or serious injury should be imprisoned for life, with no time reduction for "good behavior." If such an offender is found not guilty by reason of insanity and sent to a mental institution, the criminal justice system will have lost control over him. He will be released whenever the psychiatrists at the hospital find that he is not mentally ill. They have no authority to hold people who are not mentally ill and dangerous. The power of civil institutions to incarcerate a person because of his mental state is wisely limited. The criminal justice system is the proper forum for determining on the basis of the evidence of the crime whether the criminal should be incarcerated and for how long. This is not a decision to be made privately in the office of a psychiatrist with none of the protections of a public trial, right of counsel, confrontation of witnesses, and all the elements of due process.

The results of psychiatric decisions to hold or to release allegedly mentally ill persons are fraught with danger both to the individual and to the public. A few years ago, Ida was on trial for murder. She had performed a crude caesarian operation with a butcher knife on a woman acquaintance who was more than eight months pregnant. The woman died; the baby lived. The evidence was conclusive as to what had occurred. The accused pled not guilty by reason of insanity. Two psychiatrists testified that she had such an irrational and pathological longing for a child that she committed this crime in order to obtain a baby for herself. She was found not guilty by reason of insanity and sent to a mental hospital. A year later, the hospital released her. The doctors found that she was no longer mentally ill. The horrified judge protested. But the woman had been acquitted of the crime by reason of insanity. The criminal justice system no longer had any jursidiction over her. Under civil law a mental hospital cannot hold a patient against his or her will unless the patient is both mentally ill *and* dangerous. The criminal justice authorities have no standing to protest the release from a mental hospital of a person who, the hospital authorities declare, is not mentally ill.

Most homicides where the victim is a stranger to the criminal and which are not committed in the course of robbery or burglary are irrational. Lamar asked a stranger on the subway for a match. The man did not have one and Lamar stabbed him to death. There was absolutely no reason for this crime.

Why should the courts attempt to assess Lamar's mental state? It is evident that he is dangerous. He has randomly killed one person for no reason. If released, there is at least a strong probability that he may kill others. I see no moral or ethical problem in incarcerating for life a person who has without justification taken the life of another. The only purpose of an inquiry into Lamar's sanity would be to have Lamar committed to a mental hospital (from which he might be released) instead of to a prison. There can be no doubt that a sentence of life imprisonment would not be disproportionate to the crime, nor would it be cruel and unusual punishment. On the contrary, it would be appropriate.

Fortunately, most people are rational. Even though they may have strong reasons for taking vengeance they seldom do so. Every day people are killed and maimed on the highways. Rarely, if ever, does a member of the family of the victim of an automobile accident slay or even beat up the negligent, drunk, or reckless driver responsible for the tragedy. I have never heard of the family of a patient who was killed or crippled by the negligence of a physician wreaking vengeance on the doctor. People who have lost their life's earnings through the chicanery or faithlessness of a partner or business associate sometimes commit suicide. They rarely kill the author of their misfortunes. That is because most people are reasonable. They know that an act of vengeance will not restore their losses and will only cause themselves much trouble, most likely a prosecution for murder.

When courts attempt to deal with the issue of responsibility, they become involved in questions which neither judges nor juries can decide on the basis of evidence adduced at trial and through principles of law. In these cases courts are attempting to decide theological issues. Is it morally right to punish a person who either did not know what he was doing or that it was was wrong? This is one of the definitions of insanity. I have never encountered an accused who did not know that the act of killing or rape or arson was wrong. The usual question of responsibility is whether it is morally right to hold a person responsible who did not have the free will to choose between committing the act and not committing it. Was the accused brainwashed? Was he suffering from some illness which made it impossible for him to control himself? Did the accused have some physical or genetic defect that prevented him from exercising free will? A deprived economic, social, or emotional background is also included by some people in the category of conditions which inhibit this hypothetical free choice. Today, after a century of psychiatric research, who can say that anyone is in a position to exercise free will? Who has not been shaped by the circumstances of his birth, sex, race, ancestry, family, education, war, poverty, and all of the events which befall an individual?

Anna Russell, in a psychiatric folksong entitled "Jolly Old Sigmund Freud," describes the treacherous quicksands of responsibility in an age of psychiatry:

At three I had a feeling of
ambivalence toward my brother,
And so it follows naturally,
I poisoned all my lovers.
But now I'm happy; I have learned
The lesson this has taught,
That everything I do that's wrong
Is someone else's fault.

I suggest that courts limit their inquiry in cases of irrational offenders to the factual question: Did the accused do the act? Irrational offenders should be tried promptly in a court of law with all the protections of due process of law. They should not, however, be tried for the common-law or statutory crimes of murder, or assault with intent to kill, or in some cases rape and arson. To convict an accused of such crimes the judge or jury must determine the accused's state of mind at the time of the act and decide whether or not he intended to kill, whether he had the capacity and will to form such an intent, and, depending on the test for sanity in that jurisdiction, whether he was mentally ill or insane at the time of the alleged offense. All these questions are extremely difficult and require the testimony of psychiatrists. In very few cases do the psychiatrists for the prosecution and the psychiatrists for the defense agree even though their conclusions are based upon the same facts. Why should the law require, as it now does, that the state prove beyond a reasonable doubt that the accused was sane at the time and that he had formed a premeditated intent to kill?

Mr. Justice Holmes declared: "The law is made to govern men through their motives and it must, therefore, take their mental constitution into account." This principle has been used both to acquit the insane and to require consideration of intent. If the law considers the "mental constitution" of offenders it should be for the purpose of determining whether the offense is rational or irrational. If the offense is found to be irrational, violent, and dangerous, then the prosecution should have to prove beyond a reasonable doubt only that the accused did the act.

The judge or jury would decide only two issues. Was the slitting open of the pregnant woman an irrational act? If this question is answered "yes," then the jury should decide whether Ida committed the act. Was it irrational to kill and dismember the young student and place his body in a trunk? If that question is decided in the affirmative, then the only other question is whether Alvin committed the act. I propose that a new crime be established: the irrational commission of a violent or dangerous act resulting in death or serious bodily injury. Such a new statutory offense would eliminate as an element of the crime "mens rea," intent, premeditation, sanity, and mental capacity. The penalty for such crime should be life imprisonment without parole or early release. Under existing laws, except for habitual sex offenders, the length of the sentence is limited to a fixed number of years. The judge may not increase the penalty even though it is apparent that the offender will present a grave danger on his release.

Present law carefully grades some crimes, such as homicide, by intent. Murder in the first degree, in most jurisdictions, is the willful, premeditated, malicious killing of another. It is characterized by hardness of heart and wickedness of purpose. Felony murder is the killing of another in the course of committing a felony. If a robber shoots his holdup victim and kills him, he is guilty of felony murder even though he had no intent to kill the victim. Killing in hot blood, the crime of passion, is subject to a lesser penalty because the victim's senses were so inflamed that he could not exercise reasonable judgment. Accidental killing, such as death resulting from a motor vehicle accident, receives a lesser penalty because there was no evil intent. In all these homicides, the unfortunate victim is dead. The law considers not the fact of death but the circumstances surrounding the killing to determine the appropriate classification of the crime and the consequent penalty. No one suggests that under the rubric of justice as fairness or crime prevention or any other rationale that all killers, regardless of motivation, be found guilty of the same offense.

My proposal is simply to create another category of crime: the irrational and dangerous offense. If the crime is irrational, then courts cannot and should not apply the usual tests of motivation and intent to classify the offender by categories which are established on the basis of conduct of reasonable people. In the crime of passion, for example, it is presumed that the offender acted under sudden overwhelming emotional pressure. If the outraged spouse or lover does not act on the spot but waits to take revenge until the next day, the law considers the killing willful and premeditated murder, the most serious offense. Why is there this drastic difference in the classification of this homicide? Because the law presumes that people are rational, that after the outraged spouse or lover has time to cool down, reason and restraint should be exercised.

When we deal with the irrational dangerous offender, none of these presumptions is applicable. He is not a reasonable man. The questions which courts consider with respect to motivation, intent, mental capacity, and sanity are irrelevant and meaningless fictions in these cases. They prevent the court from deciding the real question: Did the accused commit the act? These inappropriate issues also prevent the criminal justice system from imposing an appropriate penalty.

A special offense of irrational and dangerous crime would pose no more difficult question of mental state or condition than existing law now requires judges and juries to decide. In most cases the mental condition of the accused—rationality or irrationality—could be deduced from the act itself. Judges and juries would doubtless find it easier to conclude that Ida was irrational than that she was insane. The jury that found Ida not guilty by reason of insanity was told that she would be placed in a mental institution. Had they contemplated that she would be released in a year I doubt that they would have returned a not-guilty verdict.

In some offenses, psychiatric testimony might be necessary to assist the trier of fact in determining the issue of irrationality. Dr. Manfred Guttmacher, the forensic psychiatrist, distinguished several kinds of arson, some rational and some irrational.[4] Arson committed for the purpose of fraudulently collecting insurance is a crime motivated by greed. It indicates a degree of rationality. Arson is sometimes committed as an act of revenge against an individual. This also indicates a measure of rationality. The arsonist has a grievance; he retaliates. The act may be stupid, brutal, vicious, and dangerous, but it is not irrational. These types of arsonists must be distinguished from those who commit arson as a revenge against society. They are psychotic and likely to set more fires. They have a thirst for revenge that will not be slaked by one fire. A man who sets fire for thrills, according to Dr. Guttmacher, experiences an orgasm from watching the fire. Such a person will continue to set more and bigger fires to fulfill his emotional needs. These arsonists are irrational. A man who sets fires to collect insurance is a criminal, but not an irrational criminal. Certain acts of assaults and mayhem committed against total strangers for no comprehensible reason should also be included in the definition of irrational dangerous offenses.

There is no moral or philosophical imperative that prevents the criminal justice system from isolating or "incapacitating" people who have committed irrational and dangerous acts which have caused death or serious injury. Surely this is the type of conduct which, according to John Stuart Mill, falls within the scope of permissible social control through law in order to prevent harm to others.[5] The only impediment to such a sensible disposition of such people is the phraseology of penal statutes. As we have seen, many offenses do not require criminal intent. These are generally nonviolent offenses. The principle could be extended to a class of violent offenses. There is no constitutional barrier to the enactment of a penal law which makes criminal a homicide or an attempt to kill that is not in self defense, regardless of the killer's intent or mental capacity.

Because life imprisonment without the possibility of parole or early release is a drastic penalty, there should be the widest scope of review of such cases by an appellate court. Life imprisonment with no possibility of parole or reduction of sentence is a much less severe penalty than capital punishment. The death penalty has been imposed under the common law and under American penal statutes for centuries without any special provisions for appellate review.

The concepts of crime prevention, desert, and proportionality all demand that the irrational individual who causes death or serious injury be given a most severe penalty not because he is morally blameworthy but because he is dangerous. At present there is no statute in any jurisdiction in the United States which authorizes life imprisonment of a man like Singleton, who hacked off the arms of the fifteen-year-old girl. Nor is there any statute which authorizes life imprisonment of Wade, who attempted to kill Mrs. R. but did not succeed in doing so. None of the proposed sentencing codes or mandatory sentencing laws addresses the problem of the irrational, dangerous offender. Legislation is urgently needed to permit the imposition of a sentence of life imprisonment without release or parole for the offender who commits an irrational, dangerous, and violent crime.

CHAPTER XII

FAMILY CRIMES

Every night and every morn
Some to misery are born
Every morn and every night
Some are born to sweet delight.
—William Blake

A house in the suburbs with mom baking an apple pie, daddy dili-
gently and regularly going to work and returning home on time,
and two or three smiling children walking happily to the neighborhood
school is the picture of the typical American family. It appears in
advertisements and children's readers. It is the picture of an America
that never was and certainly does not exist today. In the United States
today 44 percent of mothers with children under the age of six are
employed outside the home. There are half as many divorces as marriages each year. The two-paycheck marriage is the norm for nearly half
of all two-parent families. Approximately 15 percent of all families are
headed by women. Almost 11 million children live in homes without a
father.[1]

The picture of a supportive, protective father and a gentle, nurturing
mother is equally belied by the facts. Although there are no complete,
reliable statistics as to the extent of crimes committed against spouses
and children within the family, the partial figures reveal a problem of
epidemic proportions. According to a Texas study more than 60,000
children are reported abused each year in America. Knowledgeable
people suggest that the actual number of children physically abused annually is between 200,000 and 800,000. Between 465,000 to 1,175,000

children are severely neglected or sexually molested each year. It is estimated that one child in every hundred is physically abused, sexually molested, or severely neglected each year.[2] Another study reports that one of every seven children is abused or neglected.[3] Every three minutes a woman is battered by her husband or boyfriend. The Center for Women Policy Studies reports these facts:

A Cleveland study found that of 600 couples applying for divorce, 37 percent of the women listed physical abuse as one of their complaints.

In Lincoln, Neb., the police handled 2,000 cases of wife abuse in 1973 alone, an average of more than five a day.

In San Francisco, the police reported that 50 percent of the calls they received were for family disturbances.

In Dade County, Fla., 457 persons were homicide victims as a result of family disturbances in the five-year period ending in 1974.

In Atlanta, domestic disputes are the most troublesome area for police on the night shift, accounting for 60 percent of all calls.

At Boston City Hospital, approximately 70 percent of the assault victims received in the emergency room are women who have been attacked in the home. Where the assailant is specified, it is usually a husband or boyfriend.

In San Francisco, a quarter of all murders in 1974 involved couples. In Kansas City, Mo., a third of all homicides are domestic cases; in Detroit, one-half. In New York City, as many people have been killed each year for the last three years by family members as have been killed in Northern Ireland.[4]

Family crime is not a peculiarly American phenomenon. Britain calls it "hearthside crime." It is a serious and widespread problem in England and other European countries. It is a social problem of epidemic proportion in the United States.

The amount of spouse abuse, like child abuse, is undoubtedly much greater than the statistics indicate. Reliable figures are available only with respect to homicides. More than half of all killings are committed by people who are related or well known to the victim.[5] The facts confirm Dr. Karl Menninger's pithy observation: "Your friends and neighbors, kith and kin/Are the ones who'll do you in." Many assaults are committed within the family usually on the wife and small children and infants.

How does the law treat intra-family crime? How do the theories of crime prevention, rehabilitation, desert, and presumptive sentencing apply to such crimes? Astonishingly, neither the legal system nor the theoreticians see intra-family crime as a distinct and separate problem from other types of crime. Under the law, the accused spouse or parent or member of the family is arrested, charged, and prosecuted the same as any other offender. The penalties prescribed are the same for homicide of a stranger as for homicide of one's own child. Blindfold justice sees neither the offender nor the victim. This theory is as patently fallacious as the myth that the law is colorblind and, therefore, unprejudiced. In fact, the law treats intra-family crime more leniently and neglectfully than any other type of crime. The view that violence perpetrated on a member of the family, whether it be a legal marriage or a "relationship," is really not a crime permeates the entire criminal justice system. Unless death occurs, police are loathe to make arrests and prosecutors are reluctant to press charges. When such cases are brought to court, the sentences are far more lenient than those imposed for crimes committed against non-family members.

Although most people would consider an adult who beats a child to death or a person who throws his or her spouse down the stairs irrational, the intra-family offender is very different from the irrational criminals we have examined. Unlike irrational criminals who randomly attack strangers, those who commit crimes against their relatives, paramours, and children do so with the intent to hurt or punish the victim or to protect themselves. Horrifying and dismaying as the facts are, family crime is not a cause for unmitigated despair. Something can be done to prevent many of these serious injuries and fatalities. Family crime is totally different from irrational crime. The irrational criminal randomly strikes strangers. It is difficult to identify him. Usually he is not apprehended until after he has injured or killed several people. There is little that the criminal justice system can do to prevent the series of dreadful acts committed by irrational criminals until by accident or luck their identity is discovered. In family crimes the perpetrator is known; his whereabouts are no secret. The family criminal rarely begins his crime career with a homicide or crippling injury. These are the culmination of long history of abuse against the children or spouse. Occasionally the victim is a parent or parent-in-law. In cases of interspousal violence, often the male abuser is himself slain by the desperate woman who had endured many beatings, kickings, and other brutal attacks over a long period of time. Both the abused and the abuser could have been saved if help had been available before the final crisis.

When the law acts, it is usually too late to help the victim or the abuser. The principal legal tool in cases of intra-family violence is criminal prosecution. This is, of necessity, a slow procedure. First, there must be a complaint. Protection for children must come from neighbors, friends, or medical personnel who treat the injured babies and children. The adult victim often makes a complaint, usually by phone. The police respond to the call. They seldom make an arrest. The parties continue to live in the same home together. The victim is subject to more abuse. The abuser now feels even more free to continue the pattern of violence. If there is an arrest, the accused is entitled to a preliminary hearing at which the victim or someone who observed the crime will testify. The hearing officer must find that a crime has been committed and that there is probable cause to believe that the accused has committed the crime. At this point many charges are dismissed for lack of legally sufficient evidence. If the accused is held for court, he is entitled to bail. Unless the victim is dead or seriously injured and in the hospital, bail will not be high. The magistrate or judge who holds this hearing is often not a lawyer. The position is not one that attracts legal scholars, sociologists, or philosophers. These officials reflect the general public view. I have often heard a magistrate set nominal bail and say, "It isn't really a crime, just a family fight." The accused goes back home, where the victim is, to await trial. The hostility, violence, and fear between them increases. At the earliest, the accused will be brought to trial in four months. If he or she is convicted, then appeals follow.

The trial judge is faced with the difficult problem of imposing sentence. What sentence will prevent future crimes? What sentence can rehabilitate a man who beats his wife? What penalty does he deserve? Is it fair to sentence a parent who beats an infant to the same term of imprisonment as a man who beats another man? The judge receives no guidance to this problem from any of the sentencing codes or theories.

Wife beating and child abuse have much in common. In both instances, a larger, stronger individual attacks a smaller, weaker person. The abuser and the victim live together. The victim has no practical means of escape. The law provides no real protection. Both spouse and child abusers are to be found in all strata of society and all races. They are rich and poor, educated and uneducated. Let us see what happens when the law is invoked.

Marcella and Ron were not legally married but they had been living together for three stormy years. After a particularly severe beating Marcella called the police. When they came she told them what had happened and asked them to put Ron out of the apartment. Ron showed the officers the lease to the apartment. It was in his name.

"Arrest him," Marcella pleaded.

"We can't do that," the officers explained. "We didn't see him hit you. We don't have any evidence that a crime was committed."

"You want evidence of a crime? I'll give it to you," Marcella told them.

She took the officers upstairs and showed them a cache of heroin. Ron was promptly arrested. He was tried before me on drug charges. The abuse of Marcella was ignored by the police. They did not consider that a crime worthy of arrest.

Rosa had been beaten by her husband for years. When I saw her, she had no front teeth. Her skin was discolored, her nose misshapen. Her right arm was twisted, the result of an earlier fracture that had not healed properly. Each of these prior incidents had been reported to the police. There were numerous hospital records of the injuries Rosa had suffered. But no legal action had ever been taken against Angelo, her husband. The final episode in the twenty-year saga of abuse occurred one Saturday night. Angelo came at Rosa in a drunken rage. They were in the kitchen. Rosa stabbed him to death with a butcher knife. None of her children came to court. They had all left home at the earliest possible age. Most of them had moved far away. Although Angelo had never been arrested, Rosa was promptly arrested and charged with murder.

Hilda came into court with a black eye and one arm in a sling. She was obviously pregnant. She has two small children. Michael, her husband, is a fireman. He is a solid citizen, a good worker with an excellent rating. The family lives in a nice neighborhood. They have no financial problems. Hilda and Michael stood at the bar of the court.

"I want to withdraw charges," Hilda said.

"With prejudice," Michael's lawyer added.

With prejudice means that the case is over. If anything further were to happen, Hilda would have to file new charges. The earlier beating would be irrelevant to the new case. It would be heard before another judge who would not know about the black eye and the broken arm. I asked Hilda if her husband had, in fact, caused her injuries. She said that he had.

"Why do you want to withdraw charges?" I asked her.

"He says he won't do it again. I have no place to go. My baby is due in less than two months. Who will take care of the children and me?"

I refused to permit the withdrawal of charges with prejudice. I told

both Hilda and Michael that I would retain jurisdiction of the case but
would not hear any evidence. Hilda was instructed that if she had any
further complaints she should call me personally and I would order an
immediate hearing.

A week later Hilda did call from a neighbor's house. She was in tears,
almost hysterical with fear that she would lose the baby and that it had
been injured. The night before Michael had returned from work tired
and angry. He had a few beers. There was an argument. He struck Hilda
and she fell. Michael refused to let her call a doctor. He yanked the
phone out of the wall. As soon as he left for work the next morning Hilda
went to her neighbor and called me.

What sentence should be imposed on Michael? The maximum sentence for simple assault in most jurisdictions is two years. Hilda will be
physically safe while Michael is in jail. But that won't be for very long.
Even if the maximum sentence is imposed, he may be released early.
Parole authorities and correctional officials take a benign view of intra-
family crime. I convicted a man of first-degree murder of his wife. He
killed her in front of scores of witnesses. The psychiatrist who performed
a pre-sentence examination recommended probation. He reported that
the husband was not a "violent person" and this was his first offense.
Apparently he did not consider the slaying of a spouse an act of violence.

Child abuse follows a similar pattern. In most cases there is not a
single act for which the abuser is arrested, tried, and convicted. There
is usually a long series of acts which occur before any legal protection
is sought. Nebraska attorney Richard Hansen writes: "Abused children
who live through two hearings seldom survive to be the subject of a
third."[6] Most children who die as a result of abuse are under the age
of five. Dr. Marvin Aronson, Philadelphia Medical Examiner, sees the
age factor as significant. Children who receive their final battering, he
believes, probably were "crying from fear or as a result of a prior injury."
He finds that children who survive past five have learned how to avoid
beatings and to protect themselves. Most children who die of malnutrition or who are labeled "failure to thrive" babies are under the age of
four. Once a child is able to walk, open a refrigerator door, or even
scrounge in garbage pails he will manage to eat enough to avoid starving
to death. A child does not die instantly from malnutrition or even from
abuse. Even the most fragile baby tenaciously clings to life. Many of
these children could be saved *if* society intervened promptly and decisively.

There are many social and legal impediments to prompt action to protect children. In a democratic society, people are reluctant to have the state intervene in the home. Individuals have rights to privacy. The notion that a man's home is his castle is very strong. No one wants to have social workers employed by the state invading his home and examining his methods of child rearing and discipline. The right of a parent to beat his child under the guise of discipline is very old and very persistent. Caning resulting in physical mutilation, psychic damage, and even death was prevalent in English schools until it was abolished in 1948. In many countries it is assumed that adults have the right to strike and beat children. Sweden is a shining exception. A recent Swedish law makes it a crime for any adult, including parents and teachers, to strike children. But in the United States, the Supreme Court has upheld against claims of unconstitutionality the right of teachers to inflict corporal punishment on children.[7] The Court assumed that beating a child is an innate prerogative of adults charged with his care and education. With such societal acceptance of adult brutality toward children is it any wonder that physical child abuse is so prevalent?

Dr. Stanley Plotkin, director of infectious diseases at Children's Hospital in Philadelphia and assistant professor of pediatrics at the University of Pennsylvania, says that the prevailing attitude is "that a child is a chattel. If the parent beats a child and doesn't actually kill him, people take a tolerant view."

It is difficult to draw a legal line between a slap and a beating. Moreover, some proposed child-abuse reporting laws and many juvenile court laws give the state power to remove the child from the home when such action is in the "best interests of the child." Others define abuse and neglect as "any act of commission or omission by individuals, institutions, or society as a whole, and any conditions resulting from such acts or inaction, which deprive children of equal rights and liberties, and/or interfere with their *optimal development*... [emphasis supplied]." Such definitions are not only unworkable, they are probably unconstitutionally vague. Under such a legal mandate, juvenile and family courts would have the broadest imaginable powers to interfere in family life. Between the extremes of ordering "optimal development" of the child and permitting brutal beatings, starvation, and torture, it is possible to draft laws which authorize protection of children and spouses from serious physical injury and death.

One must recognize that there are centuries of law and custom under which the powers of husbands and fathers were virtually inviolate. As late as the nineteenth century in England a husband had the right to chastise or beat his wife with a stick, but with one no bigger than his finger. The husband had control over his wife's property and complete custody over the children. The Romans and the Athenians of the Periclean Age treated children as the property of the father. It was legal to kill unwanted babies, to expose them on mountaintops, and to kill older children at the whim of the father. Even in the early twentieth century unwanted Chinese children were exposed and left to die. The Biblical story of Abraham sacrificing his son Isaac indicates the accepted power of life and death which a father exercised over his child. When Agamemnon sacrificed Iphigenia at Aulis, she was saved by the goddess Artemis, not the juvenile court of Athens. Agamemnon was not considered an unfit father and deprived of parental rights. Nor was Abraham.

The first American legal action for child abuse was not brought until 1874. There was no legal authority for such a lawsuit. The child was treated under the rubric of a small "animal" since there was a society for prevention of cruelty to animals and laws for the protection of animals. The next year, the Society for the Prevention of Cruelty to Children was created. Until the early 1960s, problems of child abuse were handled loosely by voluntary agencies. When court action was deemed necessary, the child was treated as a "neglected" or "dependent" child under the Juvenile Court laws.

National Juvenile Court statistics reveal that in 1966 there were only 161,000 neglect and dependency cases in the entire United States. The majority of these cases involved children who were homeless and dependent due to death, absence, or illness of the parents. Abuse was not recognized by the courts as a major problem although the public was aware of the widespread serious situation.

The phrase "battered baby" became popular in the early 1960s. There was the usual American response—"There ought to be a law." Between 1963 and 1970, forty-nine states enacted child-abuse reporting statutes. Despite these laws, the juvenile courts have not seen protection of abused children as a primary obligation. In the early 1970s, the federal government sponsored a study of child-abuse reporting laws and the drafting of a model child-abuse reporting law. Countless "hot lines," foundations, and agencies to prevent child abuse have been established. Today many adults are busily employed in discussing child abuse and in raising money for this cause. But there has been no diminution in the abuse of children by relatives or persons living in the family. The reports generated by the statutes reveal that over half of the reported cases involve children under the age of four. Half of the deaths occurred in children under the age of two. In a study of 302 abuse cases, 85 resulted in brain damage, 33 in death.

The 1970 White House Conference on Children recommended that every city and town establish at public expense an office of Child Advocate to represent not only individual children but the needs of all the children in the community, and to point out deficiencies in essential services. Many communities have established such legal services. They have not been effective in reducing child abuse or in protecting battered children. There are several reasons for this failure. Many of these child advocates do not have a clear perception of their role. They are concerned with "saving the family," providing therapy for the abusers, and reducing the public financial burden by returning children to their homes at the earliest possible date. The protection of the child is only one of the goals of many child advocates.

The attention of lawmakers and lawyers has been focused on child-abuse reporting laws on the naive assumption that if incidents of abuse are reported, existing laws and procedures will provide adequate protection. The Model Child Abuse and Neglect Reporting Law, like the laws of many states, provides that "Within twenty-four hours of the receipt of a report of suspected child abuse or neglect, the Agency shall commence an appropriate and thorough investigation to determine whether a report of suspected child abuse or neglect is 'Indicated' or 'Unfounded.' The findings shall be made no later than sixty days from the receipt of the report."[8] Even if the investigation were commenced promptly, which is rarely the case, a child could suffer continued abuse and death during the sixty-day period.

After the investigation, there are three possible choices: (1) Do nothing. This is the most frequent result except in cases of death. (2) Institute a criminal prosecution of the abuser. As in the case of spouse abuse, at least four months will elapse between the time the suspected abuser is formally charged with a crime and the time he or she is brought to trial. The accused is entitled to be released on bail. If the child is still alive and not in a hospital, the abuser will return home and continue the pattern of abuse. Few children are hospitalized for months. The average hospital stay for all children except abuse cases is six days. For abused children, it is seventeen days. This indicates the seriousness of the injuries suffered. But it also indicates that the abused child will be returned to the abuser long before he or she is convicted. The likelihood that the abuser will be imprisoned is not great. In most cases he or she is placed on probation. If the abuser is the father and he is employed and supporting the family, courts are reluctant to jail him and put the family on welfare. "Family therapy" is then ordered. Meanwhile the helpless child is in the home and the focus of resentment.

The third option is to institute action in family court to remove the child and terminate parental rights. This also is a protracted proceeding and bitterly fought. Very few parents will accede to termination of rights regardless of any feeling for the child, because it is a diminution of the adult's rights and an invasion of individual sovereignty by the state. And it is permanent. Once the order is final, the child may be given out for adoption. In these cases, the abuser is entitled to be represented by counsel. The child, like all victims of crime, is not the prosecutor. In some states the child victim will be represented by counsel who may cross examine the accused and present witnesses on behalf of the child. In many jurisdictions no one represents the child. Even when there is counsel for the child, the child may not be effectively protected. The usual rules of evidence and procedure prevail in both criminal prosecutions and termination of parental rights trials. The burden is on the state to prove the charges. The accused is presumed to be innocent. In a criminal prosecution, proof beyond a reasonable doubt is required. In family court, proof by a fair proponderance of the evidence is needed to terminate parental rights.

The child, if alive, is usually too young to testify. Even if the child is old enough to speak, he is not a competent witness. A child under the age of five does not know the meaning of an oath. The testimony of an infant is not reliable. The case must be proved by circumstantial evidence and the opinions of doctors and nurses that the injuries were not accidental, that they were deliberately inflicted. It is difficult to prove that broken bones and bruises are not the result of an accidental fall. It is almost impossible to prove who inflicted the abuse unless some adult or older child actually witnessed the acts. These are frustrating and painful cases.

Denise was a small two-year-old. She was brought to the hospital with numerous bruises and several broken bones. Her parents claimed that she had fallen down stairs. X-rays revealed several healed old fractures indicating prior injuries. A child abuse proceeding was instituted in family court. The parents claimed Denise had not suffered previous abuse but that she had soft bones and the fractures were the result of falling as she learned to walk. She was returned to her parents by the court. A few weeks later she was taken to a different hospital by her parents with new injuries. This time an outraged doctor made a check of several hospitals and discovered that Denise had been hospitalized four times for "accidents" in four different hospitals. A prolonged and bitter hearing was held.

This time the pediatrician was determined to protect Denise. The hospital staff had worked night and day to save her life. Denise was a winsome little girl who had won the hearts of the doctors and nurses. Dr. S., the pediatrician in charge of Denise, retained counsel. The prosecution for child abuse was brought in family court. The parents were represented by the public defender. The Welfare Department nominally represented the child. The prosecuting attorney presented the case. Counsel for Dr. S. really had no part in the proceedings except to protect Dr. S. from ridicule by counsel defending the parents.

The prosecution offered in evidence the records from the four hospitals showing the injuries which Denise had suffered and the treatment she received. Defense counsel objected. There was no charge before the court that the parents had caused the four prior injuries. The objection was sustained. With respect to the latest injury, Dr. S. testified that it was unreasonable to suggest that Denise had broken her own arm and had put a one-inch welt across her buttocks from an accidental fall. The bruise on the buttocks obviously came from a whipping with a belt, Dr. S. testified.

Defense counsel first questioned Dr. S. about the broken arm. "Many people do fall and break their arms and legs in ski accidents, bicycle accidents, and just tripping and falling, don't they, Dr. S.?"

"But that is not what happened to Denise," Dr. S. replied.

"Not responsive to the question. Move that the answer be stricken," defense counsel stated.

"Motion granted," the court ruled.

"The bruise on the buttocks that you say is the mark of a belt—you weren't there when it happened, were you, Doctor?" defense counsel asked.

"No, I wasn't there. But I know the wound a belt leaves on a child's body," Dr. S. replied.

Defense counsel continued to cross examine Dr. S.

Q. You can't say that the father struck Denise, can you?
A. I didn't see him do it.
Q. You can't say that the mother struck Denise, can you?
A. I didn't see her do it.
Q. Thank you. That's all, Dr. S.

The attorney for the welfare department who was supposed to be representing Denise didn't ask Dr. S. any questions.

Both parents testified. They told how carefully they cared for Denise. On the day in question Denise was playing in the living room. She climbed up on a chair. Before either of them could reach her she fell. That explained the broken arm.

As for the welt on her buttocks, they testified that when they went shopping they left Denise in the care of a neighbor. She must have hit Denise. The mythical neighbor never testified. The parents did present a "family therapist" who testified that they were good and loving parents and that Denise would suffer psychological damage if she was removed from the family. He also pointed out that there was no place to put Denise. Foster parents did not want a sick baby who needed intensive care. The representative of the welfare department, which was supposed to represent Denise, testified that the hospital was demanding payment of approximately $1,800, at the rate of $100 a day for keeping Denise. There was no money available to pay for past hospital care for Denise and certainly not for future care. The court found that there was insufficient evidence that the parents had beaten Denise. She was again returned to her parents. Six months later Denise was dead. After her death, a criminal prosecution for murder was brought against the father. He was acquitted because he managed to suggest to the jury that he was not home at the time and that Denise's mother was responsible. She was not prosecuted because she was pregnant.

Another equally serious case reveals the problems of protecting children of the middle and upper classes. Lana's parents live in an expensive house in the suburbs. Her father is a high-powered young executive, a man in a hurry. He is rough and demanding. Her mother had a difficult pregnancy. She suffered post-partum depression. She was hospitalized for a few weeks and a nurse was brought in to care for Lana. The bills kept mounting. At the insistence of Lana's father, the mother was discharged from the hospital and came home to care for this infant, run the house, entertain, and cope with an angry, resentful husband. Both of these young parents were alienated people. Lana's father had an abusive father who had beaten him and his mother. Lana's mother was a gentle girl who was utterly incompetent. The house was dirty. She broke dishes; she burned the food; she cried continuously. Either Lana's mother or her father, in a fit of exasperation at the baby's crying in the night, dropped her in the playpen. In the morning they noticed bruises and discoloration on Lana's face; one eye was swollen shut. The pediatrician was called. He found that Lana had suffered severe damage to her face and permanent impairment of her sight. When he admitted Lana to the hospital he entered her as an "accident case." Lana was never reported as a child abuse case. Although child abuse occurs in all strata of society, the well-to-do are seldom reported by private physicians.

The children of the poor also suffer abuse and rarely receive effective protection. Five-year-old Alfie died in a hospital ward after what the medical examiner described as several weeks of beatings and "sadistic abuse" by his mother's boyfriend. There were 119 bruises on the body of this small boy. The boyfriend was convicted of third-degree murder and the mother was convicted of involuntary manslaughter. The court found that the mother had full knowledge of the abuse and did not protect her child.[9] The man was sentenced to three years in prison. The mother was placed on probation. In the scale of seriousness of crimes as measured by the sentences imposed, killing a child is a lesser crime. A seller of marijuana gets a heavier penalty in many states. So do purse snatchers and robbers who do not harm the victims of these crimes. Alfie lived in a densely populated area. He was not on a remote, isolated farm. Neighbors must have heard the child's cries. They must have seen him with welts and bruises. No one did anything to save him. What could they have done? Where could a concerned relative or neighbor have taken Alfie to protect him? The answer in almost every city and town is "nowhere." Vincent de Frances, director of the Children's Division of the American Humane Society says, "No community has developed a child protective service program adequate to meet the needs of all the reported cases." In most communities the only agency open twenty-four hours a day 365 days a year is the police department. The police quite properly have only limited authority to arrest on suspicion or to remove children from their homes.

After Alfie's death, society spent more than $5,000 in court and police time to convict the mother and her boyfriend. In addition, the public defender represented one of them and private counsel paid from public funds represented the other. He received a fee of $2,000. An appellate court reviewed the convictions. The state is paying almost $60,000 to incarcerate the man. Again, the law's action was too little and too late.

These senseless unnecessary deaths probably could have been prevented if there were shelters to which such children could be taken for temporary care and refuge by any concerned person; laws that grant immunity from prosecution for kidnapping to such rescuers; and provision for temporary child care without the threat against the parents of criminal prosecution or loss of parental rights.

Much child abuse is not deliberate and sadistic like the beatings inflicted on Alfie or the cigarettes burned into Tommy's small body. Kenny died at five months. He was not beaten or burned or dropped or tortured. He was simply not fed. He cried and whimpered and finally died—dehydrated and emaciated, weighing less than nine pounds. He was one of the many sickly high-risk babies born in the slums to young mothers who have not had proper prenatal care and who are themselves, perhaps, marginal people.

Such were Mr. and Mrs. R., parents of twins. In a previous generation the twins would not have lived. But excellent hospital care brought them through the first critical weeks. Then the children were discharged from the hospital. They required feeding every three hours around the clock, special handling, a great deal of skilled care. This young mother, who had three other children under the age of five, with the best will in the world was unable to provide the care that was required. At the age of eleven months, when the children were brought to the hospital, each weighed less than twelve pounds. Normal weight is approximately twenty pounds. Permanent brain damage and retardation had already occurred. At this point a child-abuse petition was filed and the children were placed with a foster mother. Another classic case of too little and too late.

Older children are also abused within the family. The most common form of abuse is sexual molestation of a girl by a father, father substitute, or other man in the household. Frequently the child is afraid to report what has happened. She recognizes, consciously or subconsciously, that the women in the family cannot or will not protect her. She is often threatened with beatings and other punishment if she does tell. The P. family is one of the city's old and distinguished families. They live in a large, beautiful house. The children are well dressed, bright, and attend good schools. Mr. and Mrs. P. and the five children attended church every Sunday. They were considered a model family. But, in the privacy of the home, behind the old oak trees, Mr. P. in turn raped each of his three daughters as they reached adolescence. He continued to have sexual intercourse with all of them until the oldest finally rebelled and told her mother, who had probably suspected the truth for some time. The mother committed suicide. The girls then went to the police. They were taken into "protective custody" by the court and kept in a juvenile detention center with delinquent girls. They were not permitted to leave this "jail" to attend school or church or even to go to the doctor. The father was free on bail and living at home with a new wife. Although the girls' mother had left property to them, the father as natural guardian had control of the property and the girls were penniless. They remained in custody until a family friend agreed to let them live with her. A court hearing was necessary in order to obtain the release of the girls. The father opposed it. The father was tried, convicted, and released on probation. At sentencing the judge remarked, "The girls will get over it." A few years later the oldest girl committed suicide.

Another shocking but not unusual case of incest involved Rosita who lived in a housing project with her mother. Her father is dead. Her uncle Sam was in and out of Rosita's apartment all the time. One day when Rosita's mother was at work, Sam raped her. Rosita was in tears, crying, screaming. She is a small wiry girl aged fourteen. She testified that Sam put his hand over her mouth, that he slapped her and threatened to choke her if she told anyone. Sam testified that he was like a father to Rosita, that she sat on his lap, that he loved her and would never harm her. Those who write about statutory rape often state that "Incest is not a violent act—the father is a loving figure—at first his fondling is rather nice."[10] Rosita and the P. girls did not find anything gentle or nice about their rapes. They were brutal and violent.

In another case of incest Dr. N. told me, "The mother is cold. She refuses to have sex with with her husband. I am trying to get her to have a better relationship with him."

"What does her refusal to have sex have to do with the fact that Mr. S. committed a crime against his daughter?" I asked. "What are you doing to protect the girl?"

"I'm saving the family," Dr. N. replied.

There are many therapy groups for prevention of child abuse. I attended one session of a program financed by public monies. There were about a dozen young women and their small children in attendance. The therapists watched while the children played. One small boy about three

grabbed a toy. His mother slapped him hard in the face. "Didn't I tell
you not to touch that?" she shrieked. The therapist watched. No one
stopped the blows. No one comforted the screaming child. Later I asked
why there were no fathers in the group. More than 50 percent of child
abuse is caused by male natural fathers or father figures. "The men won't
attend the sessions," she explained. One can only wonder whether these
children are being protected from serious abuse or death by these forms
of family therapy.

Those who are interested in crime prevention and sentencing must
recognize that intra-family crime requires different laws and procedures
from other crimes. Courts must be able to intervene after the first act
of violence. The rules of evidence must be revised to reflect the realities
of the situation so that proof of abuse does not present almost insuperable obstacles. And the victim of crime must be recognized as a party to
the litigation with the right to be in court, to be represented by counsel,
to present evidence on his own behalf, and to cross examine the accused
and his witnesses.

The law recognizes that in some situations it is not possible for
even-handed justice to prevail unless the scales are weighted in favor of
a disadvantaged person. For example, if the driver of a car is killed in
an accident, the law presumes that he was exercising due care at the time
of the accident. The deceased's representative sues the other driver who
testifies as to how the accident occurred and further testifies that he was
not negligent. Obviously the deceased cannot testify. To rectify this
imbalance, the law provides the presumption which shifts the burden
of proof to the other driver who must present evidence to overcome the
presumption.

A similar presumption should apply in many cases of intra-family
crime. Medicine recognizes that some individuals are "at risk." Because
of some physical condition they are more likely to suffer serious illness
or death from conditions which would not harm other people to the
same degree. The law should also recognize that some people by reason
of certain conditions are more vulnerable to abuse and less able to
protect themselves than the general population. The law must be
weighted in their favor in order to achieve a just result. I propose that
when there is an allegation that a vulnerable person has been abused,
attacked, or killed and there is evidence of bruises, fractures, or other
objectively verifiable injuries, the burden of proof should shift to the
alleged abuser to show how the injuries were inflicted.

A vulnerable person should be defined in relation to the alleged abuser in any of the following ways: (1) physically weaker, (2) unarmed as opposed to an armed person, (3) disadvantaged by youth or age, (4) under legal or actual control of the abuser (child/parent), or (5) mentally disadvantaged.

After the first known act of intra-family violence against someone classified as vulnerable is reported, the law should act at once to protect the victim from further attacks by the alleged abuser. Medical and psychiatric treatment should be provided for the victim. The abuser should be offered treatment on a voluntary basis.

If the alleged abuser is arrested and prosecuted under the criminal law, the victim will not receive either treatment or prompt protection from further abuse or treatment. Alternative civil remedies are needed. There are a number of established civil legal procedures which do afford immediate relief. They have not been used very often in cases of intra-family crime. The ex parte temporary restraining order is well known to the law. This is a civil remedy in which the judge issues an order to protect individuals and property *before* a trial is held. If the sheriff is about to foreclose on a property or if the highway department is about to demolish a building or a tree, the affected people can get a preliminary injunction without an adversary hearing, that is, without bringing in the other party. Under such circumstances a court will stay the threatened action for five days so that the party or the property will be protected until a hearing can be held. At that time both sides will be represented by counsel and can present evidence. Such a procedure should be made available by statute to vulnerable people who allege that they have been physically abused. A beaten spouse or paramour should be able to get the alleged abuser out of the common home for five days pending a hearing on civil charges. Several states have enacted laws which give some measure of civil relief in such circumstances. A battered baby should be removed from a place of danger to a hospital or licensed child-caring institution for five days pending a civil hearing, which should not involve termination of parental rights or any other permanent disability with respect to the parents—or criminal action against them. The purpose of these proceedings should be simply to provide immediate protection to the vulnerable person without jeopardizing the rights of any parties.

The standard for invoking this ex parte remedy should be "probable cause," which is the standard for arrest. Probable cause requires proof that a crime was committed and reasonable grounds to believe that the accused did it. With respect to abuse of vulnerable people there should be objective proof of injury and reasonable grounds to believe that the accused is the one who did it. Once these two criteria are met, a court should have authority to issue a temporary restraining order removing the alleged aggressor from the victim's home, or removing the victim to a non-penal hospital, shelter or residence. If the victim is a competent adult, the abuser should be removed and the victim permitted to remain in his or her home. At this point, psychiatric examination and therapy should be offered on a voluntary basis to the alleged abuser. If the abuser is not in danger of criminal prosecution or deprivation of rights, he or she will probably be more amenable to accepting help. Of course, help should immediately be provided for the victim at no cost, if the victim is indigent or does not have control of his own funds. Children, mental incompetents, and elderly people often are entitled to social security welfare, pensions, and trust funds. But control of the funds may be in the hands of the alleged abuser. A court can order the appointment of a guardian ad litem to take control of the victim's funds or entitlements pending a determination as to whether the allegations of abuse have been proved under civil law by a preponderance of the evidence sufficient to overcome the presumption.

Once the temporary relief is granted, the accused will have a civil trial. At this trial the victim is the plaintiff and entitled to all the rights of a party. The state does not prosecute the case. Proof beyond a reasonable doubt is not required. The victim need prove only that it is more likely that the act of aggression occurred than that it did not. The difference is not mere semantics. It can often make the difference between success and failure in the prosecution of a case. The victim of abuse who is a vulnerable person should not be faced with the burden of proving guilt beyond a reasonable doubt in order to obtain relief. The criminal sanction, as we have seen, gives no remedy to the victim. A civil action can give the remedy of a permanent injunction requiring the abuser to stay away from the victim. Violation of such an order constitutes contempt of court which is punishable by an indeterminate order of imprisonment. A civil action can also awarded damages to the victim for all the injuries, losses, and pain and suffering. Shelters for abused women are now available in some communities where women and their children can find sanctuary when they have no money, no family, and no lawyer. A civil action to remove the abuser from the home and to compel him to support his family is certainly better for the victims than requiring them to flee to a temporary shelter which is provided as an act of charity. Few communities have shelters for child victims of abuse where small children and infants may be placed temporarily before a court order is issued. If friends, relatives, or neighbors could have taken Alfie to a shelter when they heard his screams, he might be alive today. Child-abuse reporting laws grant immunity from suit for libel, slander, and all actions by the alleged abuser for one who reports suspected abuse in good faith. Similar immunity should be granted by statute to one who physically removes a child from danger and places him or her in an approved shelter.

Adequate protection for the victims of intra-family crime requires community involvement, resources, and changes in the law. Criminal prosecutions should be brought in serious cases. But the criminal sanction should not be the primary legal remedy in most cases. When the family abuser is convicted of crime, the sentence imposed should reflect the gravity of the offense. It is time for criminal courts to declare by their sentences that open season on beating wives and children is over.

CHAPTER XIII

WHITE-COLLAR CRIME

The law, in its majestic impartiality,
forbids the rich, as well as the poor,
to sleep under bridges.
—Anatole France

Crimes committed by wealthy, educated people are popularly called
white-collar crimes or economic crimes. Offenses by the poor are
usually called street crimes. These are loose definitions. Some draw the
distinction between violent and nonviolent offenses. But not all street
crimes are violent. Burglary is a street crime. It is nonviolent unless the
burglar is surprised by someone on the premises. Not all burglaries,
however, are common street crimes. Thefts of rare and valuable paintings are generally committed, or at least masterminded, by educated
people. A good definition of white-collar crime is that of Edward Sutherland, who writes that "White-collar crimes are committed by a person
of respectability and high social status in the course of his occupation."[1]
The United States Department of Justice defines white-collar crime as
an offense which is nonviolent and involves deceit, corruption, or breach
of trust. This definition would include such offenses as welfare cheating,
numbers writing, voter fraud, consumer frauds committed by small
businesses, and shakedowns and kickbacks by public employees. These
offenders are not of high social status. Such crimes are generally tried

in state courts. Multimillion-dollar frauds and breaches of trust by public officials are usually prosecuted in the federal courts. Most of the federal defendants are wealthy; they are people in administrative or professional positions. If we use Sutherland's definition, it is apparent that the law treats white-collar criminals very differently from street criminals.

The typical white-collar criminal is a white, middle-aged, and well-educated business or professional man. He is unlikely to go to jail, regardless of the extent of his crime. He may have embezzled more than a million dollars, but he will be placed on probation. The typical street criminal is young, non-white, male, poor, and uneducated. His robbery or burglary may yield only ten dollars, but he is likely to be sentenced to jail. This difference in treatment cannot be because street crimes are socially more serious than white-collar crimes. The contrary is true.

There are few, if any, hard facts about white-collar crime. We simply do not know the extent of such offenses. They are cleverly designed and carefully concealed. The white-collar crime rate rises in proportion to the efforts and funds made available to uncover and prosecute such wrongdoing. The American Bar Association reports: "Little data in the area of economic crime have been collected by the federal government; the data which have been gathered are of questionable validity. . . ."[2] Federal Judge Carl A. Muecke claims that 80 percent of the offenders are not caught. There is no question that it is difficult to unravel clever fraudulent schemes. It takes time and money. Most prosecutors' offices are barely able to cope with street crime. Nonetheless, prosecutions for white-collar crime rose 15 percent in 1975 and have continued to rise.

Economic crimes have a very great generally unrecognized impact on society. Crimes against business cost $30 billion to $40 billion a year according to a study by the American Management Association.[3] These costs are passed on to the consumers, the general public. This figure does not include crimes by business, public officials, and professionals. The United States Chamber of Commerce estimated in 1974 that white-collar crime directly costs the United States over $41 billion a year. This is two hundred times the amount of money stolen by all the bank robbers during that year. According to the General Accounting Office, white-collar crime costs the American public at least $200 billion a year, while street crimes involving property cost $4 billion per year. Representative John Conyers of Michigan reports that the United States Department of Justice devotes only 5.1 percent of its resources to combat this type of crime.[4] The FBI is now devoting more time and resources to economic crimes. Most state and local prosecutors have fraud divisions to deal with economic crimes. However, the greater number of their cases involve small business frauds on consumers and crimes against corporations committed by corporate employees. The uncovering and investigation of these crimes is generally done by the corporation. Rarely does a local prosecutor uncover crimes by corporate officials.

It is apparent that the extent of economic crimes is unknown. If one includes such disasters as the malfunctioning of the Three Mile Island nuclear plant, the nuclear fallout in Utah, and the deformities resulting from thalidomide and other drugs, the costs of economic crime are truly astronomical. Attorneys for Karen Silkwood, former employee of the McGee Corporation, contend that she was contaminated by plutonium. Testimony by former employees revealed allegedly forged health and safety documents.[5] If true, the corporation and its officials and employees involved in such acts would be liable to criminal prosecution. No one knows how many people may have been harmed by plutonium. Reporters and lawyers for injured people are just beginning to uncover similar serious violations of law committed by many corporations. The extent of harm caused by these offenses is incalculable. No one knows if any of these individuals or corporations responsible for contamination and disasters will ever be prosecuted. Careful investigation of these shocking accidents may well reveal willful and deliberate violations of law in order to cut costs and increase profits. While civil actions have been brought to recover damages for injuries resulting from such conditions, few, if any, criminal prosecutions have been instituted.

If one looks at only the conventional types of white-collar fraud and the treatment of these offenders by the criminal justice system there is a clear message: white-collar crime does pay. These are but a few of the many prosecutions brought against lawyers, doctors, brokers, and public officials for typical white-collar crimes. These cases and the sentences imposed were widely reported in all the media.

Joel Dolkart, an attorney, was convicted of stealing $2,500,000 through a calculated series of thefts and forgeries on a large scale. He was sentenced to five years' probation. The court explained, ". . . defendant's crime seems not to have subjected anyone to severe deprivation, or perhaps any deprivation." On the usual point scale of crimes, the sentence was justified. Dolkart had no prior record. He was disbarred and was presumably incapacitated from committing more similar crimes. He cooperated with the authorities. Prison, the court apparently concluded, would accomplish no useful purpose. But Dolkart kept the fruits of his crime.[6] Eugene Hollander, a nursing-home operator, was convicted of inflating medicare reimbursement claims by more than $100,000. He was sentenced to a $10,000 fine, a suspended five-year prison term, and ordered to spend his nights for six months in the correctional center. He is free during the day and weekends.[7] William Kooy pled guilty to theft of $170,000 in a classic white-collar scheme and was placed on probation.[8] Dr. Abraham Chaplan, a psychiatrist convicted of stealing almost $500,000 in medicaid payments, was sentenced to probation. This sentence was justified on the grounds that it would be "unfair to Chaplan" to senténce him to jail when Attorney Dolkart was given probation.[9]

Jerome Deutsch and Frank Mills were involved in a $530,000 kickback scheme. Deutsch was fined $10,000 and Mills $7,500. Neither jail sentence nor restitution was imposed. In a prosecution of a number of people known as the Projansky case, thirteen defendants pled guilty or were convicted of a $4,000,000 stock fraud. Of the thirteen, eight received no prison terms. The maximum sentence was one year.

A Wall Street broker was involved in a securities fraud involving $3,000,000 of excess credits upon which the broker received commissions of at least $100,000. He was sentenced to pay a fine of $6,000. Thomas F. Clendenin, an investment counsellor, was sentenced to a year and a day for defrauding his clients of some $2 million. The prosecutors staged a "sit-in" in the courtroom of Judge Howard F. Corcoran to protest the light sentence.

The Watergate criminals served minimal prison time. Despite the bluster and threats of "maximum John" Sirica, all of them emerged with their ill-gotten gains intact. Gordon Liddy, a relatively minor figure, was fined $40,000. This was the maximum fine imposed on any of the Watergate felons, including former Attorney General John Mitchell, a wealthy man. Only three other fines were in excess of $10,000: Ashland Oil, Inc., $25,000; Associated Milk Producers, $35,000; and American Ship Building, $20,000.[10] Obviously, these individuals and corporations could have paid much larger fines. Many of the Watergate felons like President Nixon, an unindicted conspirator, not only kept their illegal money but have parleyed their crimes into further profits through books, TV appearances, and financially successful lectures.

The media, the American Bar Association, and many concerned citizens are demanding that white-collar criminals be "punished." Federal judge Otto P. Skopil, Jr., observed that white-collar crime pays and "will continue to do so as long as judges endorse it through their sentencing policy."[11]

The American Bar Association report substantiates the public perception that white-collar crime does pay, that the poor and non-white will go to prison for small crimes while the rich who steal millions will get probation. In 1976, 91 percent of those convicted in federal court for bank robbery went to prison. Only 17 percent of those who were sentenced for embezzlement received a prison sentence. The committee recommends "that a great emphasis be placed on punishing economic crime offenders following their conviction."

In any consideration of the reasons for imposing criminal penalties— rehabilitation, seriousness of offense, the harm done, deterrence, justice as fairness, or the credibility of the law—certainly white-collar criminals should receive very heavy penalties. As we have seen, the law is predicated on the assumption that the wrongdoer is responsible and that he has a choice between obeying the law or violating it. The irrational criminal may well know that what he does is wrong, but he lacks this sense of responsibility. The family abuser also undoubtedly knows that what he is doing is senseless, but he does not perceive it as a crime. Such people may be unable to control themselves.

White-collar criminals, unlike these other offenders, do make a conscious choice to disobey the law. They act with forethought and deliberation. If the criminal justice system applied to theft, embezzlement, perjury, and breach of public trust, the standards of gravity and responsibility which are applied in homicide cases, the white-collar criminal would be guilty of the most serious grade of felony and receive the most severe penalty. Murder in the first degree is unlawful, willful, deliberate, and premeditated killing with malice aforethought. Every white-collar crime is also unlawful, willful, deliberate, premeditated, and committed with malice aforethought. There is no provocation, no misperception of self-defense, no acting in hot blood or passion—circumstances which reduce a homicide from murder in the first degree to a lesser offense.

Most judges when imposing sentence take into account the age, intelligence, education, and emotional problems of the defendant as mitigating circumstances. One looks in vain for any mitigating circumstances to justify tempering the severity of a sentence for privileged, educated people who willfully and deliberately cheat and betray the public. The usual plea in mitigation is "good character." With rare exceptions, the white-collar criminal has no prior record. This does not mean he has not committed other crimes. He has simply never been caught. Scores of prominent public figures come to court and testify as to the good moral character of a man who admits stealing, lying, and cheating for no reason other than money. One can only wonder at the moral character of the witnesses.

It is not only politicians and lawyers who commit these crimes. What possible excuse can there be for the doctors, psychiatrists, and dentists employed at Riker's Island prison who were charged with claiming pay for work not done and otherwise falsifying accounts? The only reason for such conduct was pure greed. Forty-eight of the 54 medical professionals employed at that prison were found to have engaged in such practices.[12]

Professors and scientists have also been found to falsify research, lie about outside employment, and commit serious breaches of trust in violation of the criminal law. The number of students at Ivy League universities who cheat is alarming. These are among America's brightest and best young people, the most privileged of all. Judges and other public officials have also been convicted of crimes, which were, in essence, lying, stealing, or betraying the public trust for money.

One must ask why these people are treated so much more leniently than ordinary thieves, cheats, and liars. One reason is, perhaps, the common assumption that prison is *the* punishment to be imposed. Prosecutor Monaco of Chicago says, "I think white-collar crime is one of the few crimes that can be deterred through prison." There are, of course, no statistics to prove the truth or falsity of this belief. Prison sentences are imposed so rarely and for such short periods that there is no basis for the belief, except the negative one that present sentencing to probation is, in fact, a green light, a go-ahead signal to other potential white-collar criminals. No one knows whether or not mandatory prison sentences would have a substantial deterrent effect. For such offenders there is always the possibility, indeed the probability, of a pardon or a deal with the prosecutor for a guilty plea to a lesser charge.

There is little serious discussion of sentencing options other than prison or probation with perhaps some form of "public service" for white-collar criminals. The press and many prosecutors demand long prison sentences. Judges on occasion yield to these demands, particularly when the offender is a public official involved with organized crime. Although there is no difference in moral culpability, illegality, or harm done by such offenders and other white-collar criminals, there seems to be a subconscious feeling that such a person is *really* a criminal, whereas the doctor or lawyer who steals, the professor who falsifies data, and the public official who lies under oath are not members of "the criminal class."

Discussions of sentencing of white-collar offenders focus primarily on the effect the sentence will have on the defendant and on other potential white-collar criminals. While some people address the question of disparities between sentences for street crimes and for white-collar crimes, they rarely consider the effect that these extraordinarily lenient sentences have on the average citizen and the problems they create in sentencing poor and disadvantaged offenders who are sentenced more severely than white-collar criminals.

After reading the remarks of judges and prosecutors and books, reports, and articles on the subject, I find that the controversy over sentencing of white-collar criminals simply replicates the arguments over sentencing in general. Little recognition is given either to the mentality of the offender or to the harm done. The victim, which is ultimately the public, is ignored.

The first argument advanced favoring prison sentences for white-collar offenders is disparity. Authorities assert that sentencing is disparate, that the poor and non-white are more severely punished than wealthy white offenders. Although federal prosecutor Silbert finds little disparity, United States Deputy Attorney General Tyler, a former judge, says that white-collar sentences are too lenient in comparison with sentences imposed on blacks and Hispanics. New York prosecutor Whitney North Seymour, Jr., states, "There's a traditional difference in sentences for different types of crime and it tends to discriminate against the uneducated, unloved, social reject—The guy who steals packages from the back of the truck is going to get four years and the guy who steals $45,000 is going to get three months."[13] There is no question that street criminals are more likely to be sentenced to prison than white-collar criminals and that they will serve longer sentences.

They also go to different prisons which are separate and grossly unequal. Street criminals will go to state or local prisons that are, by and large, miserable and brutal places. A cartoon by Flanagan, "Like, Now," reveals the public perception of classes of criminals. At a national conference on prisons the speaker says, "Obviously if we're going to lower the crime rate in our prisons, we're going to have to put a better class of people in there." Federal Judge Jack B. Weinstein told Eugene Hollander, "I want you to serve time in the Correctional Center—these are dismal surroundings." Compare this with the description of Allenwood Prison Camp where most federal white-collar offenders are sent. The Berrigans, the Hollywood Ten, the Watergate felons, and similar offenders spent brief terms at Allenwood. Thomas F. Clendenin said of Allenwood federal prison where he served a brief sentence, "This is a piece of cake." Others agree that if you must do time, Allenwood is the place to do it.

The second argument might be considered desert. It is assumed that street criminals must go to prison for their crimes but that white-collar criminals do not have to be imprisoned to be punished. Some judges believe that it is enough of a penalty that an offender who is a lawyer is disbarred or a public official loses his office. Some convicted lawyers, however, are not even disbarred. I have never heard of a doctor losing his license to practice medicine because he has been convicted of cheating on medicare or medicaid payments. Some convicted public officials are re-elected to public office. It is a common belief that all the lawyers, doctors, businessmen, and stockbrokers who commit crimes are disgraced.

I find little validity in the "disgrace" theory as to any offender. Most poor non-white offenders have prior records. So do their friends and associates. They feel little opprobrium because of the fact of conviction. Neither do most white-collar criminals. Few, if any, of them, are asked to resign from their clubs. They are not shunned socially or politically. Most of them continue their financial activities successfully. The fact is that most of these offenders do not consider themselves criminals. President Nixon and the Watergate felons are a conspicuous example of the fact that the public does not look on white-collar criminals with scorn or opprobrium. Even after a prison term these felons are in demand on talk shows and college lecture circuits. They make a financial success of their crimes and they become public celebrities. Richard Helms, former director of the CIA, who was convicted, boldly stated to the press: "I do not feel disgraced at all." He declared that his conviction for perjury was a "badge of honor." Helms was acclaimed by CIA employees.[14] Merely to convict white-collar felons without imposing a real penalty is in effect to condone their illegal conduct.

Deterrence is the third principal argument. There are those who claim that prison is the "ultimate penalty," that fear of prison will deter the white-collar criminal. Prison has not deterred street criminals. There is little likelihood that it will deter white-collar criminals. In fact, there is solid evidence that corporate crime is not deterred by criminal prosecution. The Environmental Protection Agency has learned that many companies prefer to fight anti-pollution regulations rather than to comply with them because it is cheaper to pay the fines than to install control devices. EPA proposes that the fines equal the cost of compliance.[15] This still gives corporations the option of fighting or complying with no real penalty for failure to comply.

Judges faced with the in or out alternative are obviously dissatisfied with these two options. The prisons are overcrowded. Unless the white-collar felon is sent to Allenwood, a prison sentence may certainly not be good for him. A middle-aged, middle-class, sedentary white man is certainly at risk if he is sent to a prison where most of the inmates are strong, young, black men hostile to the world which the white-collar felon represents. If the white-collar prisoner is not physically molested, he is probably going to have to buy his security from the inmates. He will find himself engaged in illegal enterprises within the prison, providing small luxuries or perhaps drugs for the other inmates. Those who survive even a year or two in state prisons or local jails return aged at least ten years.

Middle-aged and middle-class judges—both black and white—are understandably reluctant to send people like themselves to prisons where they know what is likely to happen to them. Sentencing commissions and guidelines recognize the difference between violent and nonviolent crimes although the justice as fairness theory requires that all felons of the same class of crime—whether violent or nonviolent—receive the same prison sentence. Even though white-collar crime is nonviolent, surely the taking by deceit of a million dollars deserves as much, if not more, of a penalty than a burglary or robbery of eleven dollars. Neither prison nor probation is a satisfactory penalty. Prison may be undesirable and dangerous for the white-collar offender. But probation, with nothing more, erodes the credibility of the law and offends any notion of retribution or that people should atone for their wrongdoings.

Alternative sentences, well intentioned though they are, in my opinion do not satisfy any of the goals of the criminal justice system. They promote, rather than decrease, disparities in sentencing. Judges should not have to devise penalties to fit the crime. The sentence should not depend upon the personal beliefs or imagination of the judge. The judiciary is not a position where individual innovation is desirable. Penalties, whatever they may be, should be established by the legislature and the judge should, within these limits, impose the precise penalty taking into account the crime, the criminal, the harm done, and the victim.

If we look at the offenses that white-collar criminals commit, it is clear that the primary motivation is greed. There is also a desire for power which money brings. Some politicians do favors not for money or votes but for the satisfaction of having the public recognize their power. I recall a powerful local politician-lawyer who was frequently asked by clients and friends to "fix" their parking tickets. He never refused. In those days the fine was only five dollars. He paid these fines himself. It was a small price for the gratitude and admiration he received. Others, of course, use power to put compliant people in office, to get legislation favorable to their interests passed, and other acts which are contrary to the public interest.

In some cases, white-collar criminals also enjoy the thrill of the enterprise. Like bored street criminals, they look for excitement in crime. Most white-collar offenders are solid citizens. They are good family men. The majority of the anti-trust electric company violators who were imprisoned in 1960 were prominent church members before their convictions and jail sentences and after their release from prison. Like federal judges Watson and Johnson who were convicted in the 1930s for bribery and corruption, their private lives were unimpeachable and probably rather dull. They lived in nice suburban homes, commuted to work every day in pin-stripe suits, and carried briefcases. None of them was in need. Crime may have added a fillip of excitement to their otherwise exemplary lives.

White-collar offenders act cautiously with deliberation and careful forethought. They plot and plan their crimes and their coverups. These offenders have a true cost/benefit calculus. Such cautious people probably could be deterred from committing these crimes if they were convinced that criminal conduct was unprofitable. There is a paucity of research on the deterrent capabilities of criminal sentences. Most studies have involved either of the extremes of the criminal spectrum: the death penalty and penalties for minor misdemeanors such as parking violations. It is reasonably clear that the death penalty, which is imposed only for murder or habitual criminal conduct, has not been proved to be a deterrent to other homicides. It is also reasonably clear that people will not park illegally if the fine is substantially greater than the cost of parking in a lot.[16]

Illegal parking is certainly not comparable to breach of public trust, illegal stock transactions, bribery, corruption, and other typical white-collar crimes with respect to either the harm done or the moral turpitude of the offender. There is a similarity, however, in the fact that both white-collar crimes and parking violations are deliberate, rational decisions in which emotions play no part. Nor do urgency or need substantially influence the decision to violate such laws. Occasionally a person will park in a no-parking place because he must catch a plane, go to a hospital, or do some other necessitous act and he has no time to find a parking lot. Such cases probably constitute a negligible percentage of violations. Likewise, very few drivers park illegally because they do not have money to pay for a parking lot. Most white-collar criminals are not desperately in need of money. They and their families do not face eviction or starvation. The etiology of the decision to embark on a course of embezzlement or manipulating stock deals or giving or accepting bribes may be varied. But one factor is present in almost every decision to engage in this kind of illegal activity: the desire for money.

It would seem to be an obvious conclusion that the way to prevent or deter white-collar crime is to make it so unprofitable that the risks outweigh the possibilities of gain. I do not believe that criminal sanctions can change the moral attitudes of people who believe that the end justifies the means and who find no repugnance to illegal acts or unconscionable deals. The rehabilitation of such people is beyond the capacity of the criminal justice system. The most that judges can hope to accomplish in sentencing such offenders is to make sure that their crimes do not pay. To impose that kind of sentence is far easier than meeting the needs for rehabilitation of the violent offender, the psychiatric problems of a wife beater, or the training and educating of young street criminals.

A monetary penalty—fines or restitution—is the simplest penalty to impose. It is the cheapest penalty for society to enforce. Expensive prisons are not required. Neither are costly programs of treatment or rehabilitation. The probation department does not have to undertake the difficult task of hunting probationers who have no office, no telephone, and no fixed residence. A probation officer simply has to keep a record and see that the white-collar convict pays the prescribed amount on time.

For a sentence which imposes a monetary penalty to constitute punishment, to have deterrent capacity, to be what the offender deserves, or to make the law credible, it must exceed by a substantial amount the illegal gains. The risk of loss must outweigh the likelihood of gain. Every sentence imposed on a white-collar offender should at least require forfeiture of all illegally acquired money, stock, and other items of value. In addition, I suggest a mandatory fine of treble the amount of the illegal gains.[17] The prospective criminal would know in advance that if convicted he would lose four times the amount of his gain. With odds like that, there would not be nearly so many players in the games of illegal stock deals, influence peddling, and other white-collar crimes. This, in my view, would promote deterrence and crime prevention. It would also give an objective measure for penalties. Everyone who gained $100,000 by any illegal means would be subject to a penalty of $300,000 and forfeiture of the $100,000. Simple arithmetic would give equal penalties for all white-collar offenders, both wealthy influence peddlers and poor users of stolen credit cards. Such penalties would meet the standards of the justice as fairness theory.

A study of sentences of white-collar criminals by Edward Browder, who is serving a twenty-five-year sentence for a white-collar crime which he claims cost his victims only $15,000, reveals that thirty-seven convicted defendants who stole or mismanaged an average of more than $21 million each received only small fines, suspended sentences, or probation. Others involved in crimes of millions received sentences of less than three years. Certainly such sentences are utterly insignificant when compared with the harm done.

Judges, who, generally speaking, are sensible people, recognize that ten years in prison will be no more efficacious, rehabilitative, or deterrent than three years. The additional seven years will simply cost the taxpayers that much more money. Long prison terms for white-collar offenders may satisfy public outrage but they serve no useful social purpose.

Treble civil damages are imposed by statute for many violations of state and federal laws. The most common use of treble damages is in anti-trust cases. The damages are paid to the competitors who suffered from the illegal price fixing. There is no reason why this well-established and effective remedy cannot be applied as a criminal penalty.

Consumers are frequently overcharged by business enterprises in violation of usury statutes and other laws. Although the amount of overcharge to the individual is small, in the aggregate it may be very substantial and highly profitable to the business. These overcharges are usually uncovered not by law enforcement agencies but by clever, enterprising lawyers who bring class actions to recover the hundreds of thousands of dollars illegally mulcted from the public. Of course, the individual who was overcharged fifty cents or five dollars will rarely know about the fact or bother to claim his refund. It would be impossible in the overwhelming majority of such illegal charges, stock frauds, and other swindles to locate and repay the individuals who were cheated. In the typical class action the plaintiff's lawyer recovers a substantial fee; those members of the class who can be located recover small sums. The offending corporation must disgorge the sums it received illegally. These cases are really criminal prosecutions brought in the form of a private civil suit. They do perform a useful monitoring of business at no cost to the government.

The class actions tried before me are no different from any other class actions brought in state and federal courts. In these cases, the defendant corporations overcharged their customers in violation of law. The amount of overcharge to each customer was small. A large proportion of the customers could not be located and given the refunds to which they were entitled. It was suggested by counsel that I designate some charity to receive this money. Charity, like motherhood, is always looked upon with favor. But which charity should receive a windfall and why? Does this do any good for the community? It appears that the $.5 million which the Olin Corporation was sentenced to contribute to charity in New Haven did little good and created many problems regarding the selection of the recipients.

There is an appropriate and well-established way to deal with moneys of this kind. Under the old English common law doctrine of bona vacantia—goods belonging to no one—such property escheated to the King. In the United States, such property escheats to the state. In civil class action suits, I order that these overcharges which cannot be refunded to the individuals be paid to the state.

A similar policy should certainly apply with respect to crimes. Every crime is an offense against the state or the federal government as well as an injury to the individuals affected. If restitution cannot be made to the individual, it should be made to the government for the benefit of all crime victims.

Although many judges and prosecutors urge long, stiff prison sentences for white-collar criminals, others propose alternative service types of sentences. Offenders are placed on probation and required to donate a certain period of time to charitable institutions. United States District Judge Carl A. Muecke of Phoenix, Arizona, sentenced five dairy executives convicted of price fixing to serve the poor in charity dining halls in lieu of prison and ordered the corporations to contribute milk in lieu of fines. Federal Judge Robert Zampano in New Haven, in March, 1978, ordered the Olin Corporation to pay five hundred thousand dollars in reparation to the people of New Haven in lieu of other sentence for illegal arms sales to South Africa. Other judges have ordered white-collar offenders to make speeches about the evils of price fixing, to hire and train ex-convicts, and to engage in other types of charitable service in the community. A college president was sentenced to give lectures. Executives of a meat packing firm were sentenced to provide services to a youth training program. The idea is spreading. James M. H. Gregg, acting Law Enforcement Assistant Administration administrator, believes the programs are important because fines and jail terms are often not in the best interest of society.[18] I believe that lectures by a convicted felon are neither a punishment to the offender nor a benefit to the audience. On the contrary, the speaker is the embodiment of the fact that crime does pay. The message is certainly not a desirable one.

Columnist Art Buchwald has noted the use of alternative sentences in white-collar crime. He reports that two contractors were found guilty of giving bribes to the General Services Administration. The prosecutors maintained that one defendant cheated the government out of $200,-000. The judge fined each of them $5,000 and put them on probation for three years with the requirement that they do two hundred hours of unspecified community service.

Buchwald suggests that the appropriate public service for these offenders would be to teach people in the slums how to bilk the government out of $1.2 million and wind up with nothing more than a $5,000 fine. He advocates a course for the poor would-be criminal that covers drawing up phony contracts, getting paid for work that was never done, handing in invoices for overruns that do not exist, mastering methods of disguising faulty work which does not meet government specifications, and opening a secret Swiss bank account. If the students find the subjects difficult, Buchwald proposes a special class in remedial cheating. The final lesson would be devoted to beating the rap if one is caught, including guilty pleas for light sentences as well as negotiating for immunity. The purpose of the course would be to teach the poor that the criminal justice system is kinder to those who steal large sums than those who only cheat on welfare and food stamps.

Another popular scheme to avoid prison sentences is diversion. Ostensibly, diversion is designed to protect poor, young offenders who have committed less serious crimes from what is considered the undesirable effects of contact with the criminal justice system. Diversion requires the accused to give up his right to a speedy trial in return for an agreement that the charges will be dropped if he is not rearrested within a specified period. Unlike a trial which is, except in rare instances, a public hearing and a matter of record and after which the accused is publicly sentenced and has a right of appeal, diversion is a procedure initiated by the prosecution in private consultation with counsel. Diversion operates unequally and unfairly because its benefits are denied to suspects who have a prison record even though it is granted to others accused of the same offenses. Those who are poor, young, non-white and from high crime areas are most likely to have prison records, including juvenile records. They are denied diversion. Those who are white and middle-class rarely have a criminal record. They are able to avoid trial, conviction, and punishment by this device. Diversion is an astonishing innovation which has not been studied by scholars or reviewed by the United States Supreme Court. It does not meet the goals of justice as fairness or rehabilitation. It makes no provision for redress to the victims of crime.

I do not favor prison sentences for those who do not pose a threat of physical danger to the community. Nor do I believe that alternative or creative sentences or diversion accomplish any of the goals of a fair or just criminal system. Such treatment of offenders is instead a blazing signal that the courts do not deal equally with the rich and poor, and that for the rich crime does pay. It has been often said that the wallet is the tenderest part of the anatomy. The goals of deterrence, fairness, and justice can better be achieved by imposing substantial fines and orders of restitution on white-collar offenders.

CHAPTER XIV

STREET CRIME

A man who has never gone to school
may steal from a freight car, but
if he has a university education,
he may steal the whole railroad.
—Theodore Roosevelt

Street crime is what most people mean when they talk about crime. The mugger, the robber, the rapist, the man with a knife or gun is the person they fear.[1] Most street criminals act impulsively, one might say almost accidentally. It is more difficult to find means to deter those who act impulsively than those who consider the risks and benefits of their conduct. Although street criminals are impulsive, they are not irrational; there is some hope of dealing with many of them in a sensible and humane fashion that may deter crime and provide for the victim.

Within the broad category of street criminals, there are many subclassifications. Not all street offenders present the same dangers. Not all street offenders should receive the same type of penalties. Shoplifting is probably the least dangerous kind of offense. Eighty-five percent of shoplifters are women and teenage girls. They rarely carry weapons; they seldom resist arrest. In most cases they are not a physical danger to the public. Shoplifting is not, however, a negligible crime. It costs American retailers about $2 million a year. In addition, stores spend tremendous sums on security. These costs, of course, are passed on to the consumers. Neither imprisonment nor probation is a suitable or useful penalty for shoplifters or for many other street criminals.

Probation is usually a meaningless routine of reporting to the probation officer, who provides little, if any, help or guidance to the offender. Sometimes probation itself is dangerous and deleterious to the probationer. Lorraine was convicted of drug sales. She, like most women convicted of this offense, was the courier for her boyfriend who used her so that he could carry on his lucrative business without fear of arrest. Lorraine is an attractive woman in her early thirties. She was assigned by the probation department to Jack, a male probation officer. After a few months Jack called to tell me that Lorraine refused to come to her regular meetings with him which are required under the rules of the probation department. He wanted me to issue an order for her arrest. Lorraine had not, so far as either of us knew, been involved in any further illegal activities. She had a new job and a new apartment by herself. She had left the drug-pusher boyfriend. I was very reluctant to disrupt Lorraine's efforts to establish a new life with an arrest. She might lose her job. The landlady might make things difficult for her. I told Jack to write Lorraine and tell her she must keep her appointments with him. A few days later I received a frantic call from Lorraine. I was on the bench presiding over a trial when I got this message: "Lorraine N. is on the phone. She says she will commit suicide if she can't talk to you." Lorraine told me that Jack, the probation officer, insisted on having sex with her at every meeting. Lorraine said, "Judge, I wouldn't bother you if it was just normal sex. I could put up with that if I have to. But I just can't do the kinky things he wants. I'll kill myself rather than see him again."

One could never prove the truth of Lorraine's allegations. Jack had been a probation officer for years and was highly regarded by his superiors. Perhaps she was lying, but I doubted it. If the charges were true, Jack would lose his job and his pension. Another probation officer would be very hard on Lorraine if her charges were known. I sent Jack a letter ordering that Lorraine report regularly by phone. She completed her two years of probation without further incident.

Paul also complained about his probation officer. Paul was a rarity, a very rich young man on probation for burglary. Paul told me that his probation officer demanded one hundred dollars a week or he would charge Paul with a new offense, and that he paid regularly until his period of probation was terminated.

I believe that a fine rather than probation or prison is the appropriate penalty for most shoplifters. They, like white-collar criminals, are motivated by greed. Therefore, payment in money for an offense which is committed for money is fitting. A fine can be scaled to reflect the magnitude of the theft and the ability of the offender to pay. Some shoplifting cases involve trinkets and articles of cheap clothing worth only a couple of dollars. Others involve items worth many thousands of dollars. Some shoplifters are indigent; others are wealthy. In many cases of shoplifting the law operates with benign mercy on the rich and harsh punitiveness on the poor. If the penalties are limited to prison and probation they will be either very punitive or merely nominal. Neither is proportionate to the offense.

Marian is a wealthy middle-aged suburban matron, the wife of a doctor. She regularly shoplifts. She steals from grocery stores, department stores, and specialty shops. Usually the goods are recovered and the charges dropped. It is assumed that Marian is a kleptomaniac, that she is "sick." Janine is thirty years old. She is poor and black. She, too, regularly steals from grocery stores and specialty shops. It is assumed that she is a criminal who should be imprisoned because she has been arrested and placed on probation four or five times. No one knows how many times Marian and Janine have actually stolen. Should either Marian or Janine be sentenced to prison for these thefts?

Prison is a harrowing experience for most inmates. It is particularly hard on women who have young children. Most women are not accused of crimes of violence, the kinds of offenses which endanger the safety of others. Besides shoplifting, the more common crimes committed by women are various petty frauds—stolen credit cards, cheating on medicare and welfare. Fraud is usually considered a white-collar offense. But many frauds are really nonviolent street crimes. The wealthy, white offender who commits a big fraud in which he realizes hundreds of thousands of dollars rarely goes to jail. As we have seen, he will be sentenced to pay a nominal fine, be placed on probation, and perhaps ordered to do some "public service." The poor person who commits a fraud which results in a gain of a few hundred dollars is a very likely to be sentenced to prison. Even semiliterates read the newspaper headlines or hear the news on TV. They are well aware of the sentences imposed on big offenders and those imposed on their acquaintances and relatives. This pattern of disparity in sentencing seriously erodes the credibility of the law and the claims of equal justice.

One morning I had to sentence Willie Mae, a young black woman who had deliberately cheated the welfare department of approximately $1,300. This case was listed as a major felony and vigorously prosecuted by the frauds division. The case took more than three days to try. The prosecutor, a young, earnest black lawyer, in his remarks at sentencing, indicated that his office viewed this case as a very serious offense and urged a stiff penalty. I do not permit the prosecutor to make a recommendation of sentence, but he made it clear that his office wanted a prison term. The pre-sentence investigator reported that the accused had two young children. Yet the sentence recommendation portion of the report contained this statement: "There are no reasons for not imposing the appropriate penalty." Willie Mae had two prior convictions for shoplifting. The sentencing guideline gave a presumptive sentence of three to six months in jail. That very day the headlines in the morning paper reported that a prominent white male politician, who pled guilty to taking illegally over $100,000 of public funds, was sentenced to three years' probation. Three white employees of the welfare department, who had testified against the defendant, were in court eagerly awaiting the sentence. The defendant was vigorously represented by a young white attorney.

Despite the accident of race of the two attorneys, it was difficult not to see this case as a punitive action by the dominant white society against a poor black disadvantaged woman. There was no question that Willie Mae was guilty of the crime. She had no character witnesses although the evidence disclosed that she was a good mother, kept her house clean, and did not use drugs or alcohol. She was not a prostitute or sexually promiscuous. To the dismay of the prosecutor and the welfare department, I placed her on probation and made a condition of the probation restitution of the $1,300, plus a $50 fine. With the help of the probation department Willie Mae did get a job and made restitution over a period of eighteen months. At sentencing, I felt impelled to justify the sentence to her and the people in the courtroom.

"I know other people have stolen much more money than you and have not gone to jail," I said. "That does not make stealing right or acceptable. You, too, are a taxpayer. You are cheating all the people of this state—rich and poor. I will not send you to jail because it would impose a hardship on your children, who are innocent of any crime. But I must insist that you repay the money and pay a small fine. The fine will not begin to reimburse the state for what it has cost to prosecute you. I, as a representative of the people charged with enforcing the law, cannot condone what you have done regardless of the sentences imposed in other cases."

To have sent Willie Mae to prison would not only have been hard on her but would have resulted in very great harm to her children. For small children, separation from their mother is terrifying and psychologically damaging. I know the institutions to which children are sent until they can be shifted to a foster mother, who might or might not be kind and loving. There is little supervision of foster homes. Will a harried foster mother who is herself on the brink of poverty have the strength or compassion to comfort a frightened child? It is very difficult for the children and their mother to re-establish a relationship after her release from prison. The dangers of a prison sentence for a mother like Willie Mae are great. The benefits are purely hypothetical. Will she have greater respect for the law if she serves a prison term? Will any of the people who may happen to learn of her probationary sentence have any less respect for law? I believe that the answer to both of these questions is no.

The National Commission on Children in Need of Parents reports that the nation's system of foster care is an "unconscionable failure." What conscientious judge could condemn children to this system except in the most exigent circumstances? Certainly cheating the welfare department does not constitute such a circumstance. In some prisons mothers are permitted to have their infants with them. The press reports that Brenda Glass is serving an eighteen-to-twenty-year prison term for armed robbery at which eleven dollars was taken. Her infant is with her in prison. Her two other children are not.[2] A crime in which no one was injured and the amount involved is only eleven dollars should not, under any theory of sentencing, bring a prison sentence of such length. Certainly it is not intended to rehabilitate Brenda. By the time she is released, assuming that she survives and is not sexually abused or physically scarred, she will be a middle-aged woman. She will have lost her children. How can she possibly be reformed by such cruelty? Does a robbery of eleven dollars deserve such a penalty? Is it fair or just that those who steal millions surreptitiously receive nominal penalties, while those who steal a few dollars by means of a threat when no one is harmed receive a lengthy prison sentence? These cases should impel lawyers, legislators, and criminologists to look for better methods of sentencing and more humane penalties.

I believe that if a crime did not result in harm to the victim and if the offender presents no unreasonable risk of physical danger to the community then there is little justification for a prison sentence. Some other meaningful penalty should be imposed. In most such cases, a fine and an order of restitution or reparation is appropriate. Such penalty deprives the offender of something of value to him or her and in this sense constitutes a punishment. The amount can be made proportionate to the offense and, thus, roughly meet the requirement of desert. It is fair insofar as each person who has illegally acquired goods or money is fined according to the same scale—one that is some multiple of the amount illegally obtained. It is likely that fines are as rehabilitative as any other form of penalty.

Some nonviolent street crimes are not committed for money. Drug and alcohol abuse are the most common of these victimless crimes. Many legal scholars and criminologists have proposed the decriminalization of such crimes. Sex—normal and deviate—between or among consenting adults and vagrancy are other common victimless crimes. At present the principal penalties for these offenses, like all other crimes, are prison and probation. Most of these offenders are sentenced to probation and ordered to participate in drug or alcohol treatment programs. There are many costly programs and centers. Most of them are financed with public funds, many supplied by the federal Law Enforcement Assistance Administration. Some programs are operated in conjunction with hospitals or other medical facilities. Others are operated by lay people from the community. A number of these are staffed with former alcoholics and former drug addicts. Some use methadone; others rely on counselling and group therapy. No one really knows how effective any of these programs are. All that can reasonably be concluded is that prison is less likely to provide a cure for alcoholism or drug addiction than community treatment centers. It sounds humane and therapeutic to sentence an addict to treatment. But a judge who sees hundreds of people who have been through these programs without observable benefits and sees that many people running these programs seem to have few qualifications as therapists or counsellors has doubts. How effective is even the best "treatment" for an unwilling patient? Attending a clinic a few hours a day is certainly less of an infringement on liberty than a prison sentence. But a judge should at least have some reasonable belief that the program is helpful before ordering a person to spend eight or ten hours a week attending therapy sessions.

Tony is a junkie. He has been on heroin for years. He has also been in and out of prison at least half a dozen times. He was tried before me on several charges of purchases of small amounts of heroin from police

undercover agents. The prosecution admitted that Tony was not in the
business of selling drugs. He bought to feed his habit. Although many
addicts steal to feed their habit, Tony did not. He had a reasonably good
job and was able to get along. He was not on welfare.

The pre-sentence report recommended a prison term. The presumptive sentencing guideline also indicated prison. Tony had eight prior
convictions for drug purchases. He had been on probation twice and had
served six short jail sentences. Tony had never been arrested for a crime
of violence. He is a quiet, gentle person. I discussed the problem of
sentencing with him. "I know that if I put you on probation you'll be
buying drugs. At least for the time you're in prison you'll be off heroin."

He smiled at my ignorance. "Your honor, prison is just like the street.
There are always drugs for someone who wants them." Unfortunately,
that is true.

The sentencing choices for Tony are imprisonment or probation.
Probation for drug users is usually conditioned upon attendance at a
drug treatment center. These centers, like most businesses and welfare
offices, are open from nine to five, five days a week. If Tony attends a
drug center, he will have to quit his job and go on welfare. It is a matter
of pride with Tony that, except for his periods in jail, he has always been
self-supporting. Neither a drug treatment center nor prison will stop
Tony's use of heroin. He harms no one but himself. If I sentence him
to prison, he will continue to use drugs. If I place him on probation, he
will also continue to use drugs. All of us are engaged in a futile enterprise.
The state is trying to reform Tony, to make him stop using drugs. It is
another example of the confusion of sin and illegality.

Tony's crimes are illegal purchase and possession of drugs. It is clear
that Tony will not be cured of his addiction whether he is in or out of
prison. Nonetheless, Americans continue the futile pursuit of attempting to reform drug addicts and alcoholics through criminal sanctions. I
submit that decriminalization of victimless crimes such as drug abuse,
alcoholism, and illegal sex performed by consenting adults is desirable.
Purchase of drugs in limited amounts for personal use, not resale, should
be permitted.

Drug pushers and dealers are entirely different from users. They are
businessmen. They traffic in drugs the way others traffic in stocks or
grain futures. The profits are tremendous and untaxed. The risks for the
distributor—the rank above pusher—are not great. These people are
seldom arrested. Either the pushers do not know or will not reveal the

identities of the drug bosses. When drug traffickers are arrested, tried, and convicted, the penalties should be commensurate with the crime. At present the fines and prison sentences permitted by statute are much too low. A twenty-five thousand dollar fine is nominal for a dealer in heroin, cocaine, or methedrine. A "bag" of heroin is a little celophane packet about the size of a postage stamp. It is not pure heroin. It is mostly sugar. The street price for one bag may be as high as eighty dollars or more. If judges are to impose fair, just, and proportionate sentences on offenders, then the laws must be amended to increase the fines for many crimes which are now highly profitable.

Burglary is another crime which has an enormous range of variations, but the maximum penalties: the number of years in prison and the number of dollars' fine are the same for all burglars and all burglaries. In most jurisdictions the maximum fine is twenty-five thousand dollars. This is more money than some burglars will see in a lifetime. To others, it is simply small change. Some burglars, like white-collar criminals, plan their crimes very carefully. They go where they know there are valuables. They carefully arrange that the occupants of the premises will be out so that they may steal with impunity. They will not be seen. One clever burglar sent a victimized couple two tickets for a very popular musical with a card that read, "Enjoy the show. Best wishes. E." The recipients were delighted. Their joy vanished when they discovered that highly valued jewelry, silver, oriental rugs, and rare paintings had been taken while they were at the theater.

Another family returned from a dinner which had been mentioned in the society pages and found their furs, jewels, and silver missing. The well-dressed burglar had packed it in their luggage and calmly walked out the front door carrying two suitcases in full view of the neighbors. He had driven away in his car. He looked like a house guest. No one took the license number of the car.

These sophisticated burglars were never arrested. A judge sitting in a state criminal court will see few burglars like them, but many who are like Al and Morro. They are in their early twenties. Neither is married or employed. Each lives with his mother and other relatives in a housing project. They know the day that the welfare checks arrive. Mrs. L. has seven children. Her check is large. Most recipients cash their checks the day they are received. The evening of the day the welfare checks arrived, Al and Morro knocked on Mrs. L.'s door, pointed a gun at her, and announced, "Give us your money and we won't hurt you." Both robbers were wearing ski masks but Morro had forgotten to pull his down over his face. Two of Mrs. L.'s daughters were home at the time. They sat frozen in fear in the kitchen while their mother gave the burglars all the money she had. Al and Morro walked out Mrs. L.'s door and went to a corner steak store. A few minutes later the girls went to the same store to buy cigarettes. They immediately recognized the two robbers who were laughing and talking to the man behind the counter. The girls slipped outside and waited until the burglars left. Then they went back and asked the man in the store for the names and addresses of the two people who had just left the store. Within minutes the police arrested both Al and Morro.

Although burglaries are considered street crimes, it is obvious that the sophisticated burglar who sent the theatre tickets and the one who perused the society pages are really more like white-collar criminals. If such burglars are apprehended, the penalties imposed on them should be such stiff fines and orders of restitution that they will be convinced that crime does not pay. Al and Morro, who are both school dropouts and unemployed, are typical street criminals. They commit petty, stupid, and potentially dangerous crimes. In this case no one was hurt. But the possibility of serious injury or death is always present when a weapon is used.

The sentencing decision is much more difficult when the crime involves violence, injury, or the threat of violence. Unlike white-collar criminals who act coldly, with careful calculation and premeditation, most street criminals act impulsively. Certainly Al and Morro did not plan their crime very carefully or their subsequent actions. If they had, they probably would not have been caught.

Some crimes are committed so thoughtlessly and spontaneously that one might almost say that they happen accidentally. Jerry and Joe were walking the streets looking for something to do when they encountered Herman, who told them about an old woman who had won on the numbers that day. Immediately they decided to go to her home and steal the winnings. They did not know that this woman had a forty-year-old son living with her. When the boys climbed in an open second story window, the son beat them off with a chair. Jerry saw the man reach in his pocket for a gun. Before the man could shoot, Jerry stabbed him. Jerry claimed self-defense. He was convicted of burglary and aggravated assault. Jerry was not a cold-blooded criminal. He had no intention of hurting anyone. He and his friend habitually carried switchblade knives as most business and professional men carry fountain pens. Jerry thought he could get some money from an old woman who would not offer resistance. The stabbing, in his eyes, was an accident.

Lee also stabbed a man. In his case it was really a matter of mischance. Lee was walking home from a party with some friends when they encountered a group of young men from another turf. Lee heard someone shout "Thirty-fourth Street." Was this an identification? (Gangs are frequently named by streets), or a challenge? In the noise and confusion and darkness Lee felt something cold against his ribs. He pulled his knife. When the police arrived a man lay dead on the street with Lee's knife in his chest. Among those taken into the police station from the "Thirty-fourth Street" gang were several young men with guns. It was only a matter of chance as to whether Lee would be a victim or a defendant. Both Jerry and Lee were sentenced to prison even though neither one had an intent to stab or kill. Lee had no intent to commit any crime whatsoever. Most street crimes, like most white-collar crimes, are committed for money. Both types of offenders intend to steal, not to injure or kill. However, in the course of a robbery someone is often injured and, occasionally, killed. Although the motivation and intent of both offenders is the same, the harm done is drastically different. The white-collar criminal may steal millions, but he commits no violence and causes no physical injury; the street criminal, like Brenda, may steal only a few dollars.

Many victims of street crime are injured; so are many street criminals. Jeb was only nineteen years old when he held up a neighborhood shoe store. All he wanted was a few dollars to buy some wine. He walked up to the man behind the counter, who was standing next to the cash register. Jeb put his hand in his pocket menacingly; it looked as if he had a gun. In fact, he did not have a weapon. "This is a stickup," he muttered. "Gimme your cash." The terrified proprietor opened the cash register and gave Jeb all the money that he had. It was less than thirty dollars. Jeb scooped up the money, turned, and began to run out of the store. The owner took his gun from under the counter and fired one shot. It struck Jeb in the spine. He is permanently paralyzed from the chest down. I ordered him released from the prison ward of the hospital where he was guarded every moment of the day and night. Even if he could escape in his wheelchair with the help of a friend, to leave the hospital would almost certainly result in his death. The proprietor who shot Jeb had a license to have a gun in his store. The possession of handguns, both legal and illegal, is responsible for countless tragedies.

Morton also shot a man; this shooting was fatal. Morton owns a chain of laundromats. At night he makes the rounds and collects the money from each of the laundromats. One night, as he was leaving one of the stores with the money and just opening his car door, two men approached and asked Morton for directions. Morton quickly got in his car and slammed the door. The window was open. One of the men went over to the car, continuing to ask directions. When the man started to take his hand out of his pocket, Morton drew his gun and fired point blank. Neither of the men asking directions had a weapon. They were indeed strangers who were looking for a friend's house a few blocks away. The jury found that Morton had acted to protect himself and acquitted him.

In many cases, whether it is the criminal, the victim, or an innocent passer-by who is shot, it is apparent that the easy availability of guns is the cause of tragic injuries and deaths. Howard is what might be called a professional street criminal. He and his friend Zack and their two girlfriends regularly robbed dress stores. When they were brought to trial before me, they were charged with seventeen robberies. Only three cases were prosecuted because the personnel in the other stores could not identify them. The plan was simple and worked without a flaw sixteen times. The four would go into a store. They appeared to be two nice young couples. The two girls would take a few items into the dressing rooms ostensibly to try them on. One man would go to the cash register and empty it while the other held a gun. Then the four would leave. No robbery took more than three minutes. At the seventeenth robbery, Zack stationed himself near the corridor leading to the dressing rooms. Just as they were ready to leave, a fifteen-year old girl who was trying on a dress for a prom waltzed out of the dressing room to let her mother see her in her first long dress. She had no idea a holdup was in progress. As she came into the main part of the store, she jostled the gunman and the gun fired, striking her in the chest. She has had five operations. She is permanently disabled.

I watched the four defendants for the two weeks of trial trying to get some clue as to their personalities, their motives, what kind of people they were. They were all quite different. The two girls were obviously spaced out on drugs. Zack stupidly slept through most of the trial. Howard was cold and alert. There was no doubt that the jury would convict them of at least one crime and I would have to impose sentence.

To arrive at an appropriate penalty for each offender, the judge must try to understand the individual, his problems, and his motives. My picture of these four people may be purely subjective. Their character traits and behavior cannot be computerized so that one comparing the sentences will know that Howard is the ringleader—who manipulates the other three, who keeps them on drugs and subservient to him. What does each of the four deserve? There can be no equation of time served in jail to balance the destruction of a fifteen-year-old girl who is condemned to paralysis and helplessness for the rest of her life.

I imposed the maximum penalty on Howard. Nonetheless, he will probably be released before he is thirty-five years old. Who knows what other crimes he will engineer? What other people will he entrap in drug addiction and crime?

A mandatory life sentence was imposed on Barry. The jury found him guilty of first-degree murder. I could not mitigate the penalty. Nor can one say on reading the record of the trial that the verdict should be set aside because the evidence was insufficient. Barry killed a young man. At the time, Barry was only sixteen but he was tried as an adult. He gave the following statement to the police: "Two gangs were fighting. I killed the wrong person." Barry is a functional illiterate. He was expelled from school in the eighth grade. Since then he had been living on the street. Neither the school system nor the welfare department had paid any attention to Barry for the three years prior to the crime. Barry does not know where his father is. His mother did not know where Barry was until he was arrested. This was his first offense. The psychiatrist reported: "Barry feels inadequate, insecure. . . . He has a strong need to emphasize masculinity. . . ." Barry is small and wiry. In his dirty T-shirt, jeans, and ragged sneakers he looked like thousands of other slum children. Barry gazed at me with big, dark eyes brimming with tears. I think of books like *Every Child's Birthright,* and *Beyond the Best Interests of the Child.* Barry has had no love, no nurturing, no education, no religion, not even a home. What was his birthright? What is in his best interest? Could he be helped by education, a decent home, and guidance? I think so. But under the law Barry will spend at least the next twenty years—the most important years of adolescence and manhood—behind bars without hope of release. Who would try to obtain a pardon for him? He is not a cause célèbre. He is an anonymous bit of flotsam washed up on the stony beach of the criminal justice system.

There are many boys and young men like Barry. Most of them are brought to court on charges other than murder. Alphonso is also a school dropout. He lives in an apartment with his mother, but there is no mothering. He sees his father "once in a while." The gang provides his only ties. It is an ambivalent relationship of fear and need and tension. He was convicted of aggravated assault and weapons offense in a gang incident. Alphonso's IQ score is 94. If he could read, he would probably test above average. I have ordered that he must get remedial education in prison. If the order is carried out, Alphonso may be able to lead a law-abiding life when he is released. But there are many dangers ahead. He may become involved in drugs or homosexual practices in prison. The sentence is long and he may give up the struggle and not apply himself to his studies. He has no habits of diligence or perseverance. I keep in touch with him and hope for the best.

Lenny is one who did succeed. He dropped out of school in the eighth grade and lived the aimless street life of many slum youths. He rarely saw his father or his mother. From time to time he worked for a few weeks. He was arrested on minor charges three times; each time he was placed on probation. He was tried before me at age twenty for burglary of a gas station. The station was closed and there was no contact with anyone. Lenny just broke into the place at night, took money, cigarettes, and small items. He was apprehended a half-block away carrying the meager loot. Lenny had been in six different schools. He had never had meaningful contact with a teacher, a clergyman, or a counsellor. There was no adult figure in his life. But Lenny is bright. His IQ is 116, but his knowledge of anything but survival was nonexistent. Although the guidelines and pre-sentence report recommended prison, I placed Lenny on probation and required him to get a job, go to night school, and pay a small fine. I insisted that his probation officer report to me monthly on Lenny's progress in school and his job. In less than two years Lenny obtained his high-school equivalency diploma. He has a better job now. He paid the fine and he has not been rearrested.

Isaac is not a success. He is a functional illiterate. At seventeen he was big, strong, and sullen. He committed two murders within one year. He was not apprehended until after the second murder. His mother was in court sobbing. His life seemed to me to be no worse than that of many other offenders. But Isaac was clearly a different kind of person. He killed deliberately and without remorse. The second murder occurred outside a bar. Isaac thought he had not been observed. In fact, someone was looking out of the window in a room above the bar and saw Isaac slug a stranger with a blackjack. The man fell to the street. Isaac reached in the man's pants, took his wallet, and went into the bar. He was there drinking when the police arrested him. The victim died en route to the hospital. Isaac's crime was not irrational; it was deliberate, brutal and vicious. He was convicted of murder and sentenced for life. I do not know what society could have done to prevent this crime. I do not know what the criminal justice system can do to rehabilitate Isaac. It is difficult to acknowledge that with the present state of psychiatry and penology there is really nothing that one can do for him. There is nothing to do with him except to incarcerate him permanently.

Fortunately, most street criminals are not like Isaac. They steal and they rob. Sometimes they injure people in the course of these crimes. But they usually do not act viciously. There are many more Lennys than Isaacs. Most of them can, I believe, be helped. Although rehabilitation is no longer in fashion, I am confident that many offenders could be turned from a life pattern of crime to a law-abiding and self-supporting lifestyle. What the courts do with these people after conviction does make a difference. A prison sentence is most likely to provide a graduate course in crime. Probation alone will not change the offender's lifestyle. He will continue to be poor, uneducated, and unemployed. He will be tempted to steal a thousand times. Most likely he will yield to temptation, unless he has a job and money in his pocket.

For these young men I believe that a sentence of probation conditioned upon attending school, obtaining a job, and paying restitution and a small fine offers the best hope of changing the lifestyle of idleness, unemployment, and crime. It requires them to move from the world of outcast, marginal people to the world of the majority: the employed, taxpaying, noncriminal members of society. Many judges do not impose sentences of fines and restitution on such young men because these offenders do not have money or a job. Few street criminals at the time of sentencing are able to pay restitution, reparation, or a fine.

A prison sentence is operative for many years, even for life. Probation is also imposed for a period of time which usually exceeds several years. There is no reason why an order of fines and restitution cannot be complied with over a period of time. Most nonviolent offenders who are employed are placed on probation and ordered to make restitution over the length of the sentence. Such offenders are released; they go back to work. The judge inquires as to the salary of the offender and calculates how much he or she needs for subsistence. Restitution is ordered to be paid at a weekly rate commensurate with the criminal's wages or earning capacity and the property stolen. But even among these small offenders, the law bears more punitively on the very poor and disadvantaged. If a thief or burglar is unemployed and unemployable, it is likely that he will be sentenced to jail. If he is lucky enough to have a job and will make restitution, few judges will impose a prison sentence.

A sentence of probation, fines, and restitution can work with many jobless offenders, both those who have not committed violent crimes and some who have committed crimes of violence but are not vicious or hardened criminals. They can be sentenced to probation and, as a condition of probation, be ordered to get remedial education and vocational training and make payments when they have obtained employment.

Such sentences require vigilance on the part of the judge to compel the probation officer to enforce compliance with the court's order. It is easier for a probation officer simply to have a routine contact with his probationer once a month than to ride herd on him and see that he goes to remedial classes, that he gets a job, and that he pays the order of restitution and fine. But it can be done. Such sentences, I believe, promote a sense of responsibility on the part of the offender. Credibility and faith in the justice system is restored when the victim is made whole. Such sentences may even rehabilitate the offender and in a small measure act as a deterrent.

Darryl convinced me of the wisdom of this type of sentence. He was nineteen when he was tried before me for burglary. He had taken a color TV worth $600, an FM radio worth $80, a tape recorder, a typewriter, and a pair of binoculars. He sold all this loot which was worth at least $1,000, for less than $200. I sentenced him to make restitution and pay a small fine. He was required to pay $25 per week for a year. At sentencing I asked Darryl if there was anything he wanted to say.

He stood at the bar of the court, his forehead wrinkled with thought as he calculated how much money he had thrown away. He answered slowly, "I was dumb. I'll never do a stupid job like that again. You better believe it."

I do believe it. Four years have passed. Darryl did complete a course in welding; he got a job; and he paid his twenty-five dollars a week for one year as required. He has not been arrested again.

Not all street criminals will respond as Darryl did. But every offender should at least have a chance to make good. I believe that every criminal owes a debt to society and to the victims of his crime. Society also owes a debt to many offenders who have been denied a real education and a place in the community. This debt can be repaid if the sentence imposed offers the offender education, training, and an opportunity for a productive life. The alternative is to continue the futile cycle of crime, imprisonment, release, and more crime, imprisonment, and release. The result is wasted lives of offenders, losses and injuries to the victims of these crimes, and enormous costs to the public.

CHAPTER XV

CRIME IN BLACK
AND WHITE

Criminal contacts—the third most important field
of Negro-white relationship.
—Gunnar Myrdal

I n the United States, the subject of race is inextricably entwined in
every important social and political question. It cannot be ignored in
any discussion of crime. A trial judge sitting in criminal court in an urban
area is painfully conscious of the fact that there are far more black
defendants in court than white even though the majority of the people
in the jurisdiction are white. Statistics for the nation corroborate the fact
that blacks are accused of crime, convicted, and sentenced disproportionately to their numbers. Of the sentenced offenders in federal prison,
11,756 are white and 5,154 are non-white. The non-white population
of the United States, making allowance for undercounting in the census,
is only approximately 12 percent of the total. In the state prison population, 97,700 prisoners are white and 89,700 are black.[1] In county jails
the number of blacks is much higher. In the city of Philadelphia, which
is typical of urban crime problems, non-whites account for more than
75 percent of suspects arrested for street crimes although blacks constitute fewer than 40 percent of the population.[2] The victimization rate
of crimes against persons is also disproportionately black. Forty-three per
1,000 male victims are white and 53 are black. Among female victims,

20 are white and 32 are black.[3]

To draw any reasonable conclusions as to the problem of race and crime in the United States, one must seek answers to these questions: Do blacks commit more crimes proportionately than whites? Is the criminal justice system prejudiced against blacks? If so, does that bias alone account for the disproportionate number of blacks who are arrested, convicted, and imprisoned? Are the sentences imposed on blacks more severe than those imposed on whites for the same types of crime? There are few statistics that shed light on these questions. Instead there are many imponderables and unverifiable premises. Explanations, reasons, and facts are required. They are difficult to obtain.

That neologism, "racist," is frequently heard in discussions of race and crime. It cannot be ignored or dismissed. It may be an indictment of the system or of the offenders. There are those who claim that blacks are more disposed to crime. Others assert with equal certitude that it is not race but deprivation and the heritage of slavery that cause this phenomenon.

There are as many views as there are writers on the subject. They cover the gamut from Arthur Robert Jensen to James Baldwin. Some claim that crime is wholly the fault of the individual. Others blame society. But is it the black community or the white community?

Any honest chronicler of American legal history must acknowledge that the legal system in its treatment of blacks has been characterized by inequality, fictions, and slogans. By dint of vigorous litigation and political struggle one fiction has yielded place to another. In the early census one black person was counted as three-fifths of a white person. After the Civil War, the courts declared that the Constitution required "separate but equal treatment" for blacks. The treatment, in fact, was separate and unequal. The law was later declared to be "colorblind." In fact, people of normal vision are not colorblind and can easily distinguish most blacks from most whites. Discrimination prevailed in fact if not in law. "Benign neglect" had its moment of popularity. Neglect cannot be favorable. The phrase, like every oxymoron, is, as Webster's dictionary declares, "pointedly foolish." Compensatory treatment, affirmative action, and other slogans find their way into the law and will eventually be replaced by others. But throughout these changes in slogans and perspectives, the fact remains that the criminal justice system has borne more heavily and more punitively on blacks than on whites.

Until the Civil Rights Revolution, the entire criminal justice system including police, judiciary, probation departments, and prisons was staffed predominantly by white men. Today there are large numbers of blacks and Hispanics in the police forces of most communities where there is a substantial black or Hispanic population. There are also Chinese, Japanese, and Jewish police officers as well as the Irish and Italians who have traditionally staffed police departments.

It is difficult to know whether today there is racial bias in the arrest process. Many non-whites claim that they are stopped and questioned by the police without probable cause. Such illegal stops rarely result in arrests unless contraband or weapons are discovered. Illegal arrests are usually quashed and the evidence obtained excluded from trial. Even if there is a substantial amount of discriminatory action by the police, it alone cannot account for the large number of convictions of blacks.

Child abuse is a crime which is committed by blacks and whites, rich and poor. The *New York Times* reports that blacks and whites abuse children equally but that blacks are more likely to get caught.[4] This would seem to indicate prejudice in the arrest process. Child abusers, however, are not arrested on sight by the police. They are usually apprehended after a report of suspected abuse is made and a warrant is issued. Most reports are made by hospitals and clinics. Wealthy and middle-class people take their injured children to private physicians who rarely report child abuse unless it results in death. Consequently, these well-to-do child abusers, most of whom are white, are rarely arrested. Since proportionately more blacks than whites are poor, there are more arrests of blacks for this crime.

As to police bias in the arrest process, there is considerable evidence, though little of it is verifiable, tending to show that the police treat black suspects brutally more often than white suspects. There is a similar absence of evidence tending to prove racial bias in the treatment of convicts in prison. Black prisoners have equal opportunities for education, training, and recreation in prison. But, as we have seen, federal prisons are vastly more pleasant and humane places than most state prisons and county jails. Many white, middle-class, middle-aged convicts are in federal prisons. Most black, poor, young offenders are in state prisons and county jails.[5]

In examining the judicial process to see if there is racial bias in convictions, one must look at the offender and the judge or jury. Fewer than 5 percent of criminal cases are tried before juries. Again, there are no statistics reporting racial factors with respect to the conduct or composition of juries. For many years blacks were systematically excluded from juries. Such exclusion is now illegal. In most northern cities today there is no discrimination in the selection of the jury panel. Admittedly some white prosecutors, if not stopped by the trial judge, will try to exclude blacks from the jury when the defendant is black. It is my impression, however, that black jurors are at least as likely to convict a black defendant as white jurors. Most juries in urban communities are racially mixed. It has been my experience that juries really do not believe in the concept of reasonable doubt and that they convict many times when a judge might well find that guilt had not been proved beyond a reasonable doubt. Such convictions occur with respect to both black and white defendants.

Occasionally one can draw some inferences from the conduct of juries.

Lorita, a black woman accused of welfare fraud, was tried before me. She worked for the welfare department and also legally received a supplemental welfare allotment for a sick child. Her bi-weekly payments varied from check to check. Lorita had in fact received $732 more than she was entitled to over a period of several years but the overpayment may well have been the fault of an inefficient bureaucracy. In order to be guilty of a crime, a welfare recipient must knowingly and wilfully defraud the state. There was only the flimsiest inferential evidence that Lorita knew what she was entitled to receive or that she had wilfully made a false statement to her welfare worker. Nonetheless, a predomi nantly black jury convicted her of fraud. Perhaps they were aware of the tremendous amount of welfare cheating but simply did not understand, despite careful instruction, that the state has to prove beyond a reasonable doubt that the recipient wilfully and knowingly made a false statement. After hearing the evidence against Lorita, I had such a doubt.

Willis, a black youth, was convicted of robbery by a predominantly black jury. In his case, there was a serious question of identification. The victim had seen the robber only fleetingly on a dark street. Willis was apprehended a few minutes after the robbery in an alley about a block from the scene of the crime. When the jury retired to deliberate, the two alternate jurors were excused. Both were well-dressed, polite, middle-aged ladies. One was white, the other black. We walked down the corridor together. "Do you think he's guilty?" one of the ladies asked me.

"What do you think?" I responded.

The white alternate juror answered slowly, "I must say, I have a reasonable doubt. The defendant said he had just stepped into the alley, as he put it, 'to take a leak.' That explains what he was doing there." "Nonsense," the black alternate juror snapped. "I've heard that excuse before. He was guilty."

There is insufficient evidence to draw any conclusions as to racial prejudice on the part of juries.

In more than 95 percent of state criminal cases, there is either a guilty plea or a trial before a judge without a jury. In most jurisdictions, except for first-degree murder, the judge imposes the sentence. Until recent years, the overwhelming number of judges in both federal and state courts were white, male, middle-class, and middle-aged. Despite recent appointments and elections to the bench of blacks and women, the judiciary is still predominantly white, male, middle-class, and middle-aged. Two questions must be asked with respect to judicial conduct: Is there racial bias in convictions? Is there racial bias in sentencing? There are no national, comprehensive statistics that bear on this subject. All that the census figures and Department of Justice studies report are the race of the offender and that of the victim. A careful study made by two reporters for the *Philadelphia Inquirer*, "Crime and Injustice," reveals that 32 percent of blacks accused of crime in Philadelphia who are tried by black judges are convicted and 42 percent of blacks accused of crime who are tried by white judges are convicted.[6] If one examines the behavior of individual judges, no conclusions as to racial bias can be drawn. There are "hanging" black judges and "hanging" white judges. There are fairminded black and fairminded white judges. A study of attitudes toward crime shows that it tends to be a function of political, philosophical, educational, and socio-economic background.[7] The evidence is at best tentative.

There is some dismaying evidence with respect to racial bias in sentencing. Before the death penalty was held unconstitutional by the United States Supreme Court, the number of people executed for crimes was disproportionately black.[8] Most egregious was the number of black men executed for the crime of raping white women. Significantly, there were very few convictions or executions of white men for raping black women. In the federal courts, blacks who are sentenced to prison serve on the average four months longer than whites convicted of the same crime.[9] The *Philadelphia Inquirer* Report reveals that 64 percent of the blacks who commit violent crimes in Philadelphia are sentenced to prison while only 42 percent of the whites who commit the same crimes receive a prison sentence. The report indicates neither the race of the judges who imposed sentence nor whether the black and white offenders had similar records of prior criminal convictions.

There are some explanations for this disparity in sentencing between blacks and whites. In some inner-city neighborhoods, most black boys have at least one police contact before age eighteen. This is not the fact in predominantly white neighborhoods. Prior criminal record is a most significant factor in deciding whether or not to impose a prison sentence. Unless the crime is heinous, most first offenders are sentenced to probation. Also, if a juvenile or young adult offender who has not committed a serious crime has a responsible relative who comes to court and promises to provide a job, housing, and some supervision for the young man, most judges will not impose a prison sentence but will place him on probation. Economics and social class play an important part in sentencing decisions irrespective of race. Poor blacks and poor whites who have no friends or relatives who can give them a job are much more likely to be sentenced to jail than those who are better off financially. Since more blacks are poor, blacks are more likely to receive prison sentences than whites.

Race does occasionally influence sentencing. Two young boys, aged nineteen, were accused of committing together a series of burglaries. It was a second offense for both. Both were represented by the same private attorney who was retained by the employer of the father of one of the boys. This attorney rarely appears in criminal court. He and the assistant prosecutor assigned to the case came to me to discuss a plea bargain. Arrangements for restitution had been made. We were in the robing room, which is a small office to the side of the court room. I told the attorneys that I believed a short prison sentence was required because of the prior record of the defendants and the premeditated nature of the crime. Defense counsel, who was white, did not disagree.

The prosecutor, a young black attorney, said, "Judge, you can't send Howard to jail. It wouldn't be safe."

I opened the door to the courtroom and looked at the two defendants. Wilbur was a big husky redhead. Howard was a small, slight boy with silky hair and smooth cheeks. He looked no more than fifteen.

"You're right," I agreed. I had no doubt that Howard would be brutally molested in any jail or prison to which I could order him committed. "Is he a homosexual?"

Both attorneys assured me that he was not. It would not be right to put Howard in the homosexual wing of the prison. He would probably not be safe there either. Wilbur could take care of himself in a prison where most of the inmates are strong, hostile, young black men. Howard obviously could not. Since both Howard and Wilbur were guilty of the same offense, both were placed on probation.

Such anomalous cases and the instances of actual racial prejudice, however, cannot account for the grossly disproportionate number of blacks who are convicted of crime and sentenced to prison. It is, I believe, necessary to look at the types of crime which are committed most often by blacks and whites respectively to understand this phenomenon.

In 1883, Sir James Fitzjames Stephens, writing of the state of the criminal law in England, observed, "It must be remembered that most persons accused of crime are poor, stupid and helpless."[10] This has always been the fact. It is true today. Some 80 percent or more of all persons tried in state criminal courts are represented by a public defender or a court appointed and publicly paid lawyer because they cannot afford to retain counsel. Before the landmark decisions of the Warren Court, persons accused of crime had few legally enforceable rights despite the Constitutional provisions mandating due process of law and equal protection of the laws. Until 1963, accused persons who could not afford attorneys were not entitled to be represented at public expense.[11] Although there were some defender offices which represented indigents, this was an act of charity and available only in certain communities and only for certain offenses. Although the Constitution guaranteed the right to bail, only those who could afford to post bail were able to obtain their release before trial so that they might gather evidence and prepare a defense. Confessions were coerced, often beaten, out of suspects. The police were not required to advise suspects of their rights. Indeed, they had very few rights. Suspects could be held for long periods of time on the flimsiest pretexts. Arrests were made without probable cause. No one had a right to trial by jury for minor offenses. Blacks were routinely excluded from juries.

In 1932, Professor Borchard of Yale Law School shocked the legal profession with his book, *Convicting the Innocent.*[12] It is no wonder that many innocent people were convicted under the conditions which then prevailed. Today the indigent accused has more rights. But he still does not have equal protection. Today every person accused of crime is entitled to counsel. If he cannot afford counsel one must be furnished for him at public expense. But the accused cannot choose his own attorney. Although there are many able and dedicated lawyers employed in defender offices, most of them are overworked. Usually these attorneys see their clients for only a few minutes the day of the trial. Contrast such representation with the meticulous preparation by private counsel representing wealthy clients both in civil and criminal cases. Even the United States Supreme Court has recognized the inadequacy of legal representation of the poor. A prisoner wrote to the Court inquiring about his appeal. It was evident from the record that his court-appointed counsel had failed to file an appeal. In an unsigned opinion the Court wrote, "This prisoner's story of his appointed counsel's indifference to his legitimate request for help is all too familiar."[13] Poor clients with such legal representation are more likely to be convicted and to plead guilty than those who have more thoroughly prepared lawyers, better investigation of their cases, expert witnesses, and all of the costly back-up which is required to obtain an acquittal. Although today there are bail projects in most communities to help poor people obtain release before trial, the county jails are filled with people who cannot post fifty or a hundred dollars bail to obtain their freedom.

As Sir James Stephens pointed out, criminals are not only poor and helpless before the law, "they are stupid." It is my experience, however, that many poor offenders are not stupid. In fact, many are bright but uneducated. It is the crimes that most poor defendants commit which are stupid. They rarely yield enough to make them worth the effort or the risk. Moreover, these offenders do not take care to avoid detection.

Nelson was arrested inside a large clothing store at three o'clock on a Sunday morning. He had climbed in through a skylight. He gathered a quantity of clothing, primarily for his personal use, and put these items in a store shopping bag. When he attempted to open the front door of the store, the alarm went off. Nelson was trapped inside because he had no knowledge of modern locks and burglar alarms. He did not know that the door would not open.

Donald held up a bank. He passed the teller a note written on the back of his phone bill. The teller scooped up a few dollars from a drawer and gave them to Donald. She pressed a concealed silent alarm button. Donald walked out of the bank into the arms of a waiting policeman.

It is not difficult to apprehend and convict criminals like these. It is much more difficult to prosecute and convict public officials and officers of wealthy corporations accused of receiving kickback and bribes and of perpetrating complicated frauds. The number of convictions for these crimes is extremely low.

We have looked at street crimes and white-collar crimes (see Chapters XIII and XIV) and have seen that corporate and white-collar crimes cause infinitely more havoc, misery, and death than street crimes. These crimes cost at least $400 billion a year. Most of these offenders are white. But they are rarely visible. They have no contact with the victims of their crimes. One should include in this category of crimes which are largely unreported and rarely prosecuted a number of other white-dominated groups such as manufacturers of machinery which is unsafe and causes mutilation and death to countless people; the owners and managers of improperly constructed and operated nuclear plants; and violators of pure food and drug laws whose products cause cancer, physical and mental deformities, and other diseases in tens of thousands of people. Scientists and researchers who falsify the results of their tests, experiment on innocent and unsuspecting people, and lie to them are also guilty of crimes even though they are rarely prosecuted. But few people think of scientists and professors as criminals. The extent of harm which is done by these law violators is simply incalculable. The diseased and injured people and the families of the dead rarely know the cause of the illness, injury, or death. Even when they happen to find out, the criminal is a faceless corporation or institution. The policies of these corporations and research foundations were, of course, designed and carried out by people who knew what they were doing. Most of these people in management and policy positions are rich or reasonably well-to-do, educated, and white.

The public attitude toward these two broad categories of crimes—street crime and white-collar crime—is entirely different. The treatment of the two types of criminal by the criminal justice system, as we have seen, is also markedly different from arrest through trial, conviction, sentencing, and imprisonment. When a white-collar offender is prosecuted and convicted, the common response of friends and colleagues is: "Poor X. He only did what everyone else has been doing for years." These people are not considered "criminals." Even a judge at the sentencing of a man who was found guilty by a jury of bribery, declared, "Mr. X., you are not really a criminal, so I am placing you on probation." But it is obvious that Mr. X., who was convicted of a crime, is a criminal.

This moral myopia with respect to wealthy criminals is not peculiar to contemporary society. Al Capone, the notorious Chicago gangster of the 1920s, thought of himself as a businessman. He said, "I make my money by supplying a public demand. If I break the law, my customers, who number hundreds of the best people in Chicago, are as guilty as I am. The only difference between us is that I sell and they buy. Everybody calls me a racketeer. I call myself a businessman. When I sell liquor, it's bootlegging. When my patrons serve it on a silver tray on Lake Shore Drive, it's hospitality."[14] In the 1960s college students who shoplifted for "kicks" would say they were "liberating" merchandise. They did not consider themselves criminals. But when a black boy steals, everyone considers him a criminal. When he is convicted and sentenced to prison the reaction of the public is very different. The usual response, no matter how long the sentence, is that he should be sent away forever. The robbery of twenty dollars, even if committed with a toy gun, is considered more "criminal" than the embezzlement of $20 million.

A court officer once complained to me after three months of the usual run of robberies, burglaries, rapes, assaults, and drug and weapons offenses. "Judge," he said, "this is depressing. Why can't we have a better class of criminals?" He, like most people, assumed that a perjurious congressman or a manufacturer of dangerous drugs is a better person than a mugger or a narcotics user.

If one includes in the category of criminals not simply those who have been convicted but also anyone who has violated a law, the number of criminals is legion. How many people have parked in a no parking zone, exceeded the speed limit, padded expense accounts, and inflated deductions in tax returns? Some time ago, I paraphrased the immortal Pogo and concluded: "We have met the criminal and he is us."

I believe that the principal reason for the large number of blacks who are arrested, convicted, and sentenced to prison is the fact that they commit street crimes. These are the crimes most likely to be reported and prosecuted. Stupid, ill-planned robberies and burglaries are the offenses for which it is most easy to get a conviction, especially if defense counsel is not well prepared.

The facts with respect to race, income, and employment are well established and verified. The average income of blacks is lower than that of whites. Among teenagers, the unemployment rate in 1979 for whites was slightly over 13 percent and for blacks over 32 percent. For those in the twenty- to twenty-four-year-old group, the unemployment rate in

April 1979 was 16.5 percent, but for blacks in this age group it was 34.5 percent. Six hundred seventy-seven thousand blacks aged sixteen to twenty-four are reported to be looking for work. Many more unemployed but not counted.[15]

Robert Shrank of the Ford Foundation states: "Cities like New York, where many blacks live, have become white-collar factories. Education is critical. If you are illiterate you are in a lot of trouble. The school system is turning out a lot of kids who can't read or do arithmetic."[16] Mr. Shrank's conclusions are obvious. Who will employ an illiterate? It follows that many illiterates steal by force or threat of force because they have no other means of obtaining what they want and their desires are simple and immediate.

Although the overwhelming majority of young male defendants are unemployed, they are not shivering in rags, starving, or sleeping on park benches. They have the necessities of life. Only one defendant of the hundreds who have appeared before me even suggested that he robbed for necessities. This young black man held up a bartender at knifepoint. The reason: he and his common-law wife had a little baby. They had run out of pampers (paper diapers). The mother sent him to the store to buy some and he discovered that he didn't have any money. Every other defendant, black and white, male and female, who has appeared before me charged with shoplifting, theft, robbery, or burglary had stolen for luxuries or drugs, or simply for excitement.

The lives of uneducated unemployed young men are very empty. They are not people who frequent the public library or who attend free art museums, concerts, and lectures. The choice of subjects of these lectures, concerts, and exhibits is made by members of the dominant white, upper middle-class society and rarely appeals to these young uneducated men. Most cities have a multitude of stimulating free educational and cultural events which hold no interest for them. All too often crime is simply something to do to relieve the monotony of empty days. Hanging out on a corner with no money and nothing to do is tedious. Even homicides are committed because the killer was bored. One young defendant shot a total stranger who was just walking down the street. When asked why he had done it, he replied, "I wanted to get me a body."

Rickey was convicted before me of robbery. He assaulted Mr. Y., a stranger who was walking through the park, and grabbed his wallet. In the course of the encounter, Rickey slugged Mr. Y. and broke his jaw.

Rickey's alibi witness was Walter, a friend from the neighborhood. Walter had a job with the park system. He testified that Rickey had been in the park talking to him from one o'clock until five o'clock when Walter's working day was over. They left the park together. Walter was a high-school graduate. Rickey was a school dropout who had never held a job more than a couple of weeks. After Walter left, Rickey returned to the park. He had no place to go and nothing to do. When Mr. Y. appeared, Rickey robbed him. The emptiness of Rickey's life as he described it is appalling.

Young black Curtis is a typical defendant. He was eighteen years old, charged with a weapons offense, three counts of aggravated assault, and assault with intent to kill. The facts were fairly clear. Curtis and two of his friends went to a "party." This is a euphemism for an illegal bar. Each so-called guest had to pay to attend the party which was held in a private home. Curtis got into an altercation with four other youths. After Curtis and his friends were put out of the party, they lay in wait until the four with whom they had had the dispute left the party. Curtis and his friends opened fire and shot three of the youths. One managed to run and escape being hit even though Curtis had a sawed-off shotgun and the other two had handguns.

After conviction, I questioned Curtis about himself.

Q. How far did you go in school?

A. Tenth grade.

Q. How old were you when you last attended school?

A. Fifteen.

Q. Why did you quit?

A. I didn't like it.

Q. Didn't the school authorities ever ask you why you weren't in school?

A. No.

Curtis's mother was in the courtroom. She had slept through most of the trial. Curtis's girlfriend and their one-year-old baby were also in court. I questioned the mother.

Q. Is it true that your son left school at age fifteen?

A. Yes.

Q. Why didn't you send him to school?

A. He didn't like it.

I resumed the questioning of Curtis.

Q. Can you read and write?

A. Yes.

I had the court officer hand Curtis the morning paper. He was unable to read the headlines.

Q. Have you ever had a job?

A. No.

Before he was fifteen, Curtis had spent more than a year in a juvenile correctional institution. His IQ scores indicate that Curtis is of normal intelligence. He is not a drug addict. Clearly the public school system and the juvenile court had failed Curtis. I do not say that he had failed although obviously he had not learned anything. Nonetheless, he had been physically present in public school for more than eight years and in a juvenile institution for more than one year. No wonder he didn't like school when at age fifteen he could not read at a first-grade level.

What did he do all day every day from the time he left school at fifteen until he was arrested at eighteen? What so many young criminals do: he roamed the streets; he drank beer and wine; he visited his friends; he got into trouble. The only surprising aspect of Curtis's life history was that he had not been convicted during the three years of utter idleness from age fifteen to age eighteen.

Eric, an educationally deprived white boy, was tried before me on a charge of robbery. He had dropped out of school at age sixteen. Between the ages of sixteen and twenty-one when I saw him he had been arrested five times and convicted twice. He had been placed on probation both times. He has never held a job more than a few weeks. Like Curtis, Eric spent his time roaming the streets, drinking beer, and looking for excitement. In this latest crime, Eric slugged a stranger and seized his wallet which contained less than twenty dollars. The man was badly injured.

Should Rickey, Curtis, and Eric be sent to prison or placed on probation? Can any of them be "rehabilitated" in prison? Obviously, probation had done nothing for Eric. Curtis's mother is on welfare. His father is living with another woman. Eric's parents are living together. His father works in a factory. Rickey and Curtis are black; Eric is white. Despite the differences in family background, the problems of these three young men are the same: lack of education, unemployment, and boredom. All committed violent crimes.

According to Rollo May, the appeal of violence lies in the fact that it represents "a uniting of the self in action."[17] What May calls "the ecstasy of violence" is perhaps the only ecstasy these young men have ever known. The word "anomie" comes to mind when one thinks of them. They are hollow men, frighteningly so. It is easy to look at statistics of crime, poverty, and race and find a positive correlation. It is easy to blame the absent father, the welfare mother, the inner-city lifestyle. All too often the analyses by white sociologists, criminologists, and educators find a root cause in racial difference. New York University Professor Irving Kristol is quoted as saying that the breakdown of discipline in ghetto schools (which is undeniable) is due to the increase in compulsory school attendance age and the rise in the minimum wage. "Together, these reforms insured that a great many vigorous and robust young men and women, with no academic aptitude or interests, were sentenced to confinement in the schools. . . . The results are not very different from dropping a gang of juveniles in a children's playpen. They proceed to wreck the place and make everyone miserable. . . ."[18]

Professor Kristol is not alone in claiming that "ghetto" youth have a greater propensity for perpetrating violence in the schools than their "non-ghetto" counterparts. Numerous sociological theories have emerged which state that due to restricted opportunities and frustrations, subcultural differences in values or in attitudes toward violence, members of lower socio-economic groups are responsible for higher levels of criminal incidents including crimes in schools.

"Ghetto," an Italian word which originally referred to a quarter of the city in which Jews were compelled to live, has come to be used in contemporary America as a euphemism for black neighborhoods. Given the problem of black schools and the disproportionate number of black youths arrested, declared delinquent by the juvenile court, and later convicted in adult court, it is a facile and obvious explanation. But is it not just a description of how institutions such as schools and the legal system treat these young people rather than an explanation of their behavior?

Poor unemployed young men, both black and white, living in our society desire material things even more than better educated people who seek professional or business advancement, learning, culture, and social esteem. For the uneducated and unemployed, material possessions are the measure of the man. These youths like fancy clothes and fast cars. They want to take girls out and show off before their peers—male and female. On a meager welfare allotment, they cannot possibly have any of the things they desire. The only alternative to a life without these possessions is some form of stealing—robbery, burglary, shoplifting. Much of the violence in street crime occurs accidentally in the course of attempted or successful stealing.

These young men do not know how to juggle accounts. They cannot offer bribes. No one offers them kickbacks. The only way they can get money illegally is through surreptitious theft or threat of violence. Most muggings and assaults occur in the course of robbery and burglary. These are the violent street encounters that people fear. It is what the public thinks of when the word criminal is used. A generation ago, Gunnar Myrdal pointed out that "Negroes [sic] do not commit white-collar crimes."[19]

As we have seen, blacks are disproportionally poor, undereducated, and unemployed. I believe that in crimes committed by young men, literacy and employment are the critical factors. Street crimes are committed in the main by unemployed undereducated youths—both black and white. White-collar crimes are committed by educated older men —both black and white. To test this thesis, I examined the cases of forty-five male defendants who were tried and convicted before me in a period of four months. These cases were consecutive. I did not select them. They were randomly assigned to me by court administration. All the defendants were accused of at least one major felony although some were convicted only of misdemeanors.

This compilation does not include rape and deviate sex cases although rape is a violent encounter and is one of the most serious street crimes. Rapes are committed by black, white, and Hispanic men of all ages. A sex offender usually has some kind of psychiatric problem which sets him apart from other people. Homicides were also excluded because such cases are tried more carefully and more frequently before juries. Because of the drastic penalties—life imprisonment or death—people who the judge believes are guilty may be acquitted. Often the heinous nature of the crime causes juries to convict in cases where a judge would have a reasonable doubt. Such dubious convictions and acquittals occur less frequently in non-homicide cases, which are often tried without a jury. I believe that all the men in this compilation of forty-five cases were guilty of the offenses of which they were convicted.

Female defendants were not included because their crimes are, on the whole, very different from those of men. Women constitute fewer than 15 percent of all persons convicted of crime. Their most common offense is shoplifting. While a female shoplifter may offer resistance to arrest, she seldom has a weapon. There is rarely a physical injury other than a scratch or a bruise. Women who are convicted of drug offenses and prostitution are usually used as a front by a male friend or relative. They are not professional pushers. Although women stab, shoot, and kill, the victim is almost always a husband, lover, or rival. With rare exceptions women do not attack strangers. They do not hold up stores or commit armed robberies or muggings. While illiteracy is a common problem of young men, I have never encountered an illiterate girl or young woman. Among poor Hispanics, women are far more fluent in English than the men in their families. They are, therefore, more employable.

The chart appended to this chapter reveals that of the forty-five male defendants, thirty-six committed violent offenses against strangers, theft, and car theft. Of these thirty-six, thirty were under the age of thirty. Only one was a high-school graduate and employed. He had severe emotional problems. Twenty-three were black, one was Puerto Rican, and twelve were white. The profiles of the thirty-five who were not high-school graduates were the same except for race.

Two men were convicted of wife beating; one was black and one was white. The five men convicted of weapons offenses were entirely different from the thirty-five high-school dropouts. They were convicted only of possession of a weapon. None of them used the weapon against anyone. These men carried weapons for their own protection. In the neighborhoods in which they lived or worked this was not unreasonable although it was illegal. Four were black and one was white. The paucity of white older men convicted of weapons offenses is explained by the fact that most whites do not frequent dangerous neighborhoods. All these older men were educated, literate, and employed. Two older men, one black and one white, were convicted of street crimes against strangers. Both were employed, literate, and high-school graduates. The black man's crime involved mistaken identity. He erroneously believed that the man he assaulted had molested his child. The white man who committed burglary was an alcoholic. Of the three white-collar criminals, two were white and one black. All were high-school graduates, literate, and employed.

The common factors in the men under thirty who commit street crimes are unemployment, poor education, and functional illiteracy. These characteristics are the same for whites, blacks, and Hispanics. These conclusions accord with my experience as a judge in hundreds of other cases and also with my experience as a defense lawyer representing thousands of alleged juvenile delinquents and many adults accused of crime. Significantly, when black men are educated and employed they commit white-collar crimes, not violent and physically dangerous street crimes. The nature of crime is, I believe, a function of education and class. Edward Brooke, a black senator from Massachusetts who committed perjury, has more in common with former Attorney General John Mitchell, a white man who is one of the Watergate felons, than with the average black street criminal.

Of the thirty-six young men under the age of twenty-nine included in this compilation, all but one had prior records. Despite their youth, these men had previous adult convictions as well as long histories of involvement with the juvenile court. Most of them had served some time in jail. One of the young men had a record of nine previous arrests for shoplifting. These are commonly known as "revolving door" cases.

While some of the thirty-five high-school dropouts have low IQs, none is uneducable. Probably some are brighter than their scores indicate. Illiteracy and cultural deprivation do affect intelligence test scores. Regardless of whether they are imprisoned or placed on probation, in all likelihood these men will commit more crimes. So long as they are semiliterate and unskilled they are unemployable. Few employers will consider hiring them for any work. So long as they are unemployed, their lifestyle of boredom interspersed with crime will continue.

It is apparent to me that the way to reduce street crime in the cities is to raise the level of literacy and education so that we do not have a large population of idle, unemployed young men who find themselves deprived of all the desirable material things they see around them. If we are truly concerned with crime prevention, then the only meaningful penalty imposed on such young men must include basic remedial education and job training.

When I sentence these young, uneducated offenders to prison, I inform them that they must attend school regularly. Unless the crime is heinous or very brutal, I usually impose a sentence with a short minimum and a long maximum term. I tell the offender to write to me and that I shall oppose his release until he obtains his high-school equivalency diploma. I also notify the prison authorities that the prisoner *must* attend school. Most of these offenders do write to me with fair regularity and demonstrate their newly acquired skills.

Darryl H. is one of these young men. This is his fourth letter and written much better than the earlier ones. His spelling and punctuation are reproduced.

242   CRIMINALS AND VICTIMS

Dear Judge Forer
    I'm writing you this letter pertaining to my sentence I was told that on my six to twelve months sentence that you stipulated that I get my G.E.D. [General Education Diploma] in order to be released I didn't take the test do to the fact that I was ill and I went back to school they were already finished with it now I'm told that you want me to stay and finish the test and get my G.E.D. and the next test won't be until May and the results won't be back until the middle of June which is about two and a half months after my minimum is up and that is 3/29/79 I have already been incarcerated nine months and by the time the tests are completed and everything it will be eleven months which is a long time for anyone its not that I'm trying to criticize your decision because I know your doing what you think is right but please consider my position in this case I know that you may feel that if you were to let me go to the streets that I might get out there and forget about school but if the world went without a little trust there wouldn't be much of a world left would it . . .

His letter reveals that he has learned to read and write, but not very well, and that he cleverly, artfully, and persuasively presents his request. It also shows that prison programs are not designed to foster education. The judge must continuously prod the prison authorities to see that the prisoners spend their time in school instead of working to support the prison.

I do not suggest that education will "rehabilitate" an offender. There are countless educated criminals. Nor do I believe that education is the proper "desert" or penalty for an offender. Regardless of literacy and job skills, some offenders should be imprisoned. I am convinced, however, that for the vast majority of young, uneducated youths who commit thefts, burglaries, robberies, muggings, and assaults, education and job training are essential. Idle, ignorant, unemployable youths will continue to commit crimes regardless of the severity of the penalties imposed. No amount of counselling or treatment can persuade such young men to forego their desires for material things. Unless these young, uneducated, unemployable offenders, both black and white, are taught to be functionally literate and trained to hold a job, the entire criminal justice system—police, courts, probation departments, and prisons—is engaged in a futile exercise.

The determinative factor in the criminality of young American men is not race. It is education.

CASE	RACE	AGE	I.Q.	EDUCATION	LITERACY	EMPLOYMENT	CRIME	REMARKS
1	N	21	low	10th	illiterate	no	robbery	some indication of mental problems
2	N	21	low	1cth	can read	no	burglary	no property taken—defendant is epileptic
3	N	26	low	10th	poor reader	no	robbery	9 prior convictions not uneducable
4	N	24	low	11th	poor reader	no	robbery	
5	PR	25	low	12 yrs.	illiterate	no	attempted arson	speaks English, not violent
6	N	18	82	10th	3rd grade reading level	no	stolen car	probably much brighter; pushed from school to school; diagnosed "mixed character disorder"
7	W	22	normal	grad	yes	yes	robbed bank	emotional problems

CASE	RACE	AGE	I.Q.	EDUCATION	LITERACY	EMPLOYMENT	CRIME	REMARKS
8	W	18	normal	10th	poor reader	no	burglary	
9	W	18	low	10th	poor reader	no	burglary	
10	N	18	normal	10th	yes	no	robbery	
11	W	35	normal	12th	yes	yes	burglary	alcoholic
12	N	23	normal	11th	yes	no	threats	
13	N	21	normal	12th	yes	yes	threats	
14	N	21	normal	11th	yes	no	shoplifting	
15	N	25	normal	11th	fair	no	robbery	
16	W	25	low	11th	poor	no	robbery	
17	W	23	low	11th	poor	no	robbery	
18	N	32	low	11th	fair	no	arson	
19	W	18	normal	12th	poor	no	stolen car	

CASE	RACE	AGE	I.Q.	EDUCATION	LITERACY	EMPLOYMENT	CRIME	REMARKS
20	N	43	normal	12th	yes	yes	assault	mistaken identity no prior record
21	W	24	normal	grad	poor	no	assault	
22	N	34	normal	grad	yes	yes	assault	
23	N	18	low	11th	poor	no	robbery	
24	N	23	low	10th	poor	no	robbery	
25	W	29	normal	1 yr. college	yes	yes	voter fraud	
26	W	25	normal	11th	poor	no	weapons	
27	N	34	normal	grad	yes	yes	assault with auto	alcoholic (convicted drunk driving)
28	W	18	low	11th	poor	no	theft	
29	N	29	normal	12th	yes	yes	weapons	possession only didn't use gun

CASE	RACE	AGE	I.Q.	EDUCATION	LITERACY	EMPLOYMENT	CRIME	REMARKS
30	N	19	low	10th	poor	no	theft	
31	N	21	normal	11th	fair	no	theft	
32	N	23	normal	grad.	yes	yes	weapons	cousin had been stabbed; carried gun for protection, didn't use it
33	N	24	normal	11th	fair	no	theft	
34	N	34	normal	grad	yes	yes	weapons	did not use gun
35	W	18	normal	11th	fair	no	theft	
36	N	18	normal	grad	yes	yes	weapons	did not use gun
37	W	29	normal	grad	yes	yes	voter fraud	drug user
38	W	29	normal	10th	yes	yes	weapons	did not shoot
39	N	23	normal	11th	fair	yes	burglary	

CASE	RACE	AGE	I.Q.	EDUCATION	LITERACY	EMPLOYMENT	CRIME	REMARKS
40	N	31	normal	grad	yes	yes	forgery	
41	N	19	normal	8th	yes	no	theft	transvestite
42	N	21	low	10th	yes	no	robbery	
43	N	23	82	9th	4th grade	no	wife and child beating	long prior record
44	W	34	normal	grad	yes	yes	wife and child beating	emotionally disturbed
45	N	18	normal	11th	fair	no	burglary	"adjustment reaction of adolescence" diagnosis; 5 burglaries in 1 year

CHAPTER XVI

THE CHILD
AND THE LAW

The child receives the worst of both worlds.
US v. *Kent* 383 US 541,556 (1966)

The twentieth century may be called the "Century of the Child" by future historians of Western civilization. The discipline of child psychology was invented in this century.[1] The first juvenile court was established in 1899. In the early years of the twentieth century every state established a juvenile court. Despite increasing dissatisfaction and disillusionment, no state has repealed its juvenile court law or substantially amended it. Every decade of this century the president of the United States has called a White House Conference on Children and Youth. 1979 was officially proclaimed "The Year of the Child." In many communities expenditures for the public schools equal or exceed the expenditures for all other governmental purposes.

One might conclude from these facts that Americans love children and treat them with special tenderness and affection. But if one examines the operations of the juvenile courts, child-caring agencies, and the public schools, one must sadly acknowledge that our society dislikes children. Our institutions treat children more harshly than adults and our law denies to children the rights guaranteed to every person by the Constitution.

Does this callous and punitive attitude of contemporary American law towards children reflect a dislike of children that is peculiar to our time and our society, or did adults always have similar attitudes to children? Not many scholars have considered this question. There are a few isolated facts with respect to the treatment of children in different countries and different ages. In pagan societies children, not adults, were often sacrificed to propitiate the gods. Classical Greeks, Romans, and many other peoples abandoned, exposed, and left unwanted children to die. Until the early twentieth century unwanted children were similarly disposed of in China. Although child sacrifice is forbidden in America, an incredible number of American children are killed by abuse and neglect. Until almost modern times, in many societies it was a common practice to compel young girls to marry men chosen for them by their fathers for reasons which had nothing to do with the welfare or the wishes of the girl. Many times such marriages were extremely hazardous, if not fatal, to the young bride. It was also a common practice in western countries, including the United States, to apprentice young boys to masters who were often cruel and venal. There was little, if any, legal protection for the bride or the apprentice.

Historian Barbara Tuchman, describing life in Western Europe in the fourteenth century, writes, "Of all the characteristics in which the medieval age differs from the modern, none is so striking as the comparative absence of interest in children. . . . On the whole, babies and young children appear to have been left to survive or die without great concern in the first five or six years."[2] The life of an individual such as Geoffrey Chaucer, who grew up and reared his own children in the fourteenth century, presents a very different picture of childhood. Chaucer was carefully educated by his parents and took a great interest in the rearing and education of his own children. He was, of course, an exceptional man and his attitude toward his children may have been atypical. Today, many Americans truly care for their children, sacrifice for them, and rear them lovingly and tenderly. It is impossible to know what is the norm or average attitude of parents toward their children. It is clear, however, that social and government institutions, including the entire legal system, give children far less consideration and care than they give adults, even though the children's needs are greater. Significantly, older Americans have a right to subsidized medical care based on the premise that most older people are less able to provide such care for themselves. Obviously few, if any, children are capable of providing for their own medical care. But government does not similarly provide for the medical needs of children.

As one looks back through the centuries examining the limited, objective facts, it is difficult to understand the attitude of parents and society toward children. Why did adults permit, or at least not prevent, thousands of young children from embarking on the hazardous and often fatal adventure known as the Children's Crusade? Why did parents like the Biblical Isaac and King Agememnon give their children as sacrifices? Future generations may well ask a similar question with respect to Americans in the 1960s. During these years thousands of young people left home and school and wandered aimlessly and dangerously around the nation and the world.

Although facts as to the attitude of society toward children are sparse, legal rights and disabilities of children are known and reasonably verifiable. In the Western world prior to the twentieth century, children over the age of seven were treated under the criminal law the same as adults. At common law a child under the age of seven was conclusively presumed to be incapable of committing a crime. There is a similar provision in Islamic law.[3] An older child who stole or killed or committed any other offense was tried and sentenced the same as an adult. A casual examination of the Year Books, the compilation of reported English cases beginning in the thirteenth century, discloses very few prosecutions involving children. At least only a rare case indicates that the offender was a child. Contrast this with contemporary concern with crime committed by children. In our statistical era juvenile prosecutions are well documented. Uniform crime reports reveal that in 1976 of 5,077,400 arrests, 1,218,000 were children under the age of eighteen. Possibly children in prior centuries committed an equal proportion of crimes but the fact of their age apparently had no legal or social significance and, therefore, was not mentioned.

The notion that childhood is a time of happy, carefree innocence, like the belief that primitive people lead happy, idyllic lives of goodness, did not become popular in Western Europe until the late eighteenth century. This concept was essentially part of a romantic view of the world which for the first time saw beauty in rustic landscape, idealized the lives of farmers and milkmaids, and fantasized with respect to primitive people and children, who were presumably unspoiled by civilization. This belief that childhood is a time of happiness is belied by the facts of contemporary American life. As we have seen, child abuse is of epidemic proportions. Child suicides have reached alarming figures. It is the third leading cause of death among teenagers. It is estimated that fifty-seven American children and teenagers attempt suicide every hour. Many early childhood deaths which are reported as accidents may have been suicides. The rates of childhood suicides are equally high in Japan and many Western European countries. In less developed countries such information is rarely accurately gathered so that meaningful comparisons are not possible. According to government statistics the suicide rate for white males fifteen to twenty-four years of age was 19.6 and 14.4 for black males.

Prior to the twentieth century, despite the much-publicized writings of romantics like Rousseau, children were expected to work. Except for the children of the wealthy and the nobility, children did work hard from the time they were physically able to do so. They were an integral part of the labor force, whether they worked at home or outside the home. Even today, children of sharecroppers and migrant farm workers work in the fields with their parents. In many countries around the globe children are productive members of the community and do not lead lives separate and different from adults. Llewellyn's autobiographical novel, *How Green Was My Valley*, gives a vivid picture of the life of a very young boy in a coal mining community in Wales. Life in the coal mines of Kentucky, Pennsylvania, southern Illinois, and other places in the United States was not materially different. It was not until 1913 that the United States Supreme Court sustained the constitutionality of a statute prohibiting children under the age of sixteen from being employed in hazardous occupations.[4] The case arose out of a civil action for damages for the injured child. Significantly, it was not a government prosecution of the employer for violation of the statute but a civil action for damages which raised the issue.

Until the twentieth century children were not segregated into a separate society. The concept of "adolescence" or "teenage" as being a special time and society with its own activities and conventions is a peculiarly contemporary phenomenon. In other ages children lived in an adult world. There were no special books for children. As soon as they could read, children read adult literature. There were no special church services for children or special entertainments devised for them. Children attended all the popular street events, including hangings and beheadings.

It was not until the twentieth century that Americans embraced the idea that children should be treated differently from adults in most aspects of life including the law. The juvenile court was an idealistic and humane effort to protect children from the harshness of the criminal law. At the turn of the century, criminal law in the United States was indeed harsh and lacking in what we now consider elementary due process of law. Accused persons were not entitled to free counsel; they could be held without bail for long periods before trial; confessions were routinely coerced and often beaten out of suspects; prison conditions were brutal; there were few appellate or post-trial rights for offenders.

A separate court where children would be treated not as criminals but as young people in need of guidance was a noble goal of well-meaning reformers. Juvenile court judges described their function as that of "placing an arm around the shoulders of an errant lad and gently leading him into the paths of virtue." Very soon, however, these courts became the dumping grounds for poor, disadvantaged children as they are today. But the fiction continued to bemuse judges, scholars, and the public. In the early years of this century the juvenile courts were crowded with children of immigrants. Their cases were heard quickly, in secrecy in courts which had no rules or limitations. The promise of individualized treatment soon degenerated into what the President's Commission on Crime and Delinquency describes as "the five-minute children's hour." Many juvenile court hearings at which a child was removed from his home and sent to a juvenile jail took less than five minutes. In 1974, the nation's juvenile courts heard 1,252,700 cases of delinquency but only 151,300 cases of dependency and neglect (including abuse).[5] The court had clearly become an agency to prosecute rather than protect children.

In 1967, Supreme Court Justice Abe Fortas declared that "the child receives the worst of both worlds, that he gets neither the protections accorded to adults nor the solicitous care and regenerative treatment postulated for children."[6] In 1979, more than a decade after that land-mark decision, most children appearing in juvenile court have counsel. But nothing substantive has really changed for the children. In most juvenile courts, the children still have five-minute hearings. Most juvenile courts do not have rules of procedure; sentences are arbitrary and disparate. The poor and minorities suffer disproportionately in juvenile courts as in adult courts although there is widespread recognition that crime by children of the affluent is a serious problem.[7]

The public is outraged by the fact that many boys who commit serious crimes are not incarcerated. People who are familiar with the operations of the juvenile court are aghast at the numbers of boys and girls who have not committed any crime but who are, nonetheless, jailed for indefinite periods. Children who run away from home, play hookey, and are brought into court by their parents as being "incorrigible" are routinely jailed.

Beverly is a pretty and charming girl of sixteen. She is not a brilliant student but she does acceptable work in school. I saw her in a children's shelter run by a private organization. After Beverly had been in detention (juvenile jail) for more than a month this agency succeeded in getting the court to transfer her to their group home. The entire time Beverly was in detention she had not been able to attend school. What was her crime?

Beverly's mother had petitioned the court to have her daughter declared an incorrigible and removed from the home. The mother said that Beverly stayed out late at night and was disobedient. Beverly admitted coming home late occasionally after a school party. It was apparent that the mother, who had remarried, wanted to get rid of Beverly. Boarding school is expensive. Juvenile jails are free. The judge did not question Beverly's mother as to whether she was a good and caring mother. The fact that Beverly had not committed a crime was irrelevant in his view. For Beverly's "protection" she was incarcerated and deprived of her right to liberty and to attend public school. If it had not been for the interest of this voluntary agency, Beverly would have remained in custody until her eighteenth birthday.

Beverly's case is not anomalous. As we have seen, women commit only a fraction of the crimes which men commit. The same is true of girls. But the juvenile court in its peculiar bastardized form of law and social welfare operates more punitively against girls than boys. Apparently many juvenile court judges see their function as preventing girls from having sexual relations. A girl who is apprehended is far more likely to be incarcerated "for her own good" than a boy. The Law Enforcement Assistance Administration finds: "Girls are more likely to be detained [held in custody] than boys. . . . Most girls are detained because they have been accused of so-called *children's crimes* rather than criminal offenses. Nationally, nearly 75 percent of the girls and between 20 to 30 percent of the boys in detention are held for status offenses, behavior that would not be illegal if committed by an adult. Once detained, girls are more likely to be held longer even though they are less likely to have been accused of criminal offenses."[8]

I have seen countless children like Beverly who are not criminals but who are treated by the juvenile court as if they were dangerous offenders. They are held in jails with prostitutes, thieves, and other felons. They are degraded and demeaned by the juvenile court which was created to protect them. Many times I have heard a mother or father say to the

Juvenile Court Judge, "You take her, your honor. I can't do nothin' with her [or him]."

I have never heard a judge say, "Madam, this child is your responsibility. Unless he (or she) has been proved guilty of a crime, he is entitled to his freedom. If you refuse to provide for your child you will be guilty of an offense: child neglect."

All too often a girl is really not a runaway. She is sent away by an uncaring family. All too often a child accused of truancy is really not a school dropout. He is a school pushout, pushed out by an uncaring school system.

There are few if any meaningful proposals for change. Some observers of the juvenile court strenuously advocate that noncriminal acts like truancy be removed from the jurisdiction of the juvenile court. Others advocate that the age limit of the juvenile court be lowered so that more children are tried in adult court. Most of the literature repeats the same tired debates between treatment and desert in sentencing that flourish with respect to adult offenders.[9] Juvenile judges cling to the notion that they are doing good for the child and resist restrictions on their powers. This hybrid of social welfare and law has indeed resulted in the worst of both worlds. Children do not receive either social services or a due process trial.

Although little has changed in the way the law treats children, a great deal has changed for lawyers, law schools, and social workers. Juvenile law is now taught as a separate course in many law schools. There are publicly financed juvenile justice centers around the country which study juvenile law. More social workers, judges, and lawyers are engaged in processing juvenile delinquents. Juvenile law, like correctional institutions, is a growth industry. It employs an enormous bureaucracy of adults.

Despite this tremendous infusion of money and personnel into the juvenile justice system, more young people are committing crimes and being tried, however briefly, and committed to institutions. Many of them, on release, graduate to adult criminal court and adult prisons. Juvenile crime has continued to rise. It has outpaced the increase of personnel and institutions. I do not suggest that there is necessarily a negative correlation between the crime rate and expenditures of money to control juvenile crime and to deal with juvenile offenders. The explosion of juvenile crime may well be a world-wide phenomenon in a global time of troubles when many social institutions are crumbling and patterns of life are rapidly changing. Crime by restless, dissatisfied, and alienated youth may be an inevitable response. Reports from Moscow and Peking as well as many countries in Western Europe reveal growing serious problems of juvenile delinquency.[10]

It may also be that the American legal establishment, including the courts, does not really believe that children are entitled to due process of law. Significantly in the corporal punishment cases, the United States Supreme Court held that a child is not entitled to a hearing before being beaten because "typically a child is not punished without cause."[11] To follow that argument to its logical conclusion, no adult accused of crime would be entitled to a trial because typically the police do not arrest without probable cause. Between probable cause and proof beyond a reasonable doubt, the standard for conviction of a crime, is an enormous chasm. Into this abyss the legal rights and protections of children have fallen. Few authorities link juvenile crime with the lawlessness visited on children by the juvenile justice system. There may be no quantifiably provable relationship. But a message of lawlessness and disregard of individual rights and dignity is probably not lost upon the young people who are drawn into the juvenile justice system.

During the 1960s and into the 1970s criminologists "tended to discount the significance of the sharp increase in reported crime [in the United States]. . . ."[12] Many thought that as the large population of teenagers moved into their twenties and thirties and the much smaller number of young children reached the mid and late teens the crime curve would flatten because of demography. These views were strongly espoused despite the fact that during the decade from 1958 through 1967 there was a 300 percent increase in assaults by ten-to-fourteen-year-olds and a 200 percent increase in robberies by this age group. The greatest increase in crime by children is in the fifth-to-ninth-grade age group. The FBI reports that from 1960 through 1970 adult arrests for violent crime increased 67 percent while arrests of juveniles for violent crime increased 167 percent.[13] Juvenile crime has continued to increase every year through the 1970s. Forty-five percent of those arrested for violent crime, excluding murder, are under age eighteen, although this age group comprises less than 20 percent of the population.[14] Seventh grade is considered to be the most dangerous period, when the greatest number of children are attacked by older children and vandalism is at its peak.[15]

Juvenile crime has spread from the streets into the schools. The acts committed by school children are not mere childish pranks. Public-school vandalism costs the taxpayers an estimated $200 million annually.[16] The primary victims of juvenile crime are other children who are robbed, mugged, stabbed, and shot. Teachers are frequently assaulted. In some respects, many public schools resemble prisons. The gates to the school yards are locked until the opening school bell and then locked again when the school day is over—which may be as early as 2:30 in the afternoon. The children are locked out of, not locked in, the schools. Often children are required to show ID cards. In many schools non-teaching personnel monitor the halls; bells clang throughout the school day; public address systems blare forth at any time. As many as several thousand children attend a single school. They often do not know the names of their teachers. And the teachers frequently do not know the names or faces of the children.

A conscientious guidance counsellor in a large high school plaintively asked to have the children's pictures attached to their files so that she could be sure when writing a report which child she was dealing with. This was a school with specialized teachers for each subject, non-teaching aides, guidance counsellors, many vice principals, assistant principals, and department heads. The guidance counsellors hold conferences with the teachers; the teachers confer with department heads and vice principals; but no one knows the child.

What do the schools and the criminal justice systems do when faced with these enormous and grave problems? The National Institute of Education in making its Study on Violence and Vandalism in Schools (1975–1976) asked 5578 public senior, junior, and elementary school principals what remedies they proposed. The following responses were given, listed here in the order of frequency:

Provision for employment and recreation for students after school hours and during the summer
Alternative programs for "divergent" students
Student and parent participation in decision-making
Meaningful curricula and activities for students
Increased counselling
Funding for alarm systems
Increased interagency cooperation
Increased community involvement
In-service training for teachers
Provision for discipline other than off-site suspension or expulsion

It is apparent that none of these ten remedies would change the lifestyle of the children or improve their education. "Alternative programs for 'divergent' students" is gobbledygook for getting rid of troublesome youngsters. "Meaningful curricula and activities for students" is a worthy goal. One can only wonder what curricula and activities the schools presently have. Evidently it is not meaningful. "Increased counseling" and "In-service training for teachers" are both suggestions for spending more money on adults in the hope that some benefit will trickle down to the children. The respondents to this survey have not presented a program for meaningful change in the operation of the public schools or any insights into the problems of the children which evoke such violence and crimes. There is no mention of illiteracy.

When one looks at the response of the criminal justice system to the problems of juvenile crime, there is a similar rigidity and lack of insight on the part of the bureaucracy. Inevitably there is a request for expansion of adult jobs and increased budgets. Administration burgeons. None of this additional personnel and money really touches the children.

Although there are enormous numbers of children who commit serious crimes, a large proportion of juvenile court time, staff, and facilities is spent on non-criminal children: the status offenders. These are children brought into juvenile court for acts of delinquency which are not crimes, such as runaway, truancy, and incorrigibility. They are included in the figures of delinquency. Despite numerous proposals to remove these essentially non-criminal cases from the juvenile court, the juvenile judges adamantly oppose this reduction in their power over the lives of young people.

A judge sitting in adult criminal court sees the failures of the juvenile justice system every day. Most pre-sentence reports of adult felons list not only their criminal records but also their juvenile records. I do not permit such records to be included in the reports furnished to me because a juvenile-court adjudication of delinquency is the result of a "hearing," not a due process trial with the constitutional safeguards and protections afforded an adult accused of crime; nor is conviction based solely upon legally admissible evidence and proof beyond a reasonable doubt.

The young offender at the time of sentencing usually tells me about the juvenile institutions in which he has served time. Most of these places are simply jails but with none of the protections and rules which obtain in adult prisons. Children's mail is read and censored. Solitary confinement is a common punishment. So are beatings. There are no rules as to yard privileges. In most adult prisons, the inmates are entitled to go outside in the prison yard for a certain number of minutes each day. Many children in juvenile jails spend months without ever going outdoors. There are chaplains in adult prisons. I have never seen any clergy visiting children in custody. There are law libraries and lawyers for adult prisoners. Few attorneys visit children's jails. Most significantly, there is little schooling in institutions for children. It is no wonder that young people released from such juvenile jails graduate to adult crimes and adult jails. Since its inception, this has been the record of the juvenile court.

The learned studies made of juvenile crime have been based on the children in juvenile court. These children are the raw data on which theories of juvenile delinquency are predicated. The widely read studies on juvenile crime by the Gluecks disclosed the fact that more than three fourths of the juvenile delinquents came from impoverished families.[17] Such a finding was inevitable when the juvenile court was used as a receptacle for poor, troublesome children. On this basis, half a century of criminology has found a high correlation between crime and socio-economic status. But, as we have seen in the discussion of white-collar crime, any review of all crimes reveals that criminal acts are not committed predominantly by poor disadvantaged individuals. Such people are, however, the vast majority of the people prosecuted, convicted, and imprisoned. The United States Bureau of the Census in 1923 revealed that almost three fourths of adult offenders were of lower socio-economic status.[18] Other studies indicate a high correlation between areas of poverty and delinquency.[19] It is important to remember that prior to World War II the non-white population of northern cities was much lower than it is today. The majority of the delinquents in those days were white. There can be no doubt that the delinquents in the court system then, like those today, were poor, underprivileged, and undereducated. This situation obtained long before the introduction of minimum wages and a high compulsory school attendance age. Many apologists for the failures of the school system suggest that the fault lies in the increase in numbers of academically uninterested children who cannot obtain employment and are required to attend school.

I believe that figures showing the high correlation between low socio-economic status and juvenile delinquency indicate not the incidence of juvenile misconduct but the bias of the juvenile justice system, which excludes the children of the more affluent and bears punitively on the children of the poor and disadvantaged. The monumental study, Crime and Delinquency, made by the federal government under the Johnson administration, revealed that 90 percent of all youth had committed some offense for which they could have been declared delinquent.

What should the criminal justice system do with these undereducated, idle youth who commit crimes? What can it reasonably be expected to do? These questions are seldom asked. Instead the justice system seizes upon each new proposal as a panacea, a solution that will miraculously transform problem children into models of obedience and conformity. I am frequently reminded of Mr. and Mrs. F., middle-class, white, educated people who were disgusted with Alice, their fifteen-year-old daughter. According to their litany of complaints, Alice was rude and impertinent. Her school work was poor. She stayed out late. Her boyfriends rode motorcycles. They, too, were rude. She was sloppy around the house and would not help with the daily chores. Whenever she was home there were shouting matches and slammed doors. Life was unpleasant for the entire family.

"We took her to Juvenile Court," Mr. and Mrs. F. told me. "The judge will straighten her out. That was the right thing to do. Wasn't it?"

"You have had Alice for fifteen years," I told them. "The judge will see her for, at most, fifteen minutes. What can he do that you can't do? His only options are to put her in jail with real criminals or return her to you."

Instead of recognizing the obvious limitations of courts of law, the juvenile justice system and the public continue to delude themselves with unrealistic expectations. They seize upon a scheme and adopt it with enthusiasm. When it fails to accomplish impossible goals, the system and the public just as enthusiastically and blindly embrace another plan. Let us examine a few of the more popular crime prevention programs which had their day as the great panacea for juvenile crime and then were quietly abandoned, as well as those now hailed as the ultimate solution. As each new idea blossomed, it was widely adopted before there was an adequate trial period, evaluation, and discussion of its merits and legality. Many of the plans have never been considered by the courts. Their legality has not been tested, yet they have become integral parts of the juvenile justice system, employing huge bureaucracies and processing tens of thousands of children.

The juvenile court itself was immediately hailed as an embodiment of enlightened wisdom. It was not until 1966 that the United States Supreme Court first took a small look at the operations of the juvenile court system. For sixty-seven years the juvenile courts of this country had been treating children in ways that were totally lacking in elementary due process. But, despite a few challenges to the constitutionality of its procedures, appellate courts declined to consider these issues. No one knows how many children were wrenched from their families and placed in institutions, presumably for their own good, without an adversary court hearing at which the parents and the children were given an opportunity to be heard and to present evidence. To this day there are inadequate standards and procedures under which such intervention in family life occurs. No one knows how many children were stigmatized as delinquents and incarcerated in juvenile jails as a result of a brief hearing where the child had no attorney and there was not proof beyond a reasonable doubt that the child had committed a crime. It is apparent that this cavelier treatment of children did not protect children or deter them from criminal conduct. Indeed, contact with the juvenile court may have been a contributing factor in subsequent adult criminality.

By the 1930s disenchantment with the juvenile court had begun. Children continued to commit crimes and to disturb the social scene despite the ministrations of the juvenile court. The next fad was to hold the parents responsible for the offenses of the children. During the thirties, a vast program was instituted under which parents were prosecuted in juvenile court for contributing to the delinquency of minors— their own children. This program proved futile and was abandoned after ten or fifteen years.

The contribution of the 1940s was the Youth Authority concept. In many states these special bureaucracies still flourish. The basic plan was that the juvenile court commit delinquents and young adult offenders to a state youth authority for diagnostic services and treatment. In many states the courts were required to make indeterminate commitments to these authorities. Juvenile and young adult offenders could be released only at the pleasure of the Authority. There were few rules and no due process hearings by which the offender could obtain a release. The arbitrariness of the Youth Authorities and the entire concept of indeterminate sentences fell into disfavor as juvenile and young adult crime continued to rise despite "diagnosis and treatment."

In 1958, a book with the brave subtitle "A Rational Approach to Penal Problems" was published under the auspices of the National

Council on Crime and Delinquency.[20] The rational approach proposed was the application of scientific thought (criminology) and research to the problem. We have since that time spent a great deal of money on research and collected much data showing the failures of the juvenile court. But there have been no significant changes in the operations of the juvenile courts. Significantly, the Gault decision was less than a decade in the future when this book was written. This rational approach did not recommend that children be provided with legal counsel or that they be accorded due process.

The next panacea was pretrial diversion. This concept, in essence, is to refer persons accused of less serious offenses to a social agency without having a trial to determine whether the individuals are in fact guilty of the crimes with which they are charged. This idea was current in the sixties. It was advocated by Whitney North Seymour in a book entitled *Why Justice Fails.* Many states by statute or rule of court have adopted such programs. Some have alluring nomenclatures such as "Accelerated Rehabilitation Disposition." As many of these programs now operate, they are even speedier than the five-minute juvenile court hearings. The usual pretrial diversion hearing takes approximately two to three minutes. The basic assumption is that the criminal justice system itself is crime inducing. This may be true when it treats people arbitrarily and without regard for their rights. The idea of diversion is to keep accused offenders away from the contamination of a trial. One can only wonder what rehabilitation occurs outside the court system. Most of these accused persons are simply released with a threat of trial if they are rearrested within a specific time period.

Statistics indicate that many of these accused persons are not rearrested. They may have been innocent of any offense. If the crimes were trivial, the offenders were probably not dangerous habitual criminals. For decades in adult court trivial cases have been "blown out" at preliminary hearings before a magistrate and never come to trial. But most juvenile courts do not have preliminary hearings where the state must show that a crime was committed and that there is probable cause to believe that the accused committed the offense. In many instances, diversion is used not for the benefit of disadvantaged youths but to permit middle-aged, middle-class people to avoid the stigma of conviction for offenses of which they are clearly guilty, such as driving while drunk, illegal possession of weapons, shoplifting, and other nonviolent crimes. Those who gain the benefits of diversion are principally people

with no prior record. Again the system is skewed in favor of the dominant adult society and against the young and poor.

Diversion is now popular and widely used. It has not been subjected
to careful scrutiny by the appellate courts. There has been little legislative or scholarly debate over the merits of the program, its assumptions,
and the extraordinary policy of abolishing trials. No one knows whether
it is beneficial or economical. Non-trial disposition is cheaper than trials.
But new enormous bureaucracies are employed to process these diver-
sions. Much court time is also employed in what is essentially a nonjudicial extra-legal procedure.

Other ideas are also popular. One is taking children to visit courts
during school hours. The school day is short; children have little enough
time for basic education. One wonders what benefits they derive from
watching the trial of a robber or a rapist. One day forty high-school
students sat in my courtroom and observed the trial of a wife beater. I
invited them to wait until the end of the trial so that I could explain
the procedures to them. But they left before the trial was concluded.
The teacher required them to write letters to me after the visit. Here
are a few of these letters with the students' spelling and punctuation
reproduced.

Dear Judge Forer
    Thank you for letting me sit in on your cases in court. I really had a very swell
time and really enjoyed myself and the way you handled those cases.
    If I ever decided to be a lawyer, I would love for you to give me a few pointers
(smile)"

Thank you for allowing us to visit your court.

I would like to thank you for allowing me and my class in to your court room.
I myself would be back to see you in the near future, conducting the trails [sic]

I enjoyed the trial in [sic] would like to come again if possible. I think that
the young students would enjoy visiting a trial of any kind. Thank you for leting
[sic] our class come to sit with you and watching you at work.

I enjoyed and appreciated you allowing us the students of——to visit your
courtroom. It served as a stimulating experience and incite [sic] to law and its
functions. We express our gratitude and sincerest thanks for the opportunity to
visit and hope the invitation will remain open.

These are representative letters. One might assume that they were written by fifth- and sixth-grade children. In fact, the writers are seniors in high school about to graduate.

Other fashionable programs release children from school to engage in "real work." Many of them are employed to deliver sandwiches to offices and do other menial errands. The children who participate in these programs frequently are the ones most educationally deficient.

Prison visitation is also in vogue. "Pre-delinquent" youngsters, those who live in high-crime areas, are taken to see the horrors of prison and talk to "lifers." The widely admired film, *Scared Straight,* and others like it have been shown to countless children during school hours in the belief that it would deter criminal conduct. Recent studies indicate that those exposed to the film committed more crimes than those who had not seen it.[21] Of course, those who were shown the film were probably high-risk potential offenders.

I shall not emulate the long list of eminent, sincere scholars and authorities who have proposed these various panaceas by offering another one. I am convinced that there is no simple device or plan which will transform juvenile and young adult offenders into peaceful law-abiding citizens. My premises are different. First, I believe that every person who is accused of an offense in the United States is entitled to a trial at which he is afforded the Constitutional rights guaranteed to all adults. Second, I believe that two of the basic causes of street crimes and crimes of violence committed by children and young adults are inadequate education and unemployment. Unemployment is the result of functional illiteracy and lack of skills.

The United Nations' global study of the problem of the young offender reveals that crime in this age group is extremely high throughout the world.[22] The largest percentage of the offenses committed by those aged fifteen to twenty-five is some form of stealing. The second largest type of offenses involves spontaneous acts of violence. These conclusions accord with my experience as a lawyer and a trial judge in the United States. The report further indicates that only a small percentage of crime in this age group is committed by females. This also is true in the United States.

The comment on education is interesting. "There is a paucity of data on illiteracy rates among youthful offenders but it seems safe to assume that they will be high in countries *without* compulsory and free education." The study reports that in Israel 72 percent of young adult offenders had completed no more than five grades of elementary school. American statistics clearly reveal that despite free compulsory education the educational level of the offender is directly related to the incidence of crime. Sixty-one percent of the inmates in state correctional institutions are not high-school graduates. Eighty-nine percent have had no education beyond the high school level.[23] Functional literacy is not included. I believe there is an even stronger correlation between crime and illiteracy. From my limited but representative experience, I conclude that the vast majority of juveniles and young adult offenders, regardless of the number of years they have spent in school, have no more basic skills than would be expected of a person with only an elementary school education. Many have not achieved a fourth- or fifth-grade level of literacy.

An obvious and reasonably attainable goal for the juvenile justice system is to require these young offenders to learn basic skills. A decade ago, I pointed out that school attendance laws operate like a penal sentence. When the youngster has served his time he is released from school regardless of his attainments or deficiencies.[24] I recommended that no young person of educable mentality be permitted to leave school until he had achieved functional literacy, had sufficient understanding of arithmetic to make change and do simple computations, and had the basic general knowledge required of aliens applying for citizenship. Many communities now require a basic skills test for high-school graduation. The constitutionality of such tests is under attack on the grounds of racial discrimination. But to date no state or community has made basic educational skills a requirement for legal school-leaving.

The juvenile court could, without additional statutory authority, sentence these undereducated young offenders to attend school. There is no reason to wait until they become adult offenders to require them to go to school and to learn. In sentencing young street criminals, I require them to get their high-school equivalency diploma while in prison and on release to make payments of restitution or reparation to the victims of their crimes. Similar sentences can be imposed by juvenile court judges. Restitution can be made in cash or work. Teenagers are not totally unemployable. New York City has a project, JOEY, which provides jobs for teenagers on probation.[25] School children and mentally handicapped adults have been hired to harvest apples in Michigan.[26] Both groups were found to be excellent workers. With a little imagination and enterprise subsidized employment could be found for many teenage offenders. As with young adult offenders, literacy and employment are the first steps in rehabilitation.

Education is recognized worldwide as a basic human right of all children. The General Assembly of the United Nations in 1959 unanimously adopted a Declaration of the Rights of the Child. Paragraph 7 provides that it shall be the right of a child "to receive a free education." American children receive free schooling but many of them do not receive an education. There is a material difference.

Functional literacy is not a cure-all for crime. As we have seen, many well-educated people commit very serious offenses, both white-collar crime and family abuse. They rarely commit street crimes of violence. Most of these offenders are well over the age of thirty. Real education, not merely time spent in school, may be as effective a means as we now have available for treatment of juvenile offenders and prevention of street crime.

It is futile to bemoan the ills of society, to blame the parents or the welfare state or two hundred years of discrimination. The criminal justice system cannot restructure society, it cannot rewrite history. It must deal with the people who are arrested and with their problems unless we are to continue to recycle delinquent youths and recidivist adults. Society must decide whether it wants to pay for more prisons or meet the real needs of this tremendous number of idle, undereducated, unemployed, and unemployable youth. I submit that it is not only more humane but considerably cheaper to educate and train young people to live in this society than to maintain them behind bars.

CHAPTER XVII

THE USES OF PSYCHIATRY

Psychiatrists and Juvenile Court Judges
are the only people in our society who can
lawfully lock up people who have not been
accused of any crime.
—Dr. Jonas Robitscher

Psychiatrists today are an integral part of the criminal justice system.
Judges routinely order neuropsychiatric examinations for offenders
whenever there is a suggestion of a mental or emotional problem. These
reports greatly influence the sentencing decision. Under several of the
proposals now being considered for changes in the methods and goals
of sentencing, the role of the psychiatrist would be drastically altered or
eliminated. The entire concept of rehabilitation that is now under attack
is predicated on a medical model of jurisprudence, namely, that the
offender needs treatment. If he needs treatment, he must be sick,
mentally ill. It is the psychiatrist who will diagnose, treat, and cure him.
Some psychiatrists, like Dr. Thomas Szasz, believe that mental illness
is a myth and that psychiatrists are engaged in manufacturing madness.[1]
Others are convinced that criminals are indeed suffering from serious
illness and must be treated. Some psychiatrists are concerned that psychiatry has moved from a healing art to a coercive arm of the law but
with few of the Constitutional safeguards which restrict lawyers and
judges in imposing sanctions upon individuals.[2] Misunderstandings, if

not hostility, between the disciplines of psychiatry and law are rife. Many psychiatrists believe that lawyers and judges prevent mentally ill people from being hospitalized and receiving treatment. And many lawyers and judges believe that psychiatrists attempt to coerce people into accepting therapy in violation of their Constitutional rights.

In recent years laws have been enacted which carefully prescribe the procedures which must be followed and the standards which must be met before a person can be committed to a mental institution against his will in a civil proceeding. The battles of psychiatrists which are fought in civil court are often sharp and contentious. They involve two sets of experts retained by opposing parties. These psychiatrists appear and testify in open court and are subjected to searching cross examination. They operate on a plane of equality under the adversary system of litigation. The play *Whose Life Is It Anyway?* illustrates the use of psychiatrists in civil cases as witnesses for adversary parties and also the very subjective basis for these expert opinions. Psychiatrists are frequently called to testify as to the ability of parents to care for their children, the competence of older people to live alone and manage their affairs, the competence of a testator to make a will and the possible undue influence exerted upon the testator, the psychiatric injuries inflicted upon people who have been in accidents, as well as the mental condition of individuals whose relatives seek to have them committed to mental institutions. In all such civil cases psychiatrists are called to testify for both sides, just as orthopedists and opthomologists are called as expert witnesses in civil cases involving their specialties.

In criminal cases the role of the psychiatrist is often quite different. Most modern court systems have psychiatrists on their staffs. Judges are expected to obtain neuropsychiatric reports before sentencing offenders who appear to have mental or emotional problems. These psychiatrists render opinions and give advice in writing with respect to the sentence to be imposed. Usually, they do not testify in court and are not subject to cross examination. In most cases there is no opposing expert psychiatrist who appears for the defendant to challenge these findings and conclusions. Some lawyers and judges believe that psychiatrists who recommend the sentence to be imposed on criminal offenders attempt to usurp the functions of the court and make what are essentially legal decisions. Any order issued by a court which deprives a person of his liberty is of necessity a legal decision. These orders must meet legal and Constitutional standards regardless of whether the court's findings are based on evidence regarding the offense or on an opinion as to the mental condition of the offender.

Criminal offenders were tried, convicted, and sentenced under the Anglo-American system for centuries before psychiatry was recognized as a scientific discipline and before there was a branch of learning known as forensic psychiatry. For millenia people have killed, robbed, raped, assaulted, and mutilated others in violation of law. Judges and juries have convicted such offenders and judges have imposed sentences upon them without benefit or assistance of psychiatrists. Although many in the legal profession are critical of psychiatrists, I believe that very few judges would want to eliminate psychiatrists from the criminal justice system. They may, however, wish to redefine the role of the psychiatrist and impose certain legal safeguards. These are important issues that will critically affect many offenders. They deserve careful consideration before the criminal justice system abandons efforts to rehabilitate criminals. The alleged misuses of psychiatry to absolve killers of legal responsibility and to release dangerous offenders from custody must also be examined.

People who commit violent, brutal, and sometimes bizarre crimes are extremely difficult to understand. A judge who leads a stable, quiet, middle-class life, devoid of violence and physical brutality, is bewildered by these defendants who look normal, who speak intelligently and responsibly, but who have committed acts that defy reason and common sense. One vacillates between thinking that almost every offender is mentally ill and should be given therapy, and thinking that all people must be held responsible for their acts. I believe that many of the people who appear before me as defendants in criminal cases did not behave in a rational fashion when they committed these crimes. I hesitate to use the word abnormal since one does not know what the norm of behavior is. At least eleven million crimes were committed in 1978. According to the President's Commission on Mental Health Preliminary Report issued in 1977, "At any given time 25 percent of the population is under the kind of emotional distress that results in symptoms." Is crime a symptom of emotional distress? Perhaps. But what effect, if any, should this have on the criminal prosecution, the culpability of the offender, and the sentence imposed upon him? Today psychiatrists render opinions which affect all of these issues. The psychiatrist speaks with an aura of expertise and scientific truth. His opinions, as required by law, are couched in the language of "reasonable medical certainty." It is difficult for a judge to disregard the opinion of a board-certified psychiatric expert when there is no opposing opinion rendered by another psychiatrist.

Nothing in the education or background of most judges equips us to deal with mental illness, emotional instability, and incompetence. Judges are lay people in the field of psychiatry. But it is our duty to make decisions affecting offenders even though they appear to have mental problems. As individuals we see shades of gray in the areas of mental competence, responsibility, and need for therapy, but the law requires answers in black and white: sane or insane, competent or incompetent, responsible or not responsible, mentally ill or well. Judges who have been criminal defense counsel have had experience with many people similar to the accused persons who appear before them in court. We know that many of these people are unpredictable. We know that our own clients have lied to us, that many of them have killed and shown no remorse or regret. We also know that many people who have committed one horrible crime have not committed another, or at least have not been apprehended for or accused of other offenses. Some of our former clients have been arrested for another crime as soon as we have obtained their release for the previous one, just as we have seen clients go from one bad marriage to another equally bad and still a third and a fourth.

I have heard intelligent, experienced lawyers and judges say, "You can always tell a criminal by the way he walks," or "I can spot a liar; just look him squarely in the eye." Although Lombroso's theories have been repudiated for many years, some people in the criminal justice system still believe that there is a "criminal type" and that they can detect criminals simply by looking at people and talking to them. Most of us, however reluctantly, admit that even though we have known scores of people who have killed and hundreds who have robbed and mugged, such individuals look no different from other people and they behave no differently from others except in the commission of that crime. We really do not understand why offenders commit crimes. Indeed, we are never absolutely sure despite seemingly unimpeachable evidence and confessions whether the accused person really did commit the crime. On occasion, three or four people have confessed to the same crime. Only one person did it. Which of them was it? Or was it someone else, someone no one suspects?

Being a defense lawyer is not easy, despite the TV shows and the books by famous lawyers relating their brilliant victories. Lawyers seldom write about routine cases in which the defense lawyer does not have enough time or money adequately to investigate the crime or retain experts to examine the physical evidence or obtain an in-depth psychiatric study of the accused. Lawyers and judges know that sometimes crime laboratories have given false reports on physical evidence[3] and that many persons' memories are unreliable and their perceptions of space and time are erratic. At least, however, the lawyer's role is clear. He or she has only one duty, to defend the client, not to decide whether he is guilty or innocent, responsible or irresponsible, mentally ill or not. If the client is convicted, these other issues will be brought to the attention of the court at sentencing. So it has been for generations.

A judge has a much more difficult and complex role. Some see the function of the judge as being merely the fulcrum on which the scales of justice hang. The prosecution and the defense each fills one pan of the scales with evidence favoring his side; the trier of fact, the judge or the jury, if there is one, determines the balance. Others see the role of a judge as more than a mere arbiter ruling on questions of law. They believe that a judge has a duty to pursue truth and to ensure that a just and lawful result is obtained. More than 90 percent of criminal and civil cases are not tried before a jury. The judge must decide the facts and rule on the law or accept a guilty plea or, in civil cases, approve a settlement. A judge, of course, decides on the basis of the evidence presented in- court. In evaluating that evidence the judge cannot expunge from his or her mind the experiences of a lifetime. As the United States Supreme Court observed, "We cannot ignore as judges what we know as men."

Sometimes, for example, a witness states positively that he saw the accused, a robber or mugger, face to face for at least five minutes. During that time, the man said, "Gimme your money or I'll blow your head off." The victim said, "Here it is. Don't hurt me," and handed the robber his wallet. The robber immediately fled.

I will say to the victim who is testifying, "I'll start timing you and you tell me how long this encounter took. Begin."

The witness sits in the chair. His lips move silently as he repeats the exchange of words. He reaches in his pocket, removes his wallet, and holds it in his hand.

"That's it. That's just how much time it took," he says.

The entire incident took fifty seconds, not five minutes. A witness may say, "He was fifty feet away from me."

Usually counsel will ask, "Was he farther away than the end of this courtroom or closer?"

The witness replies, "Closer."

The room is only forty feet long.

Counsel will then say, "Well, point to something in this room that is as far from you as he was."

The witness will point to a chair or a person who is less than thirty feet from him.

Obviously it is not easy to ascertain objective facts from testimonial evidence. To probe the mind of another—his intellectual capacities, the state of his mental health, and, if you will, moral sense—is well nigh impossible. It is understandable that sensitive, thoughtful judges have sought guidance from the experts, the people who make a study of the mind. Judges turn to psychiatrists for expert advice in these matters. I believe that most judges welcome expert psychiatric testimony on these difficult questions.

Psychiatrists are called upon for expert testimony with respect to the accused's mental condition at four critical points in the criminal process. The first is his mental condition at the time of trial. Is he competent to stand trial? The second is his condition at the time of the incident. This is the defense of not guilty by reason of insanity. The third is his condition at the the time of sentencing. Should his mental condition affect the sentence to be imposed? The fourth is when the offender requests release under an indeterminate sentence. At each of these times the tests imposed by law are different and the purposes for which psychiatric testimony are offered are different.

The desert theory and presumptive sentencing do not touch the first issue: competency to stand trial. Psychiatric opinion and advice would continue to be used at this first stage under these proposals. Some proponents of the desert theory would abandon the "not guilty by reason of insanity" defense and eliminate the use of psychiatric opinion at the second stage. Both the presumptive sentencing proposal and the desert theory would eliminate the use of psychiatry at the third stage: sentencing. Flat-term sentencing would eliminate the need to consider the mental state of the offender at the fourth stage: the time of release. The felon would have to be released when his sentence expired regardless of his mental condition.

With the proposed abandonment of the goal of rehabilitation and the substitution of desert or justice as fairness as the aim of sentencing, or the substitution of a sentencing commission, many of these perplexing problems would be ignored but they would not disappear. Mentally ill and incompetent people would continue to commit crimes, be tried, sentenced, and ultimately released. In order to predict the effects such drastic revisions of sentencing theory would have on most offenders, it is necessary to see how psychiatric evidence is now used in the criminal justice system.

A judge first encounters a psychiatrist in the course of a criminal prosecution when counsel for the accused comes into court and says that he or she is unable to defend the client adequately because the accused cannot cooperate with counsel and participate meaningfully in his own defense. Obviously, due process would not permit the court to try a raving lunatic. The defendant must be present in court during the entire trial. If he does not know what is going on, his mere physical presence is not enough. Philosophically this is an important issue. Practically, it is insignificant. There are often obstreperous, disruptive, and difficult defendants in court. One has only to recall Bobby Seale, who was tried while gagged and shackled to a chair in the courtroom. However, very few wild maniacs are brought into court. I have never seen an accused who could not comprehend either that he was in court or the nature of the offense with which he was charged.

An attorney who has difficulty communicating with his client and who is unable to get enough information from him to prepare a defense may ask for a psychiatric examination. If the psychiatrist diagnoses the client as schizoid or having personality disorders or suffering from some other presumably severe mental illness, a mental health commitment is requested. The petition is filed by the defendant's own lawyer; it has attached to it the certifications of one or two psychiatrists attesting to the mental condition of the defendant. Some judges routinely grant these petitions.

The judge's reasoning goes like this: I am only a lawyer. I am not an authority on mental illness. Twenty or thirty years ago I had a college course in psychology. True, I've read some books since then. But I really don't know any more about the workings of the human mind than I know about the functioning of a space ship. Fortunately, the adversary system of law does not require me as a judge to be an authority on all the social, scientific, and medical questions that come before me. I listen to the testimony and arguments on both sides and decide on the basis of the evidence presented. It is not my function to go and find the evidence. If one side presents a petition and the other side does not oppose it, it is my duty to grant the petition unless a statute or the Constitution forbids it. Petition granted.

The prosecution rarely opposes petitions for mental health commitments. The prosecutor is often relieved to have one fewer case to try. The law of most jurisdictions authorizes temporary mental health commitments for the purpose of examination. Since the accused will be in custody in a secure mental institution there is no risk that he or she will commit other crimes before being brought to trial. If the petition is denied and the defendant is found guilty, the issue of competence to stand trial might then be raised on appeal. The safe course for the judge is to grant the petition.

However, there are real problems of legality and fairness in locking up someone who has not been convicted of a crime. The Constitution guarantees every accused the right to a speedy trial. How does a mental health commitment affect this right? Moreover, under recent Supreme Court decisions it is unconstitutional to punish a person for his status or condition.[4] In other words, no one can be incarcerated simply because he is mentally ill. In order to commit a person civilly to a mental institution he must be both mentally ill and dangerous. In order to commit him under the criminal law he must have been found guilty of a crime. If John Doe hasn't been tried, he can't be guilty. Some psychiatrists think this is a Catch-22 situation in which the mentally ill are deprived of treatment. I, however, think it is a Catch-22 situation in which the individual can be held in custody without a decision having been made as to whether he committed a crime or whether he is mentally ill and dangerous. If the Court doesn't know whether Doe shot Smith, it can't find that Doe is dangerous. Therefore, Doe cannot be committed civilly. If the court doesn't know whether Doe shot Smith, he can't be convicted of a crime and imprisoned under criminal law. The solution: lock Doe up on a series of temporary commitments because he is incompetent to stand trial.

Everett's attorney filed a petition to have him placed in a mental hospital because the attorney believed that Everett could not adequately cooperate in his own defense. He alleged that Everett was unable to confer with his lawyer and participate meaningfully in his defense. When this critical question of liberty or confinement was argued before me Everett was not in the courtroom.

"Where is Everett?" I asked the prosecutor and defense counsel.

"In custody," the prosecutor replied.

"I want him in court before I grant this petition," I told them.

"That's not necessary," defense counsel declared. "We have the opinion of the psychiatrist." He handed me two certifications, one by the psychiatrist employed by the Defender Association, the other by a psychiatrist employed by the court. "I am satisfied that he is mentally ill and unable to cooperate in his defense," the lawyer declared.

"But I am not satisfied," I insisted. "Everett has a right to appear in court and speak for himself before any order incarcerating him is entered."

Everett was ordered to be brought down from jail the next day. Both lawyers fumed at the time being wasted on this routine matter. The next day Everett appeared in court. He was an average-looking man who sat quietly until his case was called. I had him sworn and questioned him myself. He promptly answered all questions correctly. He gave his name, his age (thirty-four), date of birth, address, and social security number. He knew what date it was.

I asked him if he knew where he was. He replied, "In court, of course." He looked at me as if I were crazy for asking such a stupid question.

I continued:

Q. Do you know why you're in court?

A. Yes. They say I stole this watch from the ___ store [naming it], but I didn't. I only took it out of the case to examine it.

Q. Do you want to be tried?

A. Yes. I've been in jail three months and thirteen days already. I should have been tried long ago.

Q. Do you know Mr.___[the attorney]?

A. Yes. He says he's my lawyer. But I don't want him.

Q. Why not?

A. He doesn't believe me. I want a lawyer who does believe me.

Q. Do you know Dr.___[the psychiatrist who had examined him]?

A. Yes.

Q. He examined you, didn't he?

A. No, he didn't give me no examination. He just asked me a lot of damn fool questions until I stopped talking to him. Then he left me alone.

I refused to sign the petition. We were at a stalemate. I offered to grant defense attorney leave to withdraw from the case if he wished. If he withdrew, I would have appointed another lawyer to represent Everett. The lawyer said he would consult with the psychiatrist. The next day Everett and the lawyer appeared in court.

"We're ready to go to trial, your honor," the lawyer announced.

"Did you consult with the psychiatrist?"

"Yes. He advised me that Everett is in a state of remission now and is capable of standing trial."

I asked Everett if he had seen the psychiatrist since he was in court the previous day. He said he had not seen him. Diagnosis without examination of the subject is not uncommon. Even if he was guilty, Everett had already served more time than most judges would have sentenced him to for the technical theft of a cheap watch which was not even removed from the store.

All too often those presumed to be mentally ill are held in custody without even having a hearing. Ernest was held in jail for more than four months without being brought to trial. A judge had signed a commitment for him on the petition of his lawyer. Ernest finally wrote to another lawyer who brought him before me on a writ of habeas corpus. His former lawyer and the psychiatrist on whose opinion he had been committed were in court under subpoena. Both of them testified that Ernest refused to talk to them despite their best efforts. The new attorney showed me the letter Ernest had written to him. It was logical, coherent, and neatly written. When Ernest's case was called he stepped forward. At his request, he was affirmed, not sworn. Then he answered all questions as to his identity, residence, and so forth correctly.

What was his offense? Theft of services. In plain English that means he did not pay his fare on the subway. For theft of a subway ride which cost forty-five cents, Ernest had been in custody more than four months. During this time he had been brutally assaulted by another inmate.

Ernest is a soft-spoken young man of twenty-two. He has a nervous twitch. He is physically unattractive, fat, and soft looking.

I questioned him. "Is it true that you refused to speak with the lawyer and the doctors who came to see you?"

A. Yes.

Q. They came to jail to help you. Why wouldn't you talk to them?

A. The law is corrupt. I won't cooperate with a corrupt system.

Q. Where were you going when you were arrested?

A. I was coming home from work. I had the money to pay for the subway.

Q. Don't tell me about the alleged offense. Just tell me about yourself.

Do you live alone?

  A. Yes.

  Q. Do you have any family?

  A. A father and a brother.

  Q. Do you see them?

  A. No.

  Q. Why not?

  A. They were cruel to my mother.

  Q. Where is your mother?

  A. She died two weeks before I was arrested.

  Q. And you haven't been in touch with any of your family since then?

  A. No.

  Q. If you are released now, do you have some place to live?

  A. Yes.

I promptly granted the petition. His first lawyer and the two psychiatrists spoke to me afterwards. "It's miraculous," they declared. "We couldn't get him to talk at all."

  Q. And for that reason you concluded that he was mentally incompetent?

  A. Yes. What else could we do?

Those defendants who cause the most chaos and trouble in court do it deliberately. Many of them believe they are engaged in political protest. No one suggests that they are insane or mentally ill even though they scream in the courtroom and disrupt the proceedings. Neither they nor their lawyers ask for mental health examinations.

I believe that a judge can and should determine competence to stand trial from evidence adduced in the courtroom. This critical decision should not be made in a psychiatrist's office or a jail cell. The defendant should be present and have the right to confront the psychiatrist, cross examine him, and present evidence on his own behalf. The Constitutional right to a speedy public trial should not be denied except for the most compelling reasons. It is only in a very rare and unusual case that a judge may need the benefit of psychiatric testimony to assist in this decision. In such cases the psychiatrist should testify in open court, not merely sign a certificate.

The second point at which a psychiatrist is involved in the criminal process arises when it is alleged that the accused was mentally ill at the time of the crime—the insanity defense. It poses more difficult problems. The court must decide whether or not the accused at the time of the act was or was not sane. For more than a generation judges, lawyers, and forensic psychiatrists have been attempting to formulate in words a clear, precise definition of criminal responsibility that reflects the findings of psychiatry and can be used as an objective legal standard. This quest was predicated on two principles: first, that the law should not punish a person who because of his mental condition could not choose between committing a crime and not committing a crime, and second, that even though an individual may be legally responsible, the criminal justice system is obliged to treat and rehabilitate him if he is mentally ill or emotionally disturbed.

In defining criminal responsibility the classical notion of free will may be too unshaded a doctrine for the late twentieth century. Teachings of psychiatry, psychology, biology, chemistry, and sociology inevitably color the views of legislators and jurists. Contemporary science indicates that social conditioning, economic and emotional deprivation, and even chemical or genetic mistakes can affect the mind and emotions of an individual. These views have not been translated into legal doctrine. Criminal responsibility is still predicated on the belief that the individual is responsible for his actions. And conversely, if through some mental state or condition he is not responsible then he should not be punished for his acts. There are dozens of different standards and tests. But what the judge and jury and the expert witnesses must attempt to do is determine the mental capacity of the accused at a time when they did not see him and did not know him. Obviously this is a difficult task, fraught with uncertainty and the possibility if not probability of error.

Occasionally a psychiatrist has actually treated the accused before the crime occurred. I remember one man who stabbed a stranger to death. There was an eyewitness to the crime. The defendant did not deny that he had killed the man. He had been under the care of a psychiatrist who had diagnosed him as "homicidal" several months before the killing. Even this highly competent psychiatrist had great difficulty in deciding the mental state of the accused at the time of the killing in the terms required by law.

Was the accused mentally ill at the time of the killing? Was his crime the product of his illness? Did he have a mental disease or defect? Did he know the nature and quality of his act and know that it was wrong? These are some formulations of the test of criminal responsibility. None is really satisfactory. I have never encountered a person who did not know what he had done and that it was wrong.

The real question is one of policy. What should society do with these people? That question arises *after* conviction. The question of responsibility arises *at* trial. It is also one of policy. It can be phrased simply: Should the accused be relieved of responsibility for his acts because of his mental condition? No psychiatrist can or should answer that question. Judge David Bazelon, a seminal thinker, one of the towering figures in this field, has become disenchanted with psychiatry. As he put it, we come to the end of the yellow brick road and discover that the wizard (the psychiatrist) has no magic.[5]

When an accused person is found not guilty by reason of insanity he or she is acquitted of all crime and put in a mental institution under a civil commitment. Some knowledgeable people believe that there is little difference between most mental hospitals and most prisons. In both institutions the inmate is held against his will. He may or may not get more therapy or better treatment in some hospitals than in some prisons. The legal and practical consequences of a conviction and a verdict of not guilty by reason of insanity are enormous.

In the case of Ida, the woman who performed the caesarian operation on a pregnant woman in order to have a baby for herself, a psychiatrist testified that at the time the defendant performed this operation she did not know the nature and quality of her act and did not know that what she was doing was wrong. This is the classic old McNaghten test of legal insanity. The jury found the woman not guilty by reason of insanity. But it was obvious from the accused's own testimony that she knew she was performing a caesarian operation and that she did it in order to get a baby for herself. She was committed to a mental institution. The woman was released from the mental institution a year later because she was no longer "mentally ill." Under a civil commitment, no one can be held in custody unless he is mentally ill and dangerous. Once the person has "recovered," he must be released. There was nothing the judge could do. The woman had been acquitted. The criminal justice system had no jurisdiction over her. She could not be tried again. She is free from all restraint. Is she a walking timebomb who will kill again? We will not know until after she is accused of another bizarre crime. Admittedly this is an unusual case. But such things do occur more frequently than one likes to acknowledge.

The case of Robert Torsney, a white New York City police officer accused of fatally shooting a black teenager, illustrates some of the practical problems of the not guilty by reason of insanity verdict. In this case, as in most cases in which such a verdict is returned, there is little doubt that the accused committed the act. The police department sensibly wished to dismiss Officer Torsney stating that it was improper to have such an individual on the police force carrying a gun. Torsney fought the dismissal, which will cost him his medical disability pension. It is interesting that although Torsney has been found "insane" he is permitted to spend nights and weekends at home instead of in custody in a mental institution.[6] The sensible way of dealing with such a shooting would have been to let it go to the jury on a charge of homicide in which intent, malice, premeditation, and all the other elements of the crime could have been considered. The officer might then have been convicted of murder in any of its degrees or voluntary or involuntary manslaughter, and the police department would have been able to dismiss him. The officer's mental condition would more appropriately have been considered by the judge in imposing sentence. A verdict of not guilty even though by reason of insanity is in effect an acquittal which leaves the accused in possession of all his legal rights. Society and the accused have a right to a decision on the basic question: did he do the act?

The difficulties of attempting through the testimony of psychiatrists to ascertain whether the accused was sane or insane at the time of the crime were drastically revealed in the case of Frederick T. who shot and killed his brother. There was no doubt that Frederick had done it. The two brothers were seen entering the house together. A few minutes later a shot was heard; the police were summoned; they entered the house and found Frederick and the body of his brother. No one else was in the house. No one had been seen leaving the house. After Frederick was warned of his Constitutional rights, he gave a statement to the police. Frederick said that his brother was in love with Frederick's estranged wife, was having sexual relations with her, and mocked him about the fact. The wife had told Frederick that she had been raped by his brother.

Frederick was asked by the police, "Why did you shoot him?"

He answered, "Because he would mention my wife in an unnatural way."

Frederick was examined at various times by three psychiatrists and one psychologist. The first time he was found competent to stand trial. Due to difficulties of court scheduling, he was not brought to trial. When the case was listed two months later he was again examined. This time he was found incompetent to stand trial. Some time later he was examined for the third time and found competent to stand trial. He was tried before me.

The psychiatrists who examined him for competency were asked at trial to give their opinions as to his sanity at the time he killed his brother. Each of the three psychiatrists and the psychologist testified that in his opinion Frederick was insane at the time of the act, that he did not know the nature and quality of his act, that he did not know the difference between right and wrong, and that he was paranoid and had delusions of persecution. None of them had checked to find out whether the deceased brother in fact had relations with Frederick's wife. The evidence was fairly strong that he had. The court-employed psychologist who had an M.S. in clinical psychology tested Frederick and diagnosed him as a chronic paranoid.

One psychiatrist based his opinion on the examination by the psychologist.

The court asked the psychiatrist, "Dr. G., are you able to give with reasonable medical certainty an opinion based upon a description given by a non-medical person?"

Dr. G. answered, "Yes."

A different psychiatrist retracted his earlier opinion that Frederick was competent to stand trial.

A third psychiatrist testified: "My opinions are based on the examination largely of past psychiatric reports."

In all Frederick was seen by the three doctors at most for a total of three hours. If Frederick had been found not guilty by reason of insanity, who could predict when the same psychiatrists would find him sane and release him from custody?

One must ask why mental illness should relieve an individual from responsibility for his acts. The offense was committed; the harm has been done. Offenders are not relieved from responsibility for any other reasons, many of which are very compelling. Poverty, discrimination, physical and psychiatric disability all mark an individual's character and warp it to some extent. Even the most dire poverty, borderline intelligence, and a life of gross mistreatment will not excuse the commission of a crime. These other factors can be proved and verified by objective evidence. I suggest that no individual should be relieved of legal responsibility for his illegal acts. In imposing sentence, however, all of the circumstances of the individual's life and mental and emotional make-up should be considered. The real question is: Does this person pose a threat

to society? There is no reliable evidence that anyone can predict dangerousness with reasonable scientific certainty, which is the legal standard
for admission of opinion evidence. However, it is reasonable to suppose
that a person who has committed one irrational, dangerous crime may
well commit another. We know that this individual has committed at
least one terrible crime. What should be done with him or her?

Mental retardation does not constitute insanity or mental illness.
Retardation, unlike mental illness or insanity, can be tested with reasonable objectivity. Most mentally retarded people, like most people of
normal intelligence, do not commit crimes; their retardation, moreover,
does not explain or excuse criminality, either in fact or in law. The
difference in legal treatment of retardation and insanity was revealed in
Samuel's trial. Samuel is probably the most stupid and retarded individual I have ever encountered. He is a big, lumbering man. He was accused
of rape. During the trial before me he dozed on and off and seemed to
be unable to concentrate on what was going on. His foster mother
testified that Samuel had been "given" to her by the natural mother at
the age of one week. By the time he was a year old she knew he was
"slow." He was in special schools for the retarded for years. He is able
to dress himself, bathe after a fashion, and take care of his bodily needs.
He works in a sheltered workshop. The psychiatrist testified that Samuel's I.Q. was so low that he could not measure it. It was his opinion
that Samuel was unable to know what he was doing.

The policeman who arrested Samuel testified: "I seen that he was
slow, slower than most people we see."

Defense Counsel: "But you questioned him anyway?"

Policeman: "Sure, I explained everything to him in small words that
he could understand."

Q. Did you tell him what he was charged with?

A. Yea. I told him rape and I asked him if he knew what that meant.
He said, 'No.' Then I told him rape meant fucking a woman by force
against her will, when she didn't want to. He said he understood that
and that is what he did.

Q. Do you think he understood the warnings of his rights?

A. After I explained them, yes. He knew his name, where he lived,
and how to get there. He even told me which streets were one way. He
knew where he worked and how to get there. I think he knew everything
I said to him.

Stupidity is not a legal excuse. Nonetheless, one has difficulty with people like Samuel, and there are many of them, in concluding that he has the free will to choose whether or not to break the law. Samuel said that he knew what he had done and that it was wrong even though he did not know the name of the offense. In my jurisdiction that is the test of insanity. The psychiatrist, nonetheless, testified that in his opinion Samuel was insane at the time of the offense. I doubt that Samuel or anyone that retarded has the ability to restrain himself from doing an act which he knows is wrong if the commission of the act will gratify an immediate desire. But does this inability to control himself relieve the offender of legal responsibility? The desert theory spares the judge this decision.

I ruled that Samuel could not meaningfully understand the nature of his Constitutional rights including the privilege against self-incrimination. I excluded his "confession." But I convicted him on the testimony of the victim because, despite the testimony of the psychiatrist, Samuel testified that he knew what he was doing and knew that it was wrong. I believed Samuel. Had he been tried in other jurisdictions the result would probably have been the same. Samuel does not have a mental disease but he does have a defect. But was the crime a product of his defect?[7] Who could possibly answer that question? Two psychiatrists would have given diametrically opposite opinions and the jury would have had no reasonable basis on which to arrive at a conclusion.

The most difficult decision is what to do with Samuel. This is the sentencing problem. He is only twenty-two years old. If he were imprisoned for the maximum number of years—twenty—with no time off for good behavior he would be only forty-two on his release. He would not be any smarter. He would still be unable to control his physical urges. Psychiatry is of little help to the court or Samuel.

Under the justice as fairness theory there is no possibility of taking into account the mental deficiencies of the accused. Under this theory the sentence is based on the crime, not the capacities or nature of the criminal. If the justice as fairness theory were followed to its logical end, children, no matter at what a young age they committed crimes, would be sentenced the same as adults. The proponents of the theory have not made such a suggestion. However, robbery is robbery whether it is committed by a ten-year-old boy or a twenty-five-year-old man. Does equal treatment under the rubric of justice as fairness require that a ten-year-old and a twenty-five-year-old be given the same sentence? Although there are ever louder and shriller demands that children who have committed serious offenses be treated as adults, few people would deny that most ten-year-olds do not have the same sense of responsibility and judgment as most eighteen-year-olds. I believe the law should recognize these inherent differences in maturity and treat children with more solicitude than adults. Any cutoff point is bound to be arbitrary. Some sixteen-year-olds are much brighter and more responsible than some eighteen-year-olds. Should courts hear psychiatric testimony on the capacity and mentality of each accused? I think not. This practice can lead to even more injustices and less equality of treatment.

In addition to mental illness, disease, physical defects, and intelligence, there are other significant factors in criminality such as environment, education, and social background. In some neighborhoods the majority of young men have been arrested at least once. In other neighborhoods an arrest is an anomaly. Education, literacy, social and cultural deprivation, poverty, and, perhaps most significant, neglect are all very important in understanding why the offender committed the crime. Was it the product of one (or all) of these factors in his life? Probably the answer is yes. But should this unfortunate history relieve the offender of criminal responsibility? This is not a question for psychiatrists. I do not think it is a question for judges but for the legislature. It is a matter of public policy. Other than history, there is no reason to isolate one difficult, intangible, and indefinable quality—madness, which we now call mental illness—and hold that this attribute relieves an individual from responsibility for his actions.

Courts would be well advised to avoid the uncertainties of psychiatry and psychology in deciding criminal responsibility and guilt. However, the deprivations of the offender's entire lifetime—mental, emotional, financial, social, and educational—should, I believe, be considered carefully in framing a sentence which is humane, which protects society, and which provides redress to the victim.

Although an infinite amount of psychiatric and judicial wisdom has been devoted to the insanity defense, it represents a negligible fraction of criminal cases. Thousands of larcenies, robberies, burglaries, and assaults are tried every day. No one raises the issue of insanity. The insanity defense is most often raised in homicide cases, usually for the purpose of avoiding the death penalty. It would be interesting to know whether in states that do not have capital punishment the plea is raised less often. These killings are the cases reported in the press in which forensic psychiatrists do battle with each other. Usually the fact of the killing is not in question. The insanity defense is simply a means of escaping the penalty.

The most common use of psychiatrists in the criminal justice system is in the preparation of pre-sentence reports. Under the new proposals of desert, justice as fairness, and presumptive sentencing, the mental condition of the offender would be irrelevant. Psychiatric examinations would probably be eliminated. However, this is precisely the point at which I believe psychiatrists have a significant contribution to make to the criminal justice system. When there is an area of discretion in the type of sentence to be imposed—probation or imprisonment—the length of imprisonment, the institution to which the offender is to be sent, and the conditions to be imposed upon him in custody or on probation, every judge could benefit by the opinion of a qualified psychiatrist who has made a careful examination of the offender.

There are several requirements which I would impose upon the psychiatrists. First, the examination must be thorough. I always ask the psychiatrist how many times he has seen the defendant and for how long a period. Most court psychiatrists give one "forty-minute hour" examination upon which they arrive at conclusions which are of enormous significance to the offender and society. A good part of the forty minutes is spent in getting information from the offender about the offense and the offender's background. Often the information is erroneous. Second, the psychiatrist should have read a transcript of the trial and know what the facts are. Third, the psychiatrist should give an opinion as to the accused's mental condition and prognosis but not a recommendation as to the sentence. All too often none of these requirements is met.

The imposition of sentence is a legal decision, not a medical one. The judge will benefit from medical opinion as to the defendant's mental and emotional condition. But these are only some of the factors upon which a sentence is based. Several typical cases illustrate the dangers of permitting psychiatrists to dictate legal decisions.

Lester, a twenty-four-year-old man, was convicted of attempted rape of his seven-year-old niece. He was estranged from his wife and had been living in the home of his sister and her daughter, the victim. The psychiatrist recommended probation. I phoned him and told him that I was worried about his report, that I was concerned about leaving a strong young rapist at liberty. The victim was so young. It was not a case of a young man and a nubile adolescent.

"But it was only attempted rape," the psychiatrist said. I explained that Lester couldn't be convicted of rape on the victim's testimony. She did not testify that there had been penetration. All she said was, "Lester put his 'thing' in me here [pointing to her vagina]. It hurt and I cried and ran to find my mother."

"Lester has a wife. It isn't likely to recur," the psychiatrist explained. He didn't know that Lester hadn't seen his wife for two years.

The psychiatrist agreed to see Lester again. I had him brought to the psychiatric unit at once. In less than a half-hour, the psychiatrist called me back to say that I needn't worry. He was sure Lester was not dangerous.

Another psychiatrist found that Gladys S. was mentally ill and recommended that she be incarcerated. Gladys was charged with assault with intent to kill, aggravated assault two counts, trespass two counts, terroristic threats three counts, and prohibited offensive weapons. The psychiatrist knew the charges and the convictions. The case was listed as a major felony. A week of court time was cleared for this trial.

When the case was called the courtroom was jammed with well-dressed people. I expected to see a female equivalent of the Boston strangler. Gladys is a slight woman of forty-two, rather pretty. She was wearing a T-shirt and slacks. From a distance she looked twenty years old. As she sat in the witness chair about three feet from me, I could see that her face was lined. Her hair was touched up. She looked worn and harried. She has four teenage children. One is employed. The others are in school. Gladys has a steady job.

All of these horrible crimes with which she was charged arose from a neighborhood contretemps. Gladys admitted slapping her neighbor twice—two aggravated assault counts. Since the woman was not injured by the slaps, these were reduced to simple assaults. Gladys admitted striking the neighbor once with an aluminum slat from a porch chair. The slat slashed the neighbor's arm and she went to a doctor once to have the cut treated. This incident gave rise to the charge of assault with intent to kill and the weapons charge. The slat was considered a weapon. The terroristic threats were an exchange of unpleasantries over the back fence. The neighbor was a buxom white-haired lady, about fifty, wearing a print dress and a hat. Her husband was in court watching Gladys with a leering smile. I found Gladys guilty of three counts of simple assault.

I ordered a psychiatric examination because it is recommended. The state had charged that Gladys was dangerous and psychotic. The neighbors were outraged. The psychiatrist prescribed tranquilizers but Gladys refused to take medication, claiming her Constitutional right to bodily and mental integrity. To the dismay of the prosecutor and the court psychiatrist I sustained her right to refuse medication. At the sentencing hearing the psychiatrist testified that Gladys was agitated and had paranoid delusions.

"What are her delusions?" I asked him.

A. She thinks her neighbors are intent on harming her.

Q. Is that what she said?

A. Her phrase was [he consulted his notebook] 'The neighbors are out to get me.'

Q. Did you ever check with the neighbors or the prosecuting attorney to see if in fact the neighbors are 'out to get her'?

A. Of course not. I examined the subject and concluded from my observations of her that she has paranoid delusions.

Q. How long did you see Mrs. S. [Gladys]?

A. An hour.

Q. Sixty minutes?

A. No, a forty-minute hour. The standard examination.

It was Gladys's first arrest. I sentenced her to one year probation and ordered her to pay for the neighbor's medical bills which amounted to thirty-five dollars. Gladys moved to another neighborhood and has had no further involvement with the law.

The recommendations in many pre-sentence neuropsychiatric examinations cause me great concern. Fred had been tried before me on a theft charge. The psychiatrist recommended that "the subject be incarcerated until he appreciates his need for treatment."

Another report recommended that Jeffrey who had deliberately killed his wife be placed on probation because "he is no danger to society." I agree that unless Jeffrey remarries, he is probably not a danger to society. But I did not agree that he should not be imprisoned. How can a civilized society not impose a penalty on one who wilfully and deliberately takes a life?

A psychiatrist who does not have the responsibility for imposing sentence, whose only expertise is diagnosis and treatment of mental illness, should not usurp the judicial function. No expert witness is permitted to give an opinion on the ultimate question—guilt or innocence, liability or no liability. This decision is for the finder of fact. Was the automobile driver who ran into the plaintiff negligent? Was the machinery that mangled the plaintiff reasonably safe for the purpose for which it was manufactured? Was the doctor who performed an unsuccessful operation negligent? Did the lawyer who allegedly mishandled his client's case act in accordance with the standards of legal competence in the community? These are the issues which the jury or the judge, if there is no jury, must decide. Experts testify as to facts, the state of the art of medicine, law, or the machinery in question. They cannot give an opinion as to the issue which is being tried. Similarly, no expert, including psychiatrists, should give an opinion or recommendation as to the sentence.

The other critical time of psychiatric involvement in the criminal system is when the prisoner is being considered for release from prison. Usually a psychiatrist does not testify before the parole board. He simply files a report. The prisoner cannot rebut the psychiatrist's findings because he doesn't know what they are. How can the prisoner refute the opinion that he "has not made a good adjustment" or that "he has no insight into his problems?"

The parole board does not know the crime or the criminal. The parole board operates behind closed doors. No one knows the qualifications, experience, or background of its members. In most states they were not elected nor were their appointments confirmed by the legislature. They are anonymous bureaucrats. In most states they do not have to be learned in the law.

I do not favor flat sentences. There is much to be said for giving the prisoner an incentive to improve himself. After the minimum sentence has been served, the prisoner should be taken before the judge who sentenced him for a parole hearing. At this time prison officials, a psychiatrist who has carefully examined him and has read the transcript of the trial or a summary, and any friends and family who are concerned should testify in open court. The prisoner himself should have an opportunity to be heard and to rebut the evidence against him. If there are co-defendants, evidence as to their sentences and their releases should also be presented. This would provide a due process hearing for the second most important decision. The first is commitment; the second is release. In this way a decision could be made that is just and fair.

I believe that psychiatric opinion is valuable at the time of sentencing and at the time of release. The criminal justice system has a duty to society, the victim, and the offender. If the offender is mentally ill, he should be incarcerated in a place where he can receive competent therapy. If he is ill and dangerous, he should not be released on probation. If the offender still has any fixations or delusions about the victim, certainly the offender should not be released to threaten, terrify, and possibly injure the victim again. Unless the court retains jurisdiction over the offender, there is no way that he can be isolated from society or the victim. Otherwise, he will not be brought before the court again until he commits another crime.

If sentencing is to protect the public and the victim and be "fair" to the offender, the judge cannot simply follow a scheme of equal terms of imprisonment for all offenders who commit the same crimes, because all offenders are not equal. Some have serious mental and emotional problems. Some do not. In making these difficult decisions which may have such drastic consequences for the offenders, the victims, and others, a judge would be immeasurably helped by competent psychiatric opinions based upon careful examination of the offender and an understanding of the actual facts of the offender's life. For the legal system to ignore the findings of psychiatry would be as foolish and retrogressive as to ignore the findings of roentgenology, nuclear physics, and other sciences. It is many centuries since courts decided issues by ordeal or battle. Courts seek to have the most reliable evidence which contemporary learning and science can provide. In making the most significant decision which affects the offender, the victim, and society—the sentence—psychiatric findings should not be excluded.

CHAPTER XVIII

VICTIM
COMPENSATION

> Has a crime been committed? Those who have suffered by
> it, either in their person or their fortune are abandoned to
> their evil condition. The society which they have con-
> tributed to maintain and which ought to protect them owes
> them an indemnity when its protection has been ineffectual.
> —Jeremy Bentham

Recognition of the needs of the victims of crime is a very recent development in modern Western law. Less than a generation ago there was no discussion in legal literature of the notion of compensating victims of crime. The first widely recognized plan to provide help for crime victims was proposed by Margery Fry, an English magistrate, in 1951. Her book, *Arms of the Law*, [1] proposed that the offender pay compensation to the victim. She observed that although "compensation cannot undo the wrong, it will often assuage the injury, and it has a real educative value for the offender, whether adult or child." It is significant that this proposal was made by a magistrate, one who actually saw both the offender and the victim and who observed, as I do, the futility and cruelty of the criminal justice system. Her recommendation received wide publicity in Britain and the Commonwealth nations. But it was not adopted. In the late 1950s, Ms. Fry pointed out that most offenders cannot afford to make adequate reparations to the victims of their crimes. She then supported a program for state compensation of crime victims. In less than twenty years an entire body of legal and popular literature on victim compensation has developed.[2]

The failure of the legal system adequately to address the problem of the victim of crime is pointed out with increasing frequency. *The Crime Victim's Book* rightly observes that nobody in authority listens to the victim's plea and nobody rehabilitates him.[3] The co-author, a professor of psychology, urges that the crime victim be given some emotional support. As we have seen, the legal system does provide therapy for the offender but not the victim. The authors give this advice: survive, carry on, recover. They write, "When a victim makes a good recovery and comes out of the crisis with renewed strength, he or she has achieved the ultimate victory over the criminal." Columnist Joan Beck of the *Chicago Tribune* comments, "What more melancholy commentary could there be on the state of American criminal justice?"

It is indeed a sad commentary but it misunderstands the nature of crime and the legal system. The victim and the criminal are not engaged in a contest. In most street crimes the victim and the offender are strangers. They will never meet again, except in court if the offender is apprehended. The criminal is at war with society not the victim, who is often just as poor and disadvantaged and hostile as the offender. It is society which must reckon with the offender. It is society which owes protection and assistance to the victim. What most victims need is much more than psychotherapy or advice on how to survive. Most victims need money to enable them to rebuild their broken bodies and their disrupted, shattered lives. They need the equivalent of civil money damages to make them whole, insofar as monetary payments can do so.

The concept of compensation for the victims of crime has received widespread approval. Ms. Fry's original plan for compensation by the offender has been ignored by most legislators and criminologists. The first victim compensation statute was passed in 1963 in New Zealand. It was hailed as a pioneering effort in humanitarian reforms. Great Britain followed with a similar plan in 1964. By 1972, the British program had awarded almost £3 million to 8,102 crime victims. California in 1966 was the first American state to enact a victim compensation law. In the next twelve years some twenty-five states enacted victim compensation laws.

Although there are variations among these laws, the basic plan provides for a very limited amount of compensation to be paid to crime victims from general tax revenues. The offender does not contribute to the victim or the victim compensation fund. The taxpayers bear the entire cost of the compensation and the bureaucracy created to process victim claims. Each victim who makes a claim must establish his right to compensation before the victim compensation board. There is insufficient information with respect to the operation of these statutes to draw any firm conclusions. However, most laws require the victim to do more than fill out a form. The victim must prove that a crime occurred and that as a result of that crime he or she suffered certain losses. It is reasonable to assume that most victims will have to retain counsel to process these claims. Workmen's Compensation laws were designed to avoid the necessity of lawyers. This soon proved to be unworkable. Most claimants have to retain counsel in order to recover. Under some victim compensation laws counsel fees can be recovered; under other laws, they cannot.

Most victim compensation statutes restrict compensation to economic losses. There is no recovery for pain, suffering, disfigurement, and loss of life's pleasures—all of which are compensable in civil negligence cases. The crime victim cannot, as he can in negligence actions, recover for losses which are covered by insurance. Under most state victim compensation laws the maximum recovery permitted is less than $25,-000. The inadequacy of this compensation for severely and permanently injured crime victims is apparent when one realizes that the cost of simply providing catheters for a paraplegic paralyzed from the waist down is approximately $1,500 a year. A paraplegic also needs almost constant attendance even though some such persons are able to operate specially adapted automobiles, motorized wheel chairs, and other expensive devices. For many injured victims, present victim compensation laws are woefully inadequate.

Although some state statutes have been in effect for a number of years, relatively few victims have filed claims. In New York for the fiscal year ending March 31, 1977, only 3,618 awards were made to crime victims in a total amount of $2,364,435. In Pennsylvania, the record has also been disappointing. In fiscal year 1977–78, only $518,656.62 was awarded to victims of crime. In New Zealand and Canada the amounts awarded and the number of claims have also been very small.

One reason for the small number of claims is that few victims of crime are aware of these compensation laws. When a crime is reported to the police, the victim should be immediately informed of his rights to compensation and the Victim Compensation Board should be notified.

Today those who are informed of their rights by the prosecuting attorney usually do not know how to make claims and process them. Moreover, not all victims in states which have victim compensation laws are eligible to recover. For example, a person who is assaulted in a state other than that of his residence cannot under most statutes recover either from his home state or the state where the crime occurred. When a crime results in death, payments to the survivors are limited. In New York, which has one of the more generous statutes, the maximum is $15,000 plus $1,000 funeral expenses. If the family provider is killed, the dependent spouse and children cannot survive very long on such meager compensation.

The proposed Federal Crimes Code has a provision for victim compensation and allocation of federal funds to states which have compensation laws. If this provision is enacted it will doubtless encourage more states to enact compensation laws in order to share in these revenues. But there is little likelihood that many state legislatures will appropriate substantially more funds or increase the amount of compensation.

The proposed Federal Victims Crime Act of 1973 provides for 75 percent support of state programs for victim compensation.[4] This legislation contains a "means test," limiting compensation to those who could suffer "financial stress" if they were not compensated. The staff of the United States Senate Committee on the Judiciary estimated that the annual federal costs of such a program would be approximately $28 million per year unless the crime rate increased. The United States Department of Justice estimates that there were almost six million victims of crime over the age of twelve with personal contact in the year 1974.[5] This does not include victims of white-collar crime. As we have seen, many children who are victims of crime suffer serious, permanent injuries. It is apparent that $28 million is a low figure. Even if the costs of providing adequate victim compensation were $400 or $500 million a year, this amount would not be excessive for a government that in 1979 had an annual budget of $560 billion. The cost of adequate victim compensation is certainly not excessive when compared with the good that would be accomplished. Easing the suffering of innocent human beings struck by random catastrophe is a task which the United States Government and voluntary agencies undertake as a charitable obligation on a global basis. Victims of fire, flood, drought, famine, and disease throughout the world receive massive amounts of American money. Those who are stricken by crime are equally victims of random disaster.

But it is not a national or regional catastrophe. It is a personal catastrophe as great to the individual involved as any famine, fire, or flood. Any victim of disaster, including a victim of crime, would certainly prefer compensation as a matter of right to charity bestowed as a matter of grace. Preservation of dignity and self-respect for the innocent victims of crime is an important value. The credibility and fairness of the justice system is also significant.

The vast majority of crime victims need compensation simply to survive the injuries and losses which have befallen them as a result of the crime. They do, in the language of the statutes, suffer "financial distress." Uninsured or partially insured illness, permanent disability, or loss of earnings for a substantial period of time can cause severe hardship to all except the very wealthy. Even if the United States had some form of universal health insurance, victim compensation would still be needed for the majority of victims to cover their property losses and lost earnings.

A major thesis of this book is that the criminal should pay for his wrongs and that the criminal justice system should be restructured to take into account the rights and needs of victims of crime. Even if such proposed reforms were enacted into law, they would not obviate the need for victim compensation laws. More than half of all crimes are not reported. More than half of those reported will be "unsolved." No one will ever be arrested or brought to trial for these offenses.[6] The victims of such crimes have no redress except a compensation law. Unless they are absolutely destitute and eligible for welfare, they have difficulty even in obtaining charity. Most offenders who are apprehended, with the exception of sophisticated white-collar criminals, are poor people who are unable to pay adequate compensation over a lifetime of hard work. Many are unemployed and unemployable. The victims of their crimes need immediate compensation.

Under present compensation laws, every victim who has a claim must present it to the board, prove that the crime occurred, and prove the extent of his losses and his hardship. In those cases in which the offender is not apprehended and the victim has not testified in court some form of tribunal is needed to pass upon the bona fides of the victim's claims. However, in cases in which the victim has already testified in court and has established the fact of the crime and the extent of the harm done, the victim should not have to endure the inconvenience, expense, and often the emotional trauma of presenting this evidence again. There is no reason why the judge who heard the evidence or took the guilty plea could not certify the victim's claim to the Compensation Board.

I believe that sentences of restitution or reparation should be integrated with the system of victim compensation. In some states the courts order most offenders to pay $10 to the victim compensation fund. These small sums do supply a substantial amount of money. In Pennsylvania, for example, in fiscal year 1978–79, $1,660,498.61 was collected from these $10 payments. This is a useful, sensible, and Constitutional means of supporting the fund. But it fails to take into account the needs of the victim who is before the court; it also fails to relate the penalty imposed on the offender to the crime he has committed. I propose that in imposing criminal sentences, whether after conviction or after a guilty plea, the court inquire into the harm done to the victim and whenever possible impose a sentence which requires restitution or reparation to the victim, payable through the victim compensation fund. Significantly, in all presumptive sentencing plans, harm to the victim is an important factor in computing the length of the sentence. But restitution and reparation are not included as part of the presumptive sentence.

At present, when a defendant is convicted of an ordinary crime, evidence with respect to the losses or injuries of the victim are part of the prosecution's case. Let us look at a typical, run-of-the-mill case. John Doe is accused of robbing Jane Roe by threatening her with a knife, snatching her pocketbook, her watch, and ring. He is charged with robbery, assault, possession of instrument of crime, and terroristic threats. In the course of the robbery Jane was knocked to the ground and suffered a broken leg and a knife slash on her arm. At trial, Jane Roe testifies to these facts, including the length of her hospitalization, her period of unemployment, and the resulting impairment and disfigurement. All this evidence is before the court. Even if Doe is acquitted because the evidence that he was the robber is not conclusive, the fact of the robbery and Jane Roe's injuries and damages are a matter of record. It is precisely this kind of evidence with respect to Roe's injuries and losses that would be presented if Jane Roe had been injured in an automobile accident and sued the driver of the car that knocked her down. The judge, often the very same individual who heard John Doe's criminal case, would assess monetary damages in favor of Jane Roe.

When I try cases like that of John Doe, the accused robber, I ascertain the extent of the victim's damages for the purpose of imposing a sentence of reparation. If Doe still has Jane Roe's ring and watch he will be ordered to return them to her. If he does not, the value of these items will be included in the sum of her losses. If Doe has a prior record of other violent offenses, he will be sentenced to jail on one count. On the other counts I will impose consecutive sentences of probation conditioned upon payments to Jane Roe of weekly reparations within his earning capacity. If Doe can earn money in prison and make payments, which is rarely possible, he is ordered to do so. In most cases, Jane Roe will not begin to receive payments of twenty or thirty dollars a week until after the offender is released from prison. If Doe is illiterate, unemployed, and unskilled, he will as part of his prison sentence be required to attend school and to learn a trade so that on his release he can get a job and pay Jane Roe.

But Jane Roe needs the money immediately. She has doctor and hospital bills. She may need further surgery and therapy. She has lost her earnings for several months. Payments of twenty-five dollars a week for five years commencing three years after the commission of the crime will not provide adequate compensation for her. Under the laws of most states, if the judge is determined to impose and enforce an order of reparation, that is probably the most she will recover. Absent such a determined judge and a cooperative probation officer, Jane Roe will not recover any payments for her injuries and losses.

In those states which have victim compensation laws, Jane Doe would be required to file a claim with the compensation board and present evidence to support that claim. In states which do not have victim compensation laws, Jane Doe would be entirely without redress for the very substantial injuries she suffered even though she was entirely innocent of wrongdoing or carelessness.

Justice and fairness in the criminal process require at a minimum that the innocent victims of crime be made whole in so far as possible with the least burdensome procedures. Adequate victim compensation laws are essential to provide such redress. I believe that the trial judge in every criminal case should take evidence with respect to the losses of the victim. A stipulation of evidence with respect to the victim's damages should be part of every guilty plea so that the judge can ascertain the harm done and impose an appropriate sentence. After either a trial or a plea the judge should certify to the victim compensation board the victim's claim and the amount of damages which the trial judge has found were suffered by the victim. The victim could present a different or larger claim if he or she so desired. But the victim should not have to prove again facts already found by the judge presiding over the criminal trial. The compensation board should promptly make an award to the victim for out-of-pocket losses and schedule a series of payments for permanent or continuing disabilities without limitation as to the total amount. The trial judge should impose an appropriate sentence, considering all the circumstances of the crime, the losses suffered by the victim, and the needs of the offender. Included in the sentence should be an order of restitution or reparation based upon the evidence in the case. The restitution would be paid to the victim compensation fund over a period of years to be used for the redress of all crime victims.

If orders of restitution and reparation were entered on a regular basis, particularly in white-collar crimes where the amounts involved are large, there would be substantial increments to the compensation funds and to that extent the burden on the taxpayers would be relieved.

In the laudable rush to adopt victim compensation laws, Ms. Fry's original concept—to make the offender pay restitution or reparation to the victim of his crime—has been largely overlooked. Some commentators have dismissed the idea, declaring without examination that it is impractical or that judges would resist imposing such penalties.[7] I disagree. From my limited experience, I find that sentences requiring the offender to make payments to the victim can work. But a concerted unremitting effort by the judge and the probation department to compel enforcement of such orders is required. Unlike a prison sentence which the judge knows will be carried out, orders of restitution or reparation require constant vigilance. I believe the results are worth the effort. The value of penalties of restitution or reparation is far greater than the small amounts which are collected, although even twenty-five dollars a week may be significant to a very poor person. The other benefits are considerable. The victim and his or her friends and relatives recognize that there is some justice in the criminal justice system. The public is spared the substantial costs of incarcerating the offender for long periods. The offender himself is spared the degradation of prison and is given the opportunity to atone for his wrongdoing. Since the vast majority of crimes, whether they be embezzlement or armed robbery, are committed for monetary gain, taking the profit out of crime may have some preventive or deterrent effects.

No restitution plan has been in operation in the United States a sufficiently long period of time or applied to enough cases to offer any firm data as to its efficacy or the amounts recoverable.[8] In Britain since the 1972 Criminal Justice Act, compensation for property damage has been widely used with few problems.[9] From 1976 to 1978, seven American states have enacted legislation permitting or requiring restitution as a condition of suspended sentence or probation.[10] Many other states have penal codes which either expressly permit restitution or do not forbid it.

Resitution for property stolen or embezzled is not a new remedy. For many years the minor judiciary, often lay magistrates, dismissed criminal charges if the offender paid restitution. These cases usually involved the theft of items of relatively small value. Either the object itself or the equivalent in cash was returned. Most of these cases were never reported or appealed. The victim was pleased to get something back. The accused was relieved to have the charges dismissed. Accordingly, the legality or propriety of such arrangements was rarely contested.

Most restitution laws, like most orders of restitution, are limited to property losses. But personal injuries cause the most serious and devastating harm to victims of violent crimes. Money payment for injuries is technically reparation, not restitution. In the rare case in which an order requiring reparation as part of a criminal sentence has been appealed it has been sustained as a legitimate exercise of judicial discretion.[11]

Because most orders of restitution have been made by the minor judiciary and have not been appealed, there are few reliable studies on the effects of orders of restitution or reparation on the victim, the offender, and the public. A study of four Georgia restitution shelter programs established in 1974 and 1975 to relieve prison overcrowding showed the following:[12]

Most of the offenders were property offenders and probationers, nearly evenly divided between white and black. Most were less than twenty-seven years old and most showed a history of a previous felony conviction.

Restitution obligations during a one-year period totaled $207,567, but only 26 percent was repaid ($54,828)—mainly because of unemployment problems. About one-third of the participants failed during program participation by violating parole or probation conditions; 87 percent of those who successfully participated were arrested within eighteen months of release from the program.

The rehabilitative effects of restitution under these programs have not been established. This may well be because the orders were not enforced. Seventy-five percent of the offenders did not make the payments that were ordered. Probably many of them were unable to find employment. The study further points out that restitution is an alternative to prison.

According to the Judicature study there are no restitution programs in prison. I know of none. A similar situation prevails in England. Consequently restitution is possible only in the cases of offenders who have funds or offenders who are not incarcerated and are able to obtain employment. There is no reason why prisoners could not engage in gainful activities. However, most American prisons operate on a money economy. The same economic pressures and inequalities in society are also to be found in prisons. The inmates work at menial jobs for fifteen or twenty-five cents an hour. If the prisoner has no money of his own, he must work in order to buy such items as cigarettes and toiletries. Those prisoners who have money can purchase services, legal and illegal, from the less fortunate inmates. There is rarely an opportunity for a prisoner to do meaningful work or work that pays standard wages so that he can pay restitution or support his family. Often the prisoners need these small sums of money they earn in prison so desperately that they cannot afford to attend prison school. Unless the judge makes school attendance a part of the sentence, the semiliterate offender will at the expiration of his term be as illiterate and unemployable as when he entered the prison.

For an order of restitution or reparation to be effective as an alternative to prison, the offender must have a job and the court must insist upon regular payments and revoke probation if the payments are not made. Many offenders are unable to find work, particularly young, unskilled, semiliterate, non-white males. If they have no income and no resources, obviously they cannot pay.

A subsidized employment program for non-dangerous offenders is essential. It is also essential for the judge with the cooperation of the probation department to see that the payments are made. All too often probation officers do not notify the judge that payments have not been made regularly. If the probationer calls his officer once a month and is not rearrested, he is let alone. Many harried probation officers do not urge offenders to get a job or help them to find one. If restitution payments are not made, nothing is done. Some probation officers will wait until the sentence is about to expire before notifying the judge that restitution is in arrears. Frequently the officer will recommend termination of probation. He will then have one fewer probationer to worry about.

I have learned that I must insist upon quarterly reports and that I have to keep a tickler system to assure that payments of restitution and reparation are being made regularly. Whenever there is a default, I have the offender brought in to court. If he has no valid excuse, probation is revoked and he is sent to prison. After a few months in prison, most offenders manage to obtain the promise of a job and petition for release. After release they resume payments. There is seldom a second default. Many offenders who have never been employed go to work regularly if the alternative is prison.

I am unwilling to abandon the hope that many offenders can be rehabilitated. One step in that difficult process is for the offender to recognize that he owes a debt to society and to the victims of his crime. Such atonement is not made simply by serving a prison sentence, no matter how long it is or how brutal and miserable prison conditions are. Atonement requires a positive act on the part of the offender. Even offenders who are incarcerated for life could do some productive work in prison if such programs were available. The vast majority of prisoners will return to society within a few years after they have been convicted and sentenced to prison. We owe it to the communities in which these people will live, as well as to the criminals themselves, to make reasonable efforts to prepare them to live law-abiding lives upon their release. If they are unemployable and if they have made no atonement for past wrongs, it is highly unlikely that their conduct on release will be materially different from what it was before they were imprisoned. Statistics show that they will probably commit other offenses. The history of most offenders who have been imprisoned is that they commit more crimes upon release.

Present victim compensation laws do not in any way affect the offenders. They do not require atonement or repayment for the crimes committed. These statutes simply create another bureaucracy, provide limited funds for victims, and operate in total isolation from the criminal justice system. The tacit assumption is that reparation and restitution are futile and difficult to administer. Any notion of rehabilitating the offender through work, responsibility, and atonement has been ignored or abandoned.

Victim compensation laws as presently constituted are not fiscally viable. They are largely dependent upon annual appropriations by the legislature. Most other compensation plans, such as workmen's compensation, unemployment compensation, and social security are based on a principle of spreading the risk. The person compensated may recover more or less than his contribution or the contribution made on his behalf depending upon his losses. These plans do not rely, in the first instance, upon government appropriations, which, being subject to the annual mood of the legislature, are variable and uncertain. They are based upon a scheme of payments. Government is only a guarantor or insurer.

These principles can and should be applied to victim compensation. It is apparent that a young hoodlum who permanently injures his holdup victim could never, even in a long lifetime, earn enough adequately to compensate the victim. However, there are many other offenders who can pay very substantial fines which should be contributed to a victim compensation fund. White-collar offenders who have stolen, embezzled, or otherwise illegally obtained millions of dollars should, at a minimum, be required to pay fines or restitution in excess of their peculations. In the chapter on white-collar crime, I recommended fines in treble the amount of the illegal gain. Under present sentencing practices white-collar crime does pay. It is highly profitable. If substantial fines were imposed on these offenders and paid into a victim compensation fund, the fund could perhaps approach fiscal viability. Certainly when white-collar crime is costing $400 billion a year, a concerted effort to prosecute these offenders and impose substantial fines should yield several hundred million dollars a year. This is much more than estimates of the costs of victim compensation.

Most of these successful white-collar offenders are prosecuted under federal laws. Several bills introduced into Congress provide for federal sharing or participation in state victim compensation funds. With such funding, state compensation laws could afford to provide far more adequate compensation than present laws permit.

The proposed Federal Crimes Code S.B.1 provides for forfeiture of property obtained from racketeering and a non-mandatory fine of twice the gross gain derived on the loss caused by the crime. It also raises fines to a maximum of $100,000 for individuals and $500,000 for corporations. Maximum fines under present laws are much lower than those in the proposed Federal Crimes Code. For example, campaign contribution violations now carry a maximum fine of $25,000.[13] I see no reason for fines in criminal cases to be only double the amount of the sums involved when treble damages are permitted in civil cases. Criminal intent certainly should result in heavier penalties than civil misconduct. Moreover, there appears to be no reason for a ceiling on fines for crimes.

The fine should at least equal the amount gained through the crime.

Damages for civil wrongs have no limitation. If the harm done is $1 million or $10 million the wrongdoer is liable for that amount of damages. Surely, one who is guilty of wilful, intentional criminal misconduct should at least have to pay the full amount of the damage caused by his crime.

A striking example of the unfairness of small fines and limited victim compensation as compared with civil damages was revealed in a rape-murder case occurring in Washington, D. C.[14] The criminal had been released on parole from prison for a prior conviction shortly before he committed this offense. The family of the victim sued the District of Columbia for the negligence of the parole officer in failing to disclose the criminal's prior record to the employer who hired him as a maintenance man. The victim lived in the apartment where the offender worked. A judgment of $100,000 was awarded to the victim and sustained on appeal. This was much more than could have been recovered under any present victim compensation law.

The popular singer, Connie Francis, who was raped in a Howard Johnson motel, told a United States Senate Judiciary Committee that as a result of this crime she suffered a severe depression, her marriage dissolved, and her career was ruined. Five years later she was still suffering the effects of this crime. Other victims of crime have equally severe and lasting psychic injuries. Countless victims of crime are permanently disabled and impaired. Because the rape of Miss Francis occurred in a motel, not on the street or subway, she had someone to sue for civil damages. She recovered $2.65 million from the motel and her husband recovered $25,000. Few victims of crime have anyone to sue. They must look to the meager awards under victim compensation laws in those states which have such statutes or bear their sufferings without help from the law. In our mobile society where many people do not live near their relatives and close friends, they have no help in times of crisis. For them some form of compensation is a necessity.

The folly of separating civil damages from criminal sanctions is clearly revealed in the prosecution of Congressman Joshua Eilberg. He pled guilty to receiving compensation for services rendered before a federal agency and was fined $10,000 and placed on probation. The federal government is now seeking to recover these illegal payments amounting to $149,172.00 in a civil action. There is no reason why as part of the criminal sentence a penalty of restitution should not have been imposed.

This would have saved the costs of a civil suit. Moreover, in a civil action a jury swayed by sympathy may not award the government adequate damages. Under the proposed Federal Crimes Code a fine in twice the amount of the sums involved would be recoverable. Under the sentencing practices suggested in this book a fine of treble the amount would be mandatory and payable to the victim compensation fund.

The amounts of money which could be recovered from white-collar felons are not inconsiderable. For example, Philadelphia City Councilman Bellis was convicted of receiving and making illegal payments amounting to $312,000. He was fined only $6,050.[15] A fine in treble the amount of the illegal gains in this one case would have provided more than the entire annual payments from the victim compensation fund in Pennsylvania.

Many white-collar criminals, like most street criminals, may not have sufficient funds at the time of sentencing to pay large fines and orders of restitution or reparation. Fines and sentences of restitution can be paid over a long period of time out of future earnings. In sentencing street criminals and petty white-collar offenders, I usually order probation for the maximum period allowable under law and condition it upon weekly payments within the earning capacity o the offender. There is no reason why similar sentences could not be imposed on wealthy white-collar offenders.

Some of these felons have profited enormously as a result of their crimes. Haldeman, Erlichman, Colson, Dean, and other Watergate felons have made large sums from their writings and TV appearances. They are in demand solely because of their criminal experiences. That is what they write and speak about. I suggest that a criminal's future earnings be subject to criminal sanctions under a sentence of probation conditioned upon weekly or monthly payments. At the time of sentencing in many cases neither the judge nor the offender may be aware of the future earning capacity of the offender and the sentence will not include a fine or an order of restitution of appropriate magnitude. A sentence could impose a fine of a percentage of future earnings or an order of reparation based upon future earnings. The New York Crime Victim Compensation Law provides that all proceeds from literary efforts involving convicted killers must go to the Crime Victims Compensation Board for distribution to the victims' survivors and their lawyers. The contract for a book on the life of Son of Sam has been made subject to payment under this law.[16] This statute points the way to more comprehensive laws which will make a high percentage of an offender's earnings from writings, radio, television, or any other source resulting from a crime or capitalizing on the crime payable to the victim compensation fund for a period of years equal to the maximum sentence for that offense. Such a law would not only provide funds for all victims of crime but would avoid the ugly spectacle of crime being a profitable enterprise.

Victim compensation has been recommended by many people including former president Gerald Ford. Although at this writing a federal victim compensation law has not been enacted, several bills providing for compensation have been introduced and favorably received. The idea of restitution as an alternative to prison sentences has also won support from judges, scholars, bar associations, and commentators.[17] The search for imaginative alternatives to imprisonment such as various kinds of community service would be obviated by sentences of restitution and reparation payable to a victim compensation fund. A monetary fine or order of restitution based upon the harm resulting from the crime or the amount of the peculation provides an easily ascertainable, fair, and objective standard for the penalty imposed. It avoids a prison sentence for the nonviolent criminal; it establishes a moral nexus and legal responsibility from the offender to the victim; and it helps to make possible adequate compensation for all crime victims.

The victims of crime, whether they be six million people annually or twenty million (a figure I believe to be more accurate) or an even larger number, desperately need financial assistance to cope with the physical, psychiatric, and economic effects of crimes perpetrated against them. Although it is now commonplace to express concern for the victims of crime, few courts translate this concern into meaningful relief or redress. Adequate victim compensation laws and orders of reparation and restitution imposed on criminals would provide justice for the victims of crime, relieve society of the crushing financial burden of incarcerating hundreds of thousands of people, and offer offenders an opportunity for rehabilitation.

CHAPTER XIX

AGENDA
FOR REFORM

One of the most pressing issues confronting the American
Judiciary System today is the apparent failure of our penal
system. From the abhorrent conditions within many of the
institutions, the prohibitive costs of operating them, and the
extremely high rate of recidivism, it is evident that the
benefits reaped by American Society from its prisons are
minimal at best.

—Senator James Abourezk

"**S**entencing in America today is a national scandal," writes Senator
Kennedy.[1] This is not too strong a statement. Sentenced prisoners
are being released prematurely from drastically overcrowded prisons;[2]
white-collar felons who have stolen hundreds of thousands of dollars are
sentenced to give lectures on the evils of crime but are not required to
disgorge their ill-gotten gains; poor street criminals are sentenced to long
terms of imprisonment and on release promptly commit more crimes;
and the victims of crime are totally ignored by the criminal justice
system.[3]

Plans for sweeping reforms and changes are offered by many scholars.
Some of these plans have already been adopted without adequate discussion or analysis. The most popular proposals are mandatory sentencing,
sentencing commissions, creative sentences, and diversion. As we have
seen, diversion is not an alternative to prison but an alternative to trial.

Both diversion and creative sentences favor the middle-aged, middle-class white offender and discriminate against the young, poor, and non-white. They exacerbate disparities in sentencing. Mandatory sentencing and sentencing commissions ignore the needs of the offender. None of the proposals is designed to deal with the very different types of people who commit offenses. None provides redress to the victims of crime.

Before proposing new laws, abandoning time-honored rights to trial and individualized sentencing, the problems which can be alleviated must be identified. As Tocqueville observed, Americans are inclined to view every public and social problem as a legal issue. However, not every difficult problem in the field of criminal justice can be solved through sentencing practices no matter how wise or fair they may be.[4] Social injustices, lack of parental love and guidance, and conditions of slum life cannot be cured by the criminal law. There is no form of compensatory action which the law can take to redress these unfairnesses of life. The criminal law cannot deal with problems of physical health, genetic defects, brain damage, and other conditions which may materially contribute to criminal behavior. Many offenders can be helped. Some cannot be treated or "cured" of mental and emotional problems which lead to the commission of crimes. There is no known cure for the amoral belief, held by many, that the end justifies the means and that the only crime is to be caught.

Reluctantly we must acknowledge that we simply do not know how to treat violent, dangerous offenders so that they can be "cured" of violence, unreason, and hostility. Until such time as there are developments in psychotherapy, chemistry, and medicine, the legal system will have to isolate these people who pose an unreasonable risk to society. For them, prison is the only appropriate penalty. Of the 400,000 people now in prison in the United States, probably fewer than 50,000 are such offenders. The other 350,000 need not be incarcerated if we employ other meaningful penalties specifically designed to rehabilitate the offender, deter other potential offenders, and provide redress to the victims of crime.

From where I sit, I see seven major problems which could be substantially alleviated by changes in statutes and legal procedures. These proposals would deter crime, protect the public, reduce the prison population, eliminate disparities in sentencing, and provide redress for the victims of crime.

First in importance in preventing death and serious injury to victims and offenders is the enactment and enforcement of strict gun control laws. More than 6,000 Americans were killed by handguns in the first ten months of 1979.[5] This is an epidemic problem. Taking guns out of the hands of criminals and law-abiding citizens will not stop crime but it will materially decrease the injuries incurred in the commission of many crimes. None of the people who have appeared before me in cases involving shootings was a sportsman or hunter. No one had a valid reason for having a firearm. It may be argued that criminals will use knives if they do not have guns. That is true. Knives and clubs are sometimes lethal, but they are not nearly so dangerous as guns. There is a quantum difference between a fist fight and a shootout.

There is some evidence that a mandatory one-year jail sentence for anyone found carrying a gun will cause a significant drop in the use of guns. Such a law is in effect in Massachusetts. The number of homicides involving guns in Boston declined 43 percent during the two-year period following the enactment of the law.[6]

Gun laws will probably not affect professional criminals—the hit men who kill for hire. But many random aimless shootings, assaults with guns, and homicides that comprise a large proportion of the crimes tried in state criminal courts might be eliminated or be much lesser offenses if such laws were enacted.

Second in importance in the prevention of violent crime and reduction of the prison population is education. I do not mean simply compulsory school attendance but programs which actually teach young people to read and write and become employable. As we have seen in the chapter "Crime in Black and White," education and literacy are directly linked to violent street crime. Literate, employed people are much more likely to commit nonviolent crimes. Semiliterate street criminals commit violent crimes. Most of these offenders are natives of the cities in which they committed the offenses. They attended the local public schools for at least nine or ten years. Unemployed boys and young men are responsible for much of the violent street crime which terrifies the public. Day after day I see defendants who dropped out of school or were pushed out of school as early as age fifteen. Most of them are only semiliterate, if not functionally illiterate. They are unemployable except in the most menial and temporary jobs. No public or private agency pays any attention to them from the time they leave school until they are arrested. A major reduction of the prison population could be brought about by educating and training this huge population of school dropouts before they commit serious crimes.

After these school dropouts are convicted, it is the responsibility of the criminal justice system to see that they are educated and trained. It is evident that if the offender is illiterate and unemployable on his release from prison he will most probably commit other crimes.

The third significant problem is that crime is profitable. So long as crime is profitable it will continue. All white-collar crime and organized crime is committed for money. It is only common sense to take the profit out of crime.

Creative sentences have won the approval of many judges, scholars, and journalists. The United States Senate Subcommittee on Administrative Practices and Procedures of the Committee on the Judiciary held a hearing on "Creative Alternatives to Prison" at which nineteen judges, a judicial candidate, and other public officials enthusiastically approved the idea of "public service" as an alternative to prison, primarily for white-collar offenders and people of good background.[7] As we have seen in the chapter "White Collar Crime," such sentences do not constitute a meaningful penalty; the sentences are of dubious benefit to the community; they are uncertain and variable; they deny equality of treatment to offenders convicted of similar crimes. They leave the offender in possession of his illegal gains. They do not provide redress for the victims of crime.

The use of fines and orders of restitution as an alternative to prison has not been adequately explored. It has been wisely observed that the fine is the cheapest and by no means the least effective penalty. It is also probably the least studied of all forms of sentences.[8] A fine has many advantages over prison. It spares the offender the degradation, brutality, and crime-inducing experience of prison. It saves the public the enormous financial and social costs of maintaining hundreds of thousands of inmates in prison.

The limitations on the maximum amount of fines which are set by statute can be changed by statute. The proposed Federal Crimes Code substantially increases the fines for many crimes. I see no reason for a maximum dollar limitation on the amount of the fine for any crime. It is obvious that a fine which leaves the offender in possession of the fruits of his misdeeds is not a meaningful penalty. It cannot conceivably further the goals of crime prevention or deterrence. Such a penalty will not rehabilitate the offender or give him his just deserts. I propose that the only limitation on the amount of the fine for any crime be three times the value of the property or money illegally acquired or the harm done.

The fourth problem is intra-family crime, which is widespread and frequently results in death or serious, permanent injury. Fifty percent of homicides are committed against a member of the family or one with whom the killer has a close relationship. Many of these offenders are sentenced to prison. Prevention of these crimes will not only avoid tragedy but will also substantially reduce the prison population. Laws permitting immediate civil intervention to remove the abuser from the home and to remove battered babies and abused children from the abuser would save many lives.

Prevention of child and spouse abuse requires not only laws but also money. Society must be committed to spending money to protect victims instead of spending money to punish and imprison abusers. A year of care for the child is cheaper than a year of prison for the parent. Appropriate laws and shelter facilities could substantially reduce the prison population.

The fifth major problem is lack of jobs for street criminals. Most street criminals are poor and unemployed. They cannot make restitution and pay fines. Therefore, they are sentenced to prison. This is not only unfair when compared with treatment of white-collar criminals, but it also compounds the unfairness of the lives of the poor and undereducated. Some offenders who were on welfare at the time of their crimes managed to find jobs and make payments when they knew the alternative was prison. Not all criminals are able to find jobs even when they are willing to work. Many of them are unemployable on the open labor market.

I strongly suggest a publicly subsidized work program for those offenders who do not constitute an unreasonable physical danger to the public. The benefits of such a program would be considerable. Non-dangerous criminals would be spared the brutalizing experience of prison, and the prison population would be radically reduced. Moreover, the arguments of desert and justice as fairness apply with the same force to poor offenders as to rich. The shoplifters, purse snatchers, burglar and credit card theives should pay for their crimes. They should pay in money: everyone who steals $100 should repay the $100 and pay a fine of $300. This is fair, equal, and just punishment.

All employed people pay taxes and contribute to the economy. Work habits are as likely, perhaps more so, to rehabilitate an offender as the idleness of prison. The message that crime does not pay will be heard by the poor offender, as well as the rich offender. It may have a deterrent effect.

No one has estimated the cost of subsidizing jobs for 350,000 offenders a year. It is unlikely that it would amount to $1 billion, which is less than the proposed subsidy for the Chrysler Corporation. One can approximate the costs of maintaining an offender in prison. Assume that the average cost of incarcerating one inmate for one year is $20,000. This is a very low figure. In New York, the average cost is $26,000. Some youth facilities cost as much as $40,000 a year for one inmate. Assume also that the average prisoner has two dependents (again a low estimate) who will be on welfare if he or she is in prison. The costs of maintaining them, including the welfare administration, is well in excess of $7,500 a year. The public gets no benefit from these expenditures.

If the government subsidized a job program for non-dangerous offenders to be hired by private employers who would pay each convict a living wage, the public would save at least $27,500 in direct expenses for prison and welfare per offender per year. In addition, the offender would pay taxes and restitution or reparation. The value of the work performed should also be included in the savings. Such a job program should involve labor-intensive activity rather than require expensive machinery and equipment.

Would offenders work if jobs were available? No one knows because such a program has never been established for any broad group of offenders. However, many criminals who have been placed on probation on the condition that they acquire basic education and job skills, get a job, and pay fines or restitution have done so. It is worth trying. The alternative is more prisons, more disrupted families, and more wasted lives.

Publicly subsidized jobs need not deprive law-abiding citizens of employment. Convicts could be employed to perform maintenance work and rehabilitation in the inner cities and on public property, work that is not being done either by government or the private sector. The subsidized jobs would be contracted to private industry. Organized labor would have the same right to unionize these employees as any other privately employed workers. The employer could hire a mix of regular employees, whose full salary he would pay, and convicts, whose jobs would be subsidized by the government for the difference between the standard wage and what the convict employee's services were actually worth. In time, with compulsory education and on-the-job training, many offenders should be able to enter the open labor market. I believe this is the cheapest and most direct way to reduce the prison population. For those who refuse to work, prison is the ultimate penalty. It should not be the penalty of choice for the non-dangerous offender. It is also possible that a job may have great rehabilitative value.[9]

The sixth problem is that of disparities in sentencing. Unjustified disparities can be eliminated without abolishing individualized discretionary sentencing by the trial judge. Professor James W. Wilson suggests that the legal system should "most definitely stop pretending that judges know, any better than the rest of us, how to provide 'individualized justice.' "[10] A judge may not know better than professors and criminologists how to provide individualized justice, but who is in a better position to know all the relevant facts?

It has been pointed out that "the trial judge has the unique and unreproducible advantages of seeing the defendant, 'sizing him up,' and possessing from daily exposure a seasoned wisdom in the use of such first-hand impressions."[11] The judge also has the benefit of the arguments of counsel, the pre-sentence and psychiatric reports, and the opinions of the accused's friends, relatives, employer, and of other people who testify at sentencing. The judge has also seen the victim, if he or she is alive, seen the injuries inflicted, and perhaps glimpsed some of the psychic scars. Even when the defendant pleads guilty, although the judge may not hear the testimony of the victim and the other witnesses, they are usually in the courtroom. The judge sees them. The judge also has the benefit of legal training. A crime is a violation of law. It may also be a sin. The offender is a criminal. He may also be mentally ill. I do not believe that clergy, moral philosophers, or psychiatrists should make the sentencing decision. Legal training is essential. Moreover, the judge imposes sentence in open court and must assume the responsibility for that decision.

Although I favor individualized sentencing by the trial judge, the judge's discretion should not be unfettered. Judicial discretion has been exercised unwisely many times. Indeed, it has been abused. The most direct, simple, and effective means of curbing abuses and errors by the sentencing judge and of eliminating unjustified disparities is broad appellate review of sentences.[12] Almost every other ruling of an American trial judge is subject to review.

Appellate review is the time-honored procedure by which common-law courts correct errors and abuses of discretion and develop the law.[13]

The opinions of higher courts provide the rationale for decision making which guides the trial bench and the bar. It is likely that if sentencing had been reviewable during the past half century, a substantial body of law would have been created by federal and state appellate courts establishing criteria for sentencing. Legal scholars and criminologists would not today be frantically proposing drastic remedies which cut against the grain of the law.[14]

The seventh major problem is redress for the victims of crime. It is self-evident that no legal system can be just or fair that totally ignores the needs of innocent people who suffer serious harm as a result of crimes. Crime is one of the most widespread risks of contemporary life. No one is too young or too old, too rich or too poor to be the victim of crime. There is little that the individual can do to protect himself or to provide for the catastrophic costs of injury, disfigurement, and loss of income resulting from many crimes. The criminal justice system from the moment a crime is reported until sentence is imposed should acknowledge the interest and needs of the crime victim. Adequate victim compensation laws should be enacted in every state.[15] Federal support of state victim compensation funds is required. If the proposals for restitution, treble fines for white-collar criminals, and education and job subsidies for street criminals were adopted, victim compensation could be financed in large part by the offenders rather than the taxpayers.

This agenda for reform is long and complicated. To deal justly with criminals and the victims of crime and to protect the public requires the best efforts of the legal community and the legislatures. For far too long, the legal profession—lawyers, judges, and scholars—have taken little interest in the criminal law.[16] The Bureau of National Affairs, in a significant paper published in 1979 entitled "Future Law—Lawyers Confront the 21st Century," did not even mention criminal law. It should be obvious that unless the crime rate diminishes, increasing numbers of lawyers will be needed to prosecute and defend criminal cases. The taxpayers will be burdened by the costs of more prisons, and more and more people will be helpless victims of crime. The way lawyers meet these obligations and the way judges sentence offenders are problems that confront the legal system today and will be with us in the twenty-first century.

The sentence is the most significant, critical, and visible part of the entire criminal justice process. In each case a sentence should be imposed that meets the particular needs presented by the facts of the case so that the public is protected from the risks which the offender presents, the victim's losses and injuries are adequately redressed, and the criminal himself is treated humanely, fairly, and given an opportunity for rehabilitation. The goals of sentencing are the same in every case but the means are different in each case. No single formula will yield in every case a sentence that is equal to that imposed in other cases. It requires a human being, not a computer or a mandated system of penalties, to balance the many factors in each case: protection of the public, rehabilitation of the offender, deterrence, fairness, credibility of the law, and needs of the victim.

The road leading from vengeance to justice in the treatment of offenders is long and hard and the journey is far from ended. The goal cannot be reached by actions of judges alone. It also requires intelligent painstaking efforts by legislators and scholars and a public commitment to devote the resources necessary to the task.

NOTES

CHAPTER I

1. *Fair and Certain Punishment: Report on Criminal Sentencing*, Twentieth Century Fund, Inc. (New York: McGraw Hill, 1976).
2. See e.g. Marvin E. Frankel, *Criminal Sentences: Law Without Order* (New York: Hill and Wang, 1972).
3. Gordon J. Hawkins and Franklin E. Zimring, *Deterrence: The Legal Threat in Crime Control* (Chicago: University of Chicago Press, 1973) p. 24.
4. The Ford Foundation gave a grant of $537,500 for the research which resulted in Charles E. Silberman's *Criminal Violence, Criminal Justice* (New York: Random House, 1978), *Esquire*, 7 November 1978, p. 35.
5. See Richard Kluger, *Simple Justice: The History of Brown v. Board of Education and Black America's Struggle for Equality* (New York: Alfred A. Knopf, Inc., 1976).
6. See Benjamin Nathan Cardozo, *The Nature of the Judicial Process* (New Haven: Yale University Press, 1951); John Paul Frank, *American Law: The Case for Radical Reform* (New York: MacMillan, 1969); Oliver Wendell Holmes, Jr., *The Common Law* (Boston: Little, Brown & Co., 1881).
7. Exodus, 21:37; 22:1 and 3.
8. Patricia McLaughlin, "The Case of the Criminologist Who Changed His Mind," *Today Magazine, Philadelphia Inquirer*, 26 November 1976, p. 16, at p. 17.
9. Charles Fried, *Right and Wrong* (Cambridge: Harvard University Press, 1977). See also book review by Brian Barry, "And Who is My Neighbor?" *Yale Law Journal* 88 (1979): 629.
10. Herbert L. Hart, *Punishment and Responsibility: Essays in the Philosophy of Law* (New York: Oxford University Press, 1968); John Rawls, *A Theory of Justice* (Cambridge: Belknap Press of Harvard University Press, 1971); Michel Foucault, *Discipline and Punish: The Birth of the Prison* (New York: Pantheon, 1977).
11. Some historians find this a romantic gloss on the power struggle between the crown and the nobility. However, the belief in the supremacy of law has prevailed, though often in the breach, for centuries.
12. Regents v. Bakke, 438 U.S. 265 (1978); Steelworkers v. Weber, 443 U.S. (1979).
13. There are no government figures for the years subsequent to 1975. *The*

Statistical Abstract of the United States gives the following data: In 1975 there were 263,291 inmates in federal and state prisons. In 1972 there were 141,600 in city, county, and local prisons. In 1974 there were 76,671 children in public and quasi-public detention centers, shelters, and other involuntary forms of custody. This gives a total of 481,562 persons incarcerated. The numbers have increased dramatically in the past few years.

14. See Furman v. Georgia, 408 U.S. 238 (1972) in which this standard was formulated.

15. Steward Machine Co. v. Davis, 301 U.S. 458 (1937).

CHAPTER II

1. *The Legal Intelligencer,* 28 January 1974, p. 19.

CHAPTER III

1. Civil cases are settled by agreement between plaintiff and defendant, sometimes with the assistance of the court and subject to court approval. Criminal cases are disposed by plea bargains between the prosecutor and defense counsel which must be approved by the court or by open guilty pleas in which there is no agreement as to the sentence to be imposed by the court.

2. Judge Joseph P. Braig, *Philadelphia Inquirer,* 9 January 1979, p. A7.

CHAPTER IV

1. Norval Morris, "Impediments to Penal Reform," *University of Chicago Law Review* 33 (1966): 627.

2. *New York Times,* 18 March 1979, p. 3.

3. Holmes, *The Common Law,* Lecture II.

4. *Royal Commission on Capital Punishment 1949–1953 Report* (London: Her Majesty's Stationery Office, 1953), Command Publication 8932 par. 53, p. 18.

5. See Hawkins and Zimring, *Deterrence.* The authors state: ". . . the traditional question, Does punishment deter crime? This question, though not entirely meaningless, is unanswerable in categorical terms, for we confront a complex of issues about human behavior in a great variety of situations. . . ." p. 7.

6. Richard Joseph Barnet, "Challenging the Myths of National Security," *New York Times Magazine,* 1 April 1979, p. 25.

7. Most Reverend William Temple, Archbishop of York, *The Ethics of Penal Action,* Clark Hall Lecture No. 1 (Rochester, Kent, Eng: Stanhope Press Ltd., 1934).

8. Thorsten Sellin, *The Death Penalty: Report for the Model Penal Code Project of the American Law Institute* (Philadelphia: Exec. Office of American Law Institute, 1959) p. 28.

9. Evelyn Gibson and E. H. McClintock, *Robbery in London: An Enquiry by the Cambridge University Institute of Criminology,* Preface by Leon Radzinowicz (London: MacMillan, 1961).

10. *Federal Crime Control Assistance,* A Study by the Staff of the United

States General Accounting Office (Washington, D. C., January 27, 1978).
11. *New York Times*, 11 March 1973, p. 3.
12. Douglas Hay, *Albion's Fatal Tree: Crime and Society in Eighteenth Century England* (New York: Pantheon Books, 1975).
13. *New York Times*, 11 June 1979, p. A16.
14. A Report by the National Advisory Commission on Higher Education for Police Officers sponsored by the Police Foundation, *New York Times*, 3 December 1978, p. E5.
15. Increases in every kind of crime in the first six months of 1979 contradicted the predictions of experts that the national crime rate would decline. *New York Times*, 28 October 1979 p. 1.
16. Quoted in Leon Radzinowicz and J. W. Cecil Turner, "A Study on Punishment," *Canadian Bar Review* 92 (1943).
17. Johannes Andenaes, "The Morality of Deterrence," *University of Chicago Law Review* 37 (1970): 649.

CHAPTER V

1. See Russell Lynes, *The Tastemakers* (New York: Harper & Row, 1954).
2. *Philadelphia Inquirer*, 25 February 1979, p. 1.
3. Robert O. Dawson, *Sentencing: The Decision as to Type, Length, and Conditions of Sentence* (Boston: Little, Brown & Co., 1969) p. 3.
4. Arthur P. Miles, "Social Theory, Civil Rights and Crime," *Crime and Delinquency* 19 (1973): 394.
5. *New York Times*, 24 June 1979, p. E21.
6. David Fogel, *We Are the Living Proof: The Justice Model for Corrections* (Cincinnati, Ohio: Anderson Publishing Co., 1975).
7. Max Grunhut, *Juvenile Offenders Before the Court* (Oxford. Clarendon Press, 1956) p. 10.
8. *Fair and Certain Punishment.*
9. See Gerald R. Wheeler, "The Computerization of Juvenile Correction," *Crime and Delinquency* 22 (1976): 201–10.
10. See James R. Bagley, "Why Illinois Adopted Determinate Sentencing," *Judicature* 62 (1979): 390.
11. James Bennett, *I Chose Prison* (New York: Alfred A. Knopf, Inc., 1970), pp. 182–84.
12. Irving R. Kaufman, "Appellate Review of Sentences: A Symposium of the Judicial Conference of the U. S. Court of Appeals for the Second Circuit," *Federal Rules Decision* 32 (1963): 249 at p. 260.
13. *Fair and Certain Punishment.*

CHAPTER VI

1. Abe Fortas, *Concerning Dissent and Civil Disobedience* (New York: Signet Press, 1968), p. 32.
2. *New York Times*, "Criminal Justice System: Some Justice, Little System," 18 December 1977, p. E8.
3. Bernard Berelson and Gary A. Steiner, *Human Behavior: An Inventory of*

Scientific Findings (New York: Harcourt, Brace & World, 1964), p. 631; Edwin Powers and Helen Witmer, *An Experiment in the Prevention of Delinquency: The Cambridge-Somerville Youth Study* (New York: Columbia University Press, 1951); Joan McCord, "A Thirty Year Follow-Up of Treatment Effects," *American Psychologist* (March 1978), pp. 284–89, analyzing the treatment program of juvenile delinquency prevention of Dr. Richard Clark Cabot. The study compares 253 men who had been in the treatment program with 253 "matched mates" assigned to the control group and concludes that the untreated men committed fewer crimes than those subjected to treatment.

4. Com. v. Kostka, 475 Pa. 85 (1977).

5. Juvenile courts do exercise such plenary powers over children, often with disastrous results.

6. 95th Cong. First Sess. S1437 §2003.

7. Analysis by Professors Thomas I. Emerson, Vern Countryman and Carole E. Goldberg for National Committee Against Repressive Legislation, December, 1977.

CHAPTER VII

1. Bordenkircher v. Hayes, 434 U.S. 357 (1978) and People v. Dolkart, 400 N.Y.S.2d 500 (1977).

2. *New York Times*, 18 August 1972, p. 33.

3. See Willard Gaylin, *Partial Justice* (New York: Alfred A. Knopf, Inc., 1974).

4. David F. Fogel, "Justice, Not Therapy: A New Mission for Corrections," *Judicature* 62 (1979): 372.

5. Hart, *Punishment and Responsibility*.

6. *New York Times*, 23 January 1977, p. E5.

7. U. S. v. Addonizio,   U.S.   , 99 S. Ct2235 (1979).

8. *New York Times*, 4 January 1979, p. B1.

CHAPTER VIII

1. A number of states and counties now have such commissions.

2. Frankel, *Criminal Sentences*.

3. Meredith W. Watts, "Crime Control versus Due Process: Their Place in an Anti-Heterodox World View," speech presented at the First Annual Scientific Meeting of the International Society of Political Psychology, September 2–4, 1978, New York, N.Y.

4. National Survey of Crime Severity Center for Studies in Criminology and Law, University of Pennsylvania, November, 1978.

5. Zurcher v. Stanford Daily, 436 U.S. 547 (1978).

6. Merna Marshall and Saundra Dillio, "Philadelphia's Sentencing Guidelines," *Legal Intelligencer*, 4 April 1979, pp. 1, 12.

7. Carole E. Goldberg, "S1437 is a Legal Nightmare," *The Judge's Journal* 16 (1977), 3: 4.

8. Davis v. Davis, 585 F2d 1226 (1978). This case was later reversed by the court en banc, one judge dissenting. 601 F2d 1531 (1979).

9. "White Collar Justice," a Study by the Bureau of National Affairs, *U.S. Law Week* 44, 13 April 1976.
10. *New York Times*, 12 November 1972, p. 10.
11. People v. Golden, 342 NYS2d 309 (1973).

CHAPTER IX

1. *New York Times*, 26 February 1979, p. A18.
2. *New York Times*, 14 January 1979, p. 42.
3. Interview with Judge Joan B. Carey, *New York Times*, 27 March 1979, p. 3.
4. "Challenge of Crime in a Free Society" (Washington: Government Printing Office, 1967) pp. 165–71; Ronald L. Goldfarb and Linda R. Singer, *After Conviction* (New York: Simon and Schuster, 1973).
5. Hay, *Albion's Fatal Tree*.
6. Foucault, *Discipline and Punish*.
7. The pillory and stocks were less brutal than physical torture and mutilation. Like public hangings, they appealed to sadistic and vengeful impulses of the mob. Such penalties did not rehabilitate or deter. Nor did they provide redress for the victims of crime.
8. Sir William Blackstone, *Commentaries on the Laws of England*, Book IV (Oxford: Clarendon Press, 1768), pp. 369–72.
9. See Bobbs-Merrill edition in English, 1963.
10. Furman v. Georgia, 408 U.S. 239 (1972).
11. *New York Times*, 18 March 1979, p. 3.
12. Walter Berns, "For Capital Punishment," *Harper's* 258 (1979): 15.
13. See Anthony F. Granucci, "Nor Cruel and Unusual Punishment Inflicted: The Original Meaning," *California Law Review* 57 (1969): 839.
14. Aldridge v. Com., 2 Va. Cases 447 (1824).
15. Ingraham v. Wright, 430 U.S. 651 (1977).
16. Jackson v. Bishop, 404 F2d 571 (1968).
17. Rochin v. California, 342 U.S. 165 (1952).
18. Schmerber v. California, 384 U.S. 757 (1966).
19. Weems v. U. S., 217 U.S. 349 (1910).
20. *The Daily Item*, Sunbury, Pennsylvania, November 8, 1978.
21. Derrick Bell, "Inside China: Conformity and Social Reform," *Juris Doctor* 4 (April 1978): 23, for a description of Chinese law by a Harvard Law School professor.
22. See Harold J. Berman, "The Background of the Western Legal Tradition in the Folklaw of the Peoples of Europe," *University of Chicago Law Review* 45 (1978): 553.
23. Frederic William Maitland and Frederick Pollack, *The History of the English Law* (Cambridge: University Press, 1895); see also Stephen Schafer, *The Victim and His Criminal: A Study in Functional Responsibility* (New York: Random House, 1968).
24. Sir James Fitzjames Stephen, *History of the Criminal Law of England* (London: MacMillan, 1883), p. 198.

25. New York Workman's Compensation Law, Art. 2 §15.
26. Berman, "The Background of the Western Legal Tradition," fn. 22, p. 280.
27. See Ralph B. Pugh, *Imprisonment in Medieval England* (New York: Cambridge University Press, 1968).
28. Henry de Bracton, *De Legibus Et Consultudinibus Angliae* (c. 1250), translated with notes and revisions by Samuel E. Thorne (Latin text edited by George E. Woodbine), *On the Laws and Customs of England* (Cambridge, Mass.: Belknap Press of Harvard University Press, 1968).
29. Giorgio Del Vecchio, "The Struggle Against Crime," reprinted in Harry Burrows Acton, *The Philosophy of Punishment: A Collection of Papers* (London: MacMillan, St. Martin's Press, 1969).

CHAPTER X

1. Fines are payable to the state, unlike the Wergild and other early penalties that required compensation to the victim of a crime and his family to be paid by the criminal and his family. The maximum penalty for each crime is fixed by statute and bears little, if any, relationship to the harm done or the amount of property illegally taken.
2. National Center for State Courts, Research Priorities in Sentencing, Publication No. R0022, September 1975. Significantly there is no suggestion for this kind of research or program by the federal government. See U. S. Dept. of Commerce, "Federal Crime Control Assistance: A Discussion of the Program and Possible Alternatives," 27 January 1978.
3. See Glendon S. Schubert, *Quantitative Analysis of Judicial Behavior* (Glencoe, Ill.: The Free Press, 1960); Lee Loevinger, "Jurimetrics: The Methodology of Legal Inquiry," *Law and Contemporary Problems* 28 (1963): 6.
4. McCord, "A Thirty Year Follow-Up of Treatment Effects."
5. Berelson and Steiner, *Human Behavior*, p. 632.

CHAPTER XI

1. Franz Alexander and Hugo Staub, *The Criminal, The Judge and the Public: A Psychological Analysis*, second edition (Glencoe, Ill, Free Press, 1956), pp. 209 et seq.
2. Psychiatric testimony is needed in many other phases of the criminal justice system. For a discussion of the issues and questions which require psychiatric evidence see Chapter XVII, The Uses of Psychiatry.
3. *Philadelphia Inquirer*, 21 April 1979, p. 2A.
4. *Federal Rules Decision* (1965): 129.
5. John Stuart Mill, *Utilitarianism, Liberty and Representative Government* (New York: E. P. Dutton and Co., Inc., 1951), p. 73.

CHAPTER XII

1. All figures are taken from Statistical Abstracts of the United States Department of Commerce.

2. Stephan Cohen and Alan Sussman, *Reporting Child Abuse and Neglect* (Cambridge, Mass.: Ballinger Publishing Co., 1975).

3. *New York Times*, 18 February 1979, p. 58. See also Study by National Institutes of Mental Health, *New York Times*, 26 November 1978, p. E9.

4. Study supported by United States Law Enforcement Assistance Administration, *New York Times*, 3 December 1977.

5. Donald T. Lunde, *Murder and Madness* (San Francisco, Calif.: San Francisco Book Co., Inc., 1976).

6. Lois G. Forer, "Battered Children," *The Philadelphia Inquirer, Today Magazine*, 2 January 1972, pp. 6–11.

7. Ingraham v. Wright, 430 U.S. 651 (1977).

8. Section 11.

9. *Philadelphia Evening Bulletin*, 23 April 1979, p. 1.

10. Carol Saline, "The Family Secret," *Philadelphia Magazine*, August 1977, p. 111.

CHAPTER XIII

1. Edwin Hardin Sutherland, *White Collar Crime* (New York: Holt, Rinehart and Winston, 1961) p. 9.

2. Economic Crimes, Recommendations of the American Bar Association Section of Criminal Justice, Committee on Economic Offenses, March 1977.

3. *Philadelphia Evening Bulletin*, 30 January 1978, p. 9.

4. *Philadelphia Evening Bulletin*, 4 April 1979, p. 40.

5. *New York Times*, 18 March 1979, p. 26.

6. *New York Times*, 24 January 1978, p. 62.

7. *New York Times*, 5 May 1975, p. 1.

8. *Philadelphia Inquirer*, 17 March 1979, p. B1.

9. *New York Times*, 24 January 1978, p. 62.

10. These figures are taken from Leon Jaworski, *The Right and the Power: The Prosecution of Watergate* (New York: Reader's Digest Press, 1976), Appendix A.

11. "White Collar Justice," Study by the Bureau of National Affairs, *U. S. Law Week* 44, 13 April 1976.

12. Column by Sydney J. Harris, *Philadelphia Evening Bulletin*, 27 April 1979.

13. *New York Times*, 22 September 1972, p. 57.

14. *New York Times*, 5 November 1977, pp. 1, 24.

15. *New York Times*, 25 March 1979, p. E20.

16. William J. Chambliss, "The Deterrent Influence of Punishment," *Crime and Delinquency* 12 (1966): 70, reporting a study which disclosed that increased fines for parking violations and close monitoring reduced the number of violations. See also Barry Schwartz, "The Effect in Philadelphia of Pennsylvania's Increased Penalties for Rape and Attempted Rape," *Journal of Criminal Law, Criminology and Police Science* 59 (1968): 509, demonstrating that such penalties had no effect on the rate of rape.

17. Under the Omnibus Control Act of 1970 the maximum fine for fraud and

embezzlement, regardless of the sums involved, is only $10,000.
18. *Philadelphia Evening Bulletin*, 15 May 1978, p. 31.

CHAPTER XIV

1. The Federal Safe Streets Act enacted in 1968 was a response to the pervasive public fear of street crime. June 19, 1968, P.L. 90–351.
2. *New York Times*, 29 April 1979, p. E7.

CHAPTER XV

1. United States Census.
2. *Philadelphia Evening Bulletin*, 24 April 1977, p. 2.
3. Law Enforcement Assistance Administration, Criminal Victimization in the United States, 1973–1975.
4. *New York Times*, 18 March 1977, p. 38.
5. Most of the prisoners in Attica prison in New York State were blacks; most of the jailers were white. Those who studied the riot which erupted there in 1971 concluded that race was a factor contributing to the unrest. See *Attica: The Official Report of the New York State Special Commission on Attica* (New York: Bantam Books, 1972).
6. Donald Bartlett and James Steele, "Crime and Injustice," *The Philadelphia Inquirer*, February 18–23, 1973.
7. Watts, *Crime Control versus Due Process*. The author did not include race as one of the factors.
8. See the figures quoted in Furman v. Georgia, 408 U.S. 238 (1972).
9. Yakov Avichai, Geoffrey W. Peters, and Laurence P. Tiffany, "Statistical Analysis of Sentencing in Federal Courts: Defendants Convicted after Trial, 1967–1968," *Journal of Legal Studies*, 4 (June 1975), p. 369.
10. Stephens, *History of the Criminal Law of England*.
11. Gideon v. Wainright, 372 U.S. 335 (1963).
12. Edwin Montefiore Borchard, *Convicting the Innocent: Errors of Criminal Justice* (New Haven: Yale University Press, 1932).
13. Wilkins v. U.S.,   U.S.   (1979).
14. Daniel Joseph Boorstin, *The Americans: The Democratic Experience*, vol. III (New York: Random House, 1973), p. 84.
15. New York Times, March 11, 1979, p. 44.
16. Ibid.
17. Rollo May, *Power and Innocence: A Search for the Sources of Violence* (New York: W. W. Norton, 1972).
18. Education U.S.A. Special Report, "Discipline Crisis in Schools: The Problem, Causes and Search for Solutions" (Arlington, Va: National School Public Relations Association, 1973), pp. 4–8.
19. Gunnar Myrdal, *An American Dilemma* (New York: Harper and Brothers, 1944), p. 968.

CHAPTER XVI

1. See Jean Piaget and Barbel Inhelder, *The Psychology of the Child* (New York: Basic Books, 1969).

2. Barbara Tuchman, *A Distant Mirror* (New York: Alfred Knopf, Inc., 1978), pp. 49–52.

3. Louis Milliot, *Introduction á l'édude du droit Muselman* (Paris: Recueil Sirey, 1953).

4. Sturges and Burn Mfg. Co. v. Beauchamp, 231 U.S. 320 (1913).

5. Sourcebook of Criminal Justice Statistics–1977 (Washington, D.C.:U.S. Department of Justice, Law Enforcement Assistance Administration, National Criminal Justice Information and Statistics Service, 1978).

6. U.S. v. Kent, 383 U.S. 541, 556 (1966). For a description of the actual functioning of juvenile courts see the opinion of the United States Supreme Court In re Gault, 387 US 28 (1967).

7. Lori B. Andrews, "Bad Kids from 'Good' Families," *Parent's Magazine,* May 1979, p. 72.

8. "Little Sisters and the Law," report of U.S. Department of Justice Law Enforcement Administration, 26 August 1977.

9. See "Children's Rights Report," issued by the Juvenile Rights Project of the American Civil Liberties Union Foundation, No. 8, May 1978.

10. *New York Times,* 11 March 1979, p. 13.

11. Ingraham v. Wright, 430 U.S. 651 (1977). Similarly the Supreme Court assumes that parents act in the best interests of the child when committing him to a mental institution. Children are not entitled to the same kind of hearing as an adult who is being committed into a mental institution. I have seen scores of normal children petitioned into mental institutions by their parents. See Secretary of Public Welfare v. Institutionalized Juveniles, U.S. , 99 S.Ct. 2523, (1979)

12. Silberman, *Criminal Violence, Criminal Justice,* p. 448.

13. *New York Times,* 4 October 1971, p. 1.

14. "The Crime Wave," *Time Magazine,* 30 June 1975, p. 10, et seq.

15. *Philadelphia Inquirer,* 26 January 1978, p. A9, reporting the results of a federal government study.

16. "Violent Schools—Safe Schools," The State School Study Report to the Congress, Vol. I, Dec. 1977.

17. Sheldon and Eleanor Glueck, *One Thousand Juvenile Delinquents: Their Treatment by Court and Clinic* (Cambridge: Harvard University Press, 1934).

18. U. S. Bureau of the Census, *The Prisoner's Antecedents* (Washington, D.C.: U. S. Government Printing Office, 1923).

19. Henry D. McKay and Clifford R. Shaw, *Juvenile Delinquency and Urban Areas* (Chicago: University of Chicago Press, 1942).

20. Sol Rubin, *Crime and Juvenile Delinquency: A Rational Approach to Penal Problems* (New York: Oceana Publications, 1958).

21. *New York Times,* 29 April 1979, p. 47, p. E5.

22. The Young Adult Offender: A Review of Current Practices and Programmes in Prevention and Treatment (New York: United Nations, Dept. of Economic and Social Affairs, 1965).

23. *Sourcebook of Criminal Statistics 1977,* p. 616.

24. Lois G. Forer, *No One Will Lissen: How Our Legal System Brutalizes the Youthful Poor* (New York: John Day Co., 1970).

25. *New York Times,* 3 December 1978, p. 50.
26. *New York Times,* 26 November 1978, p. 59.

CHAPTER XVII

1. Thomas Szasz, *The Manufacture of Madness* (New York: Harper and Row, 1970).
2. Jonas Robitscher, "The Uses and Abuses of Psychiatry" (The 1976 Isaac Ray Award Lectures), *The Journal of Psychiatry and Law* (Fall 1977), p. 331.
3. Miller v. Pate, 386 U.S. 1 (1976).
4. Robinson v. California, 370 U.S. 660 (1962).
5. David L. Bazelon, "The Perils of Wizardry," *American Journal of Psychiatry,* no. 1. 131 (1974), 12:317.
6. *New York Times,* 14 June 1979, p. B3.
7. See Washington v. U. S., 390 F.2d 444 (D.C. Cir., 1967).

CHAPTER XVIII

1. Margery Fry, *Arms of the Law* (London: Gollancz, 1951).
2. See Herbert Edelhertz and Gilbert Geis, *Public Compensation to Victims of Crime* (New York: Praeger, 1974) and the bibliography included. See also Stephen Schafer, *Compensation and Restitution to Victims of Crime* (Montclair, N.J.: Patterson Smith Publishing Co., 1970).
3. Morton Bard and Dawn Sangrey, *The Crime Victim's Book* (New York: Basic Books, 1979).
4. 93rd Congress, S. 300.
5. See "Compensating Victims of Violent Crime," a Report by the United States Department of Justice, Law Enforcement Assistance Administration, 1977.
6. Gary Thatcher, "Disorder in the Courts," *The Christian Science Monitor,* 27 November 1978, p. 12.
7. See John F. Klein, "Revitalizing Restitution: Flogging a Horse that May Have Been Killed for Just Cause," *Criminal Law Quarterly* 20, 8 June 1978, p. 383.
8. Brandeis University has received a $200,768 grant from the LEAA to expand the University's Court Alternative Placement Program, which is designed to place selected offenders in jobs. A portion of the offender's salary is paid to victims through the courts. The plan is bravely touted as "Careers Instead of Cells." To date there is no report on the success of this very limited experiment.
9. Paul Softley and Roger Tawling, "Compensation Orders in the Crown Court, 1976," *Criminal Law Review,* July 1976, p. 422. See also James A. Canter and George F. Cole, "The Use of Fines in England: Could the Idea Work Here?" *Judicature* 63 (1979): 154, suggesting that since fines work adequately in England even for those convicted of crimes of violence that the United States should adopt the use of this penalty.
10. See Steve Chesney, Joe Hudson, and John McLagen, "A New Look at Restitution: Recent Legislation, Programs and Research," *Judicature* 61 (1978): 348.

11. See Com. v. Walton, Pa. , 397 A.2d 1179 (1979).
12. Chesney and Hudson, "A New Look at Restitution," fn. 10.
13. 18 U.S.C. §611, et seq.
14. Reiser v. Dist. of Col., 563 F.2d 462 (D.C. Cir. 1977).
15. Com. v. Bellis, 476 Pa. 128 (1977).
16. *New York Times*, 7 November 1977, p. 54.
17. See Gary Thatcher, "The Shape of Courts to Come," *Christian Science Monitor*, 30 November 1978, p. 12. Ronald L. Goldfarb, "Alternatives to Prison," *The Washington Post*, 13 February 1979; Burt Galaway and Joe Hudson, "Restitution and Rehabilitation," *Crime and Delinquency* 29 (1972): 403; and Schafer, *The Victim and His Criminal.*

CHAPTER XIX

1. Edward M. Kennedy, "Symposium on Sentencing," Part I Introduction, *Hofstra Law Review* 7 (Fall 1978): 1.
2. United States District Court Judge Robert Vamey of Alabama in September 1979 ordered fifty-five inmates released from Montgomery County Jail because of overcrowding.
3. The negative effects of prison on the offender have been documented, "Challenge of Crime in a Free Society," U. S. Printing Office, 1967, pp. 165-71.
4. Federal Judge David L. Bazelon wisely points out that sentencing laws must "not be viewed as the panacea for crime in America." Bazelon, "Missed Opportunities in Sentencing Reform," *Hofstra Law Review* 7 (1978): 57, 69.
5. *New York Times*, 6 November 1979, p. A18.
6. *New York Times*, 18 June 1978, p. D14.
7. 95th Congress Second Sess., October 14, 1978.
8. Alec Samuels, "The Fine; The Principles," *Criminal Law Review* (1970): 272.
9. The Employment Program for Recovered Alcoholics finds that a job is a major contributing factor to keeping the ex-alcoholic from reverting to his habit. *New York Times*, 4 November 1979, p. 76.
10. James Q. Wilson, *Thinking About Crime* (New York: Basic Books, 1975), p. 234.
11. Frankel, *Criminal Sentences.*
12. See also Robert J. Kulak and J. Michael Gottschalk, "In Search of a Rational Sentence: A Return to the Concept of Appellate Review," *Nebraska Law Review* 53 (1974): 463.
13. Whether the prosecution, as well as the defendant, should have the right of appeal is an issue that has generated much controversy. The American Bar Association in 1967 recommended that appeals be limited to the defense, 1967 ABA Tentative Appellate Review Standards. In 1978, the Association approved new standards allowing appeal by the prosecution, 1978 Appellate Review Standards.
14. Abolition of parole boards and sentencing authorities would also eliminate unfair disparities in the sentences actually served. The decision to release or not to release a convict serving an indeterminate sentence would be made in open

court by the sentencing judge and be appealable.

15. New Jersey has recently enacted a crimes code establishing restitution to the victims of crime and increasing fines up to $250,000 (N. J. Stat. Ann. Title 2C, New Jersey Code of Criminal Justice, enacted by laws 1978, Chapter 95, effective September 1979).

16. Most law students take only one course in criminal law. The best and brightest students avoid criminal law and become corporate or tax lawyers or professors. The United States Supreme Court reflects this disinterest. In 1928, the Court issued 129 opinions. None dealt with criminal law. Only one involved civil liberties. In 1977, the Court issued 257 opinions. Only 36 involved criminal law and the rights of offenders.

INDEX